WASH DAY
diaries

written by **Jamila Rowser**   art by **Robyn Smith**

colors by Robyn Smith, Bex Glendining, and Kazimir Lee

CHRONICLE BOOKS
SAN FRANCISCO

Library of Congress Cataloging-in-Publication Data is available.

ISBN 978-1-7972-0545-8

Manufactured in Malaysia.

MIX
Paper from
responsible sources
FSC
www.fsc.org
FSC™ C005748

Design by Neil Egan.

Additional typesetting by Riza Cruz.

10 9 8 7 6 5 4 3 2 1

Chronicle books and gifts are available at special quantity discounts to corporations, professional associations, literacy programs, and other organizations. For details and discount information, please contact our premiums department at corporatesales@chroniclebooks.com or at 1-800-759-0190.

Chronicle Books LLC
680 Second Street
San Francisco, California 94107
www.chroniclebooks.com

contents

To the Black girls around the world,
you are seen,
and you are beautiful.

WASH DAY

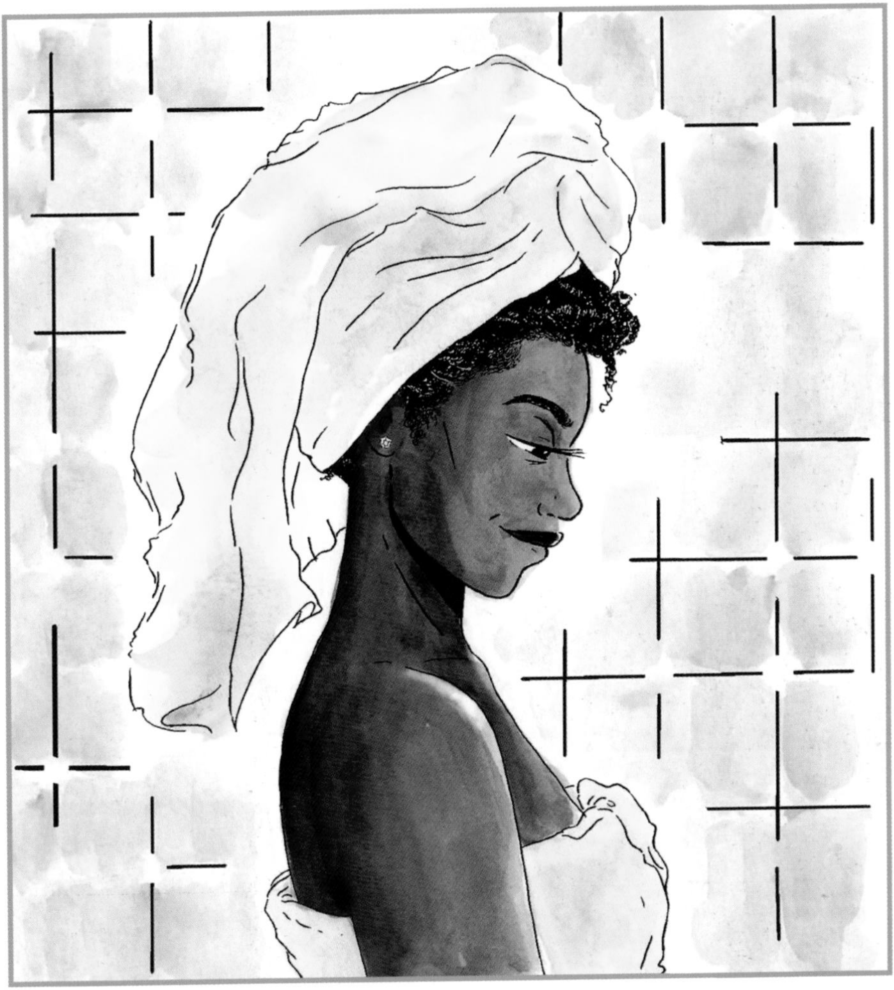

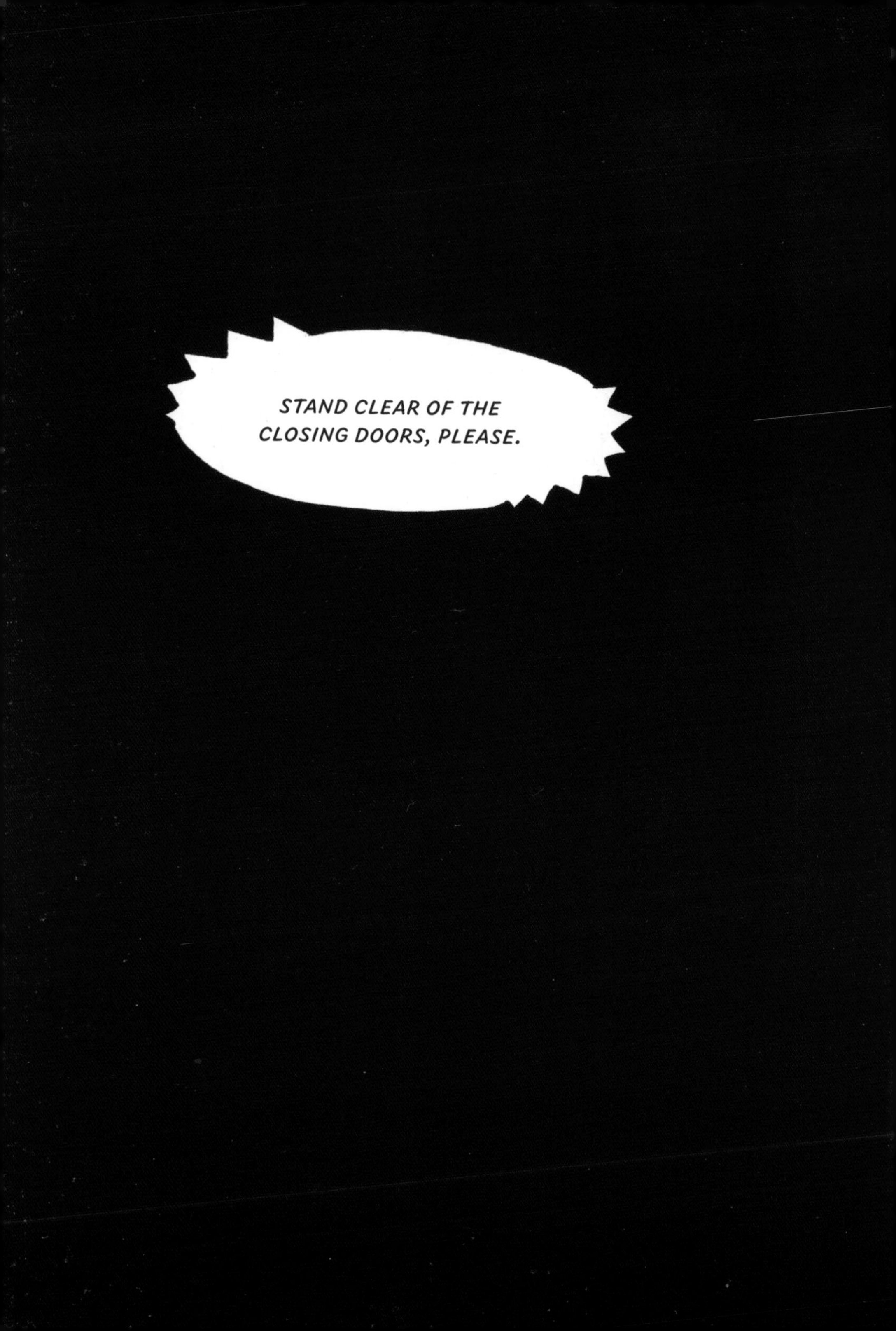
STAND CLEAR OF THE CLOSING DOORS, PLEASE.

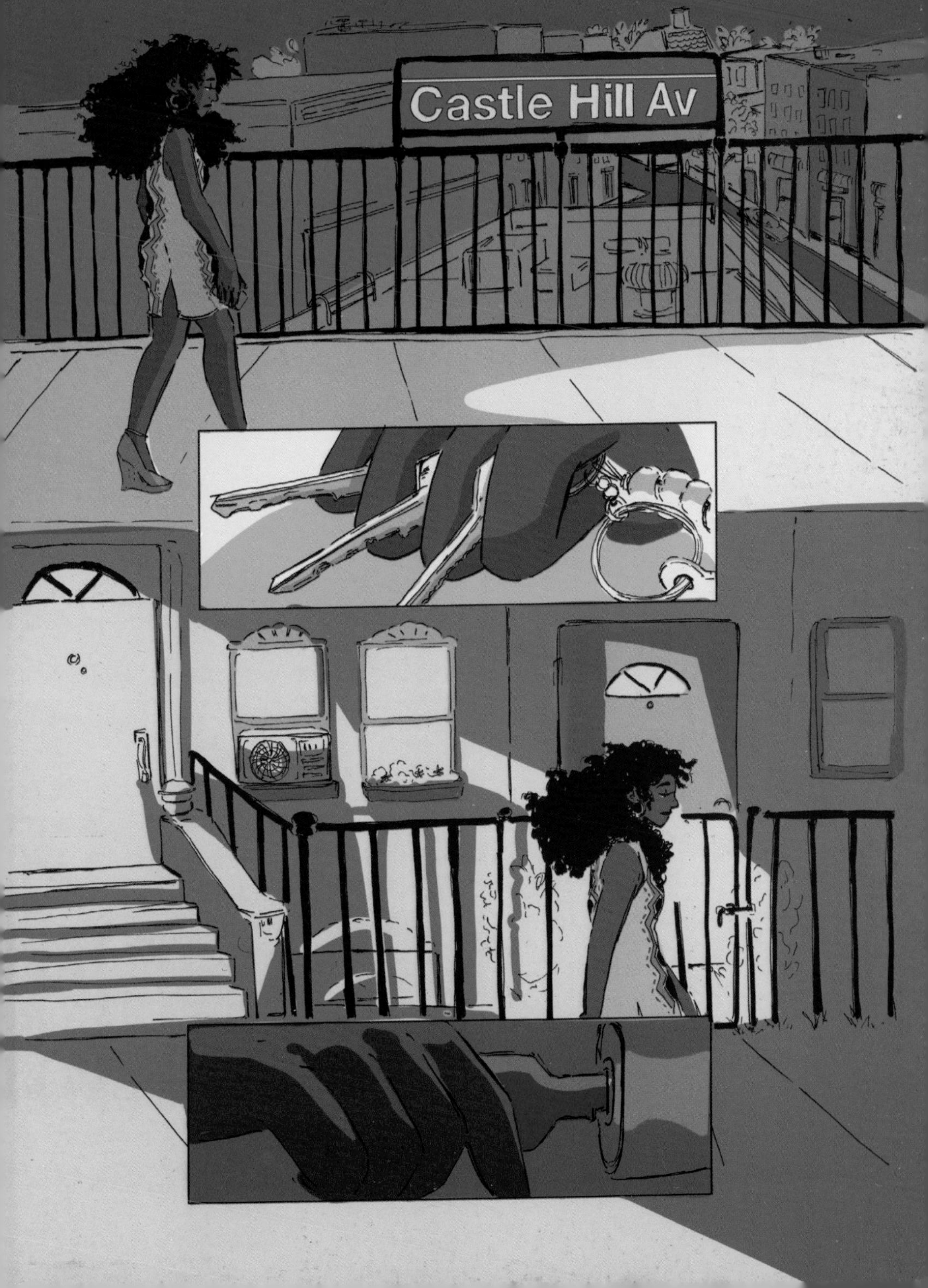
Castle Hill Av

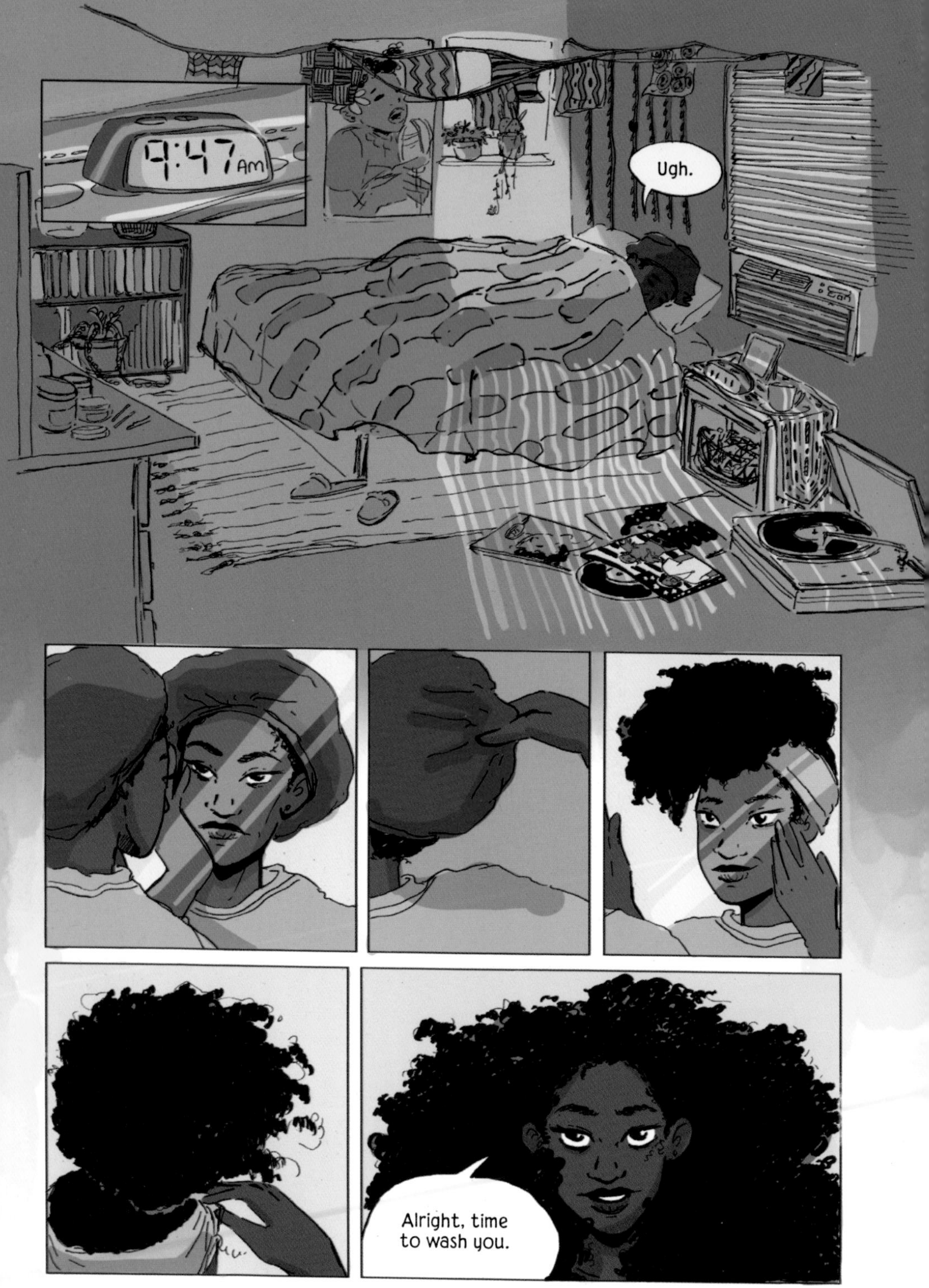
9:47 Am
Ugh.
Alright, time
to wash you.

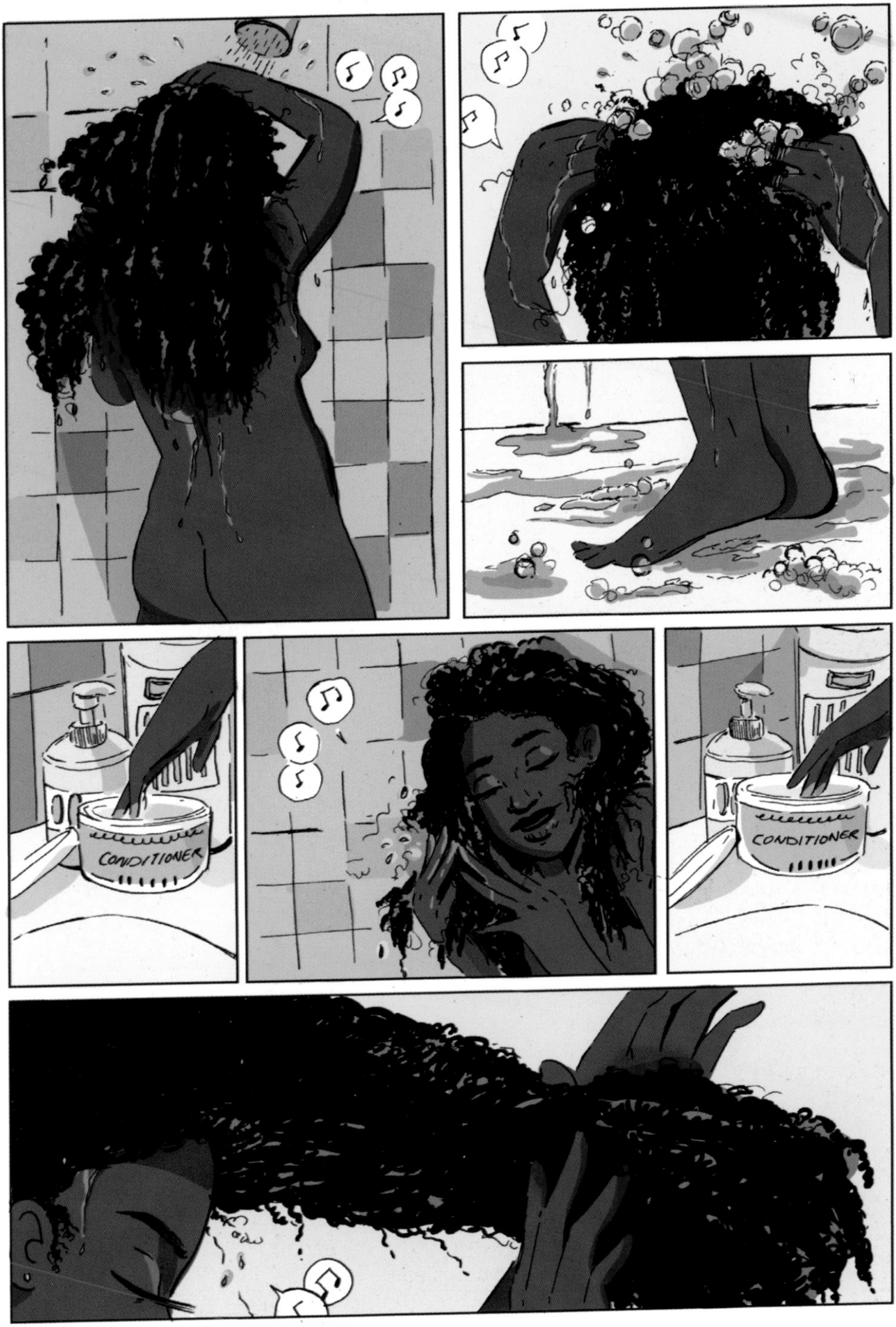
CONDITIONER
CONDITIONER

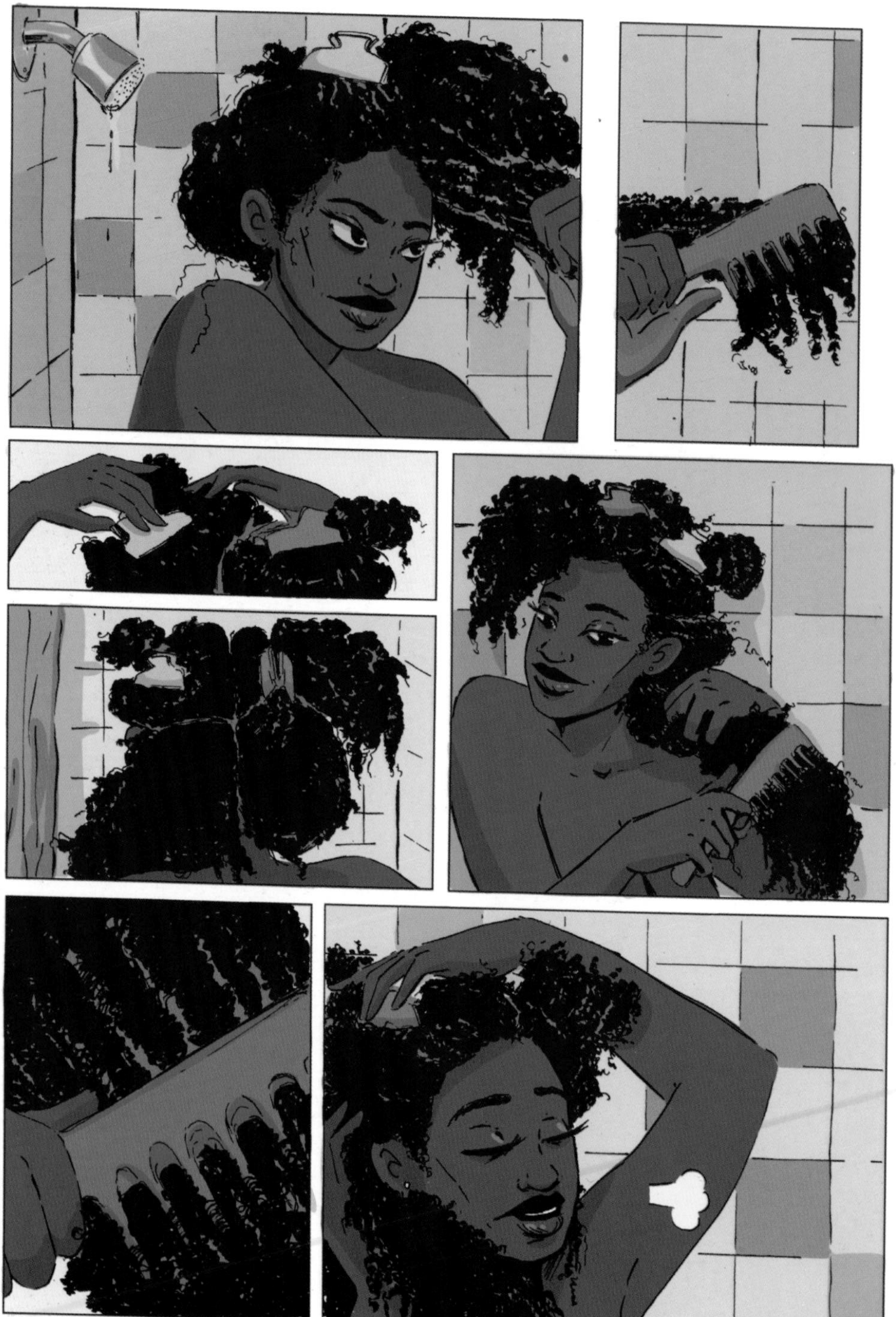

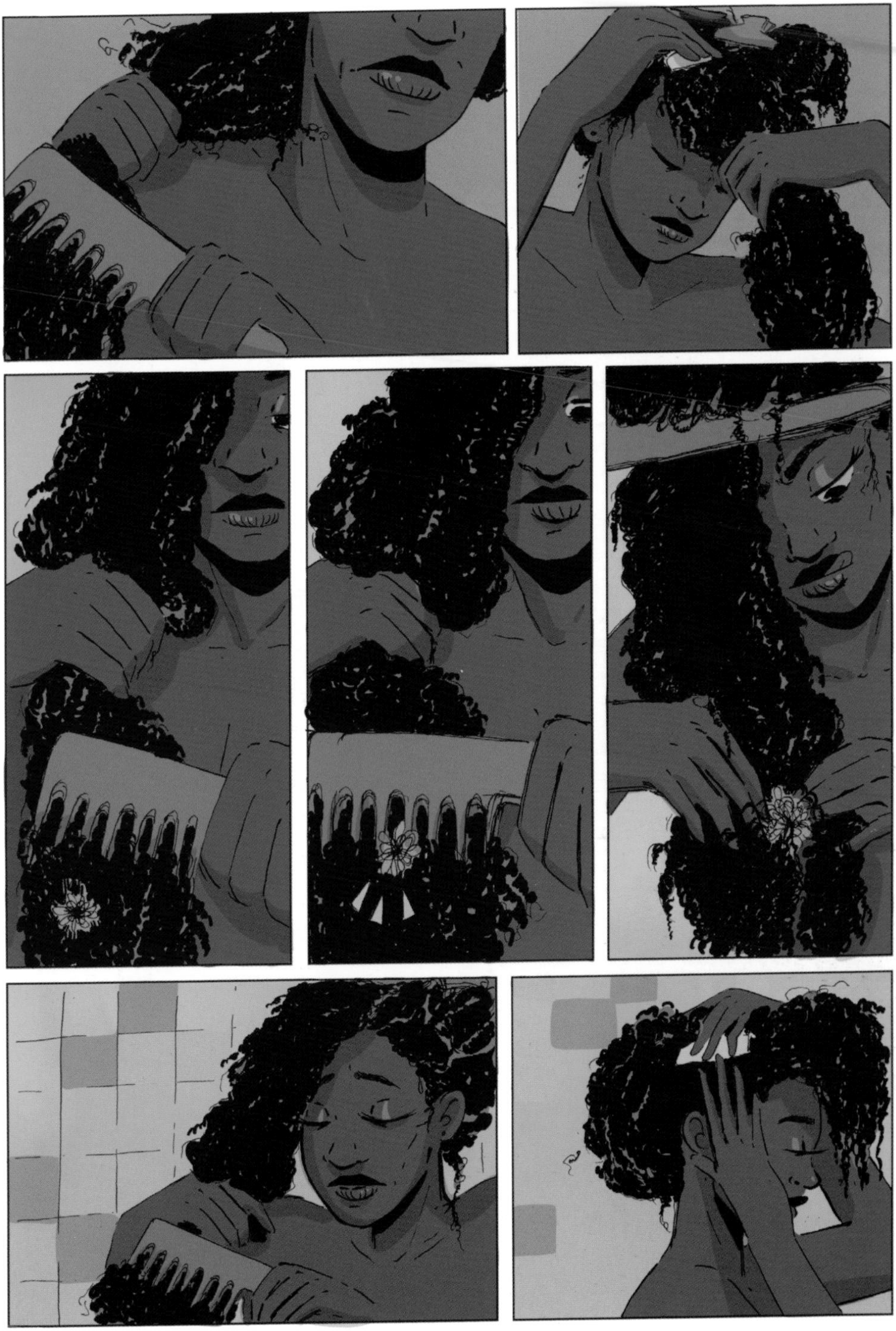

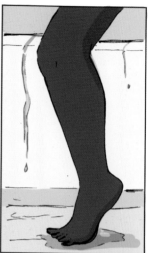

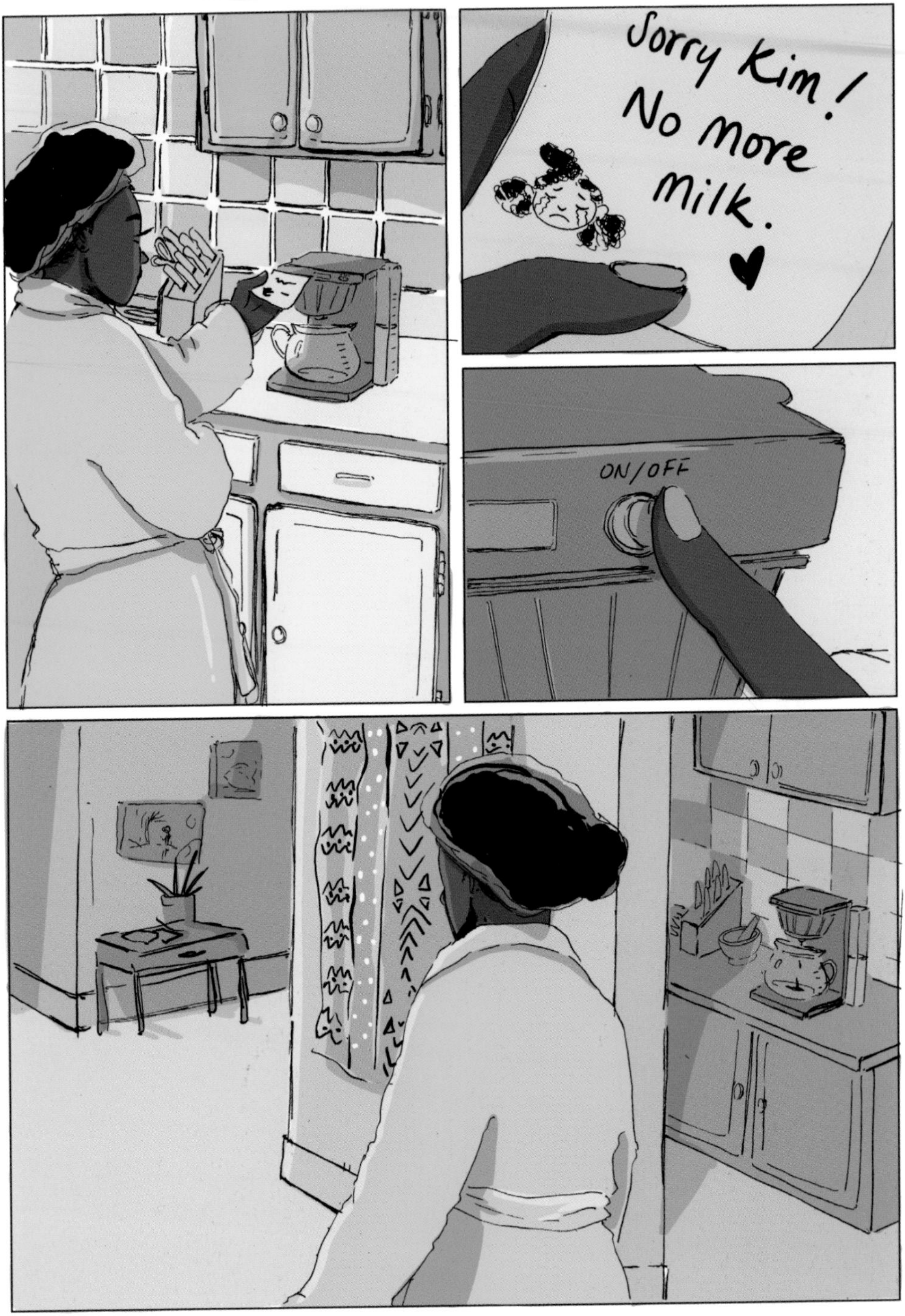
Sorry Kim! No more milk.
ON/OFF

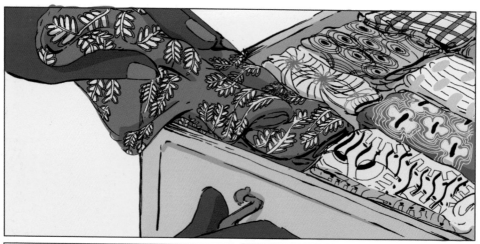

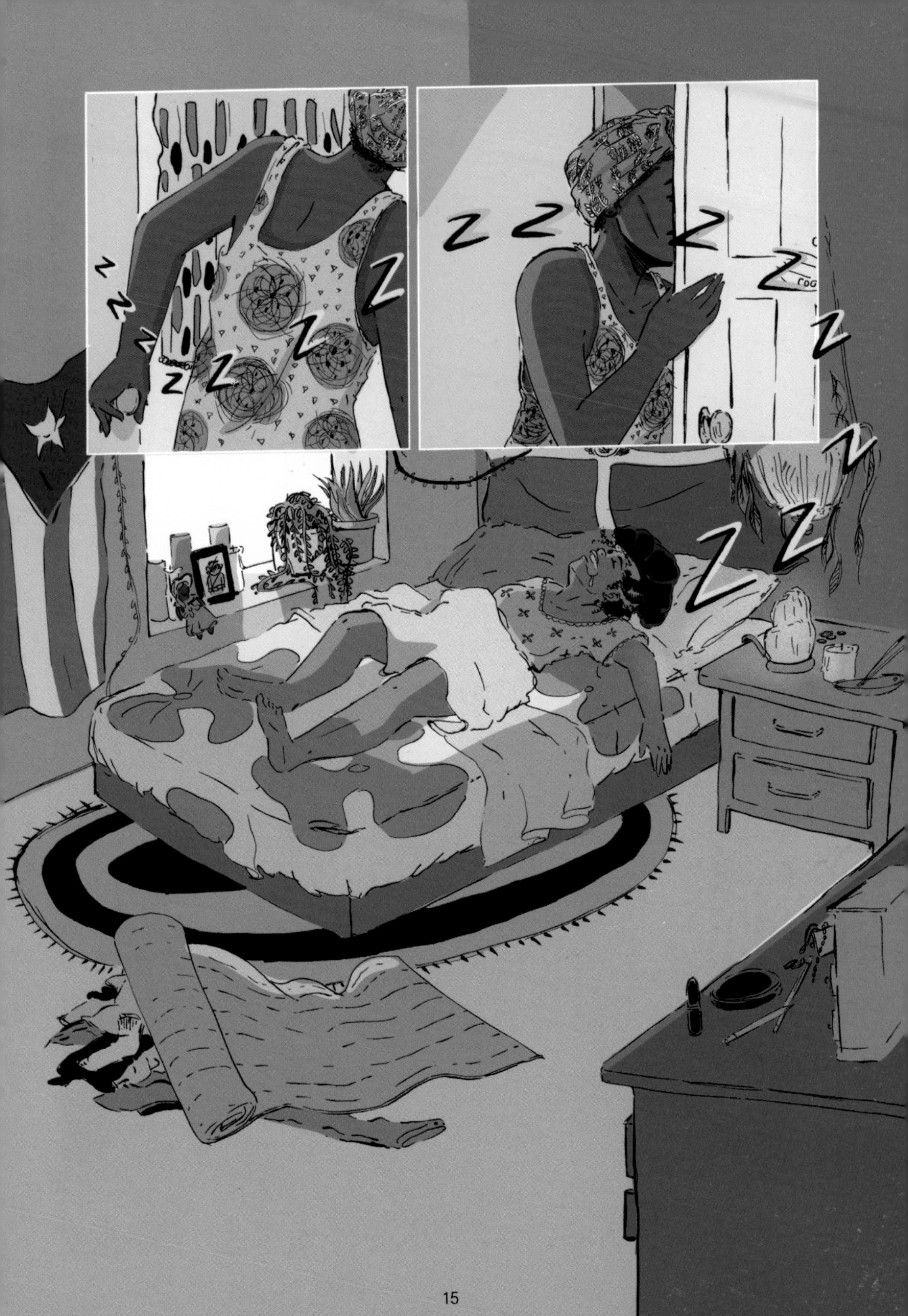
z z z z
z
Z Z
z z
z
z
Z
z
Z
Z

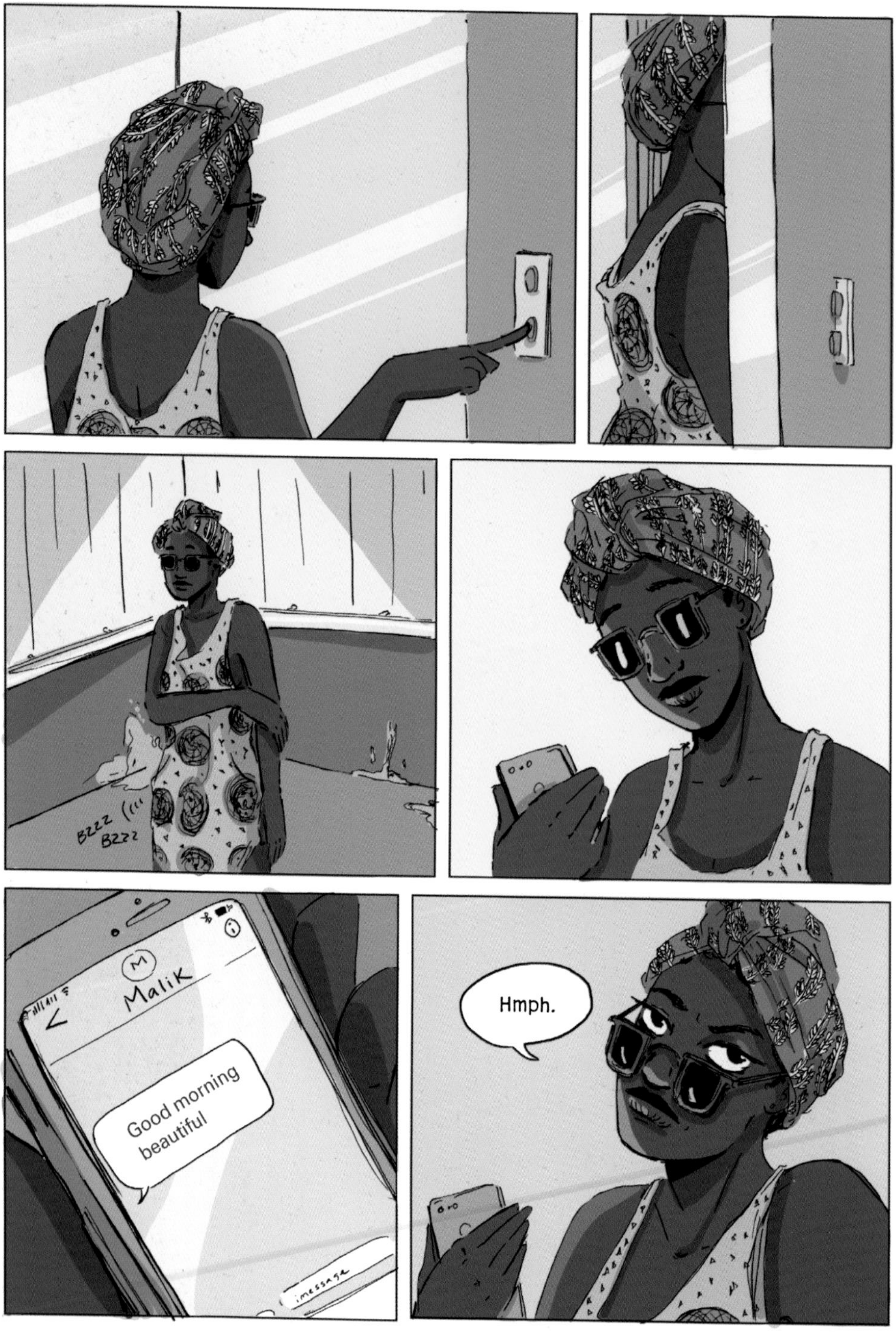
BZZZ BZZZ
Malik
Good morning beautiful
imessage
Hmph.

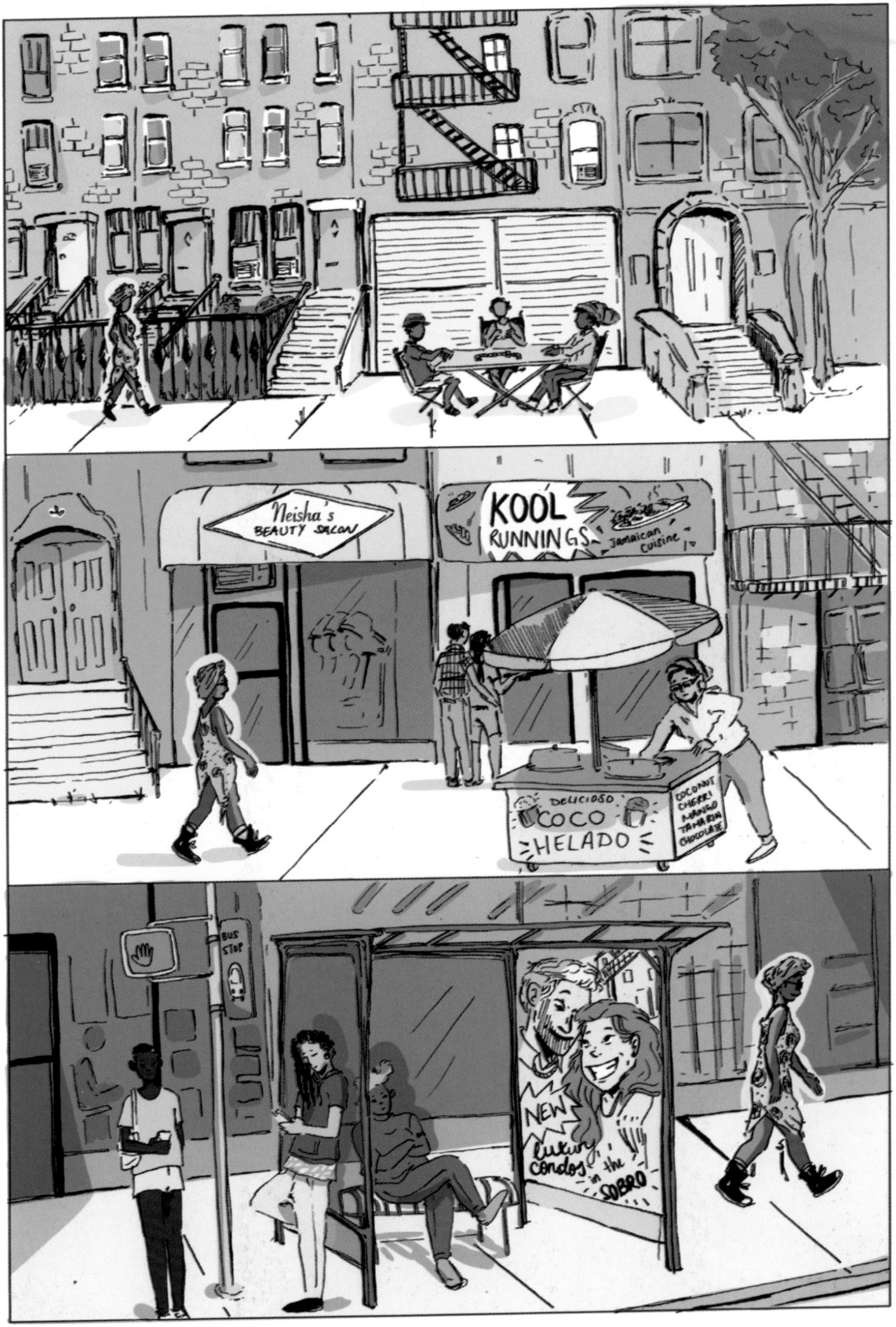
Neisha's BEAUTY SALON
KOOL RUNNINGS
Jamaican Cuisine
DELICIOSO COCO HELADO
COCONUT CHERRI MANGO TAMARIN CHOCOLATE
BUS STOP
NEW luxury condos in the SOBRO

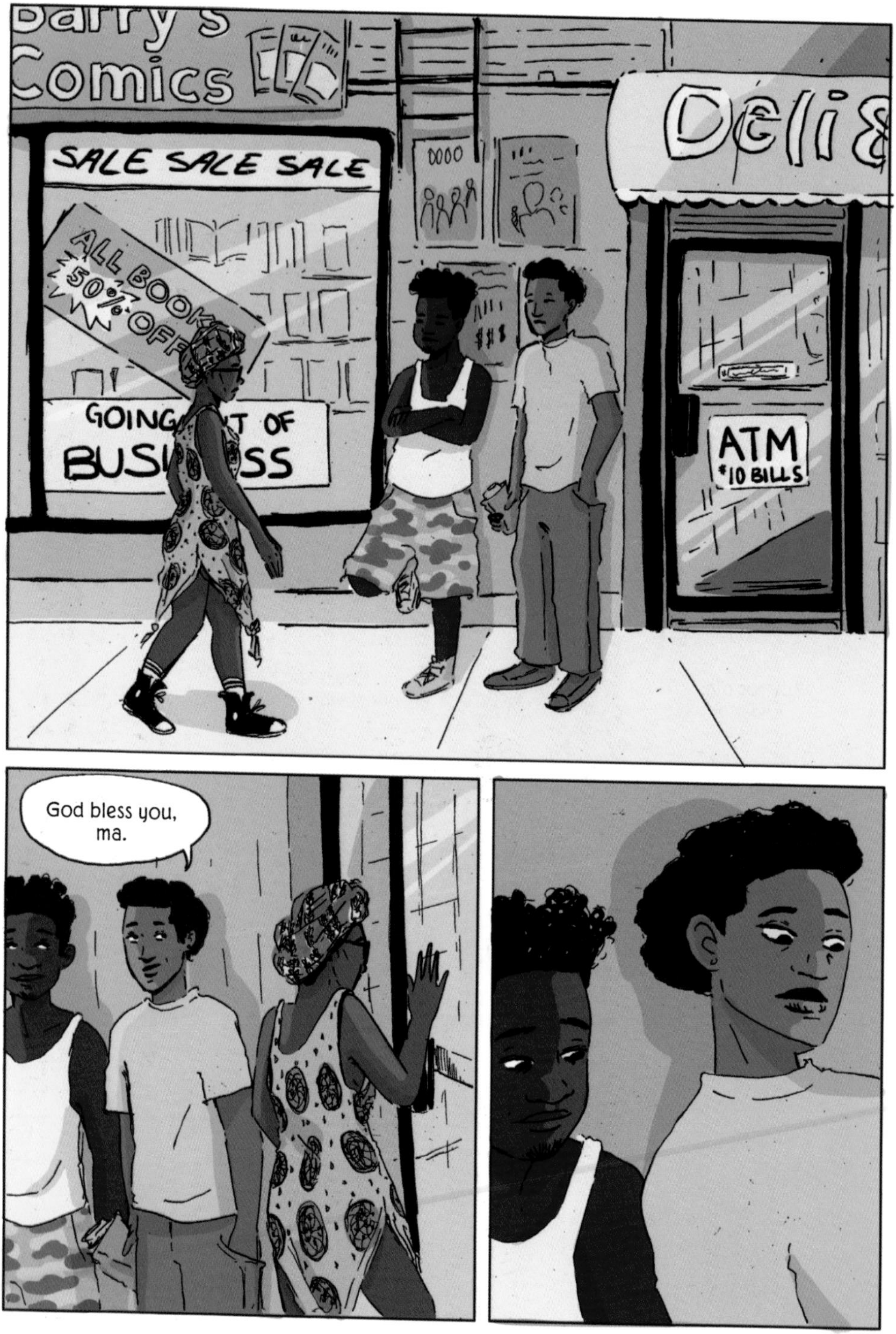
Comics
SALE SALE SALE
ALL BOOK
50%
OFF
GOING T OF
BUSI SS
Deli
ATM
$10 BILLS
God bless you, ma.

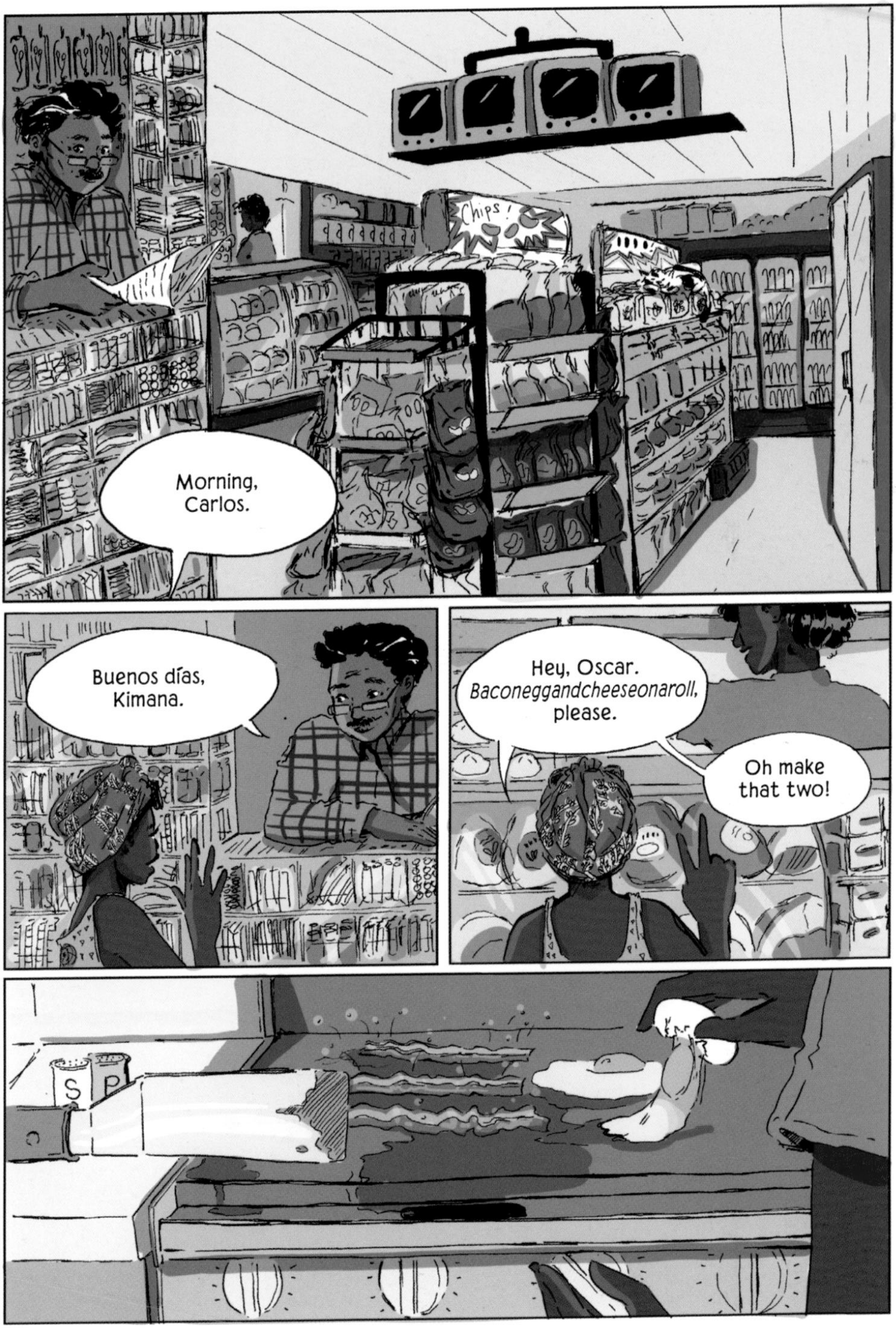

Chips!
Morning, Carlos.
Buenos días, Kimana.
Hey, Oscar. *Baconeggandcheeseonaroll,* please.
Oh make that two!
S
P

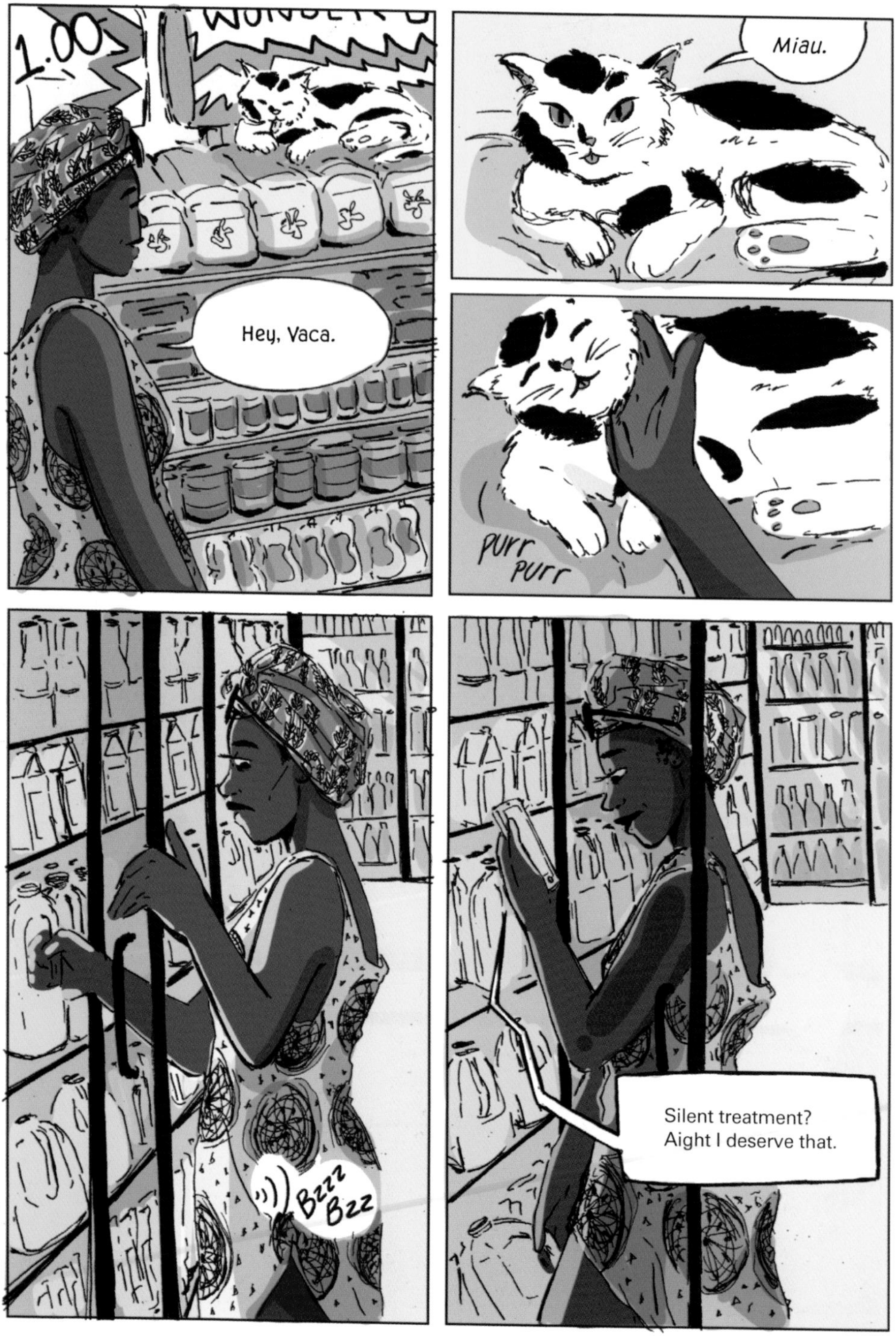
1.00
Hey, Vaca.
Miau.
purr purr
Bzzz Bzz
Silent treatment? Aight I deserve that.

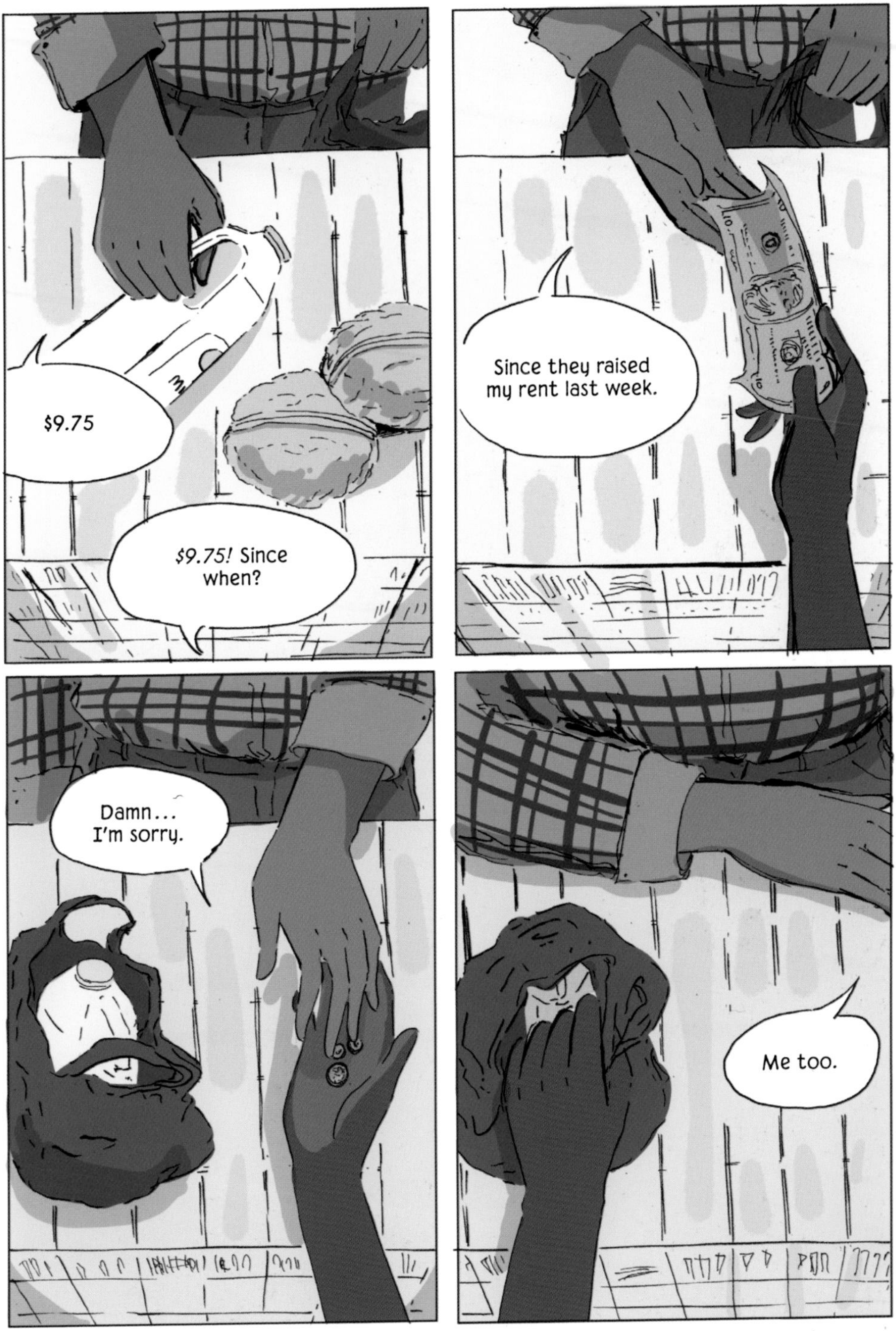
$9.75
$9.75! Since when?
Since they raised my rent last week.
Damn... I'm sorry.
Me too.

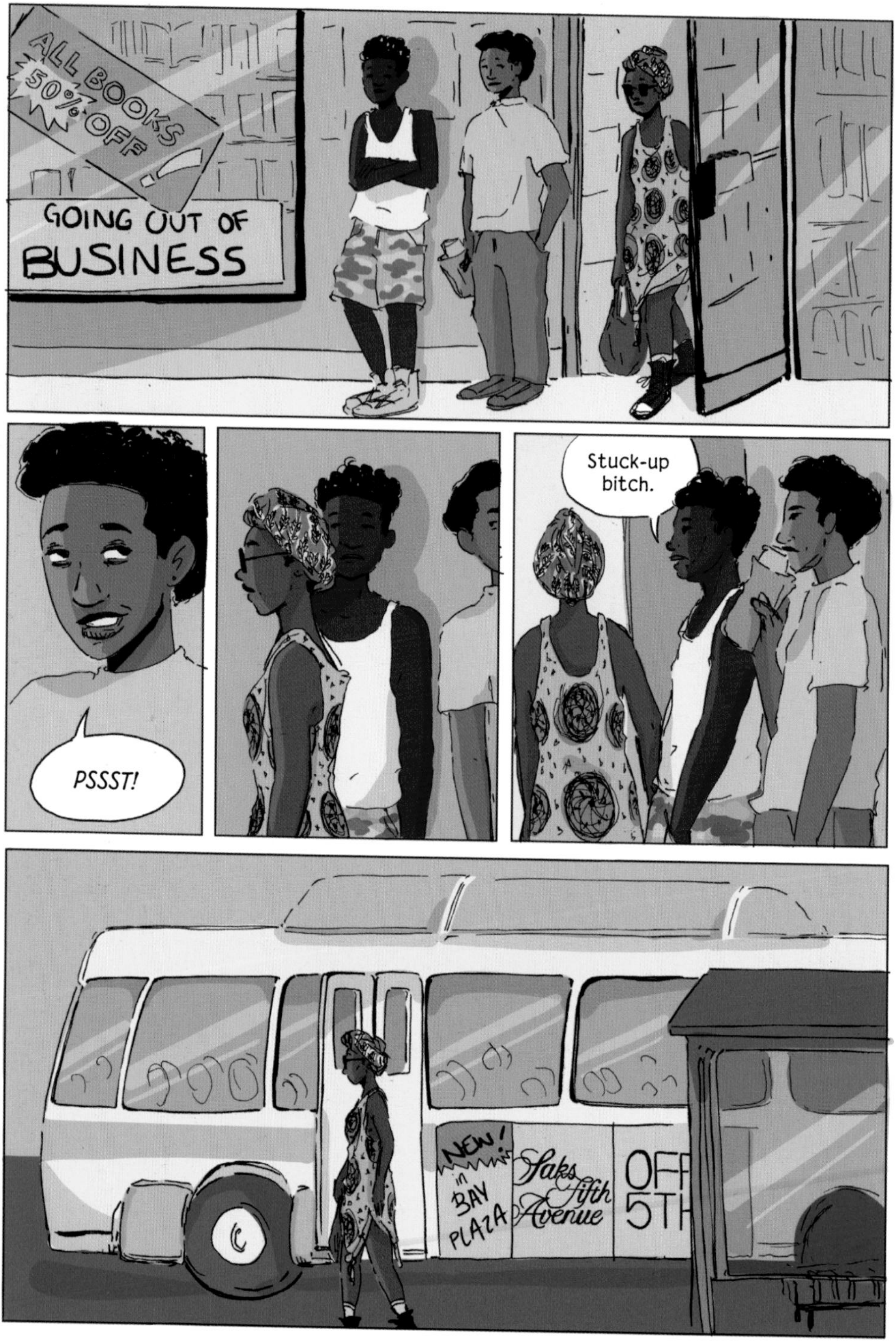
ALL BOOKS 50% OFF
GOING OUT OF BUSINESS
PSSST!
Stuck-up bitch.
NEW! in BAY PLAZA
Saks Fifth Avenue
OFF 5TH

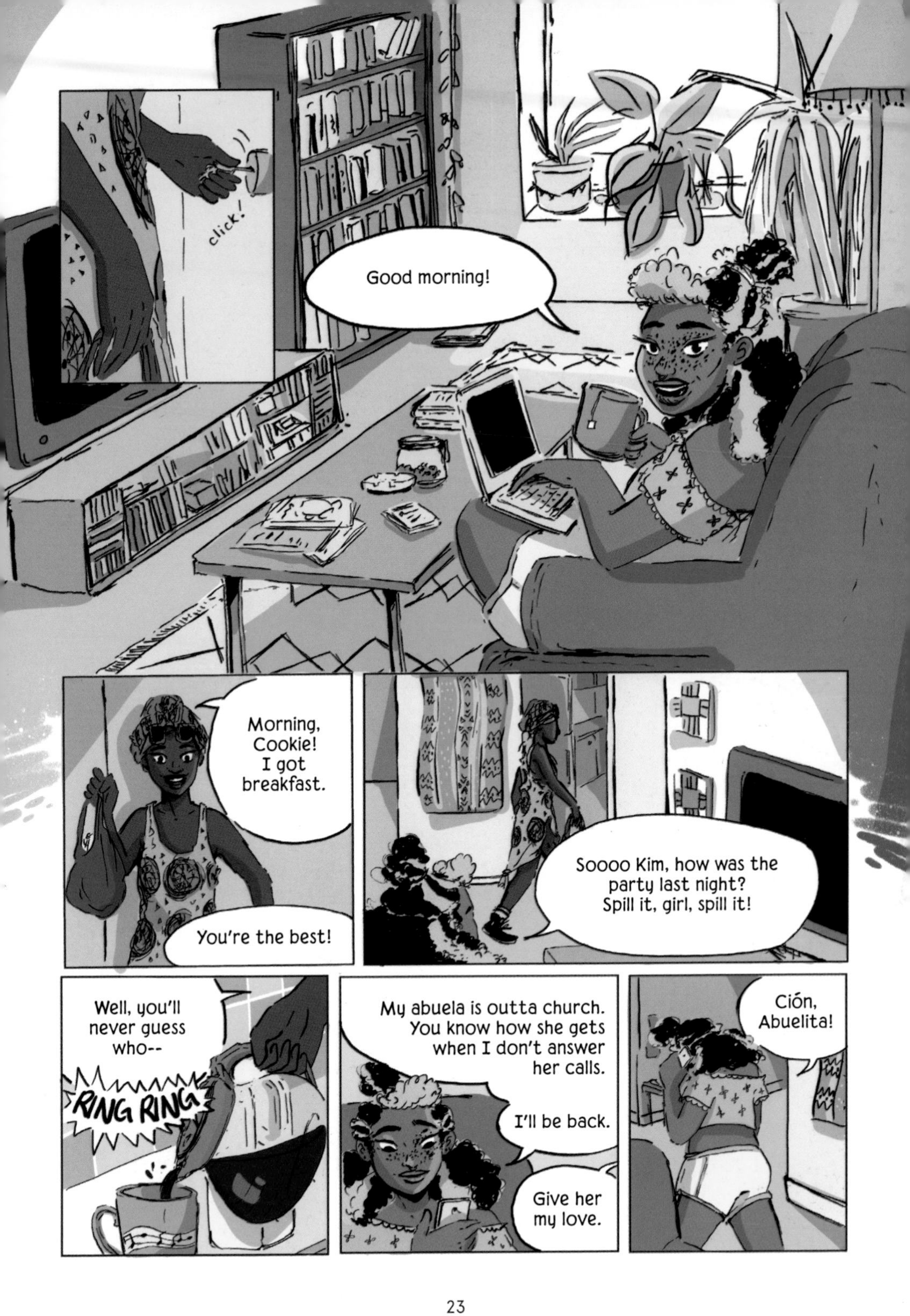
click!
Good morning!
Morning, Cookie! I got breakfast.
You're the best!
Soooo Kim, how was the party last night? Spill it, girl, spill it!
Well, you'll never guess who--
RING RING
My abuela is outta church. You know how she gets when I don't answer her calls.
I'll be back.
Give her my love.
Ción, Abuelita!

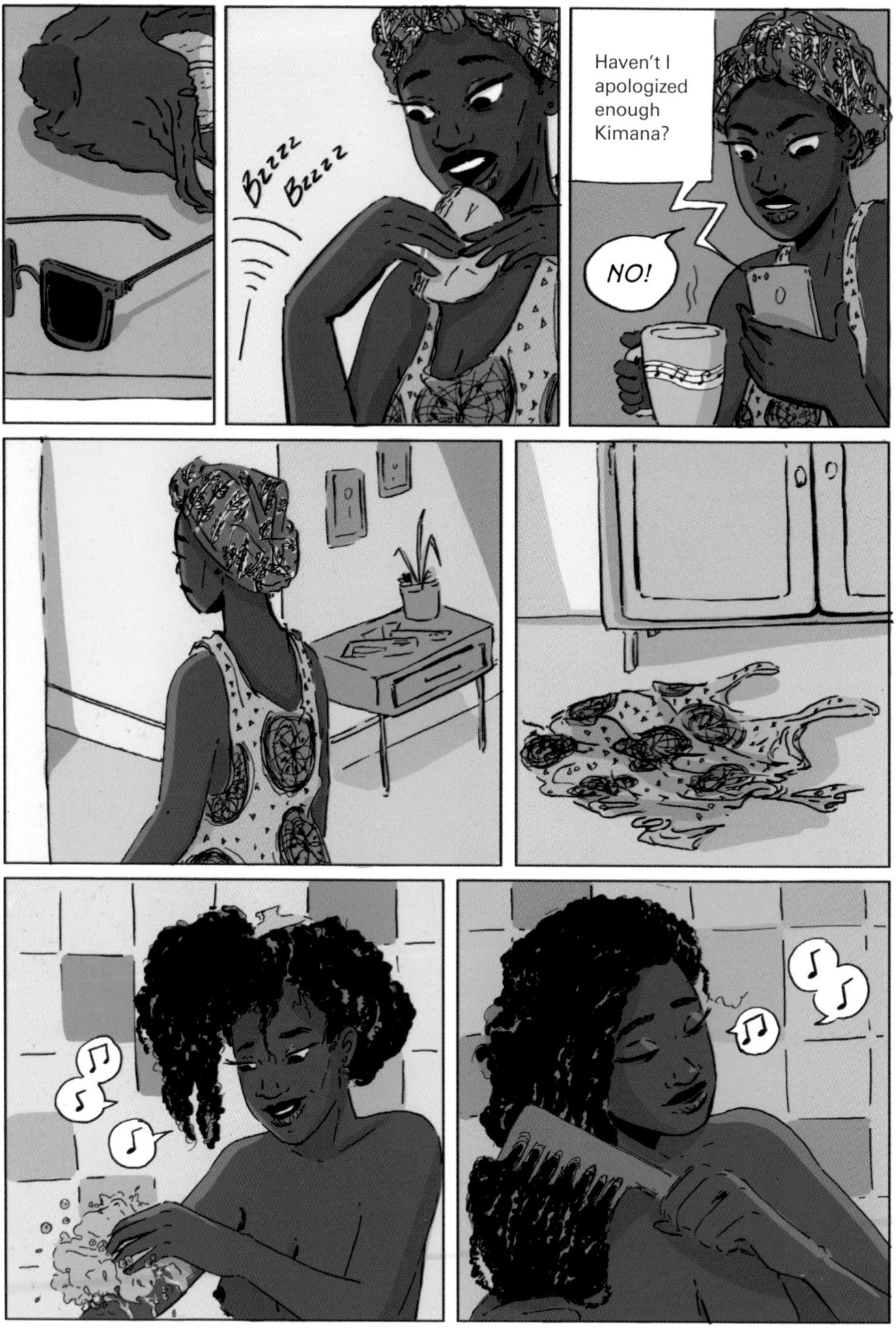
Bzzzz Bzzzz
Haven't I apologized enough Kimana?
NO!

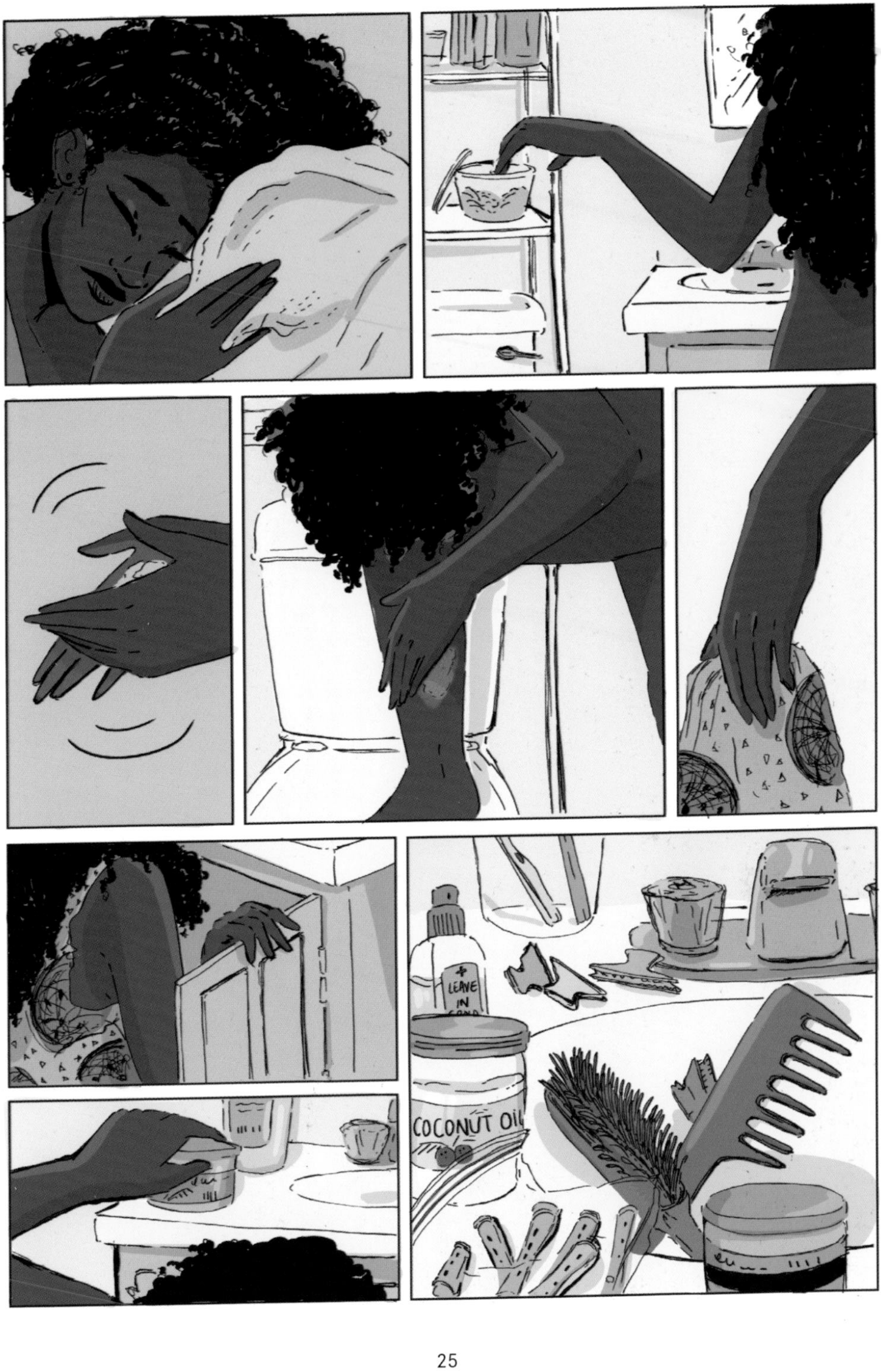
LEAVE IN
COCONUT OI

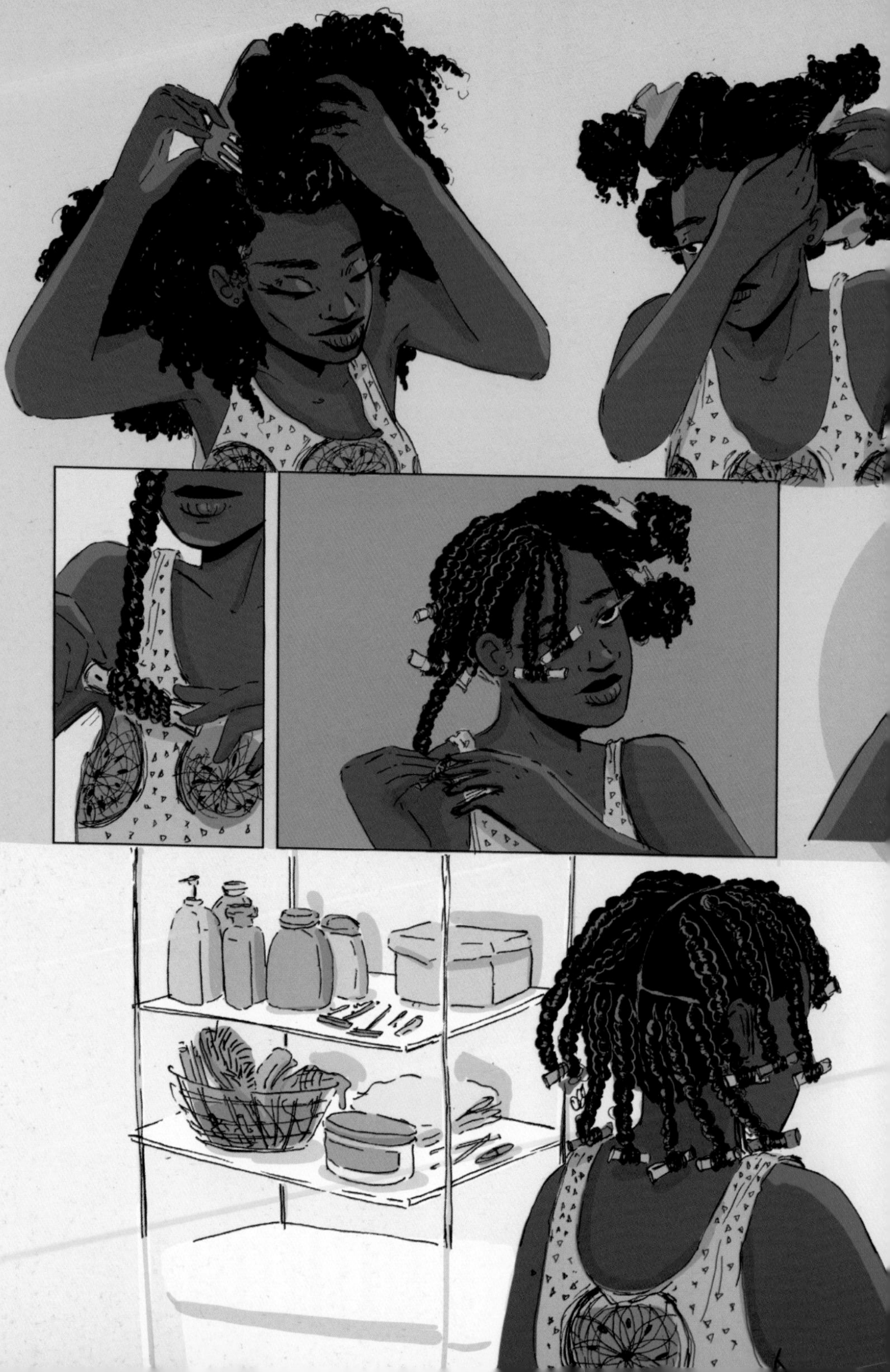

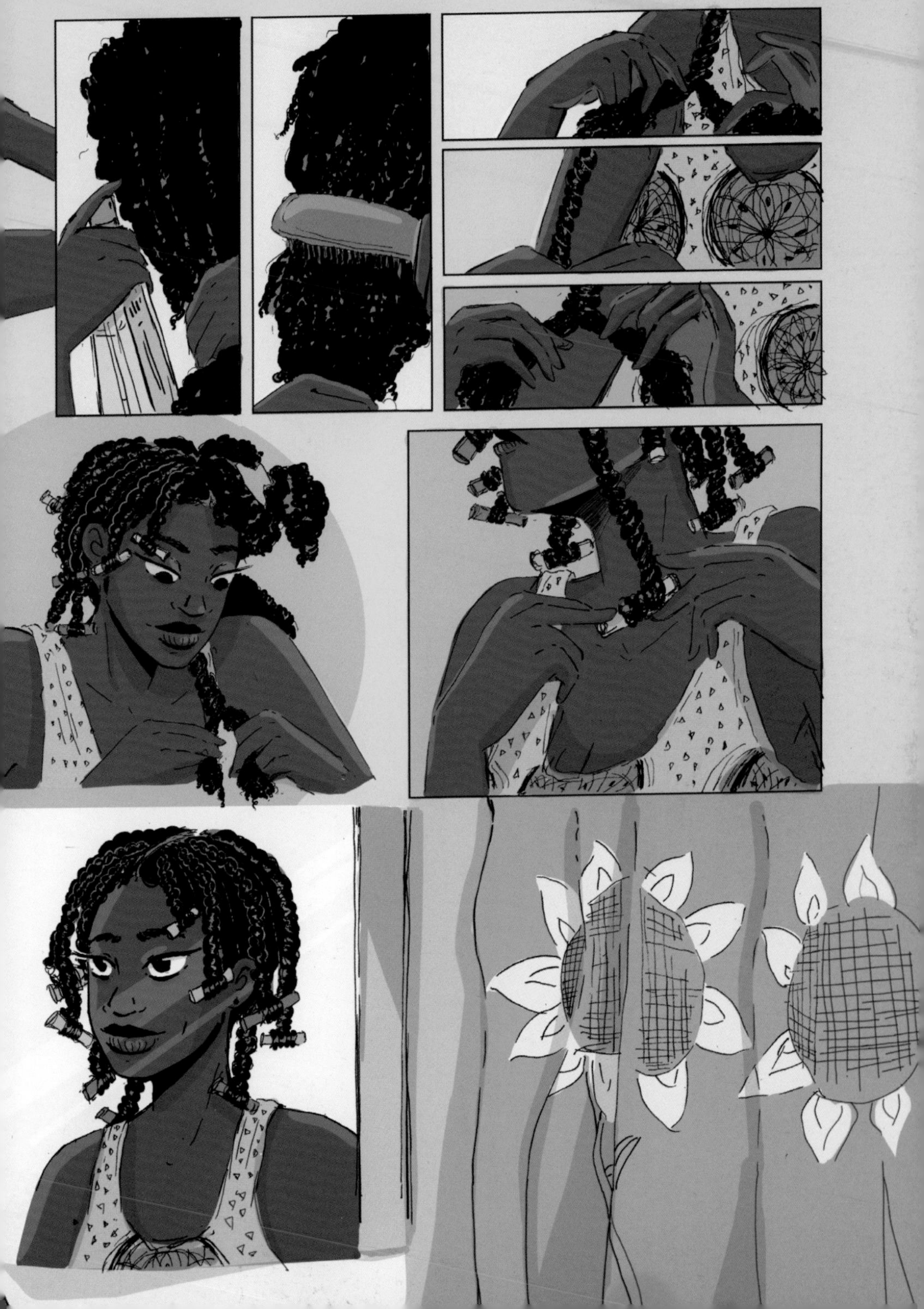

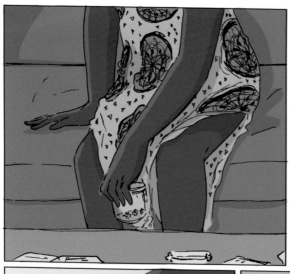
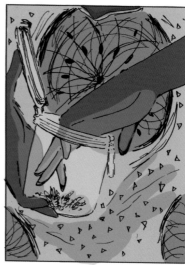

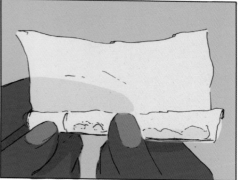

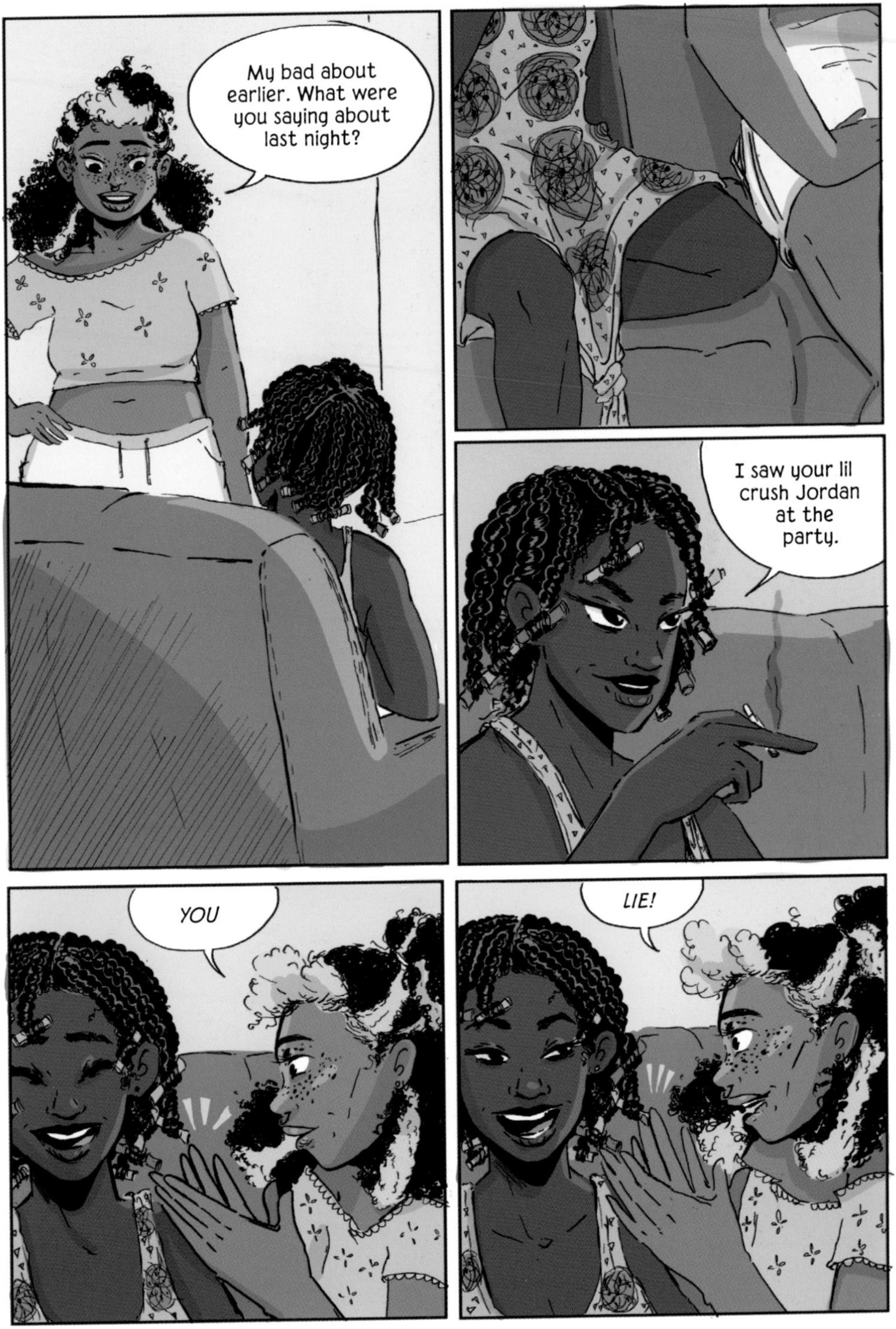
My bad about earlier. What were you saying about last night?
I saw your lil crush Jordan at the party.
YOU
LIE!

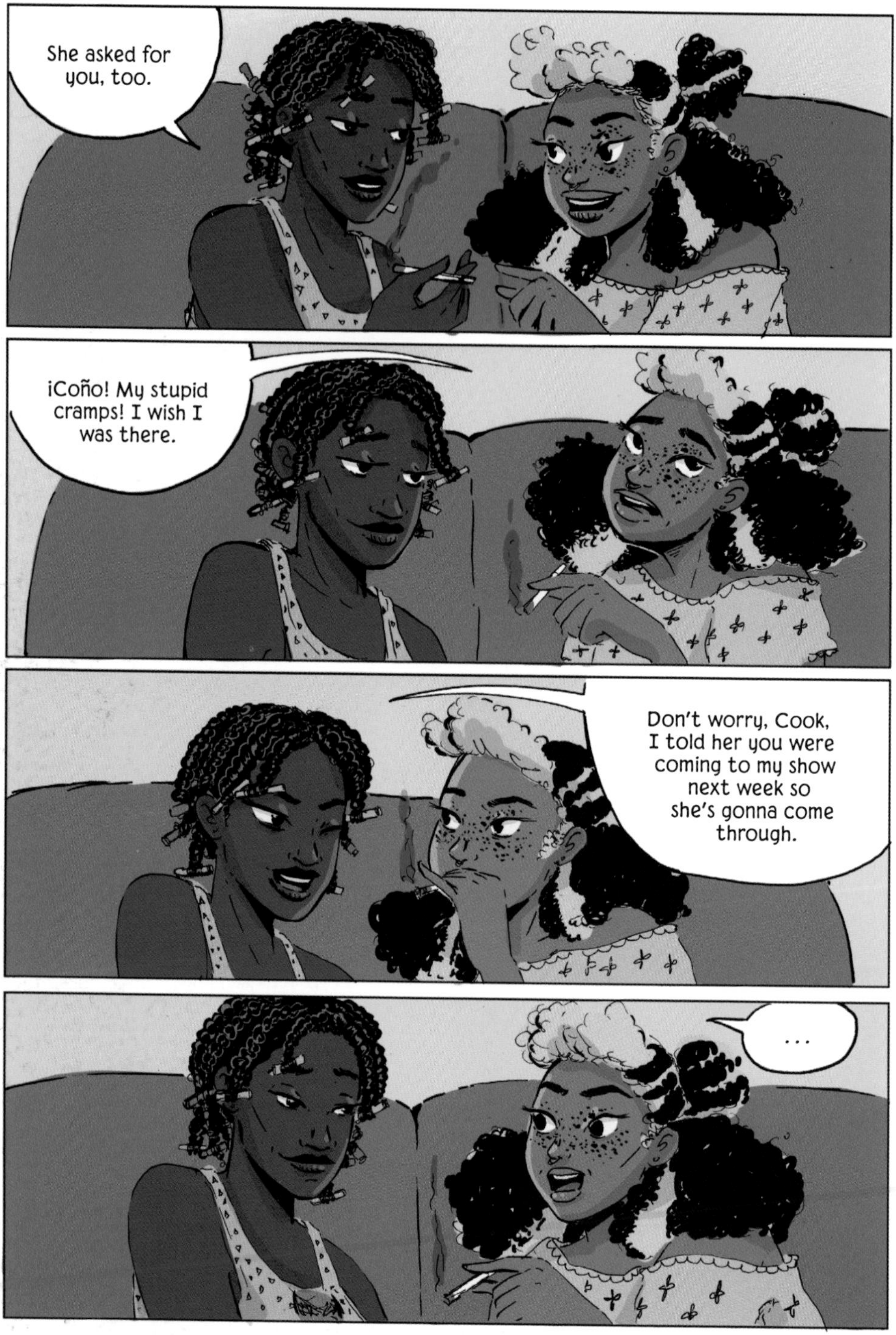
She asked for you, too.
¡Coño! My stupid cramps! I wish I was there.
Don't worry, Cook, I told her you were coming to my show next week so she's gonna come through.
. . .

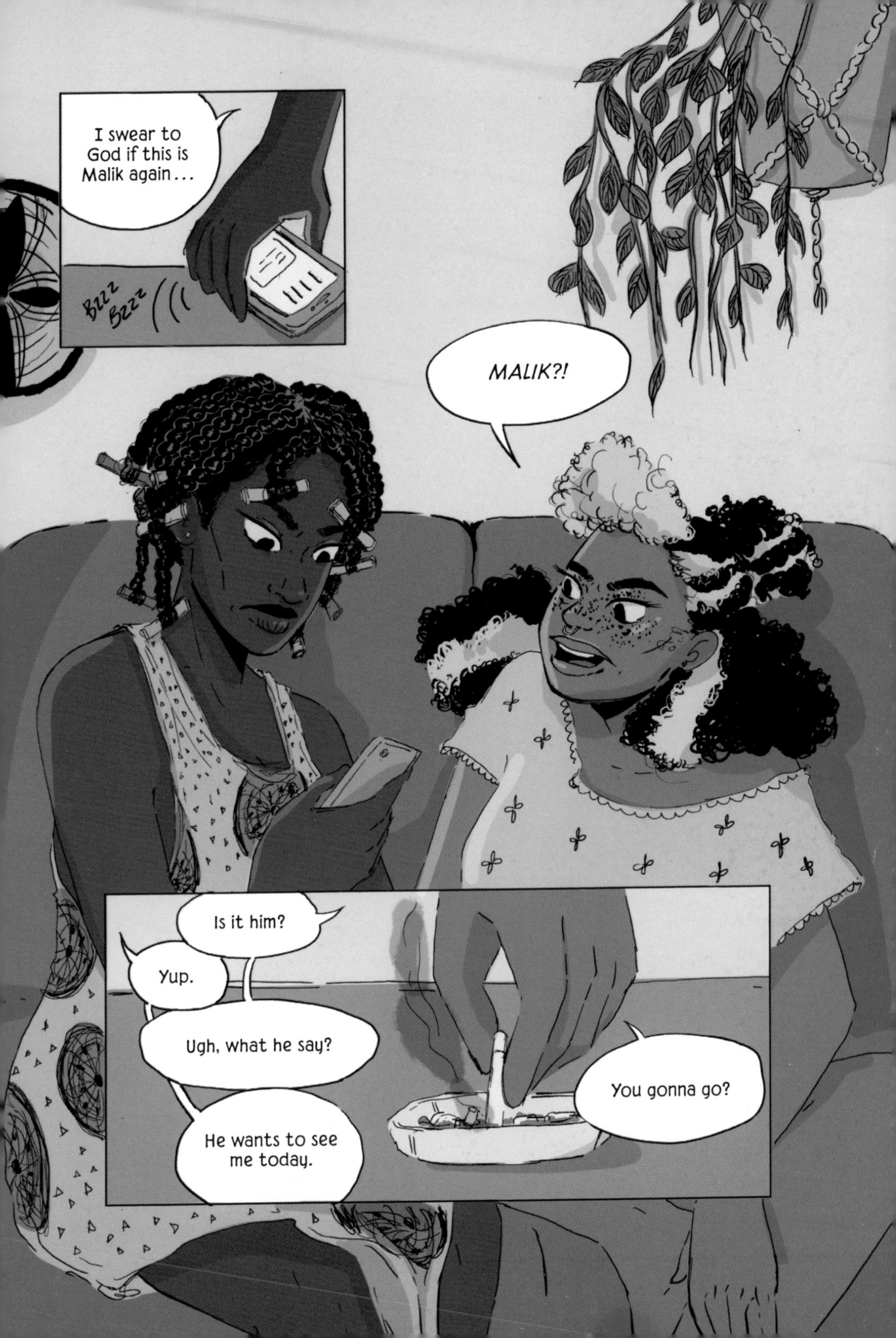
I swear to God if this is Malik again . . .
Bzzz Bzzz
MALIK?!
Is it him?
Yup.
Ugh, what he say?
He wants to see me today.
You gonna go?

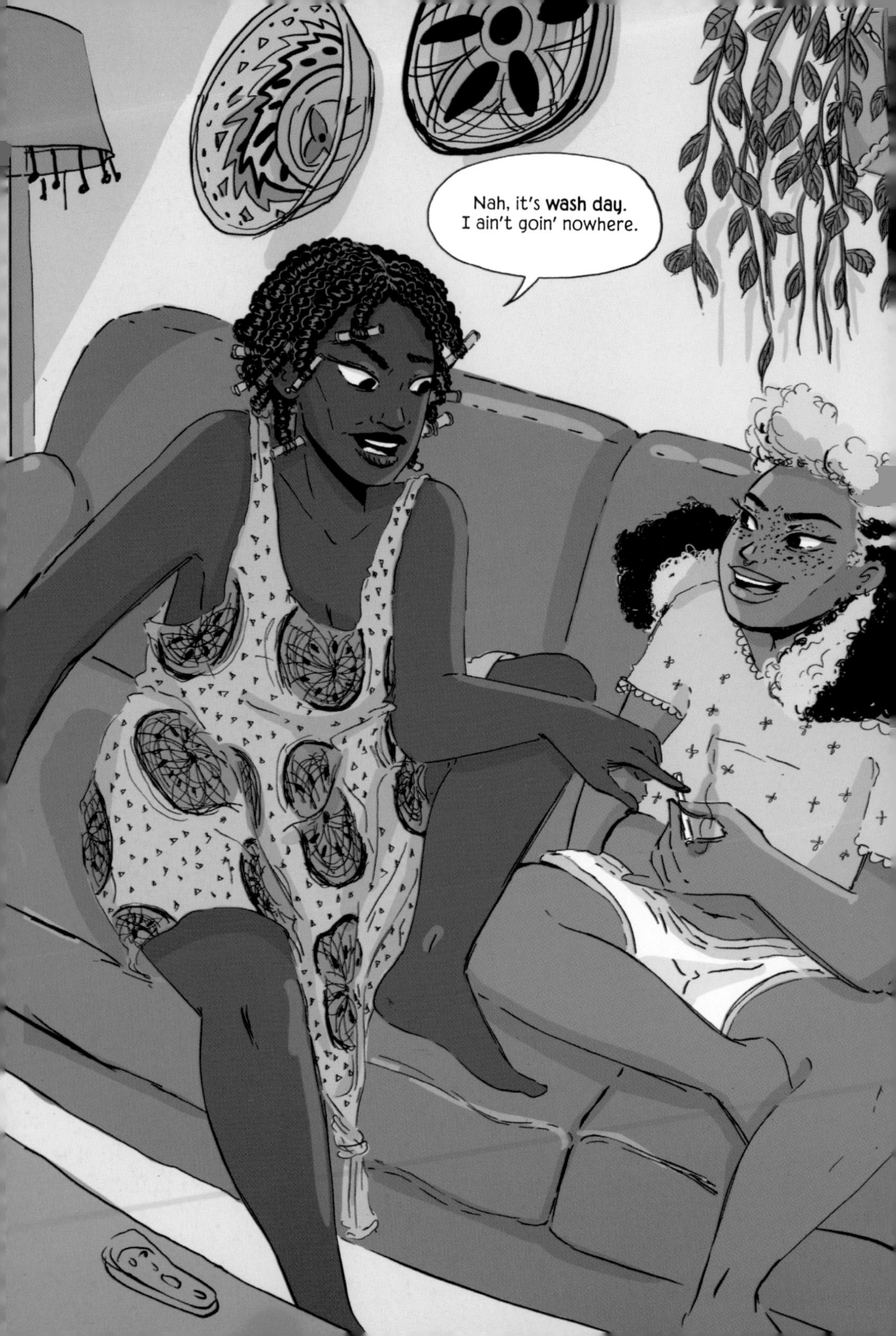
Nah, it's **wash day**. I ain't goin' nowhere.

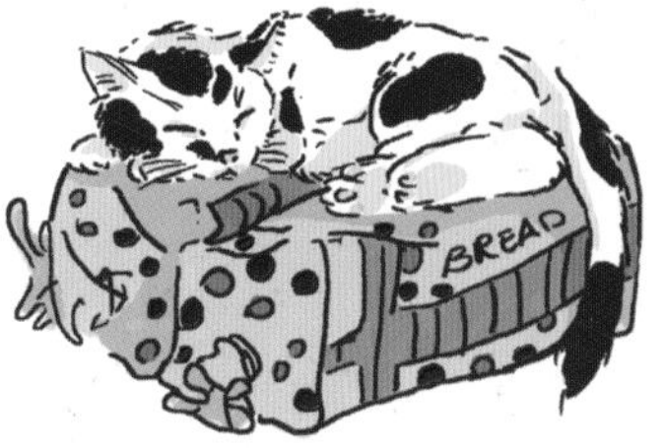
BREAD

GROUP CHAT

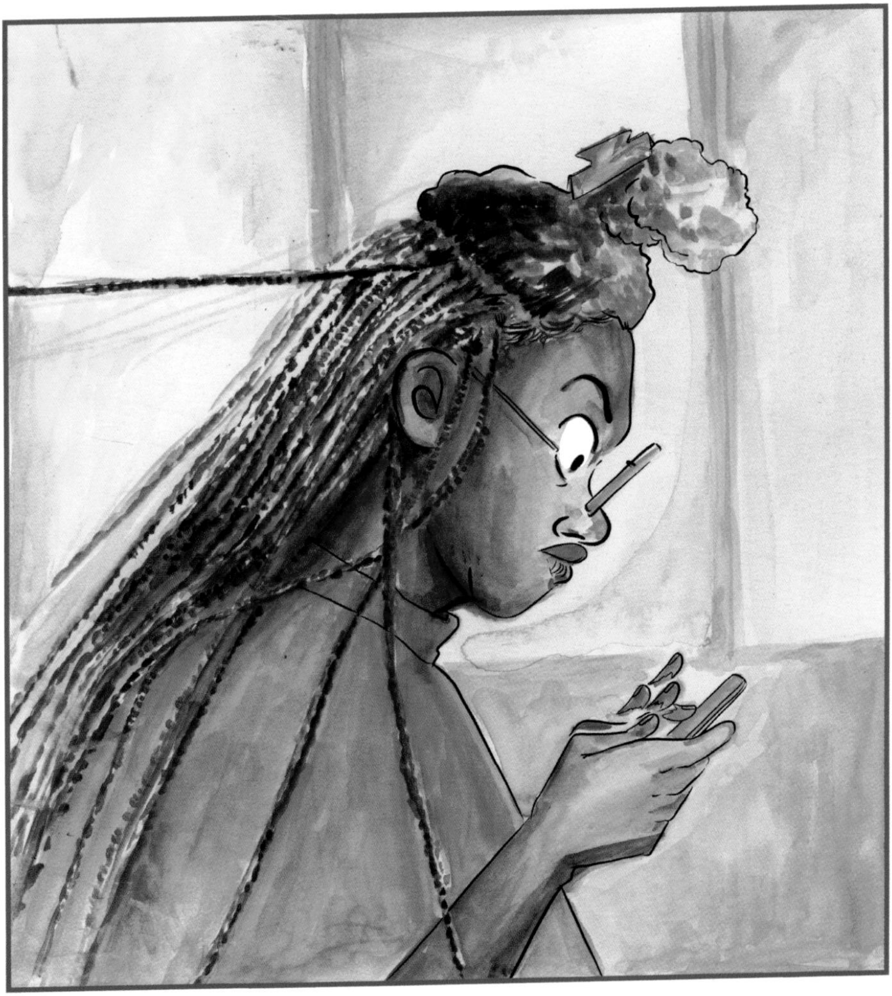

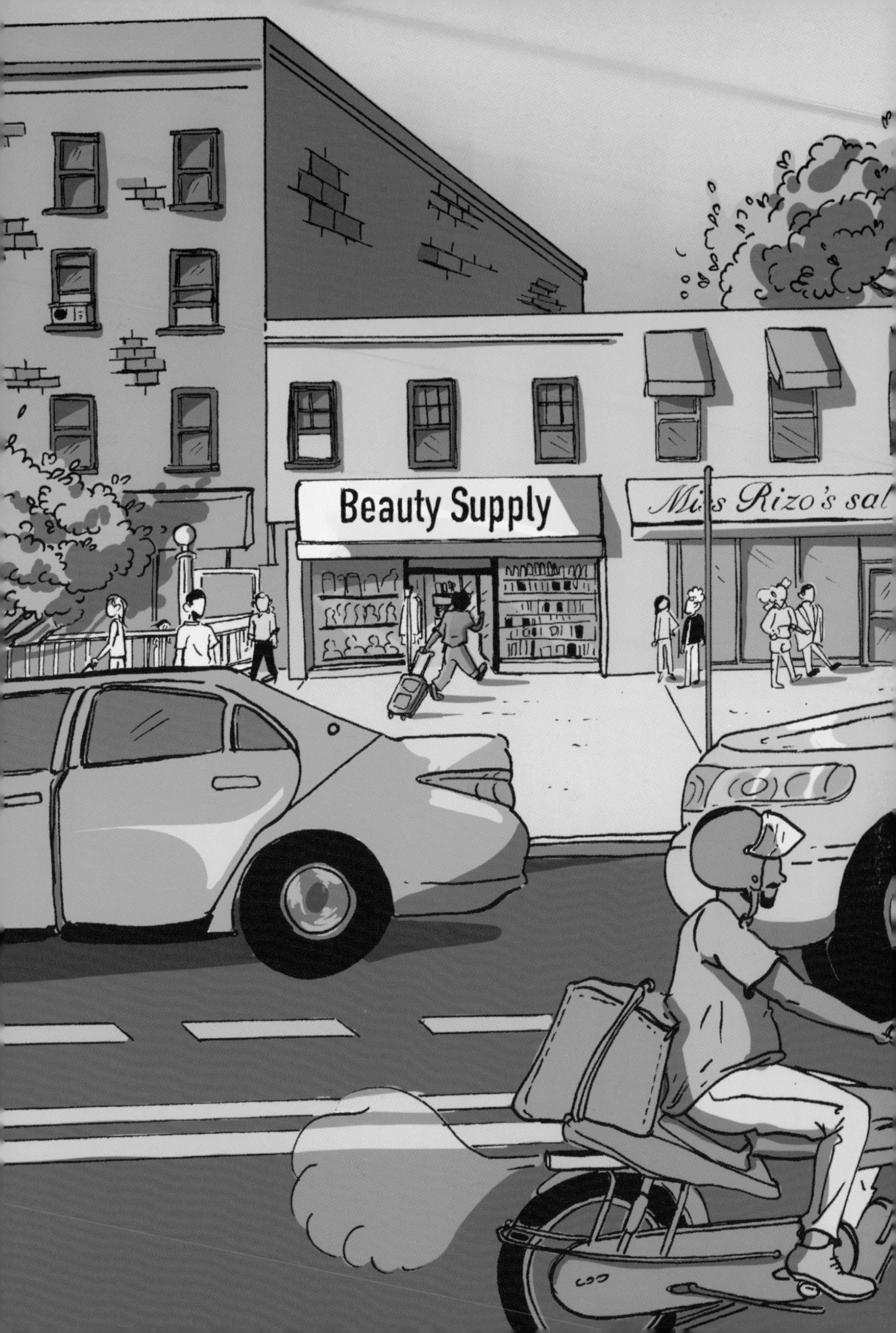
Beauty Supply
Rizo's

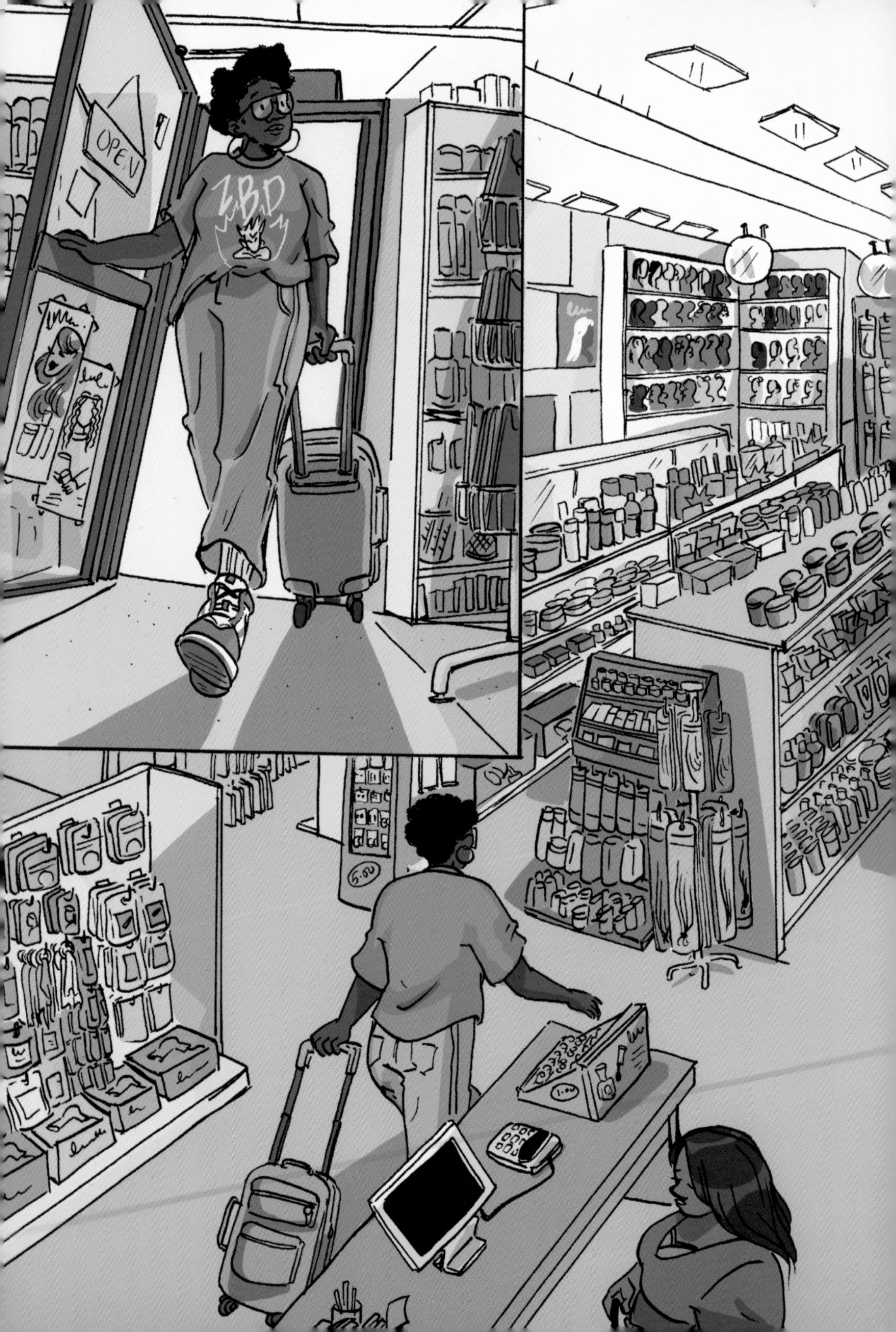
OPEN
Z.B.D
5.00
1.00

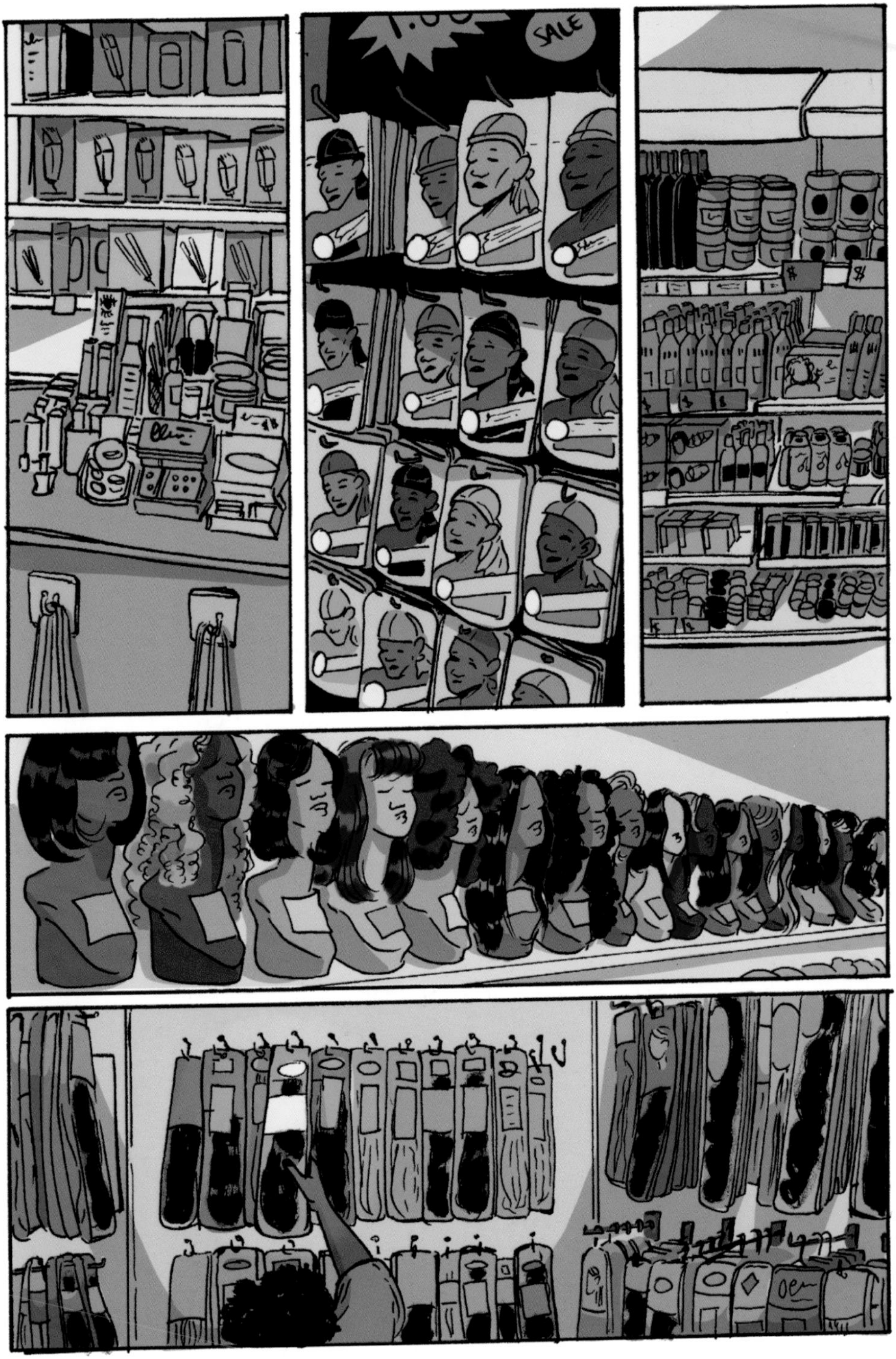
SALE

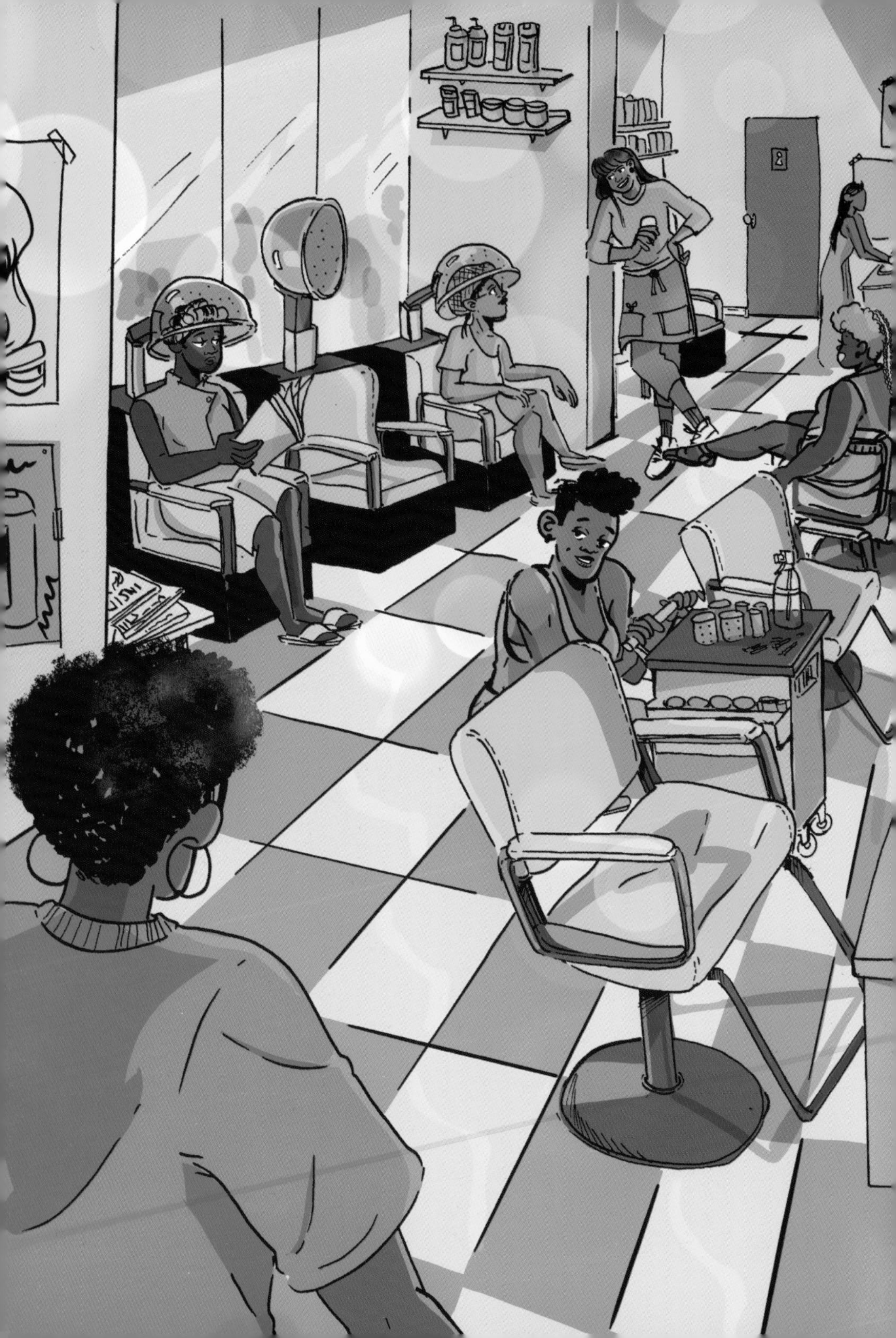

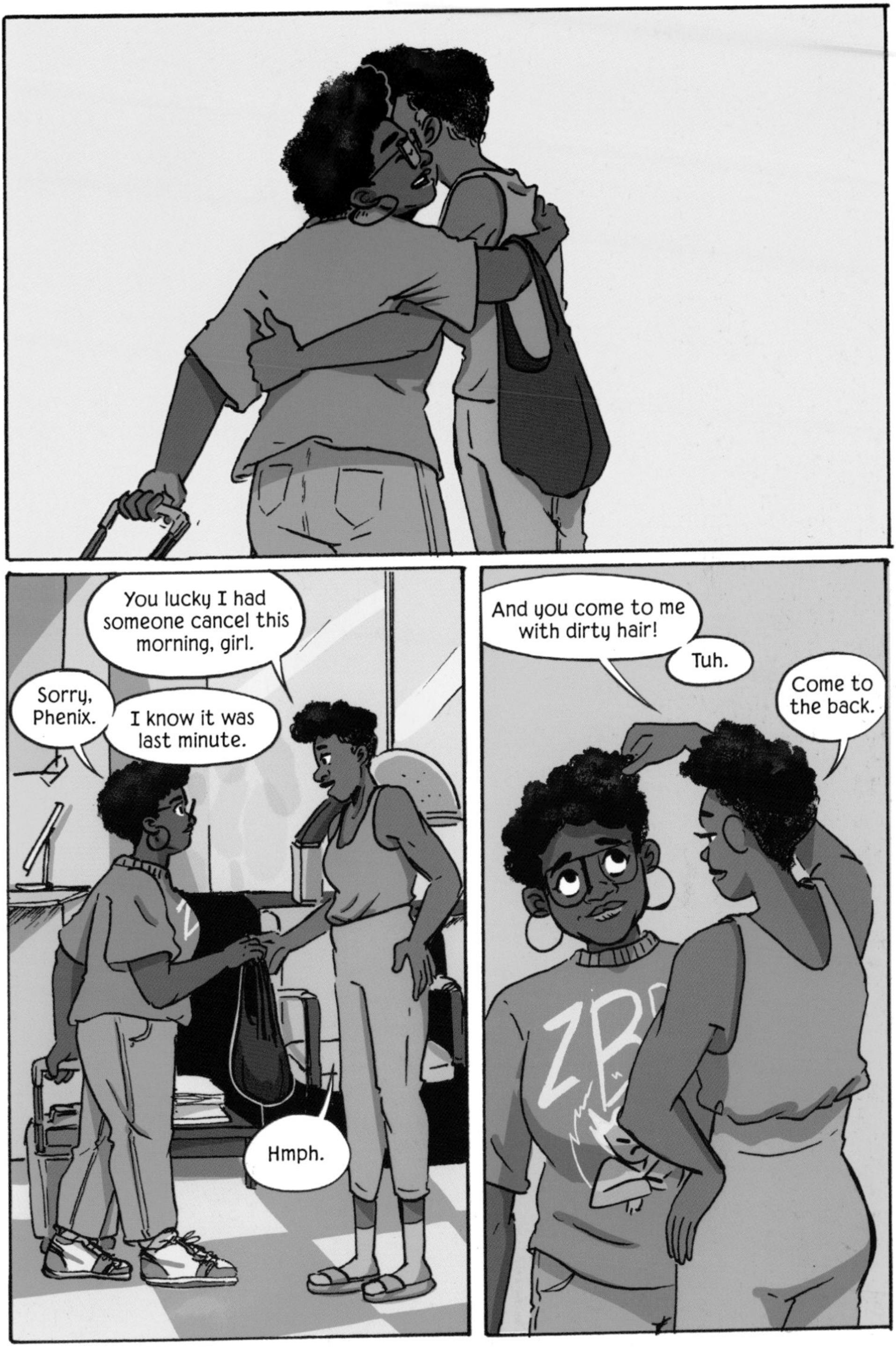
You lucky I had someone cancel this morning, girl.
Sorry, Phenix.
I know it was last minute.
Hmph.
And you come to me with dirty hair!
Tuh.
Come to the back.
ZB

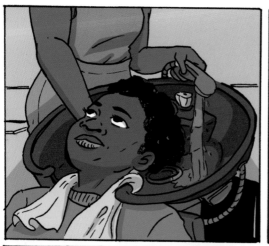

Girl, will you stay still?

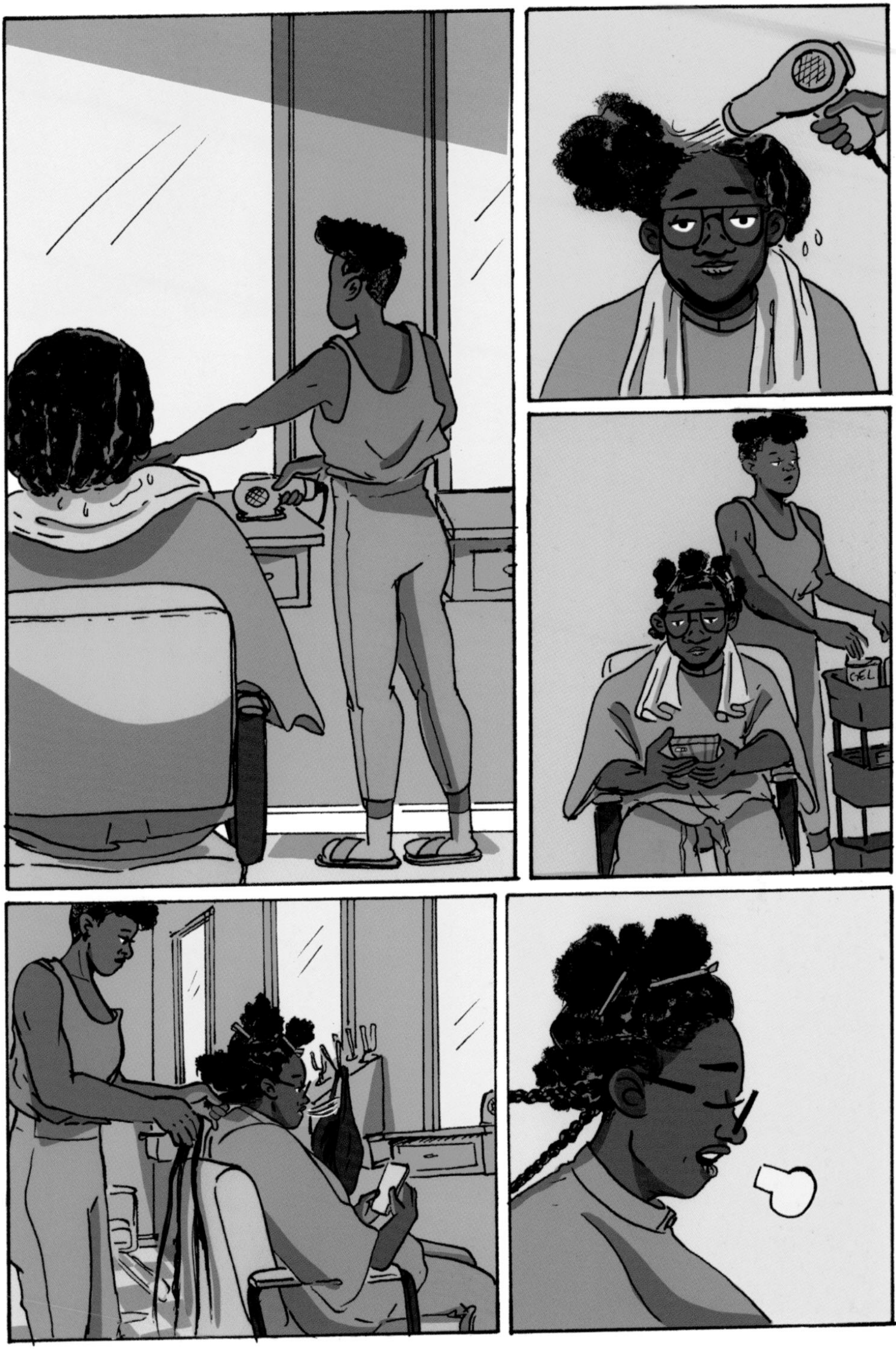
GEL

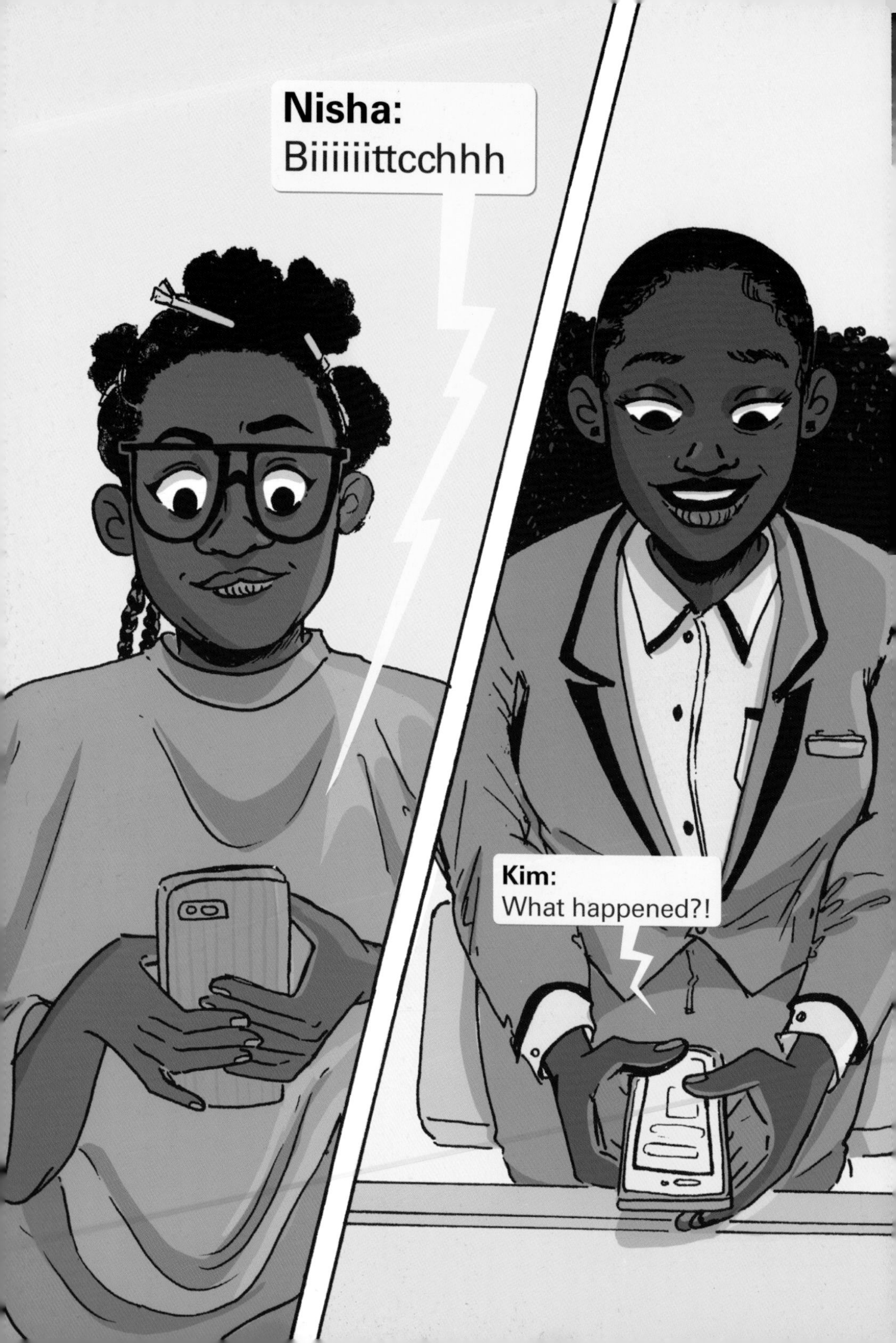
Nisha:
Biiiiiittcchhh
Kim:
What happened?!

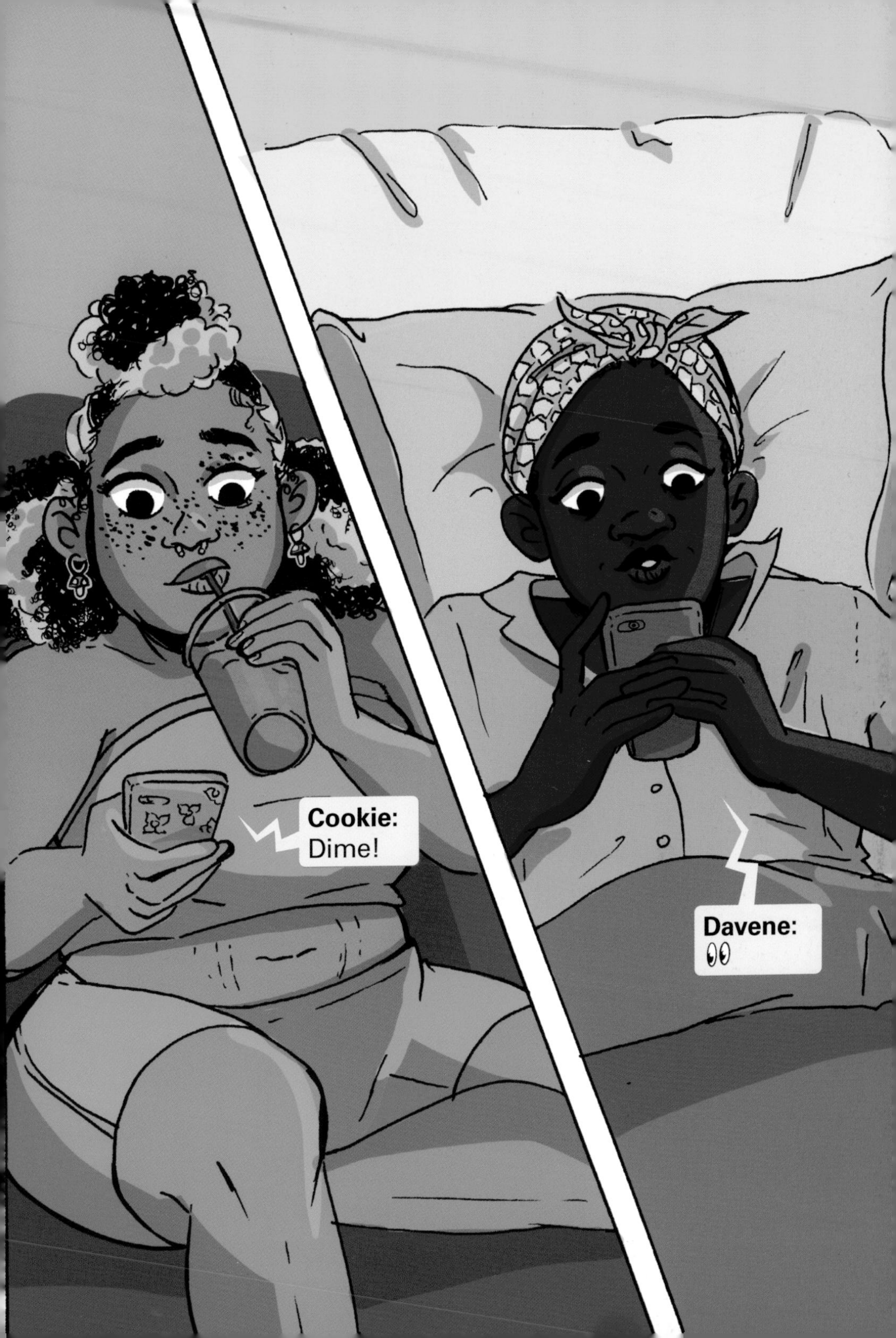
Cookie: Dime!
Davene: 👀

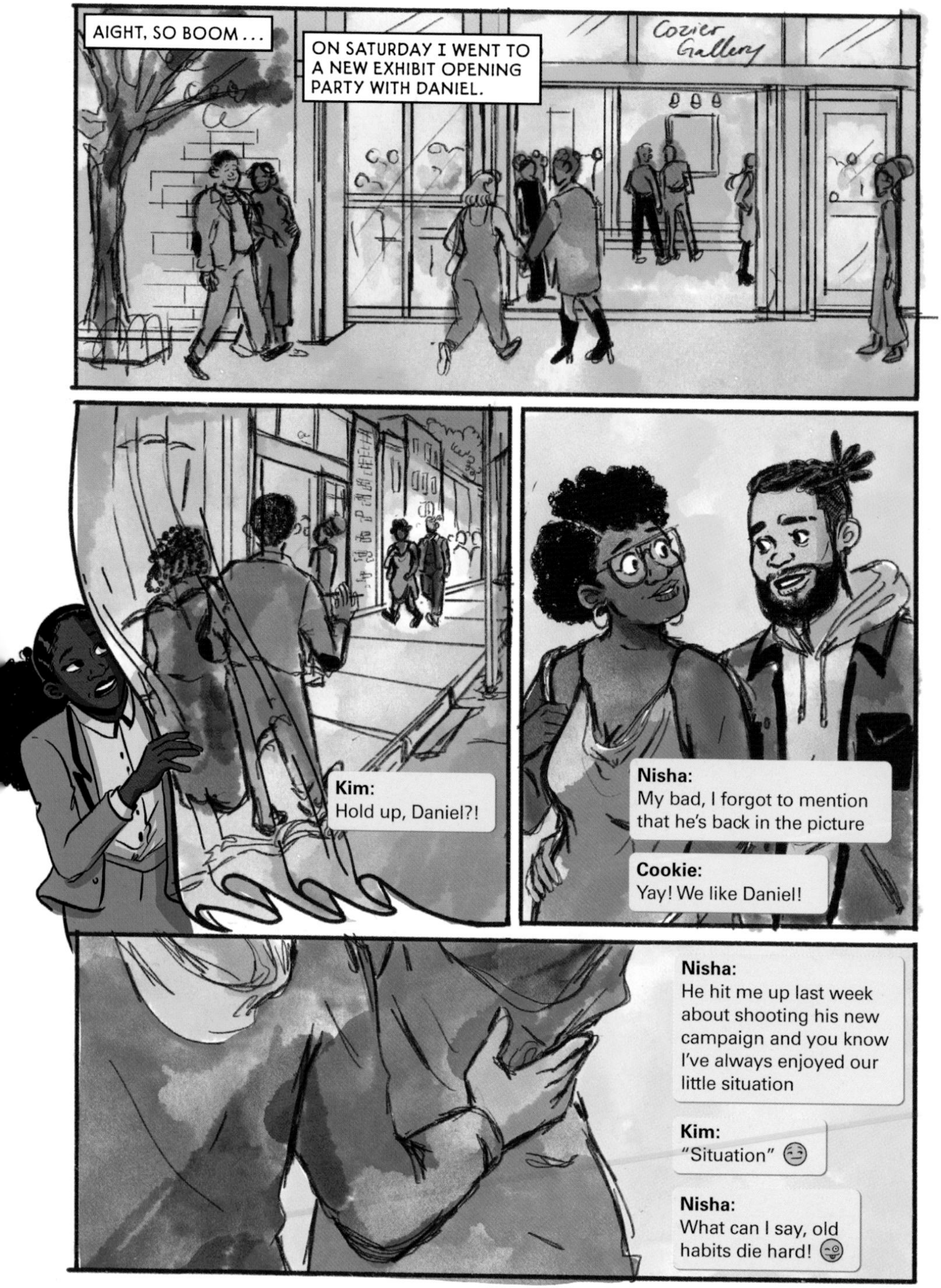

AIGHT, SO BOOM . . .
ON SATURDAY I WENT TO A NEW EXHIBIT OPENING PARTY WITH DANIEL.
Cozier Gallery
Kim: Hold up, Daniel?!
Nisha: My bad, I forgot to mention that he's back in the picture
Cookie: Yay! We like Daniel!
Nisha: He hit me up last week about shooting his new campaign and you know I've always enjoyed our little situation
Kim: "Situation"
Nisha: What can I say, old habits die hard!

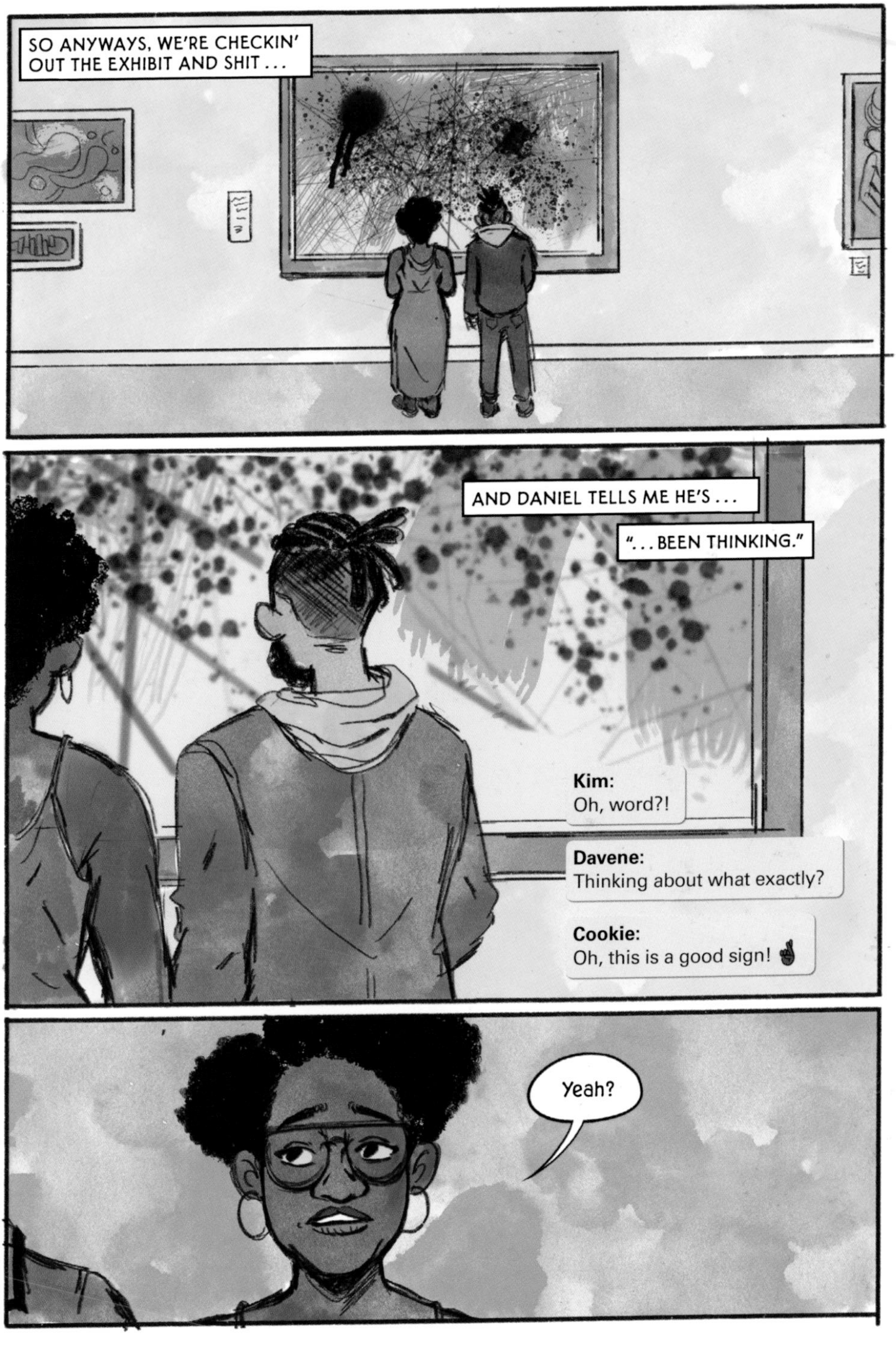
SO ANYWAYS, WE'RE CHECKIN' OUT THE EXHIBIT AND SHIT . . .
AND DANIEL TELLS ME HE'S . . .
". . . BEEN THINKING."
Kim: Oh, word?!
Davene: Thinking about what exactly?
Cookie: Oh, this is a good sign!
Yeah?

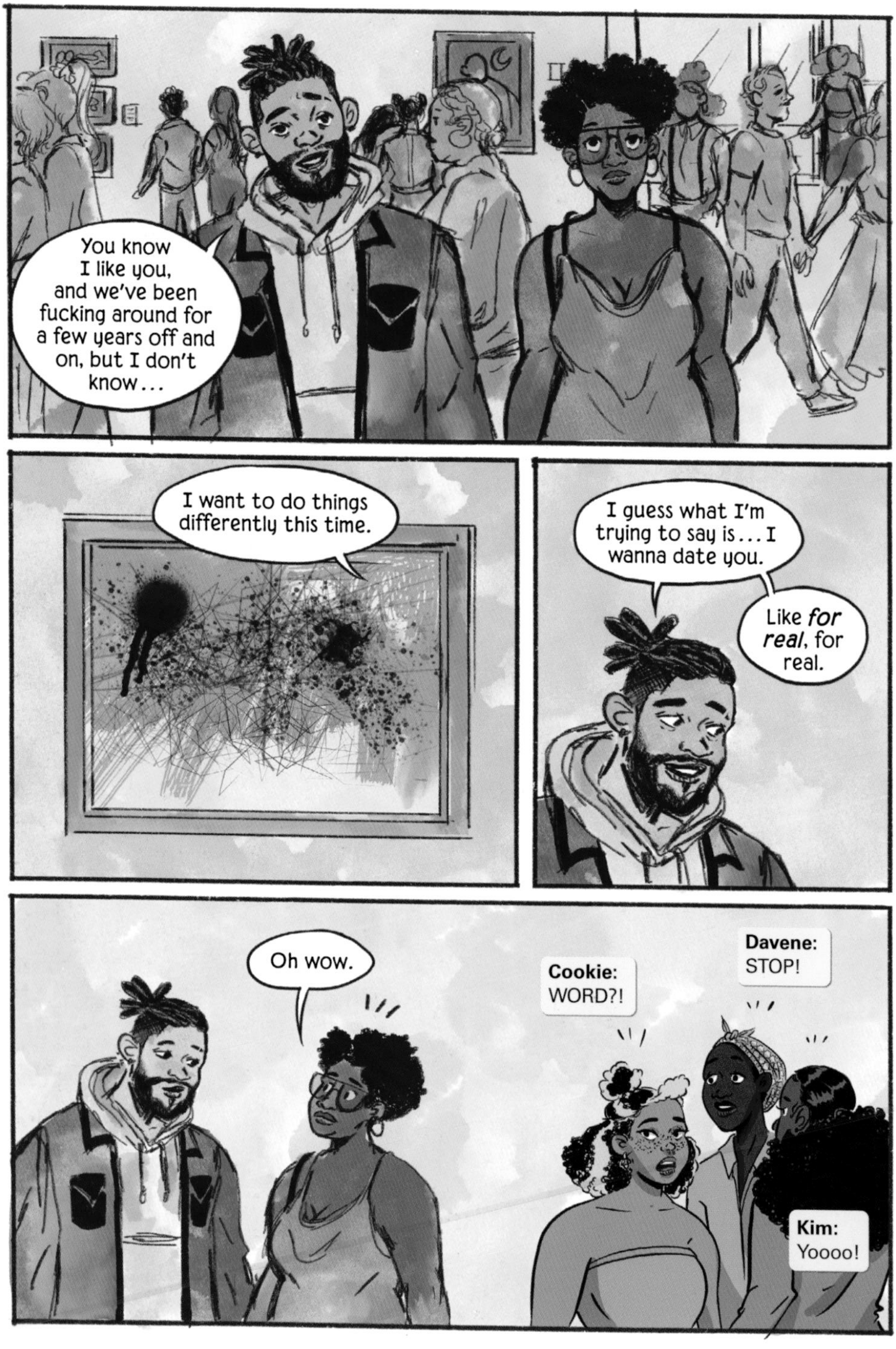
You know I like you, and we've been fucking around for a few years off and on, but I don't know...
I want to do things differently this time.
I guess what I'm trying to say is... I wanna date you.
Like *for real*, for real.
Oh wow.
Cookie: WORD?!
Davene: STOP!
Kim: Yoooo!

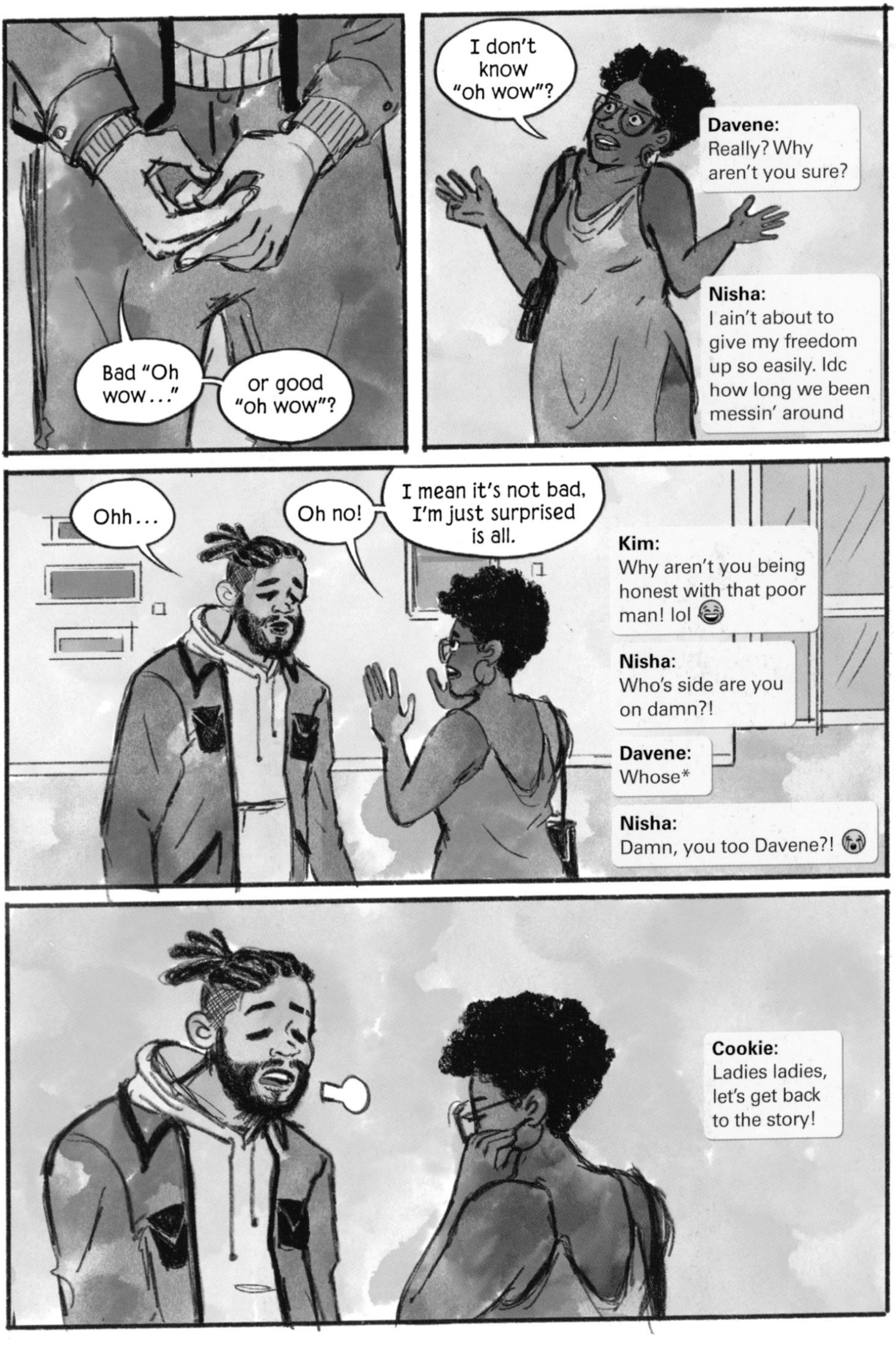
Bad "Oh wow…"
or good "oh wow"?
I don't know "oh wow"?
Davene: Really? Why aren't you sure?
Nisha: I ain't about to give my freedom up so easily. Idc how long we been messin' around
Ohh…
Oh no!
I mean it's not bad, I'm just surprised is all.
Kim: Why aren't you being honest with that poor man! lol 😂
Nisha: Who's side are you on damn?!
Davene: Whose*
Nisha: Damn, you too Davene?! 😭
Cookie: Ladies ladies, let's get back to the story!

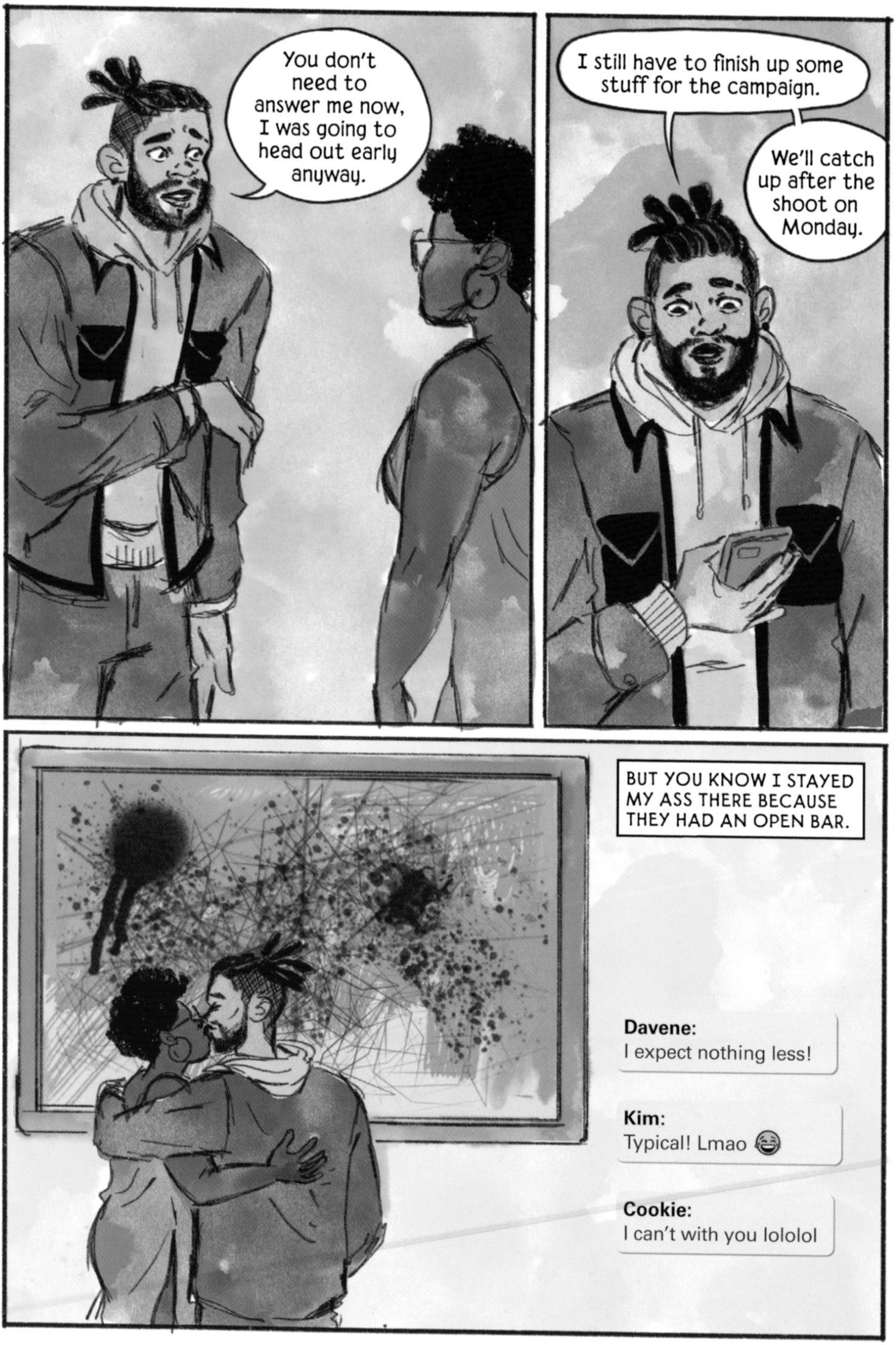
You don't need to answer me now, I was going to head out early anyway.
I still have to finish up some stuff for the campaign.
We'll catch up after the shoot on Monday.
BUT YOU KNOW I STAYED MY ASS THERE BECAUSE THEY HAD AN OPEN BAR.
Davene:
I expect nothing less!
Kim:
Typical! Lmao 😂
Cookie:
I can't with you lololol

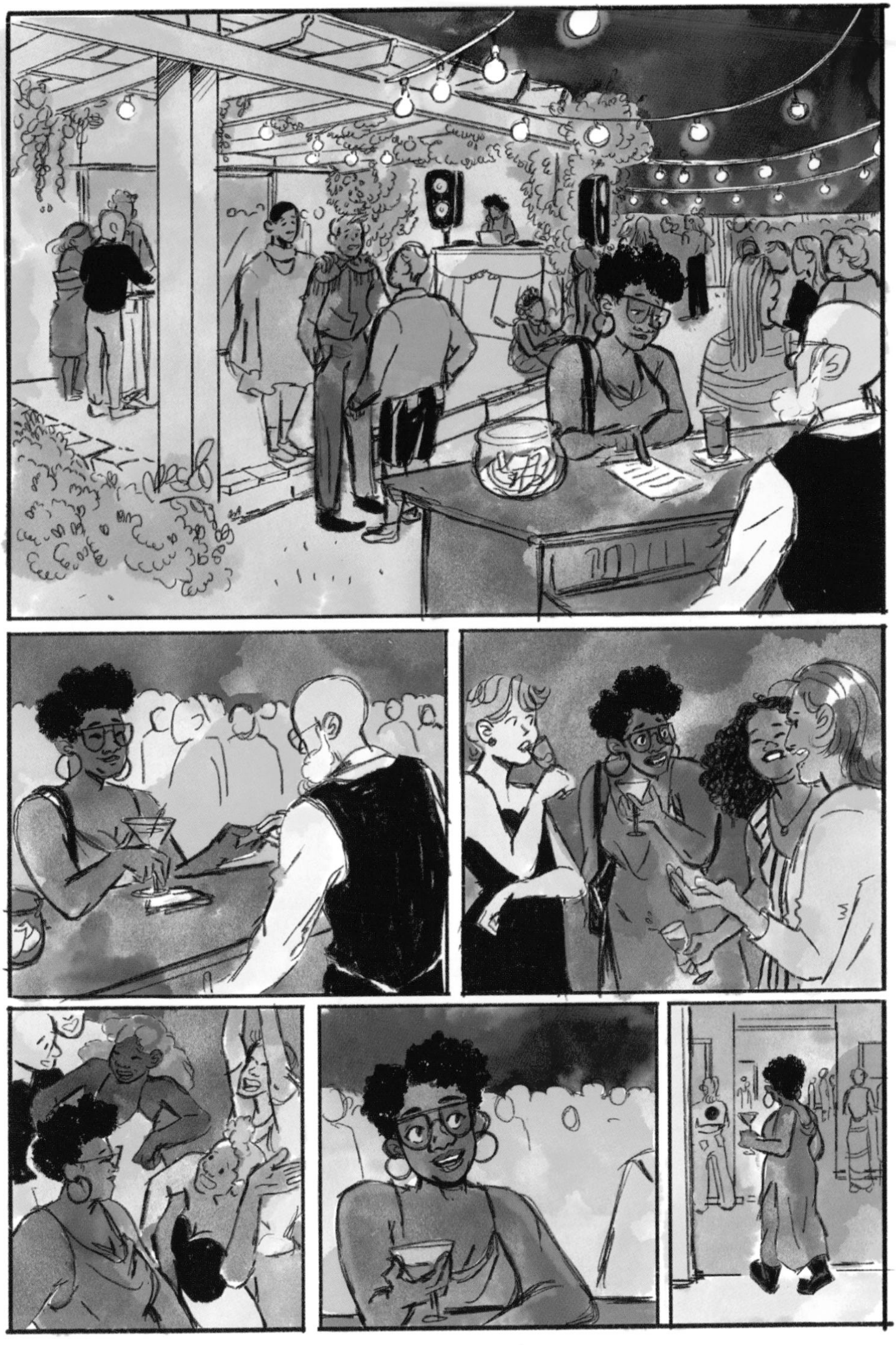

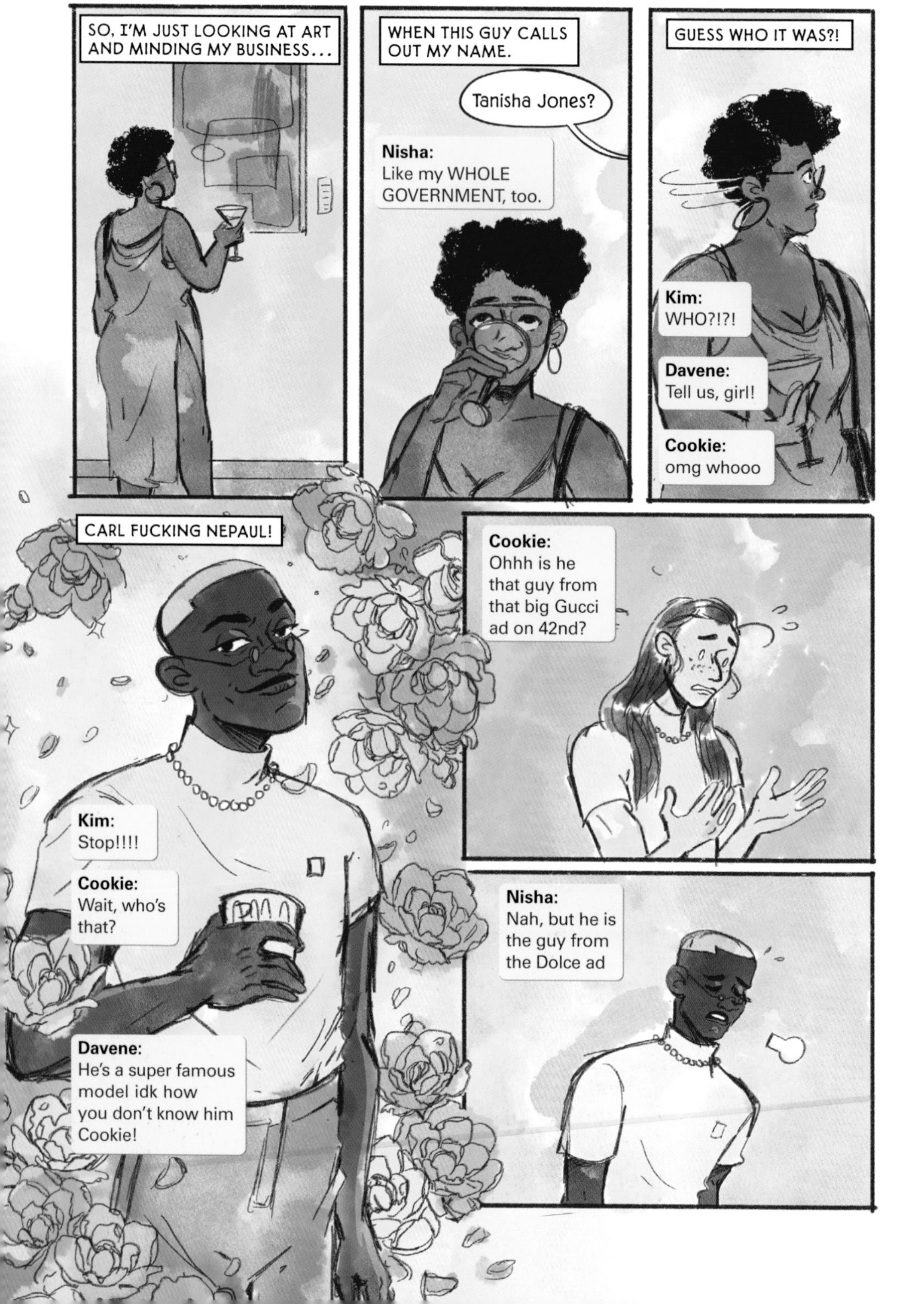
SO, I'M JUST LOOKING AT ART AND MINDING MY BUSINESS...
WHEN THIS GUY CALLS OUT MY NAME.
Tanisha Jones?
Nisha: Like my WHOLE GOVERNMENT, too.
GUESS WHO IT WAS?!
Kim: WHO?!?!
Davene: Tell us, girl!
Cookie: omg whooo
CARL FUCKING NEPAUL!
Kim: Stop!!!!
Cookie: Wait, who's that?
Davene: He's a super famous model idk how you don't know him Cookie!
Cookie: Ohhh is he that guy from that big Gucci ad on 42nd?
Nisha: Nah, but he is the guy from the Dolce ad

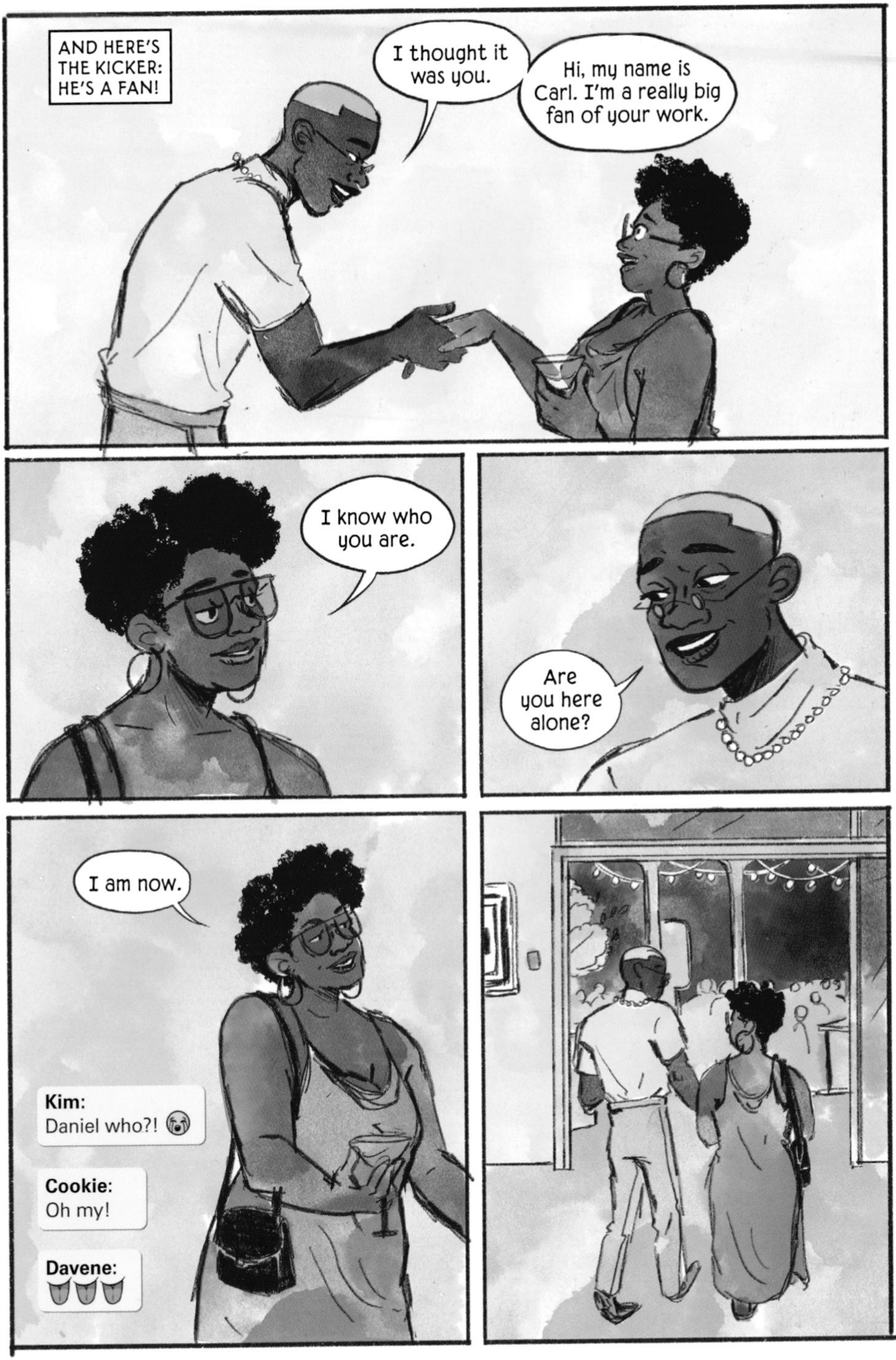
AND HERE'S THE KICKER: HE'S A FAN!
I thought it was you.
Hi, my name is Carl. I'm a really big fan of your work.
I know who you are.
Are you here alone?
I am now.
Kim: Daniel who?! 😭
Cookie: Oh my!
Davene: 👅👅👅

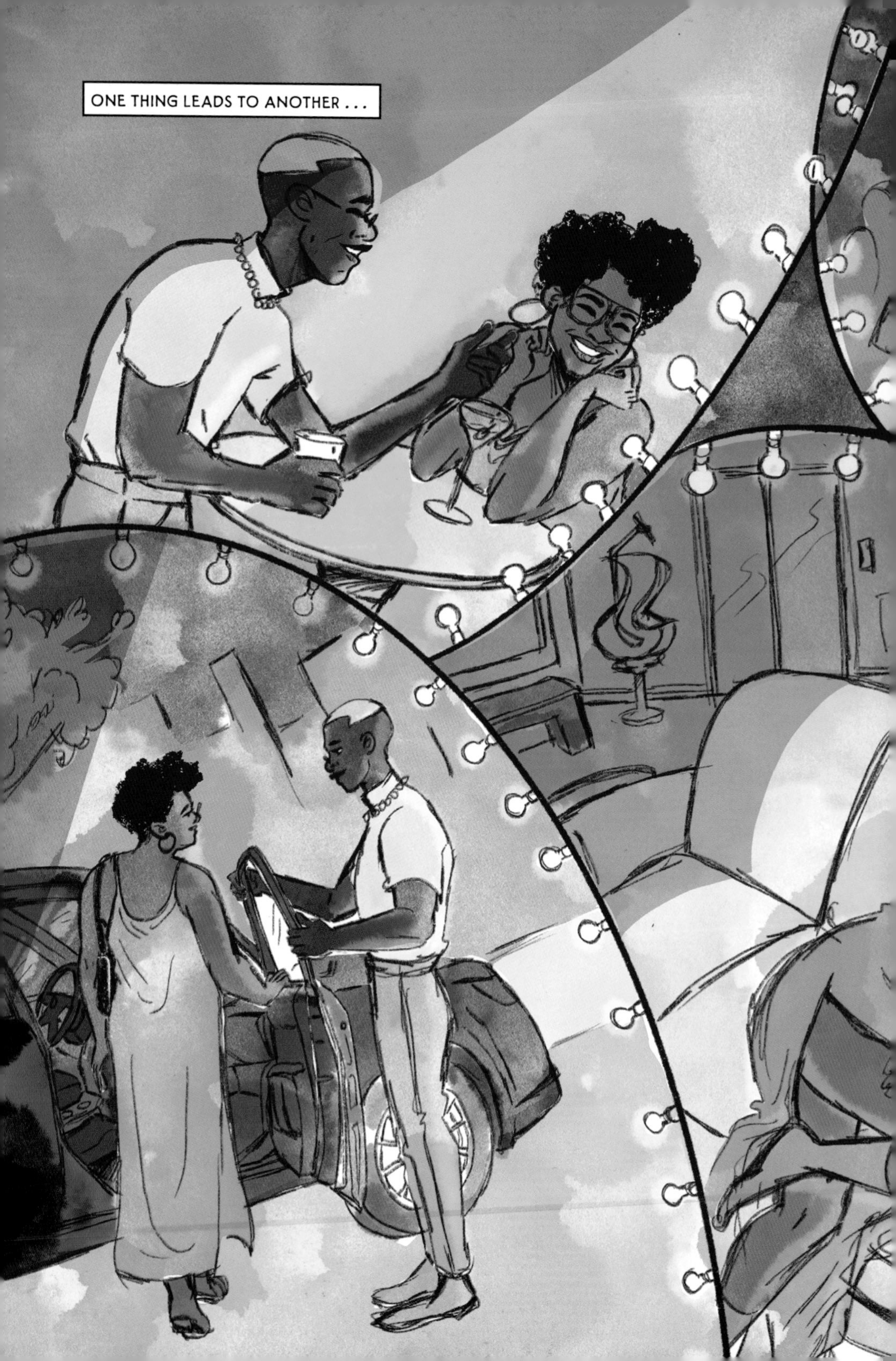
ONE THING LEADS TO ANOTHER . . .

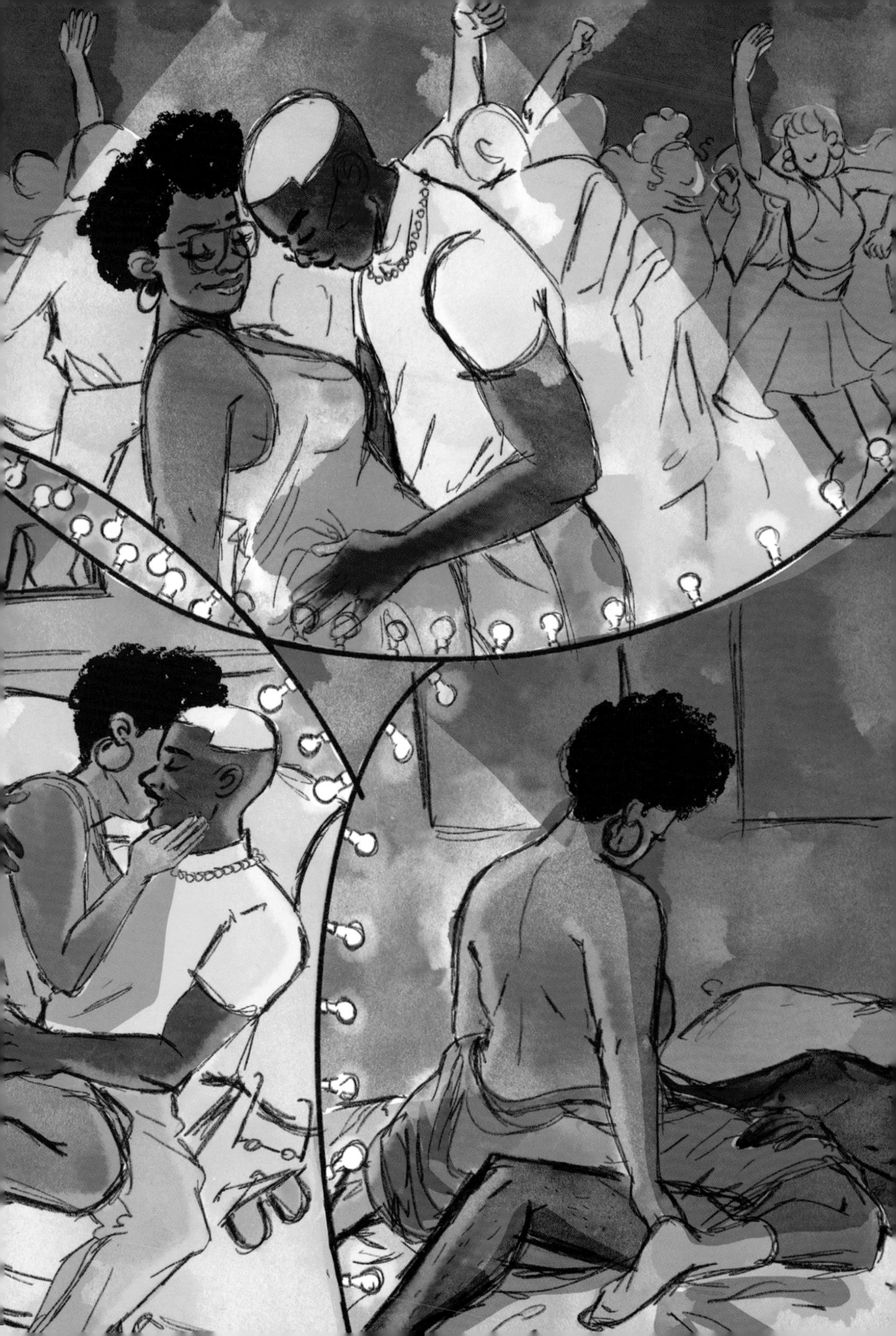

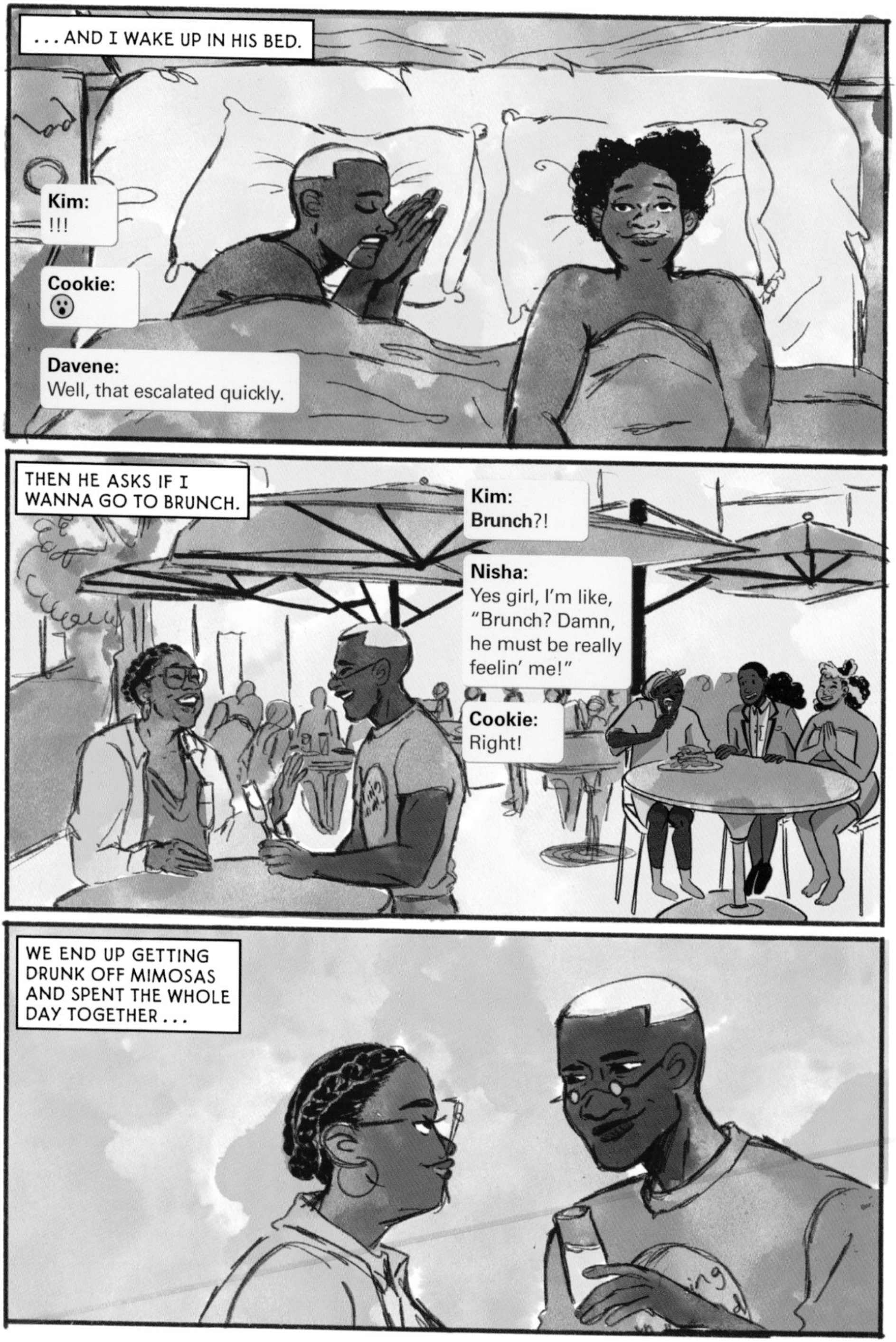
. . . AND I WAKE UP IN HIS BED.
Kim: !!!
Cookie:
Davene: Well, that escalated quickly.
THEN HE ASKS IF I WANNA GO TO BRUNCH.
Kim: Brunch?!
Nisha: Yes girl, I'm like, "Brunch? Damn, he must be really feelin' me!"
Cookie: Right!
WE END UP GETTING DRUNK OFF MIMOSAS AND SPENT THE WHOLE DAY TOGETHER . . .

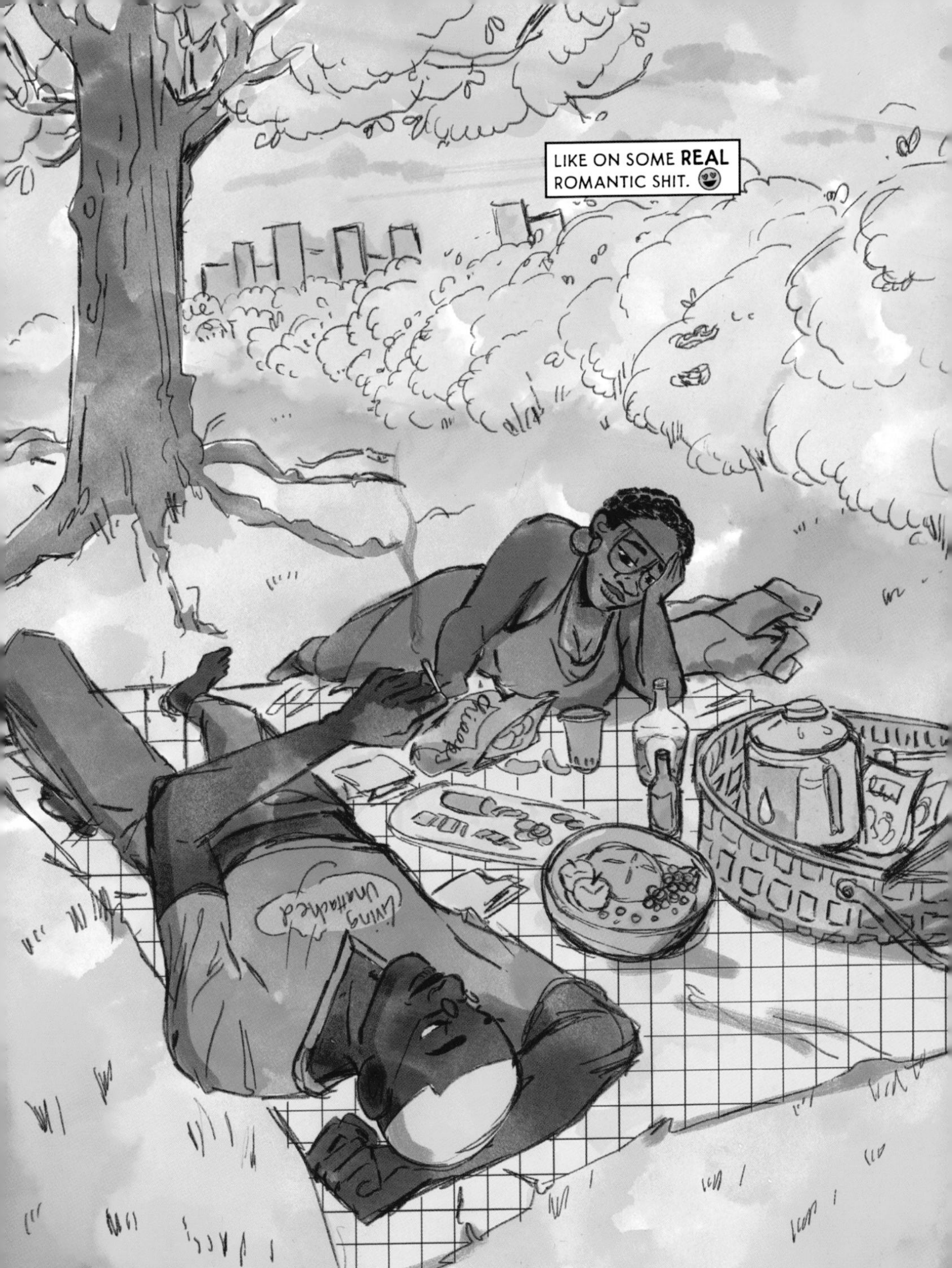
LIKE ON SOME **REAL** ROMANTIC SHIT. 😍
Living Unattached

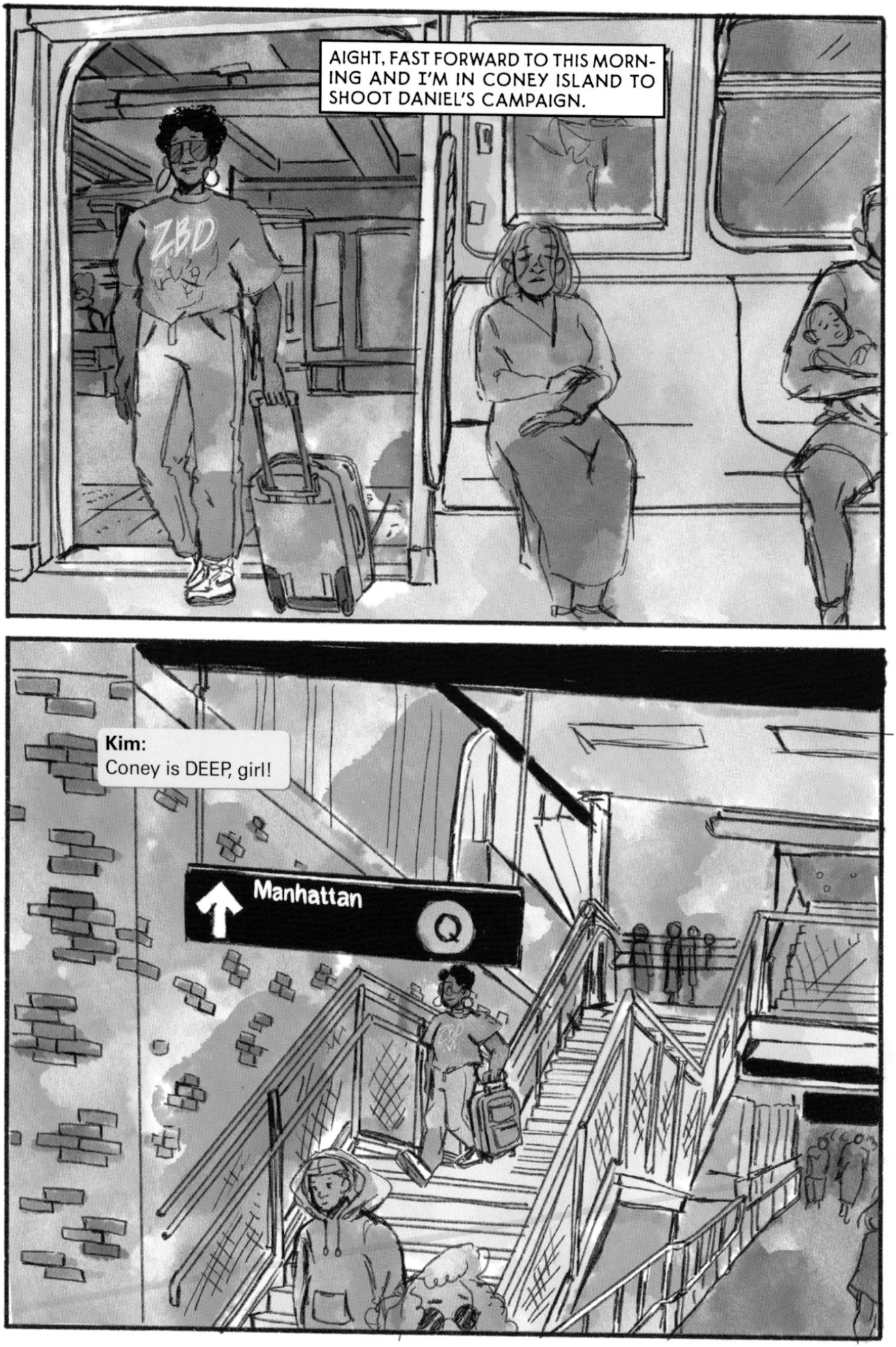
AIGHT, FAST FORWARD TO THIS MORNING AND I'M IN CONEY ISLAND TO SHOOT DANIEL'S CAMPAIGN.
ZBD
Kim:
Coney is DEEP, girl!
Manhattan
Q

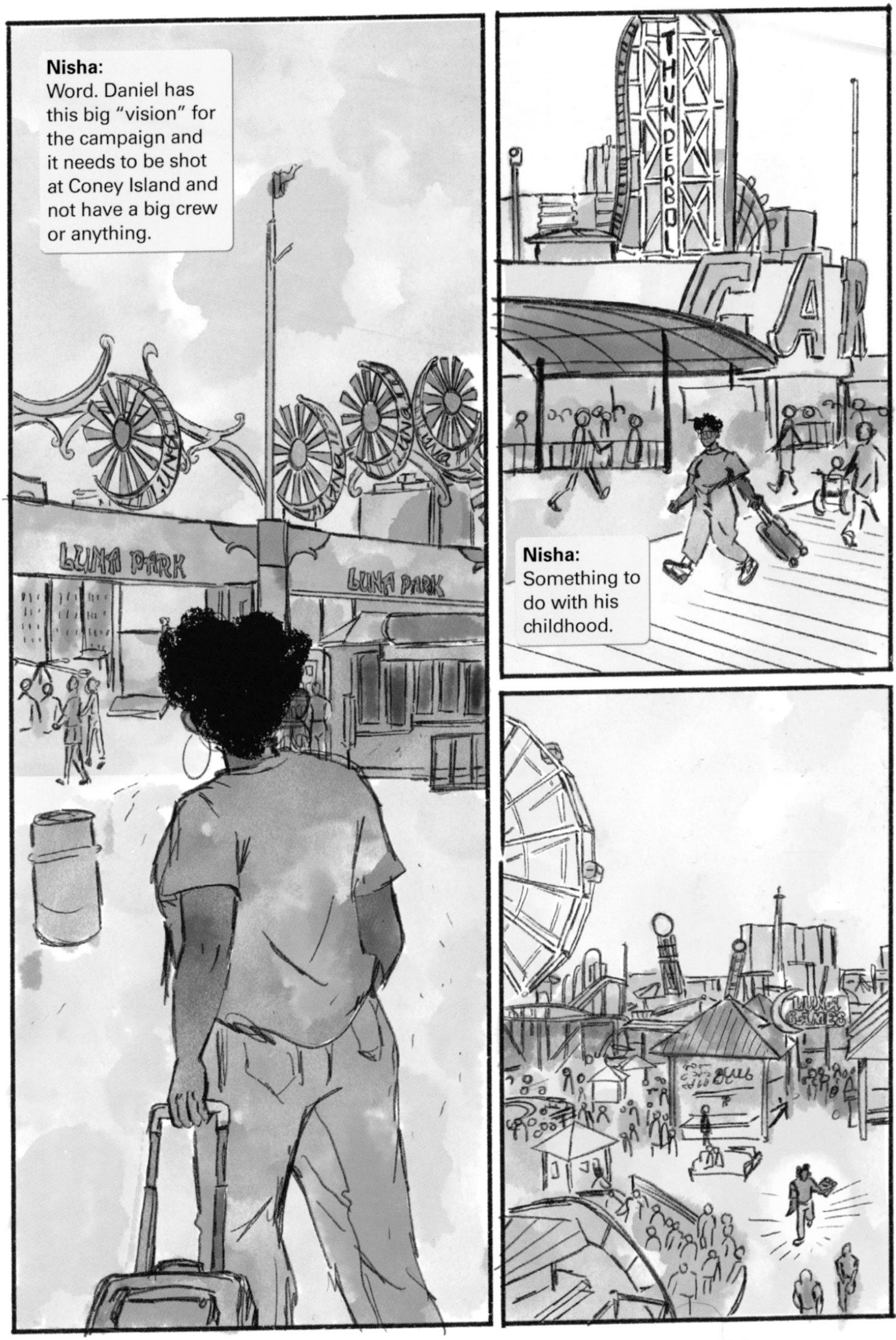
Nisha:
Word. Daniel has this big “vision” for the campaign and it needs to be shot at Coney Island and not have a big crew or anything.
LUNA PARK
LUNA PARK
THUNDERBOL
Nisha:
Something to do with his childhood.

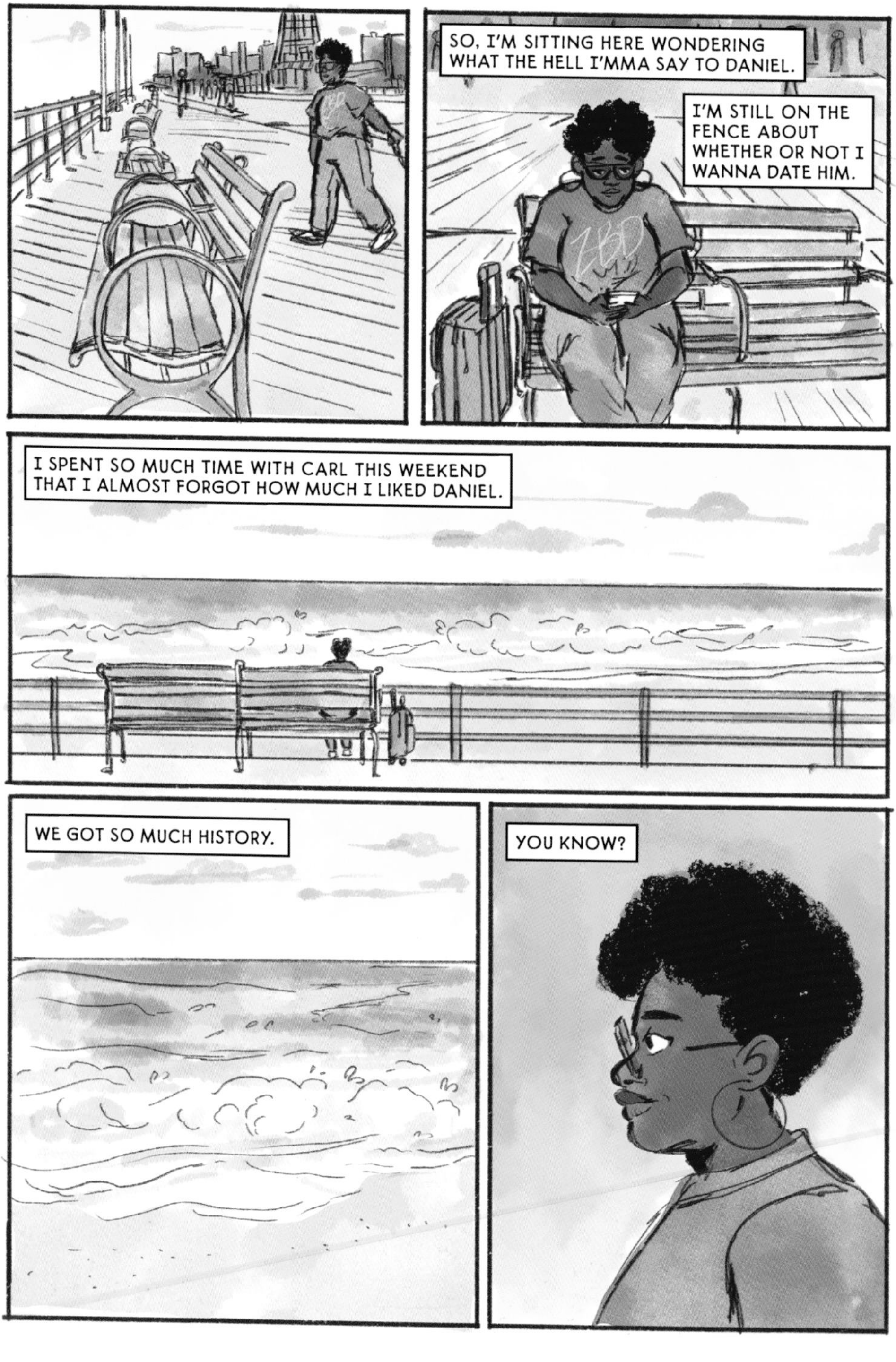
ZBD
SO, I'M SITTING HERE WONDERING WHAT THE HELL I'MMA SAY TO DANIEL.
I'M STILL ON THE FENCE ABOUT WHETHER OR NOT I WANNA DATE HIM.
I SPENT SO MUCH TIME WITH CARL THIS WEEKEND THAT I ALMOST FORGOT HOW MUCH I LIKED DANIEL.
WE GOT SO MUCH HISTORY.
YOU KNOW?

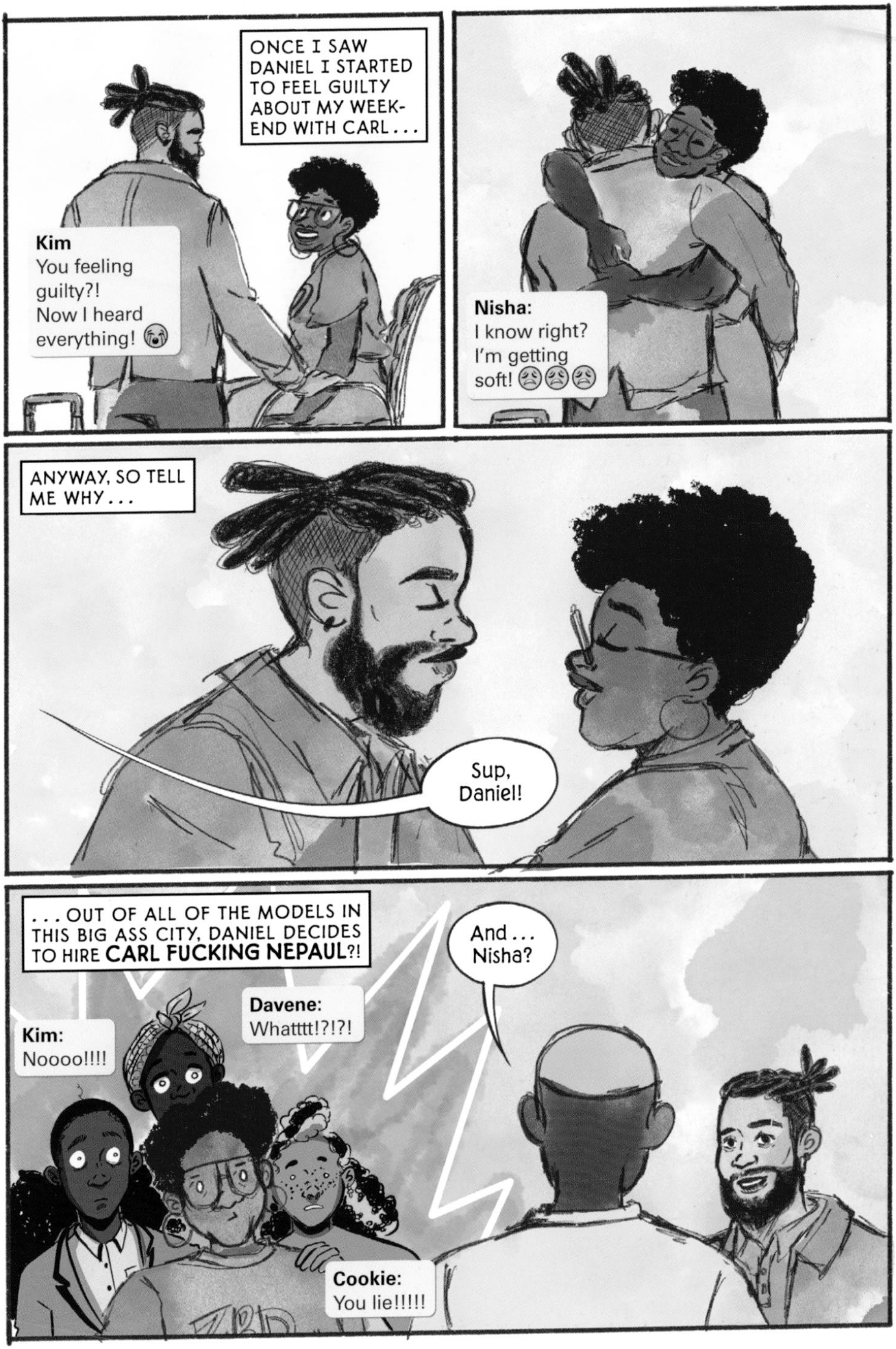
ONCE I SAW DANIEL I STARTED TO FEEL GUILTY ABOUT MY WEEK-END WITH CARL . . .
Kim You feeling guilty?! Now I heard everything! 😭
Nisha: I know right? I'm getting soft! 😩😩😩
ANYWAY, SO TELL ME WHY . . .
Sup, Daniel!
. . . OUT OF ALL OF THE MODELS IN THIS BIG ASS CITY, DANIEL DECIDES TO HIRE **CARL FUCKING NEPAUL**?!
And . . . Nisha?
Davene: Whatttt!?!?!
Kim: Noooo!!!!
Cookie: You lie!!!!!

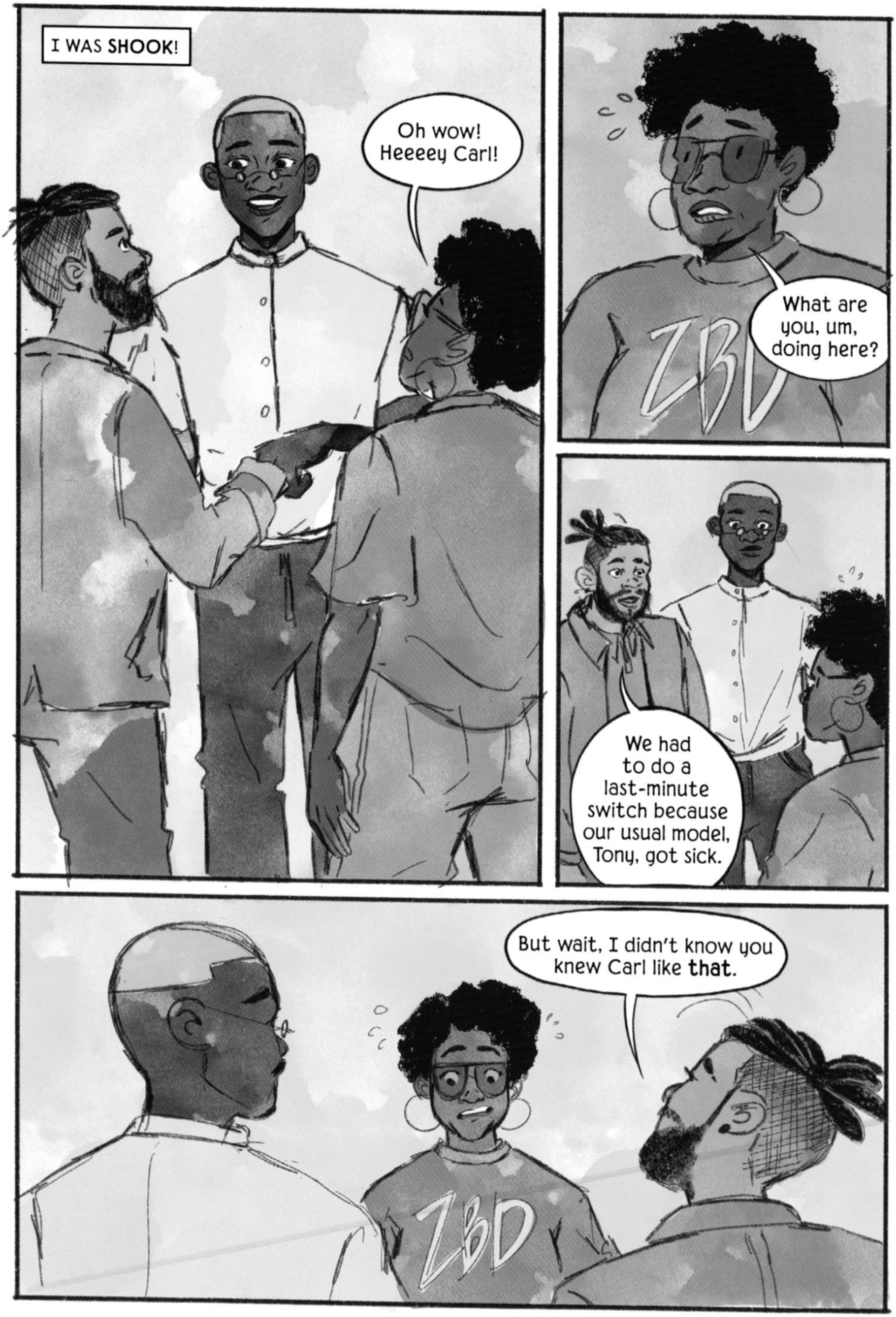
I WAS SHOOK!
Oh wow! Heeeey Carl!
What are you, um, doing here?
ZBD
We had to do a last-minute switch because our usual model, Tony, got sick.
But wait, I didn't know you knew Carl like that.
ZBD

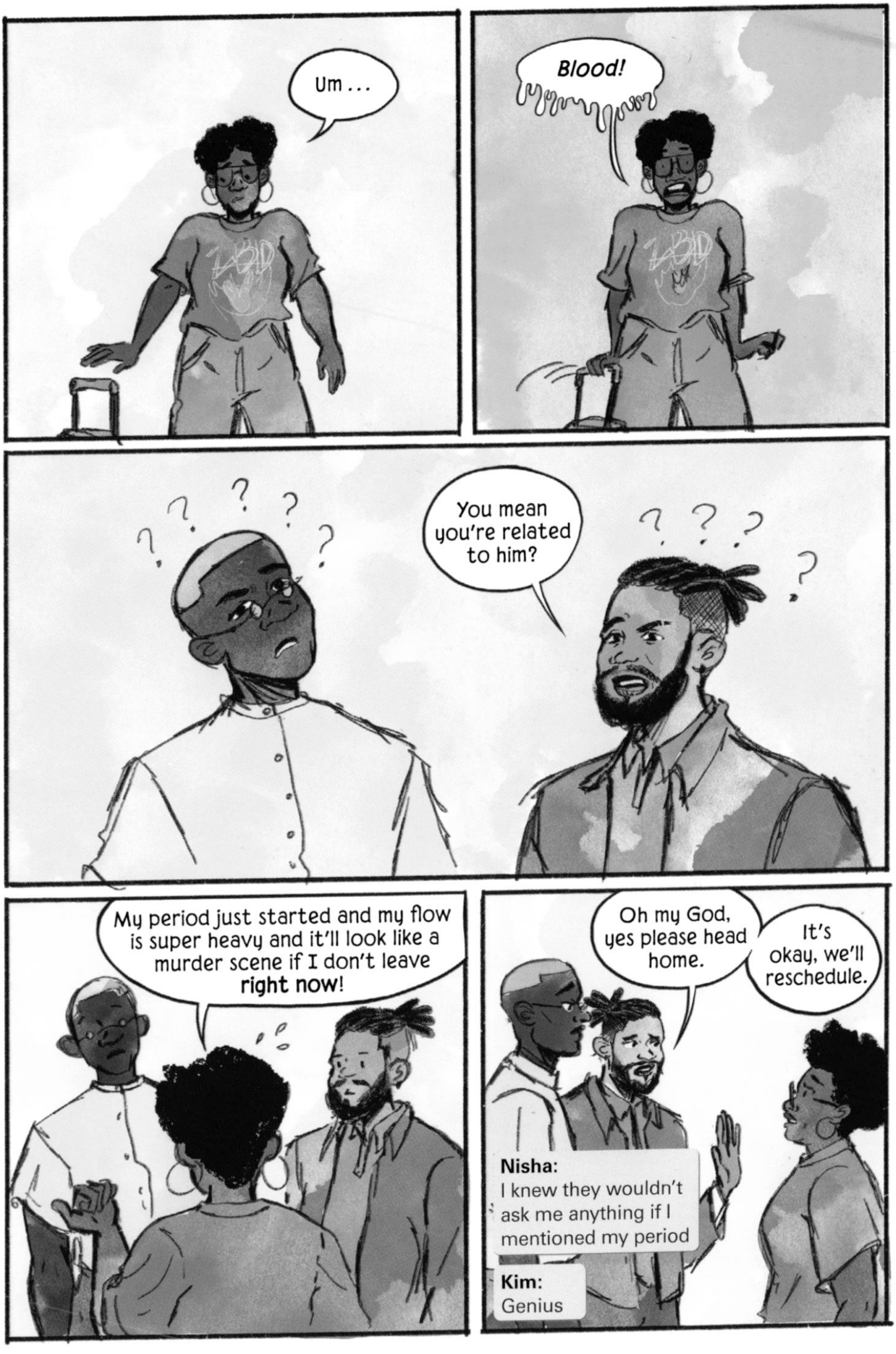
Um . . .
Blood!
You mean you're related to him?
My period just started and my flow is super heavy and it'll look like a murder scene if I don't leave **right now**!
Oh my God, yes please head home.
It's okay, we'll reschedule.
Nisha: I knew they wouldn't ask me anything if I mentioned my period
Kim: Genius

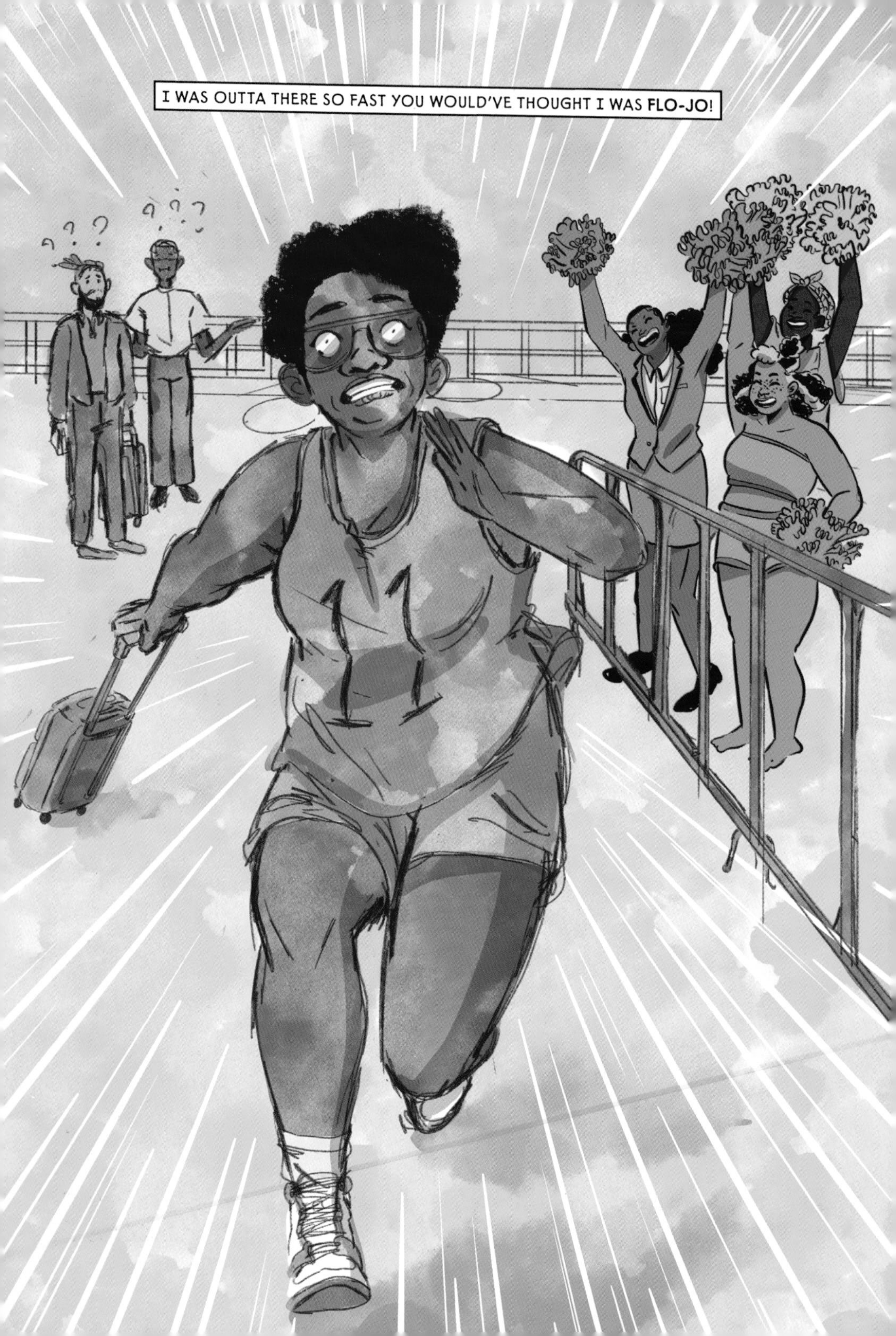
I WAS OUTTA THERE SO FAST YOU WOULD'VE THOUGHT I WAS FLO-JO!

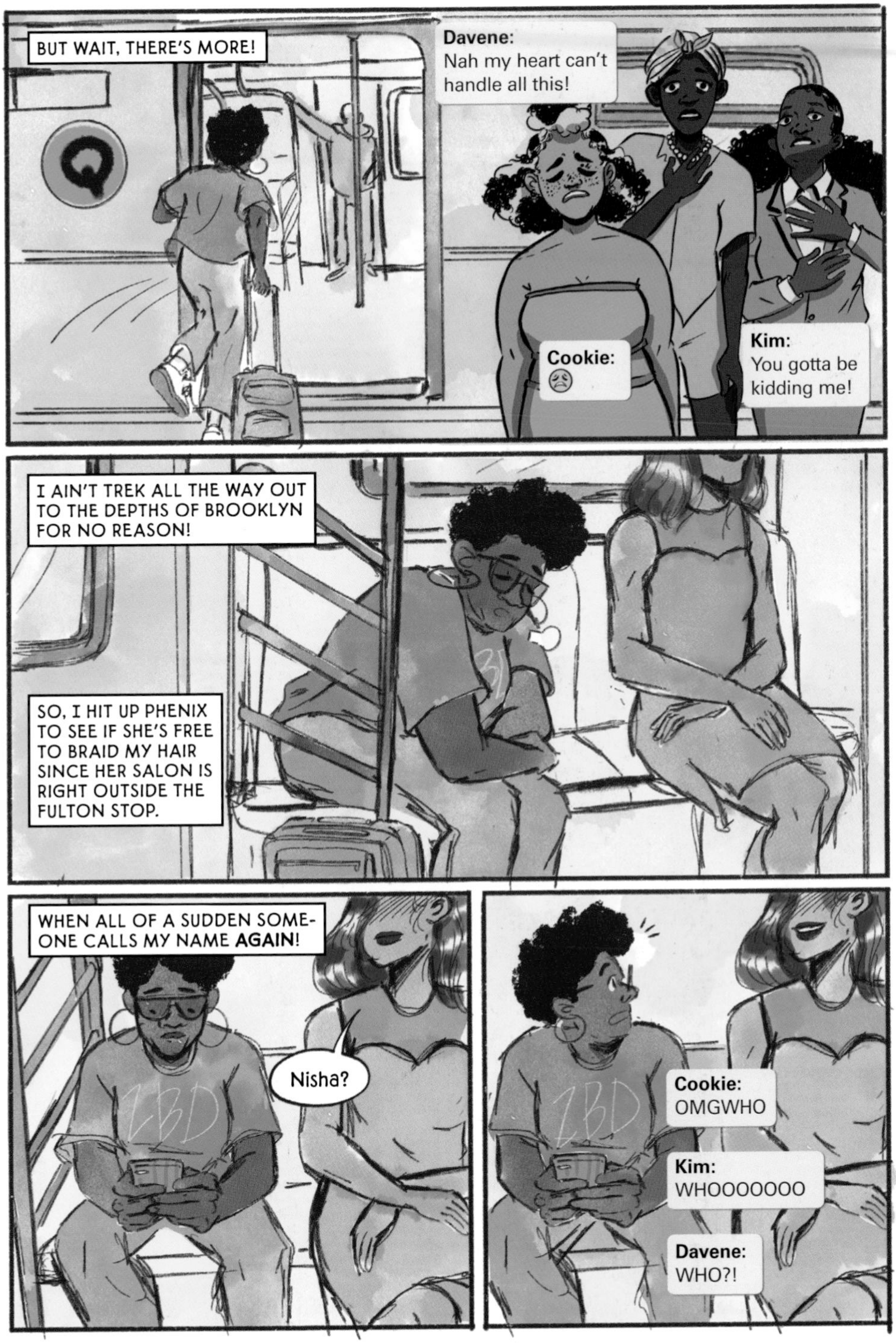
BUT WAIT, THERE'S MORE!
Davene: Nah my heart can't handle all this!
Cookie: 😥
Kim: You gotta be kidding me!
I AIN'T TREK ALL THE WAY OUT TO THE DEPTHS OF BROOKLYN FOR NO REASON!
SO, I HIT UP PHENIX TO SEE IF SHE'S FREE TO BRAID MY HAIR SINCE HER SALON IS RIGHT OUTSIDE THE FULTON STOP.
WHEN ALL OF A SUDDEN SOME-ONE CALLS MY NAME **AGAIN**!
Nisha?
Cookie: OMGWHO
Kim: WHOOOOOOO
Davene: WHO?!

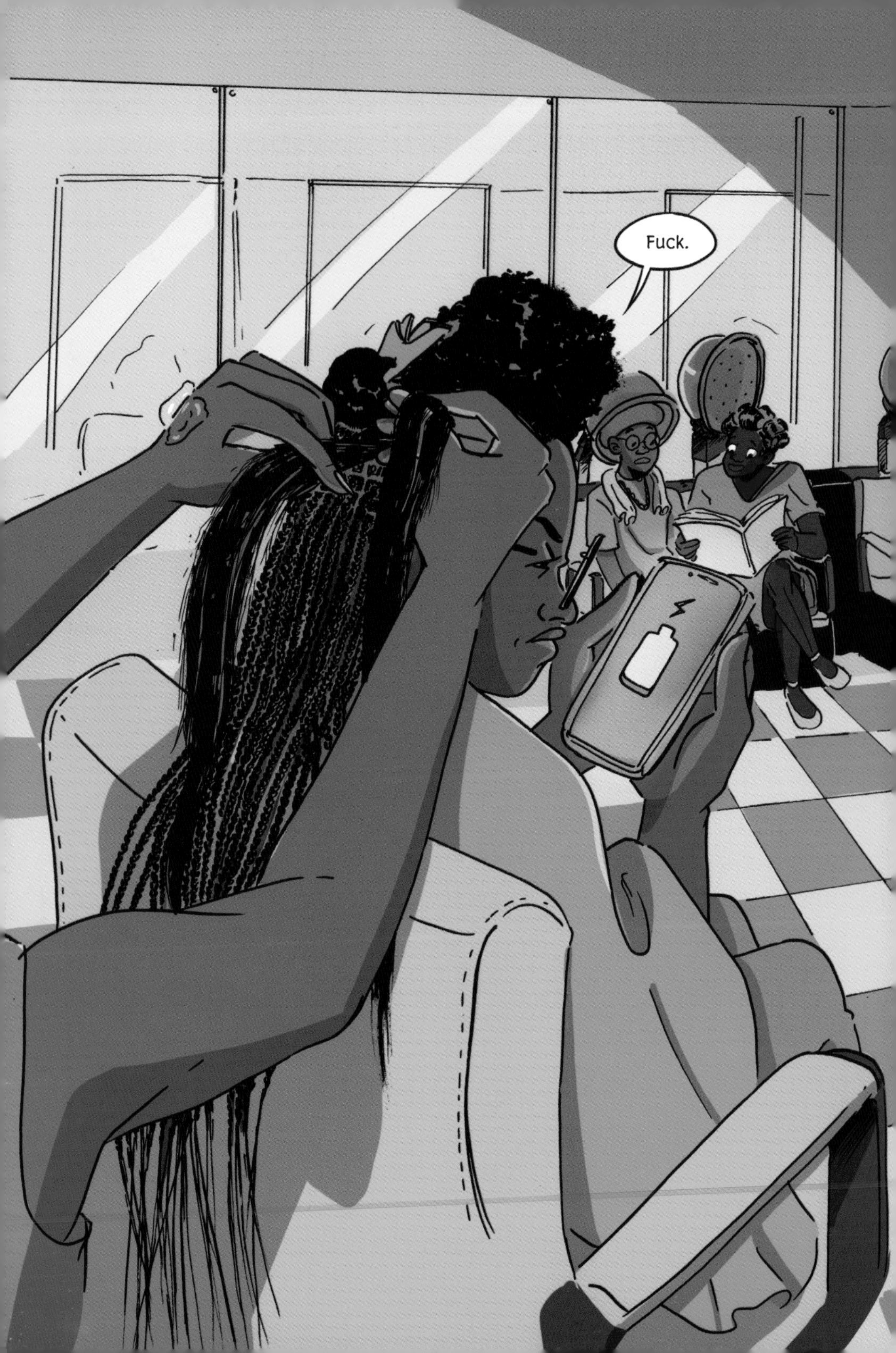
Fuck.

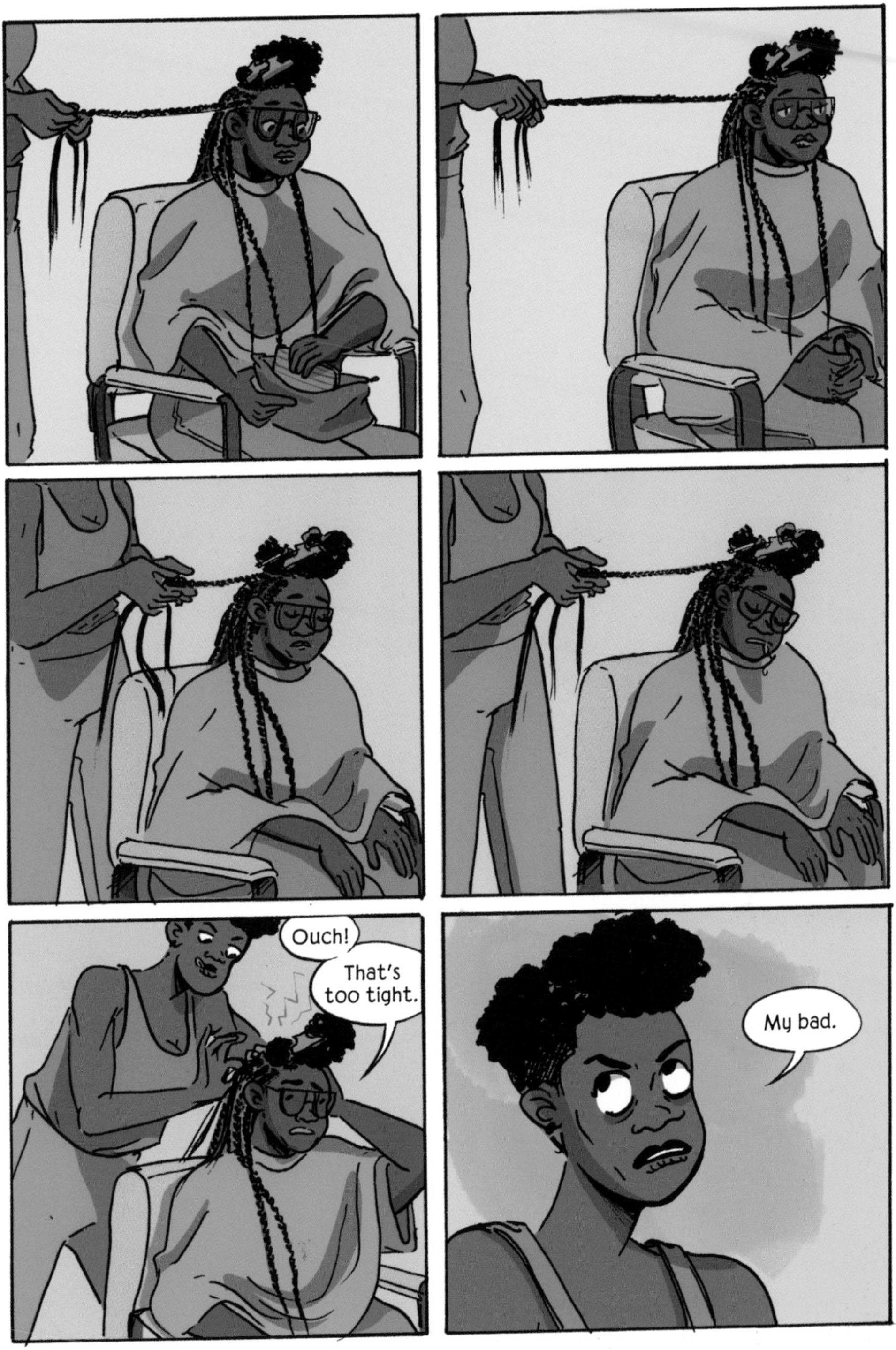
Ouch!
That's too tight.
My bad.

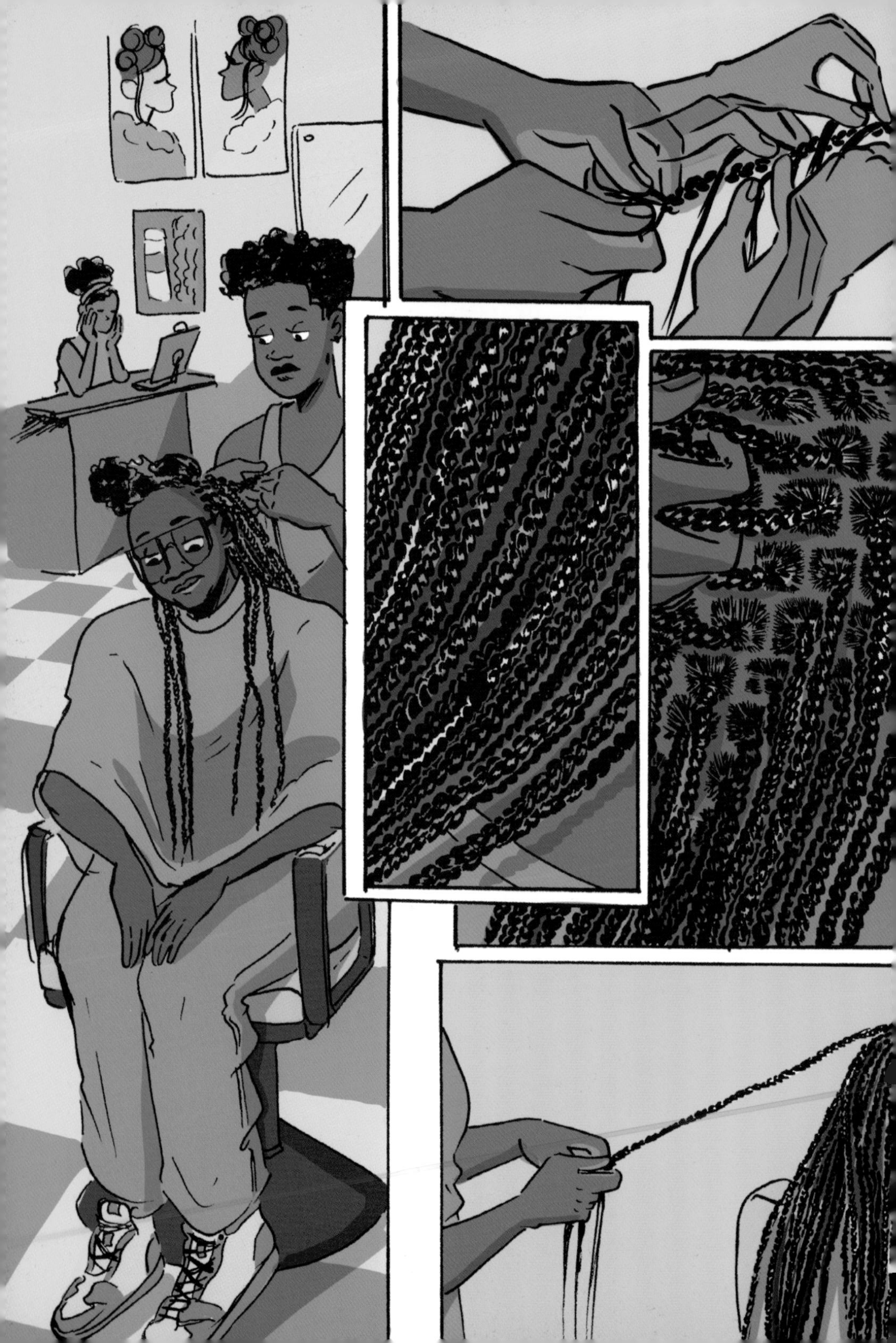

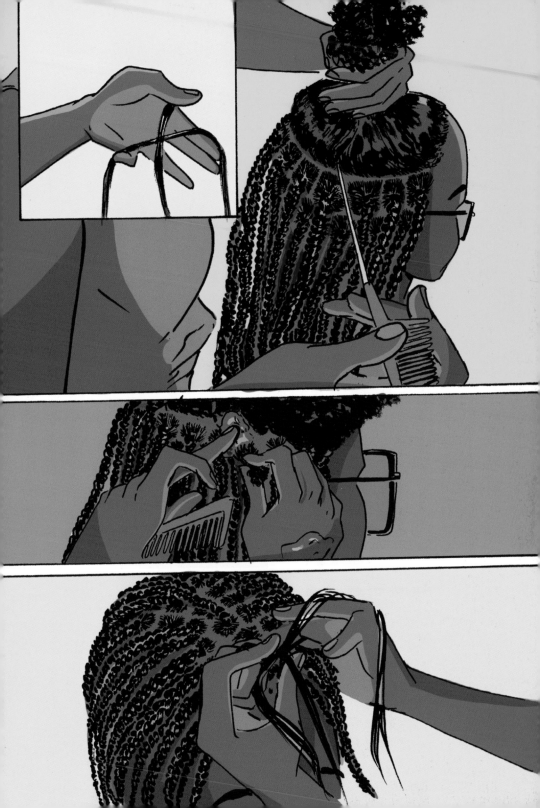

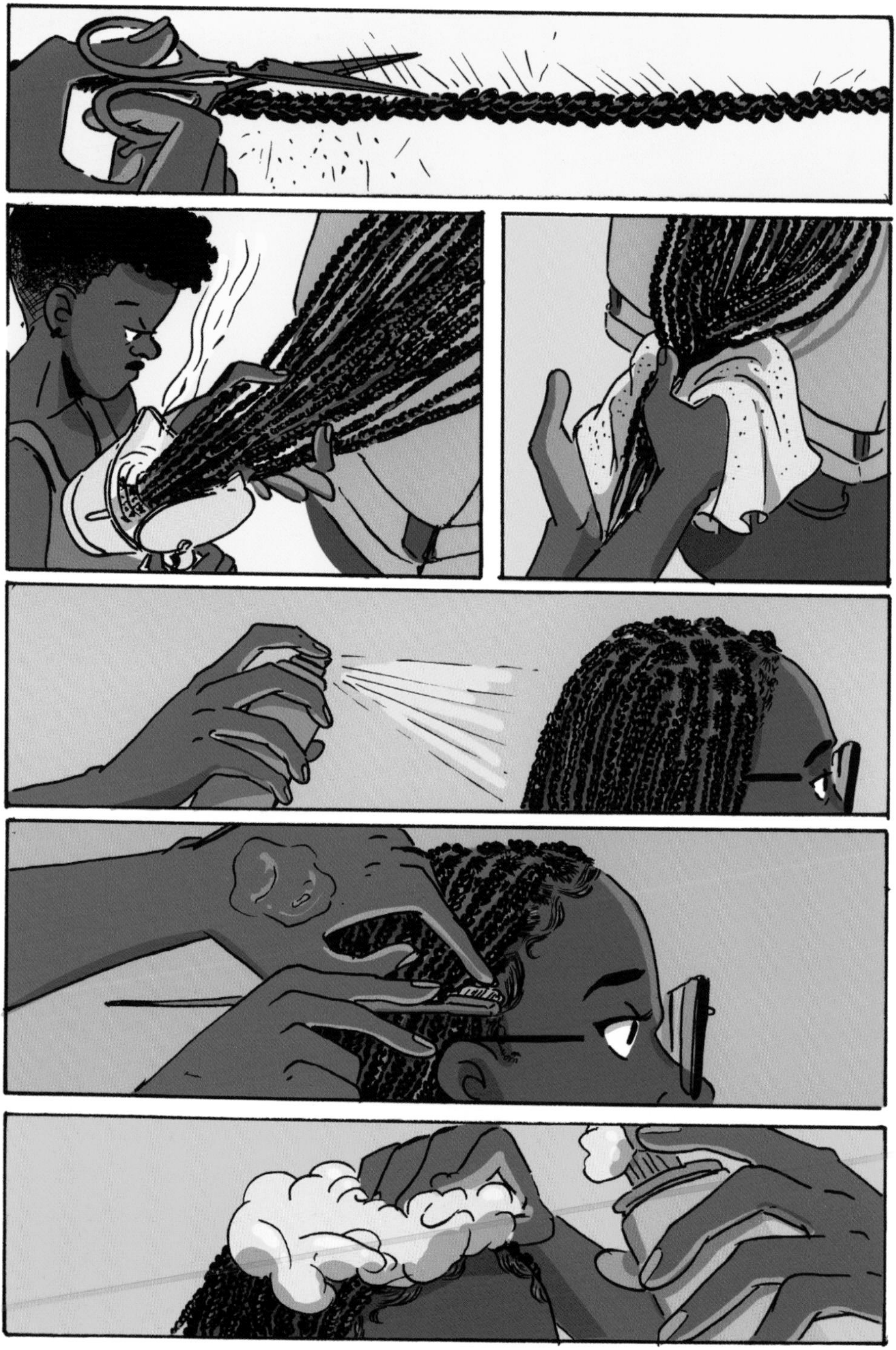

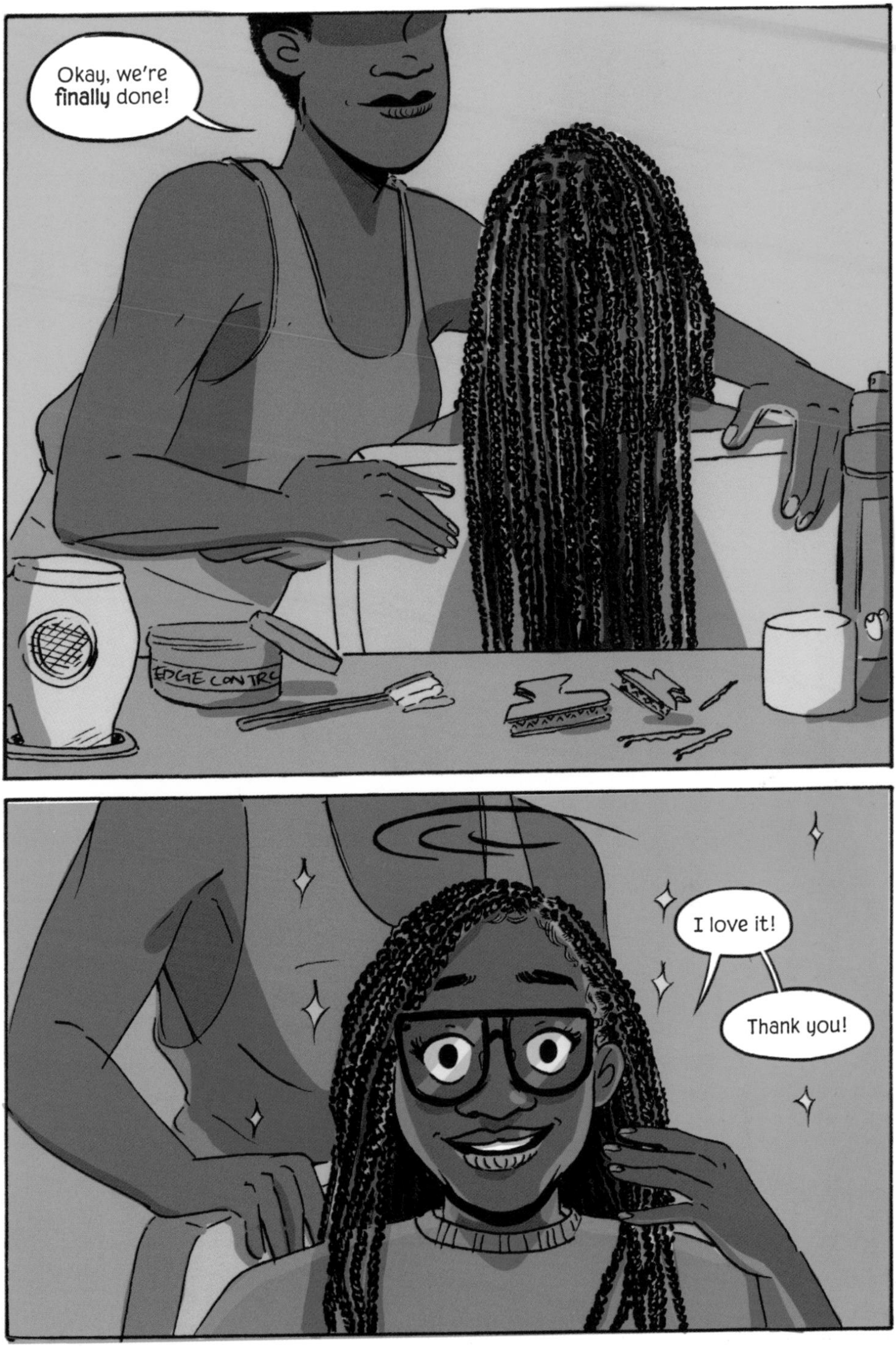
Okay, we're **finally** done!
I love it!
Thank you!
EDGE CONTRO

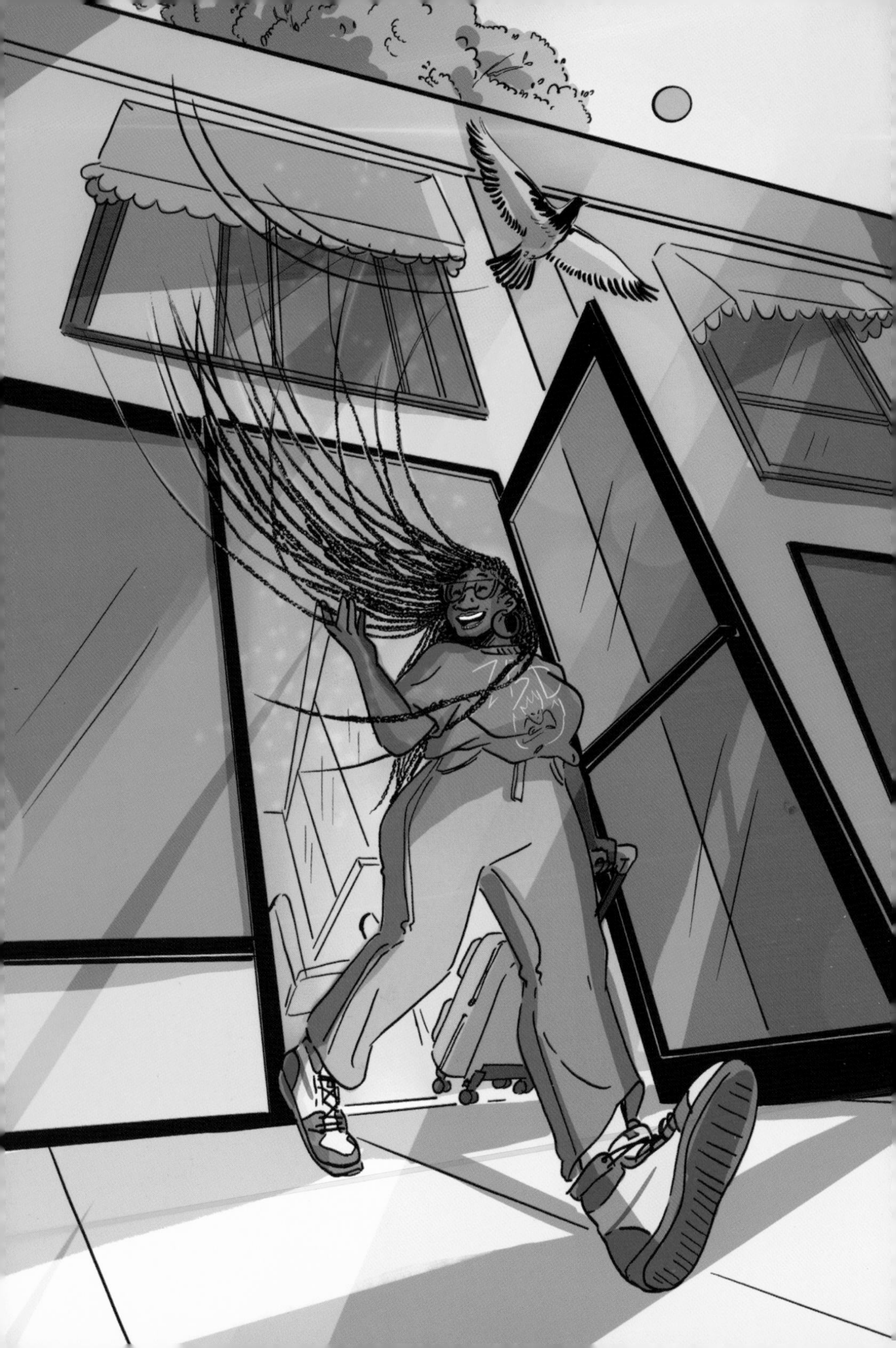

BRIGHT SIDE

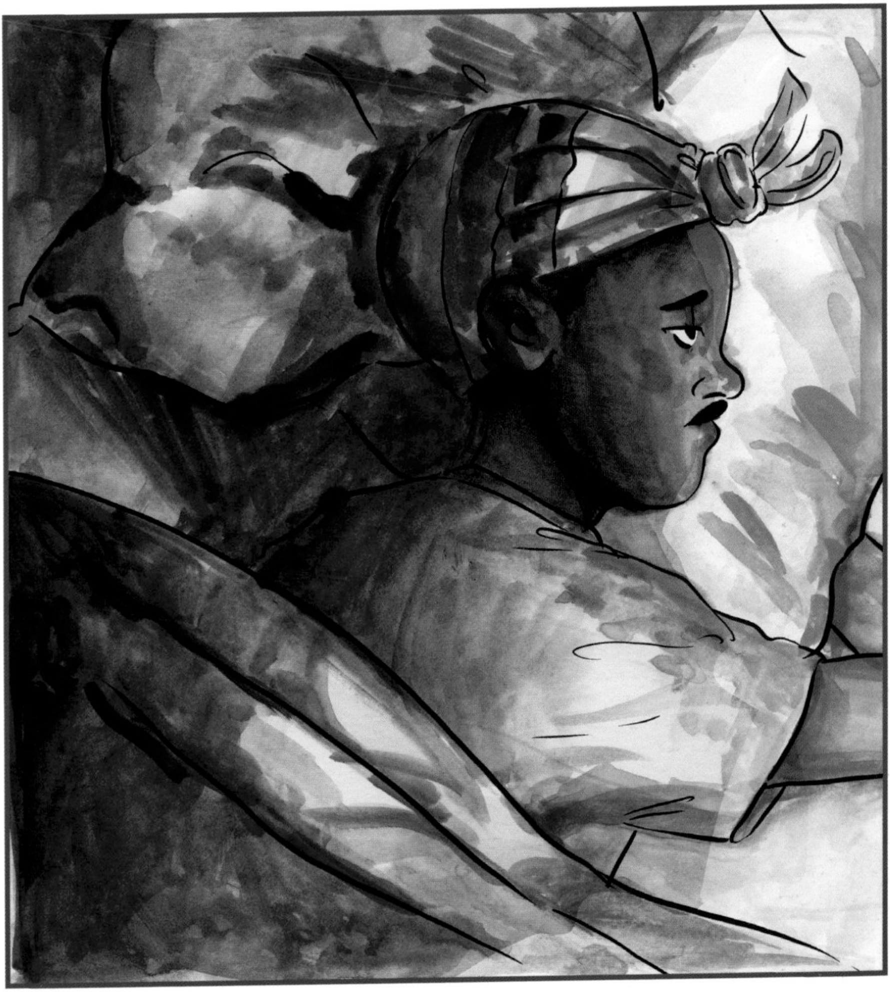

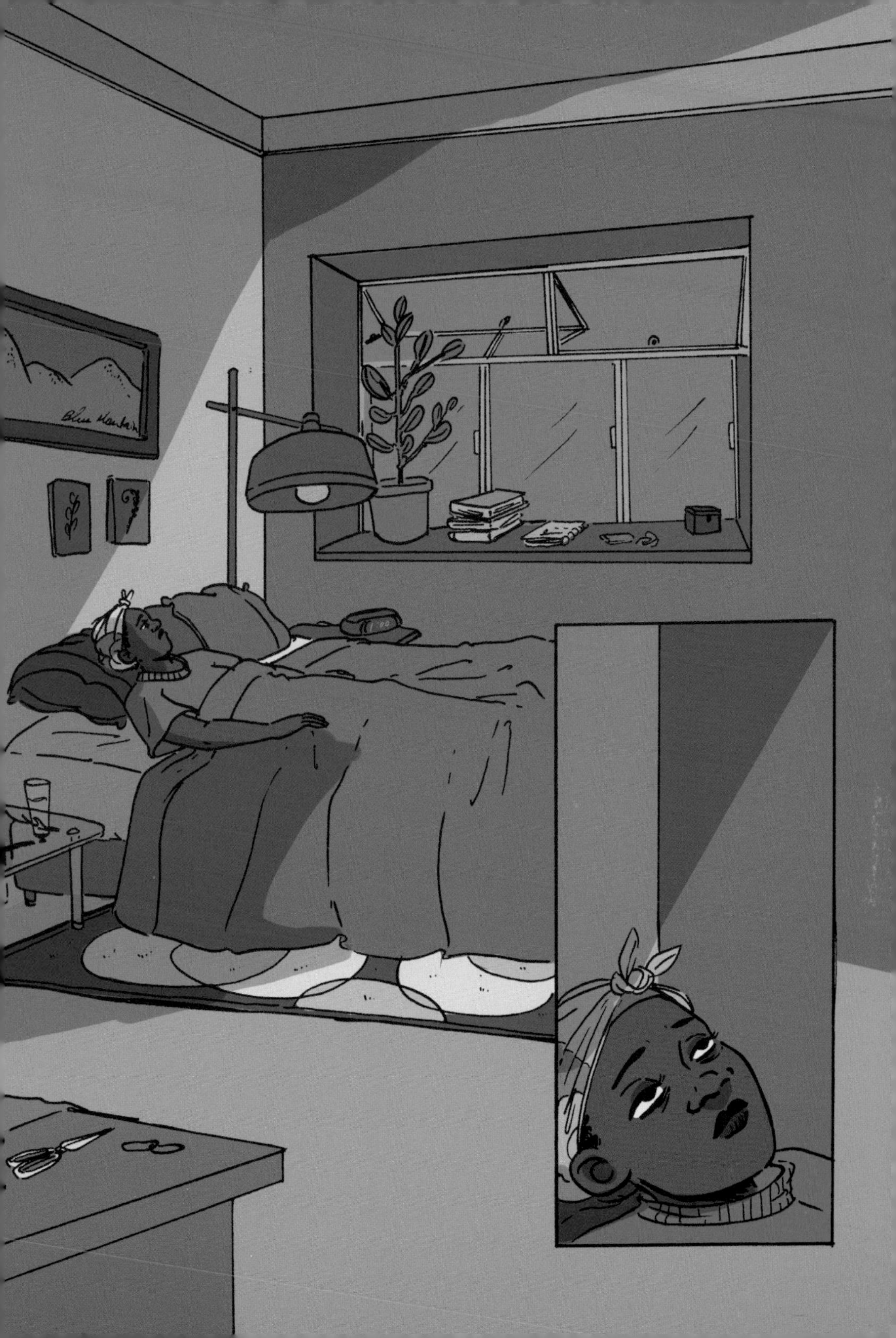
Blue Mountain

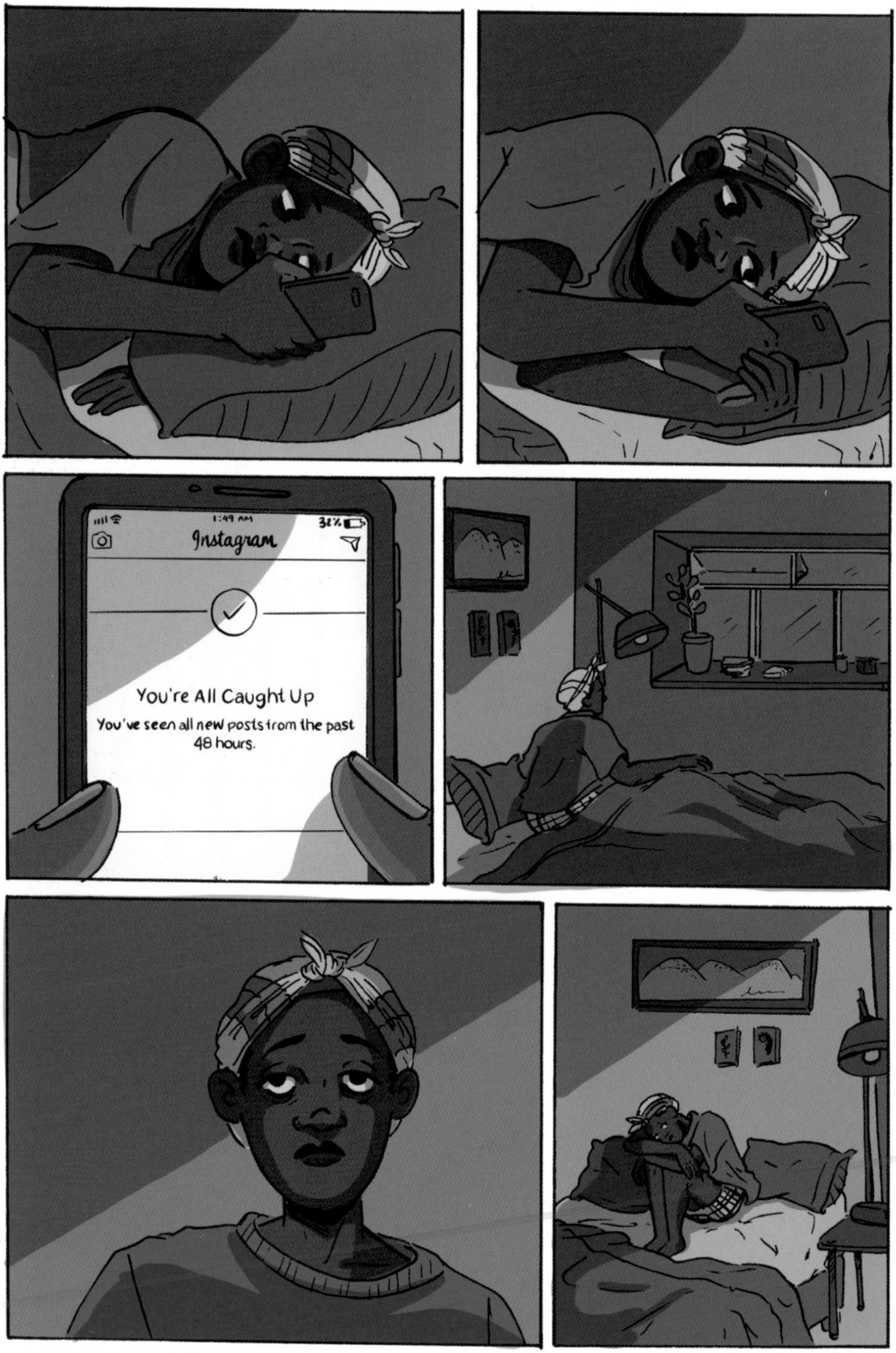
Instagram
You're All Caught Up
You've seen all new posts from the past 48 hours.

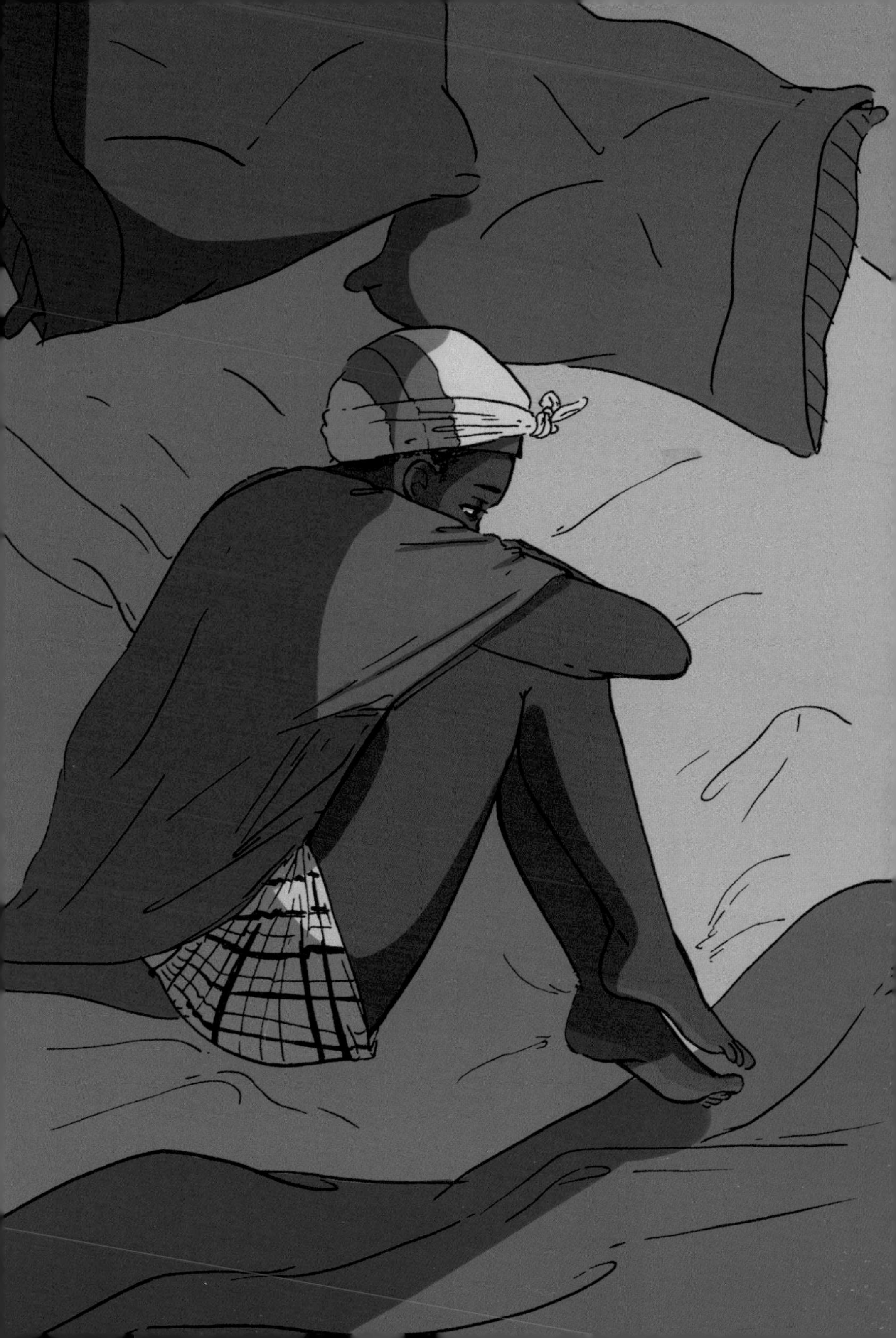

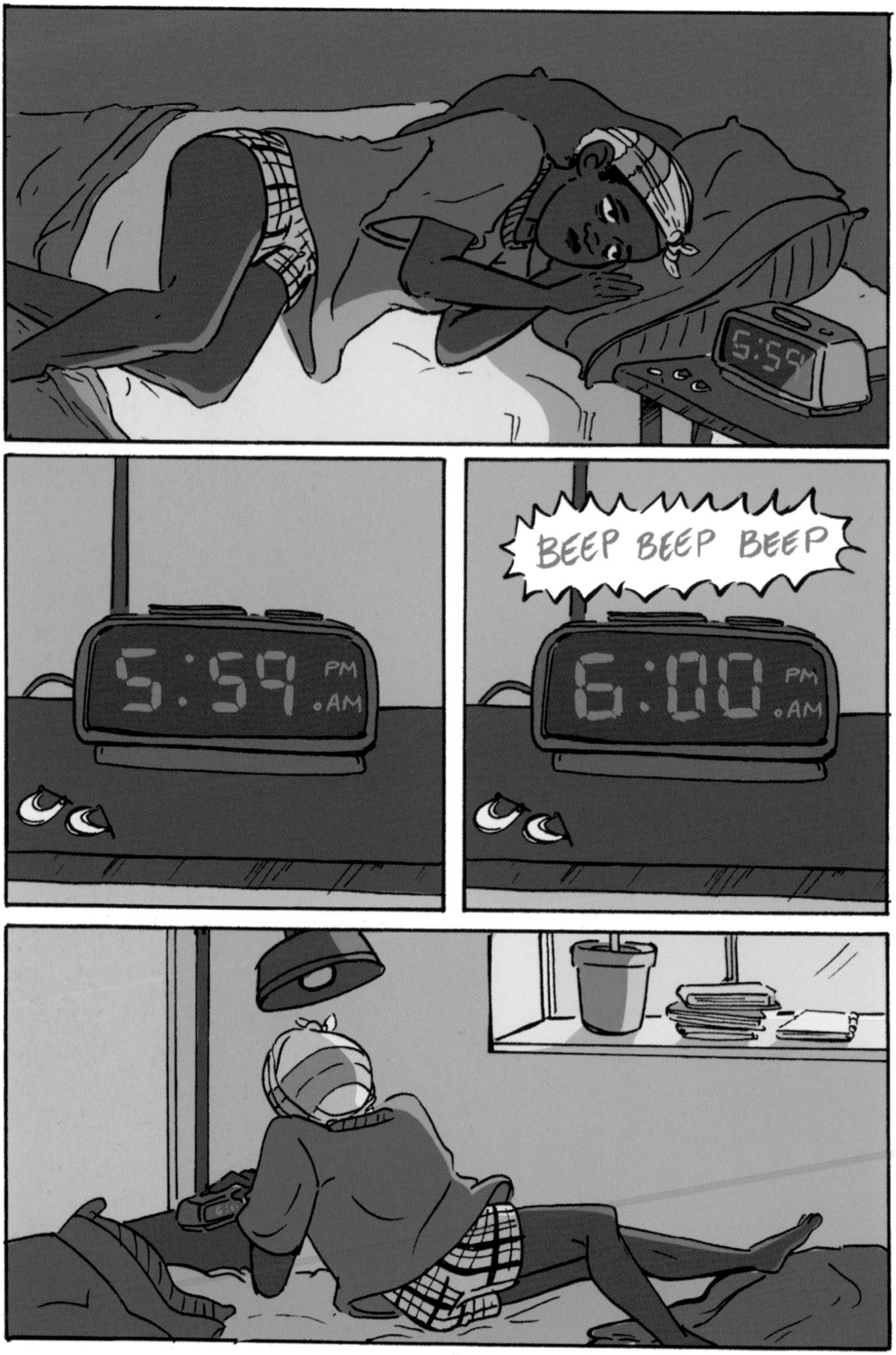
5:59
5:59 PM AM
BEEP BEEP BEEP
6:00 PM AM

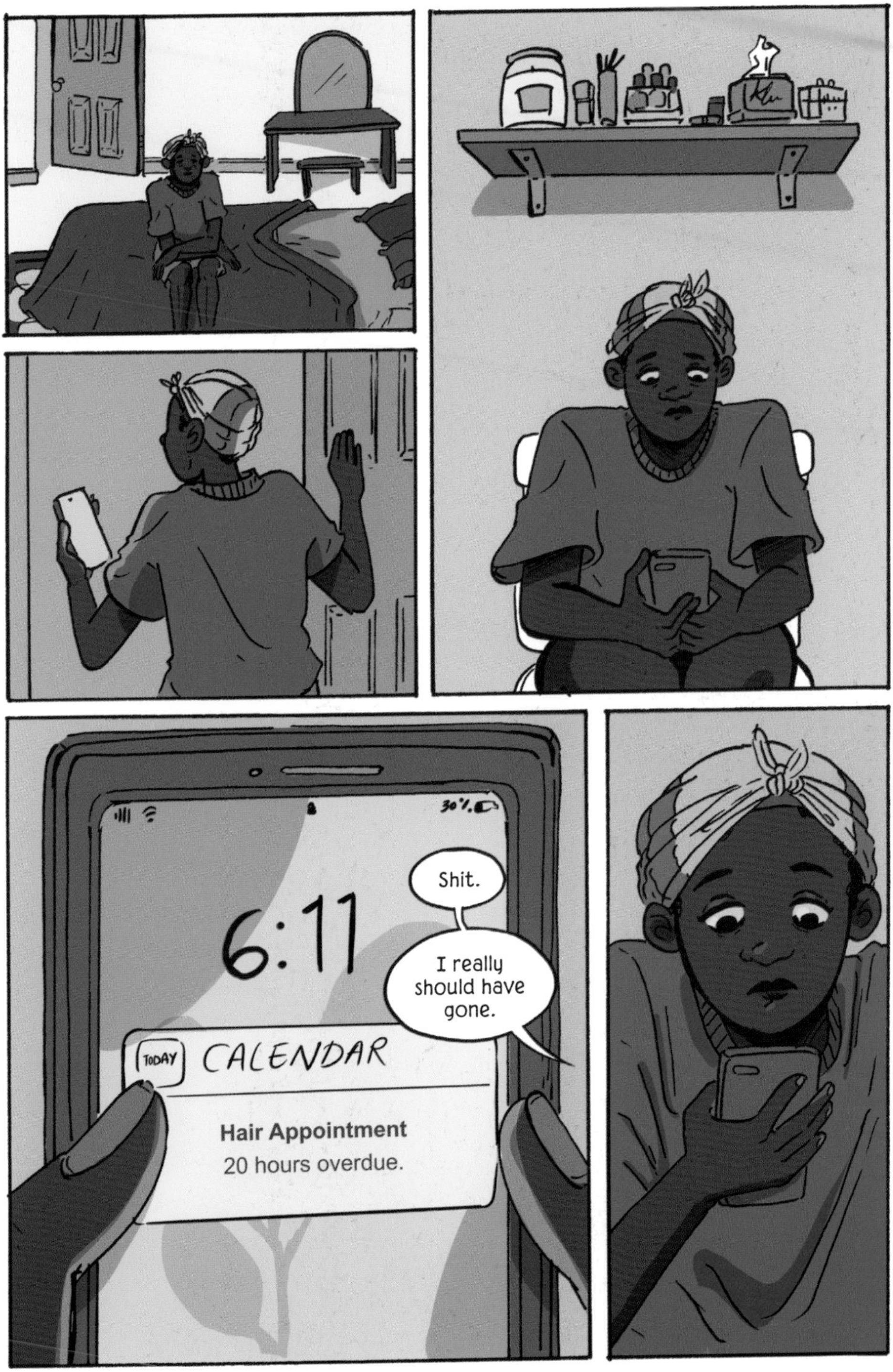
30%
6:11
TODAY
CALENDAR
Hair Appointment
20 hours overdue.
Shit.
I really should have gone.

Davene:
Morning, Michelle. I'm so sorry for missing the appointment yesterday. I wasn't feeling well this weekend.

Davene:
Are you free today?

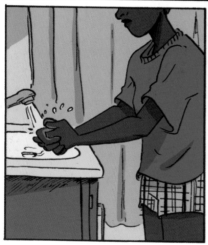

PING

Michelle:
Sorry, I'm booked until next week.

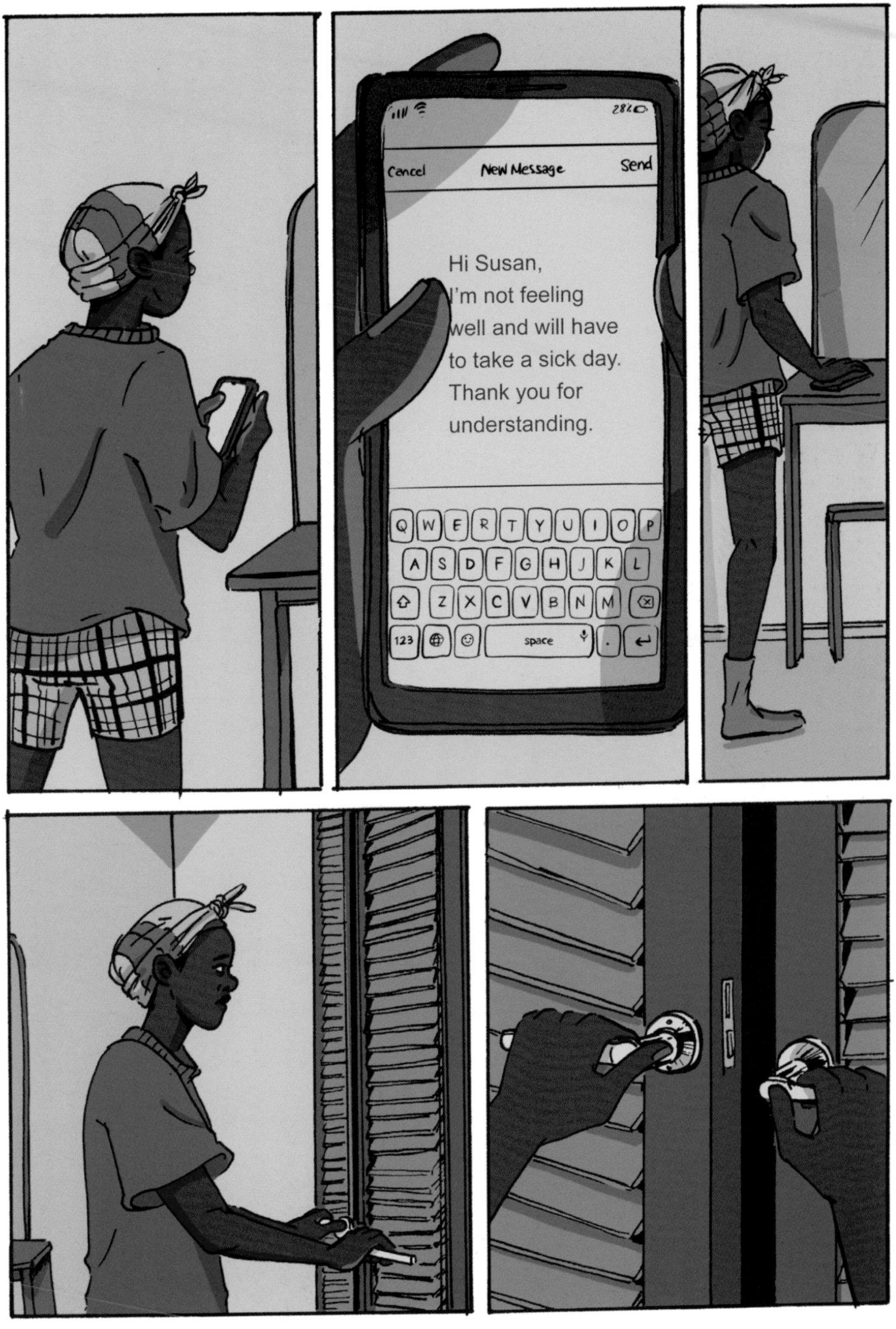
Cancel
New Message
Send
Hi Susan,
I'm not feeling well and will have to take a sick day. Thank you for understanding.
QWERTYUIOP
ASDFGHJKL
ZXCVBNM
123
space

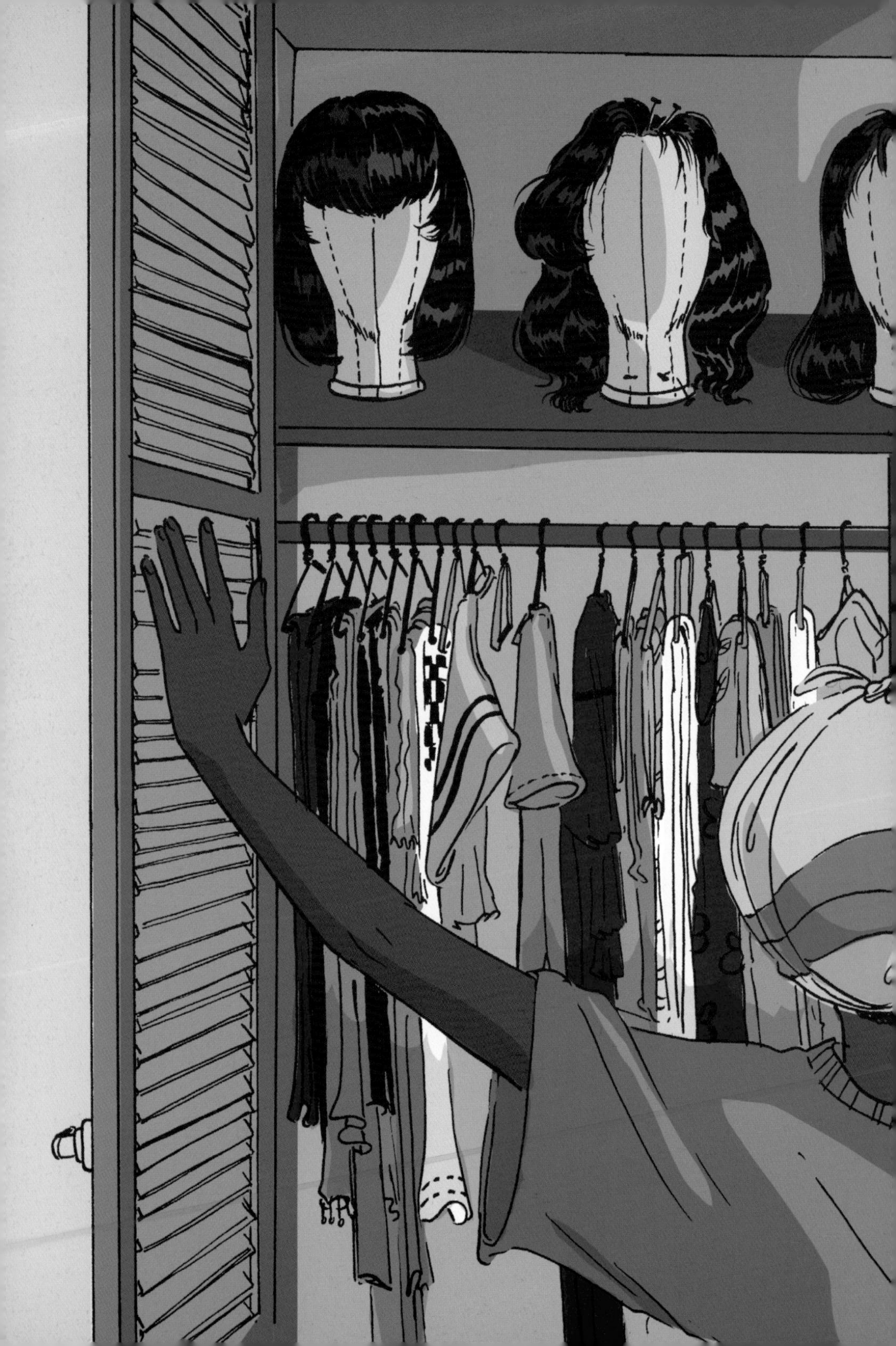

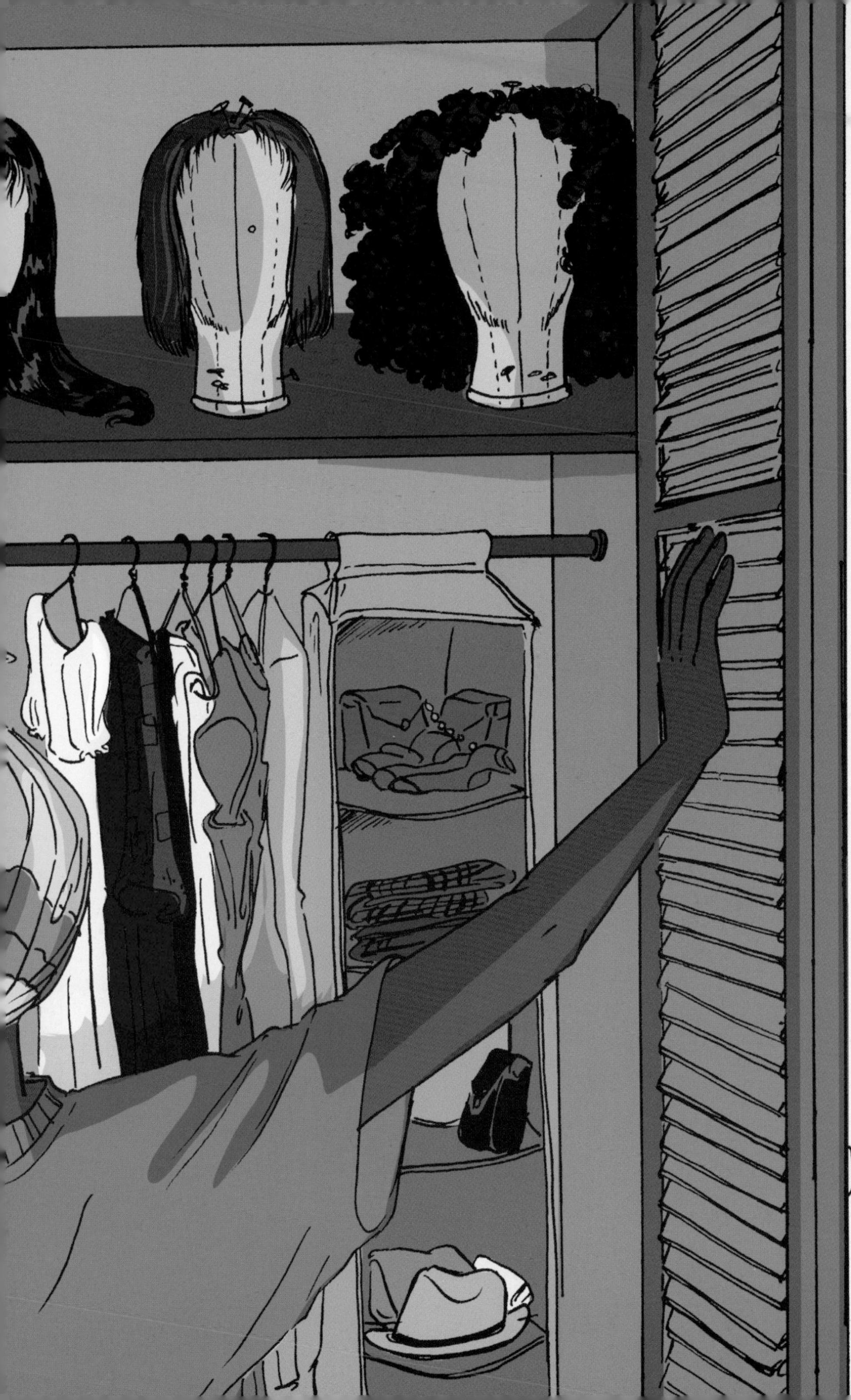

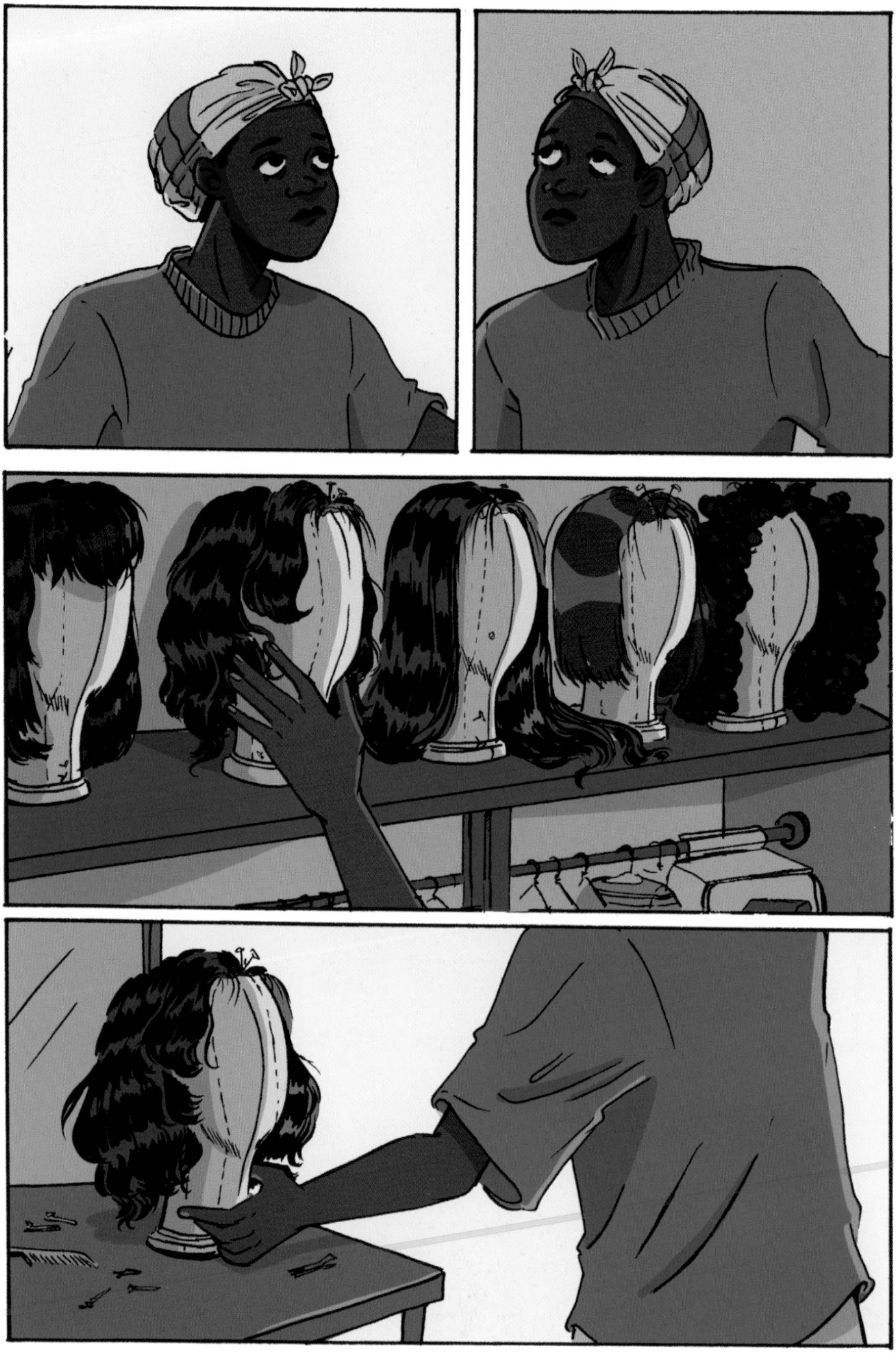

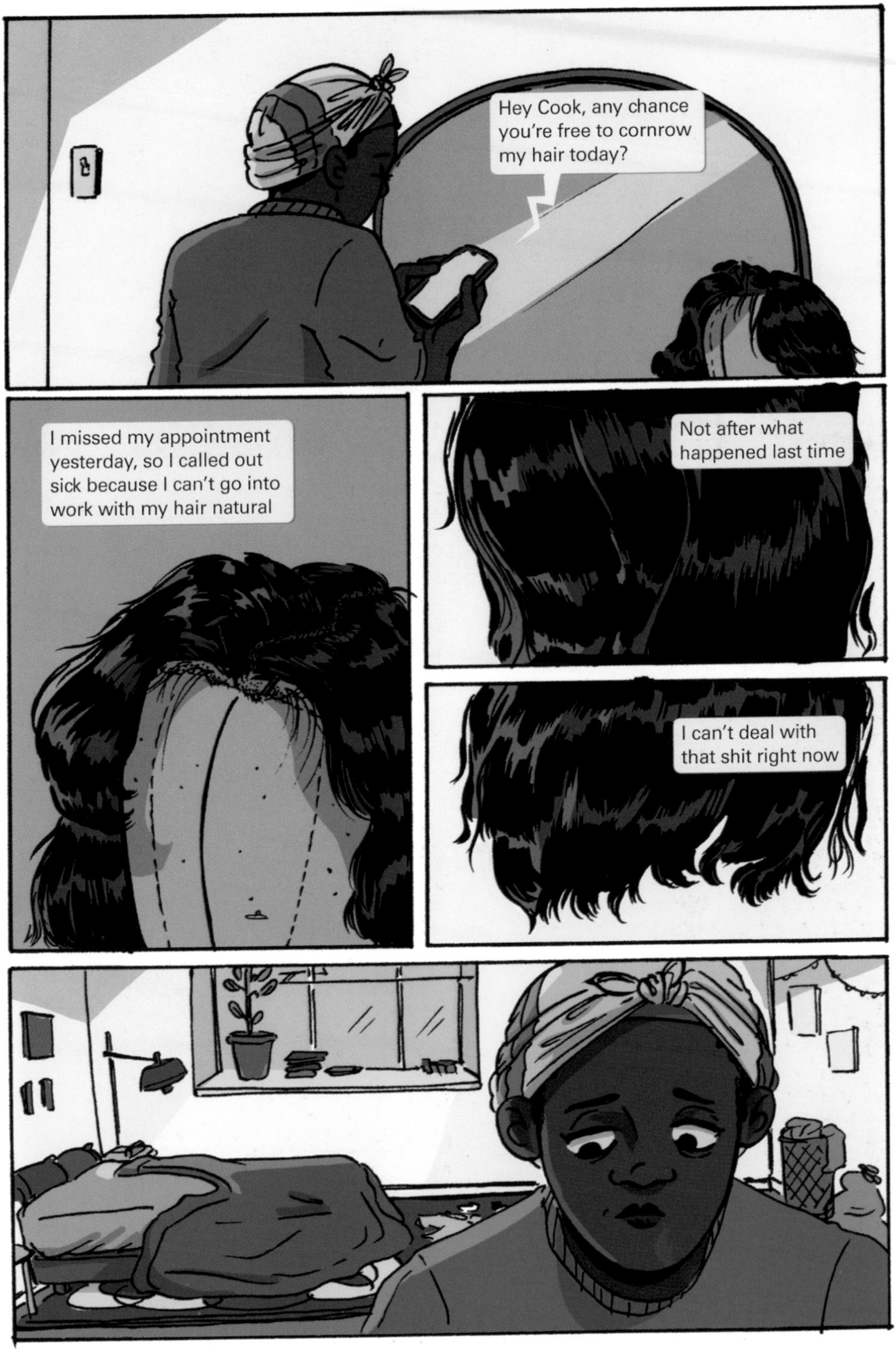
Hey Cook, any chance you're free to cornrow my hair today?
I missed my appointment yesterday, so I called out sick because I can't go into work with my hair natural
Not after what happened last time
I can't deal with that shit right now

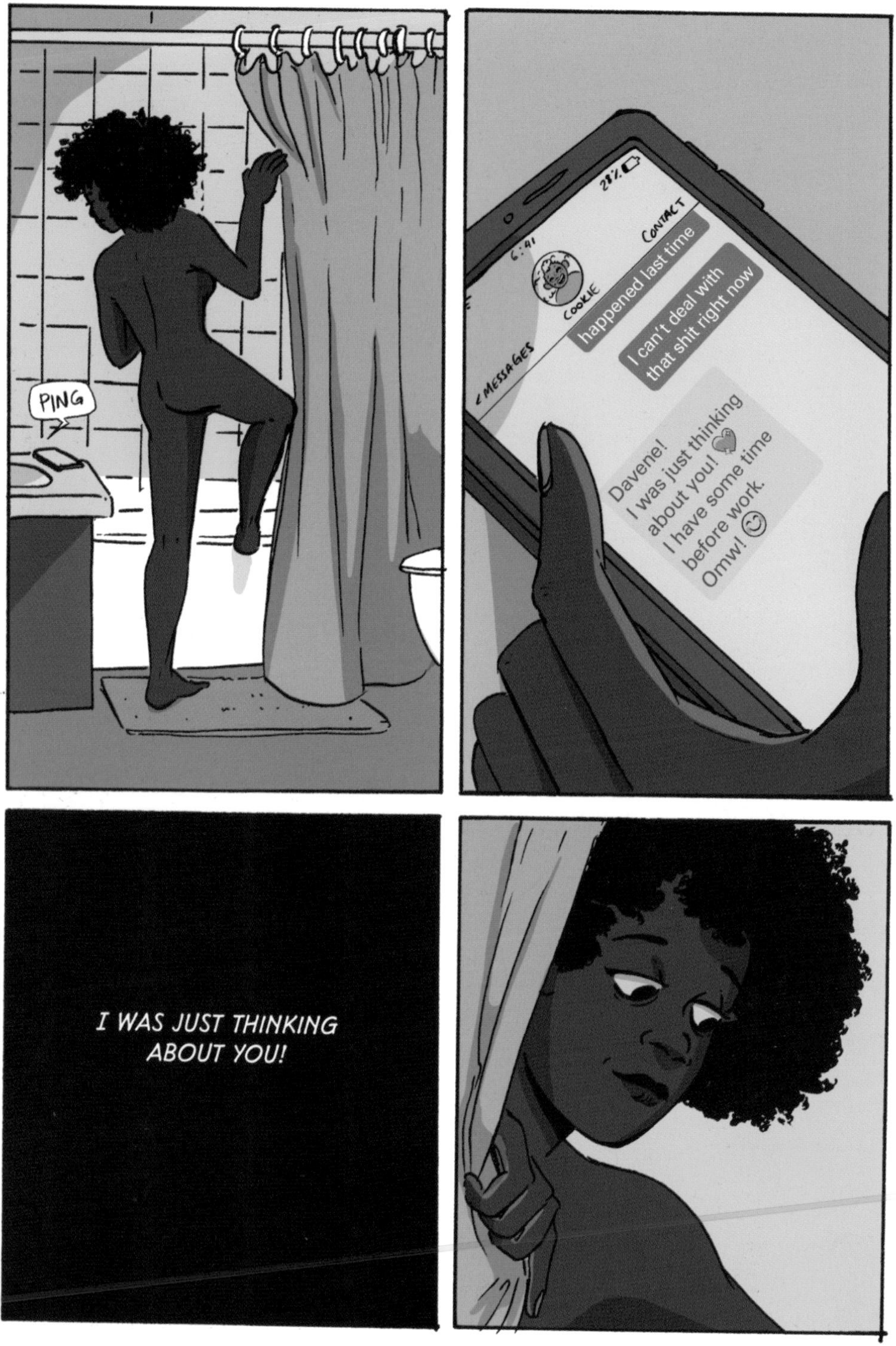
PING
28%
< MESSAGES
COOKIE
CONTACT
happened last time
I can't deal with that shit right now
Davene! I was just thinking about you! I have some time before work. Omw!
I WAS JUST THINKING ABOUT YOU!

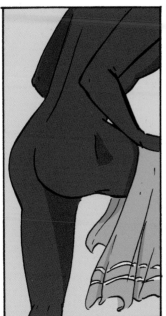

BZZZT

She's here already.

Shit.

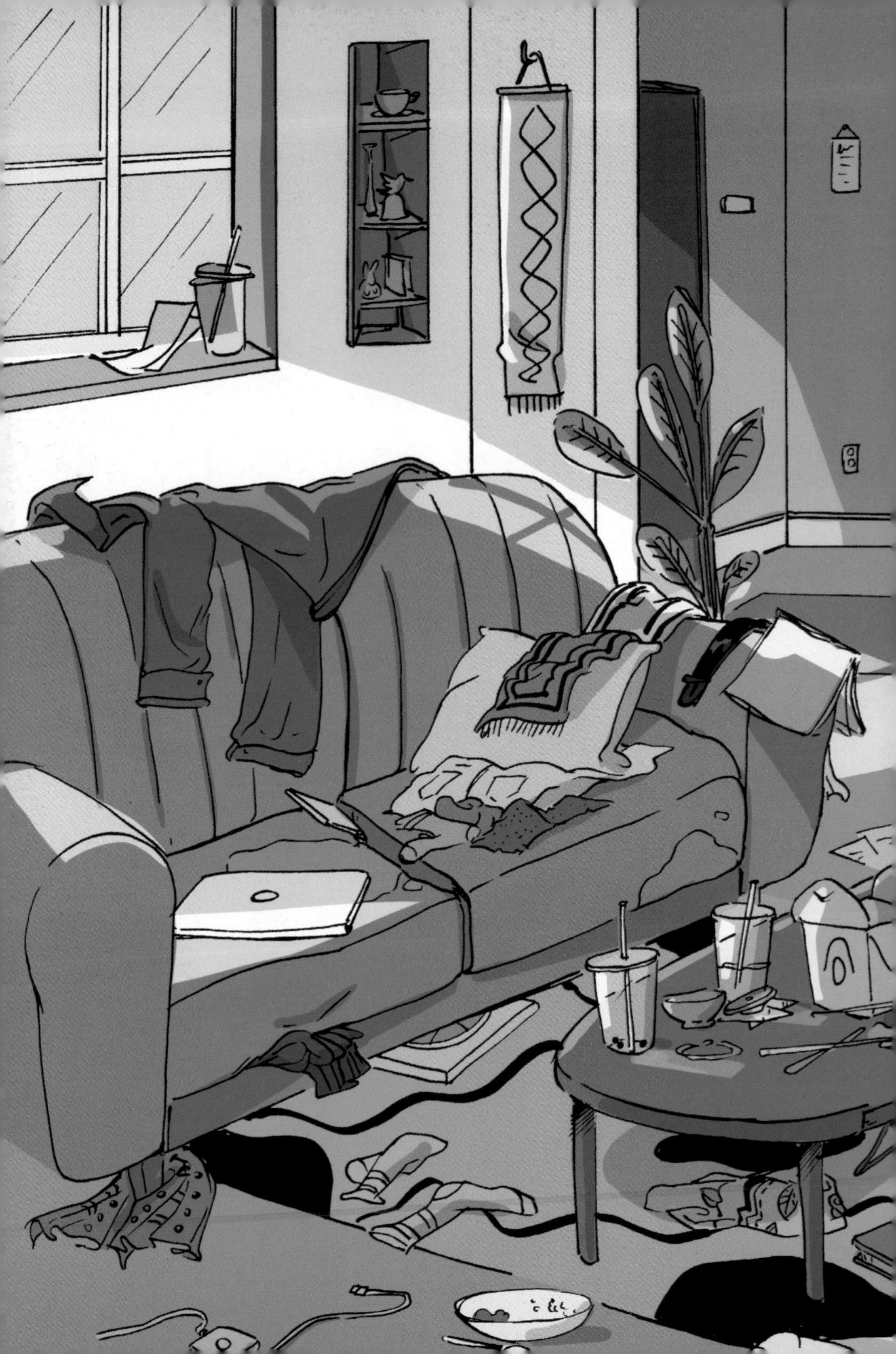

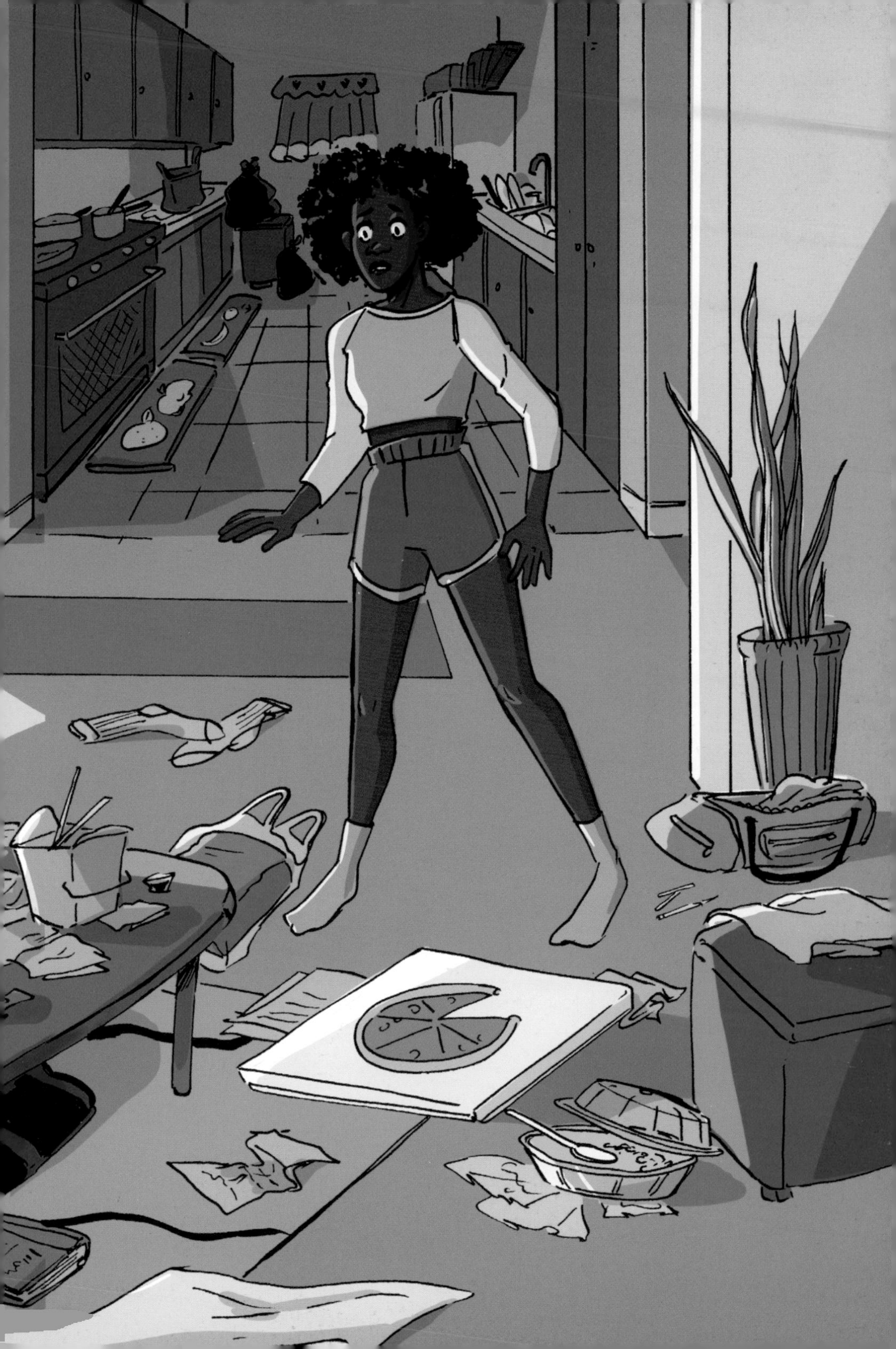

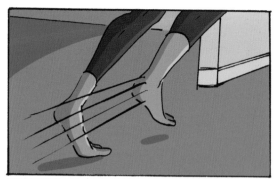

bzzzzz

DOOR   LISTEN

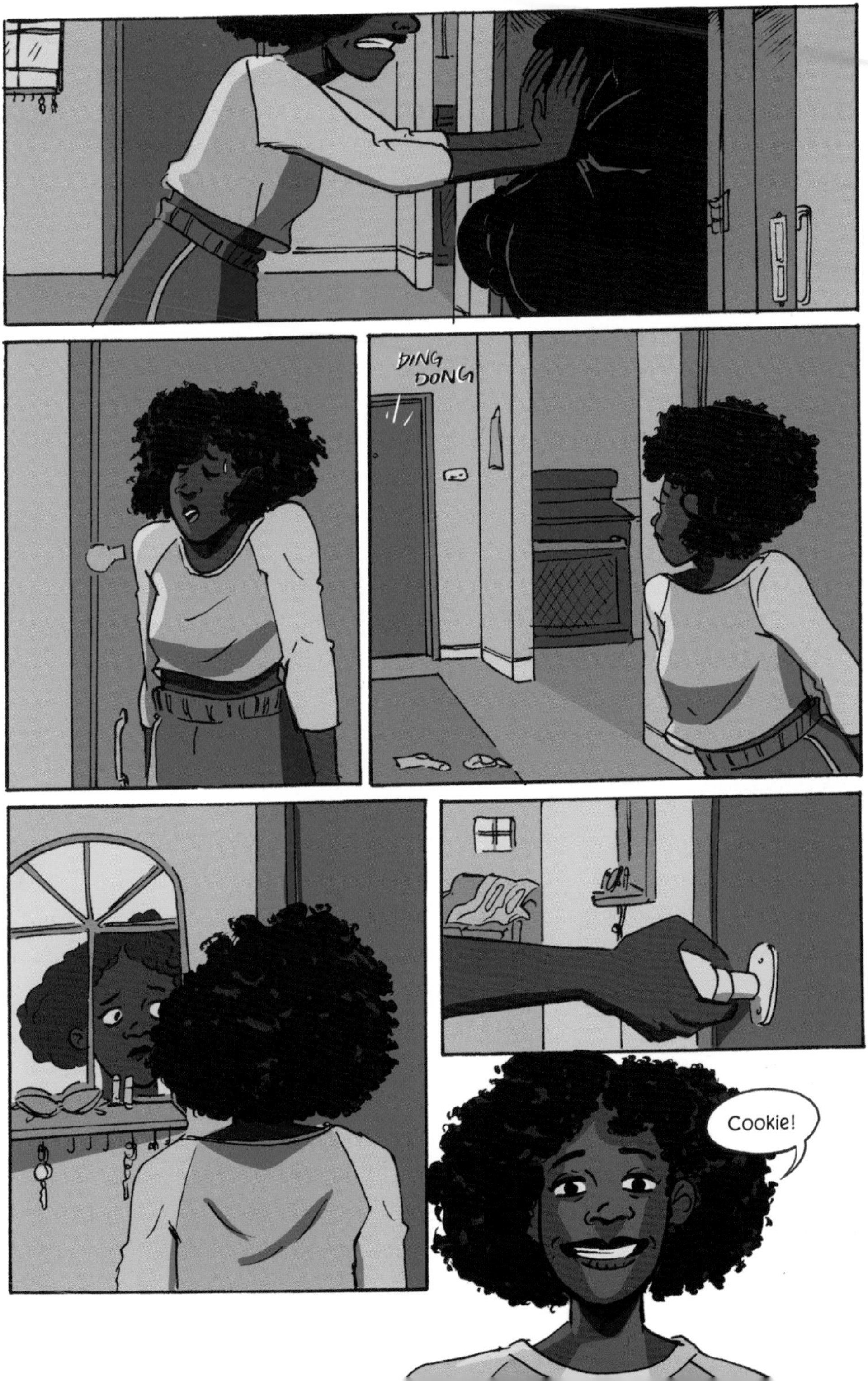
DING DONG
Cookie!

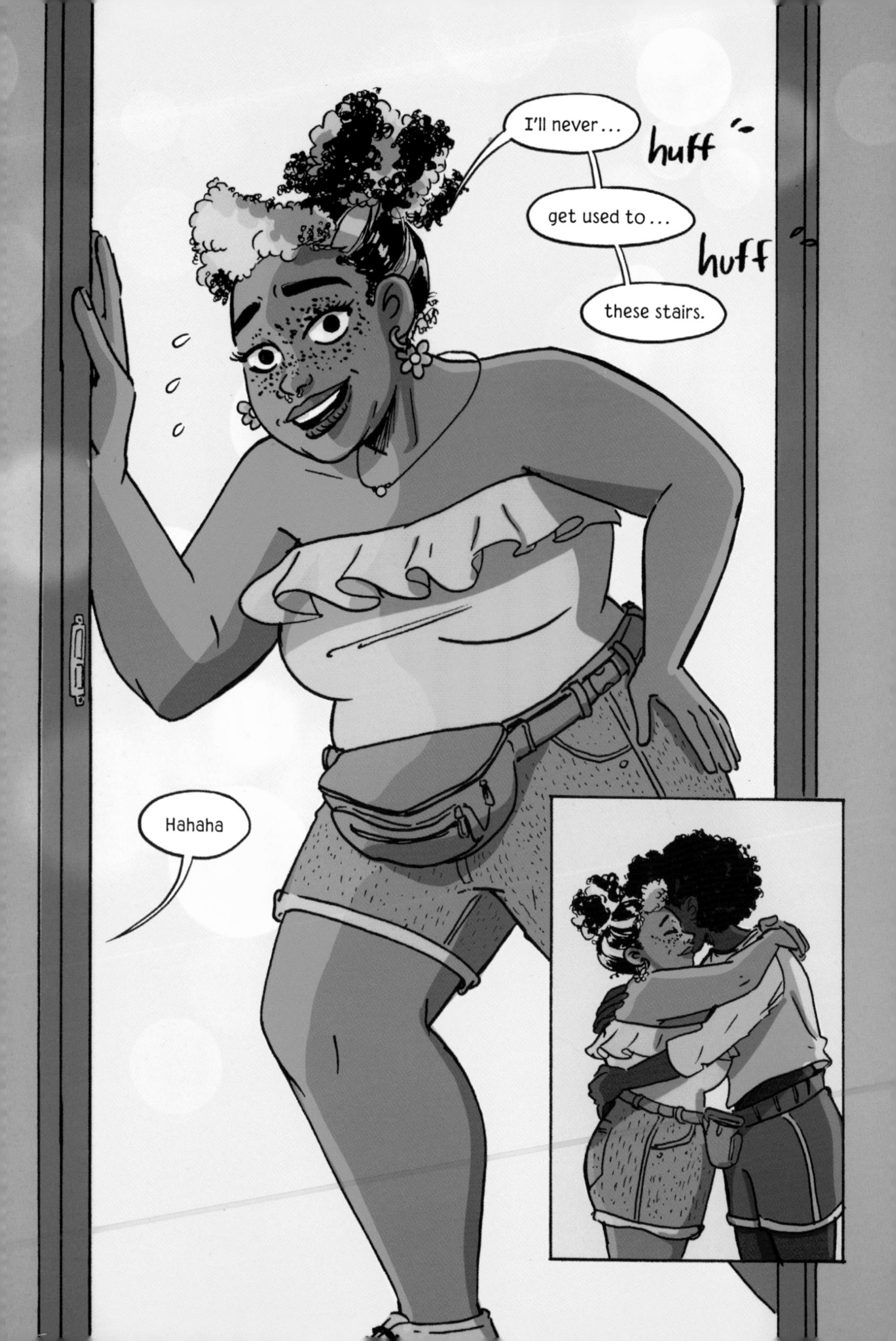
I'll never...
huff
get used to...
huff
these stairs.
Hahaha

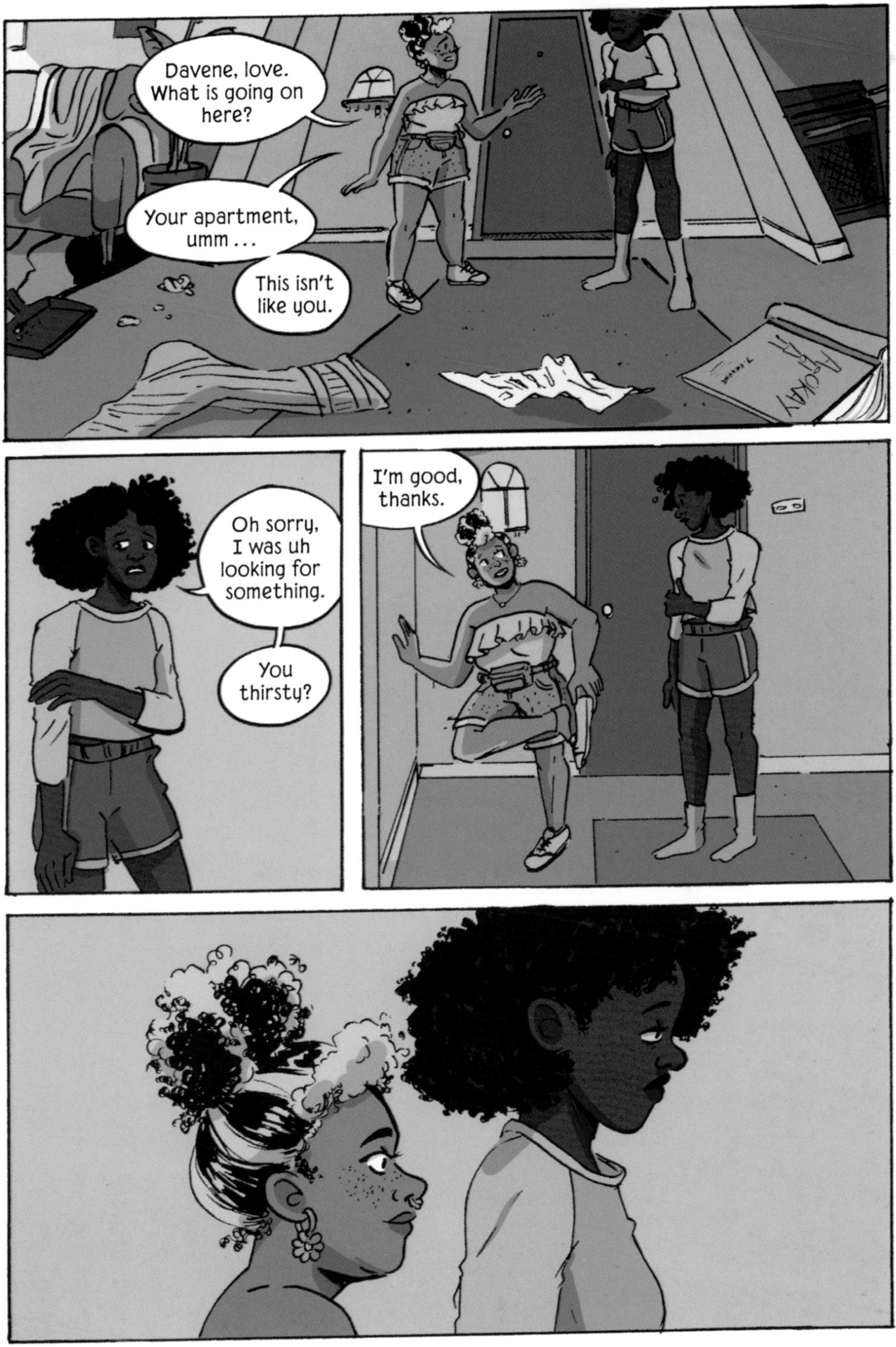
Davene, love. What is going on here?
Your apartment, umm . . .
This isn't like you.
Oh sorry, I was uh looking for something.
You thirsty?
I'm good, thanks.

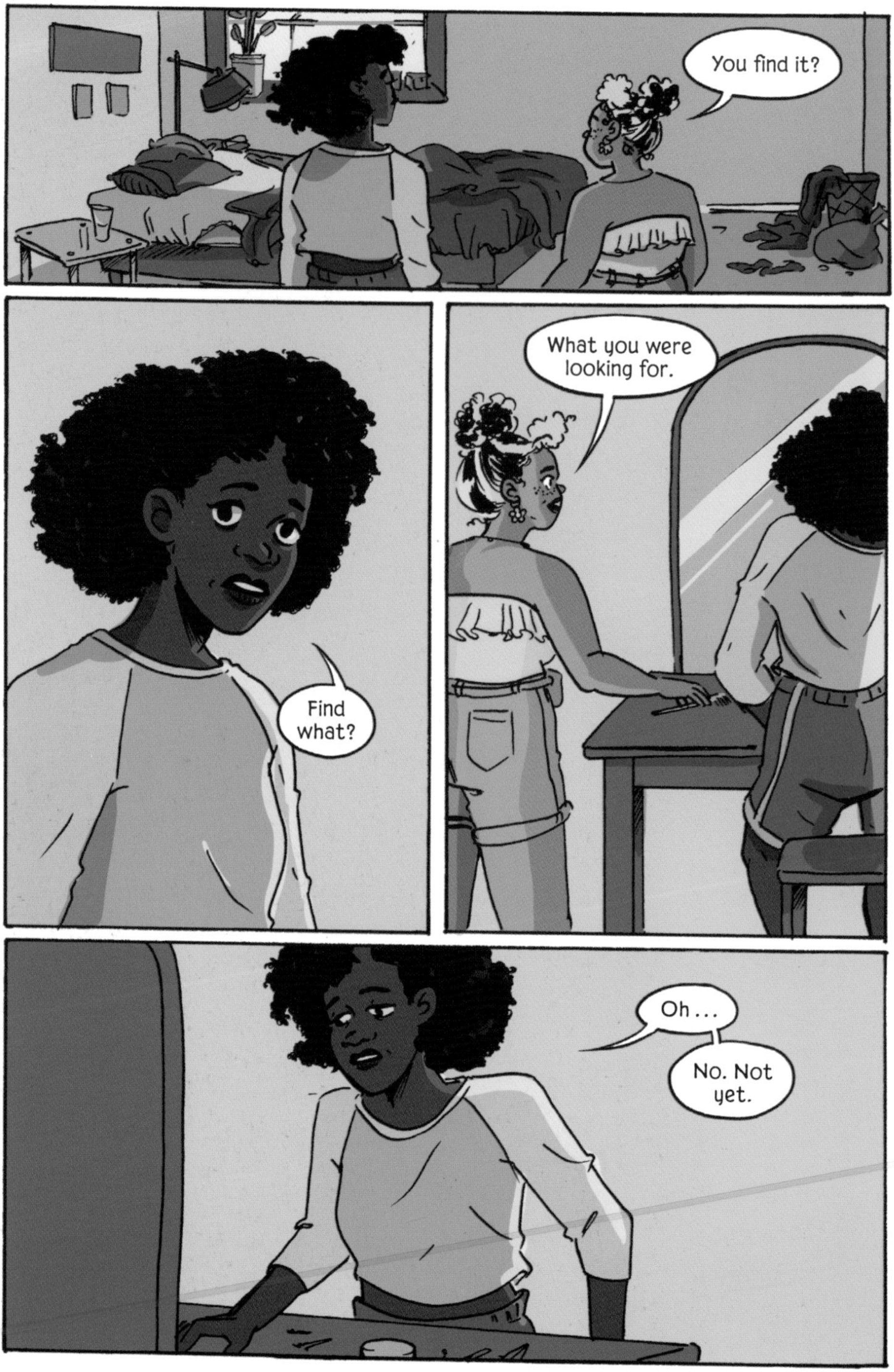
You find it?
Find what?
What you were looking for.
Oh . . .
No. Not yet.

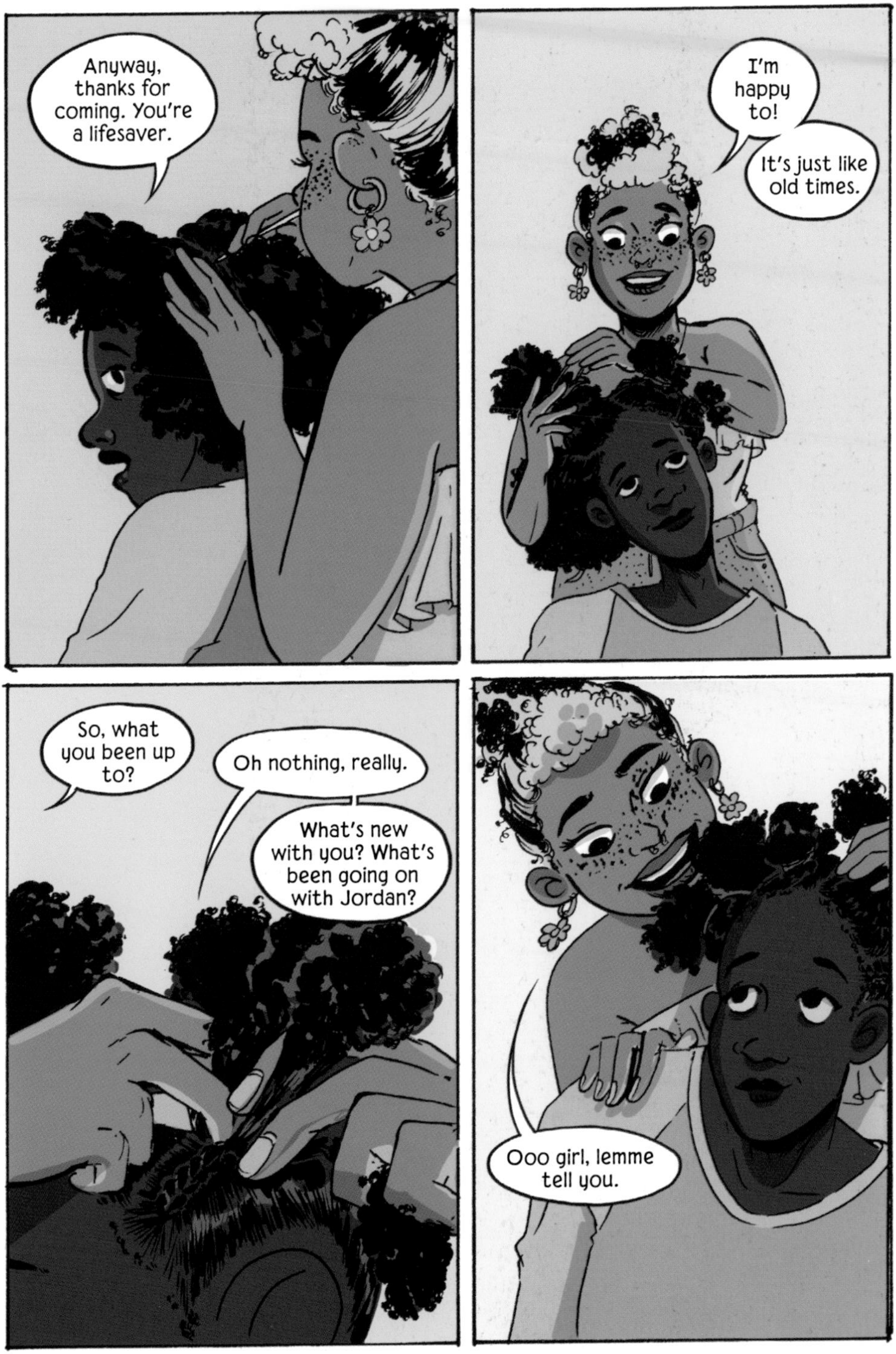
Anyway, thanks for coming. You're a lifesaver.
I'm happy to!
It's just like old times.
So, what you been up to?
Oh nothing, really.
What's new with you? What's been going on with Jordan?
Ooo girl, lemme tell you.

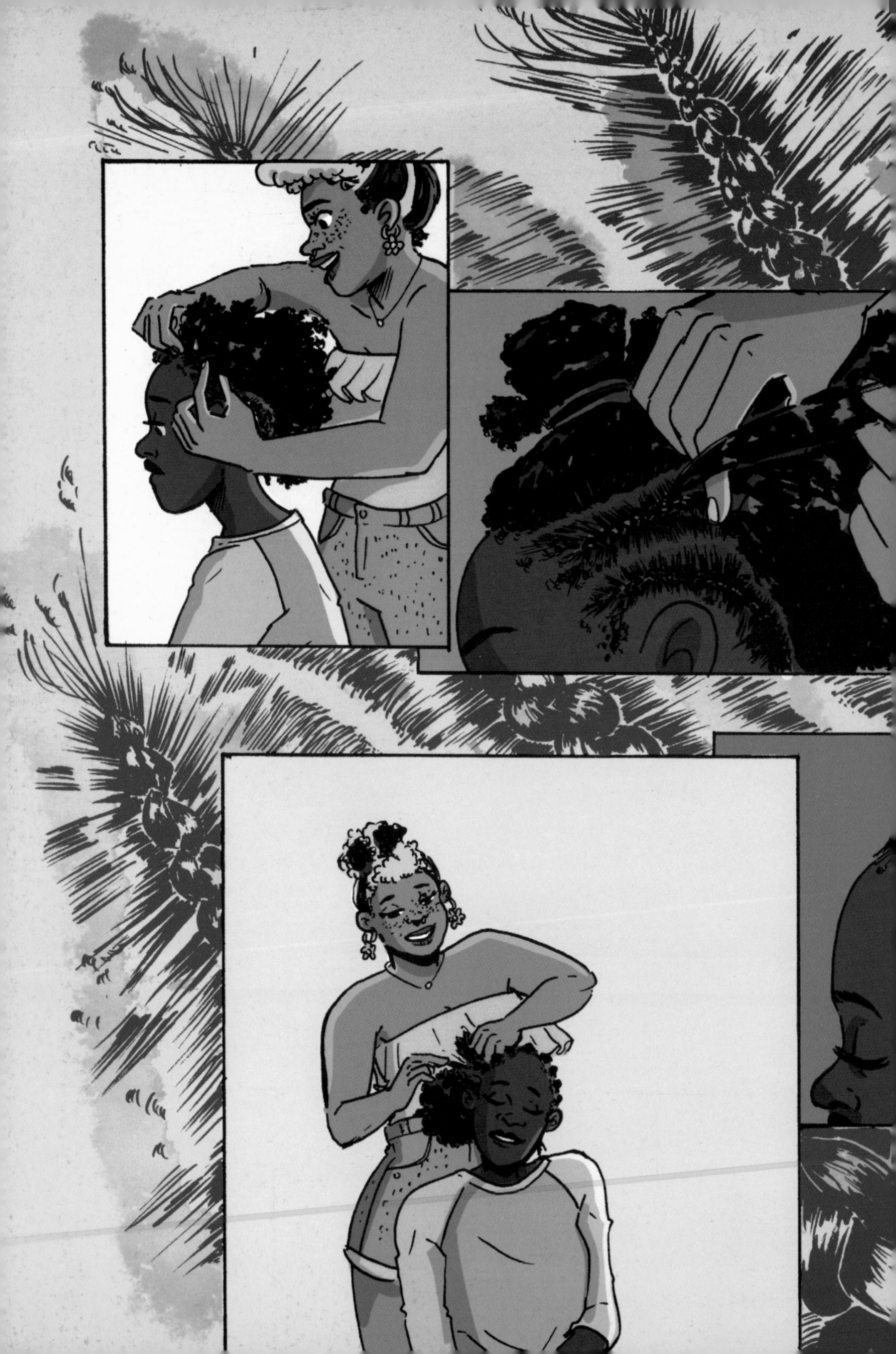

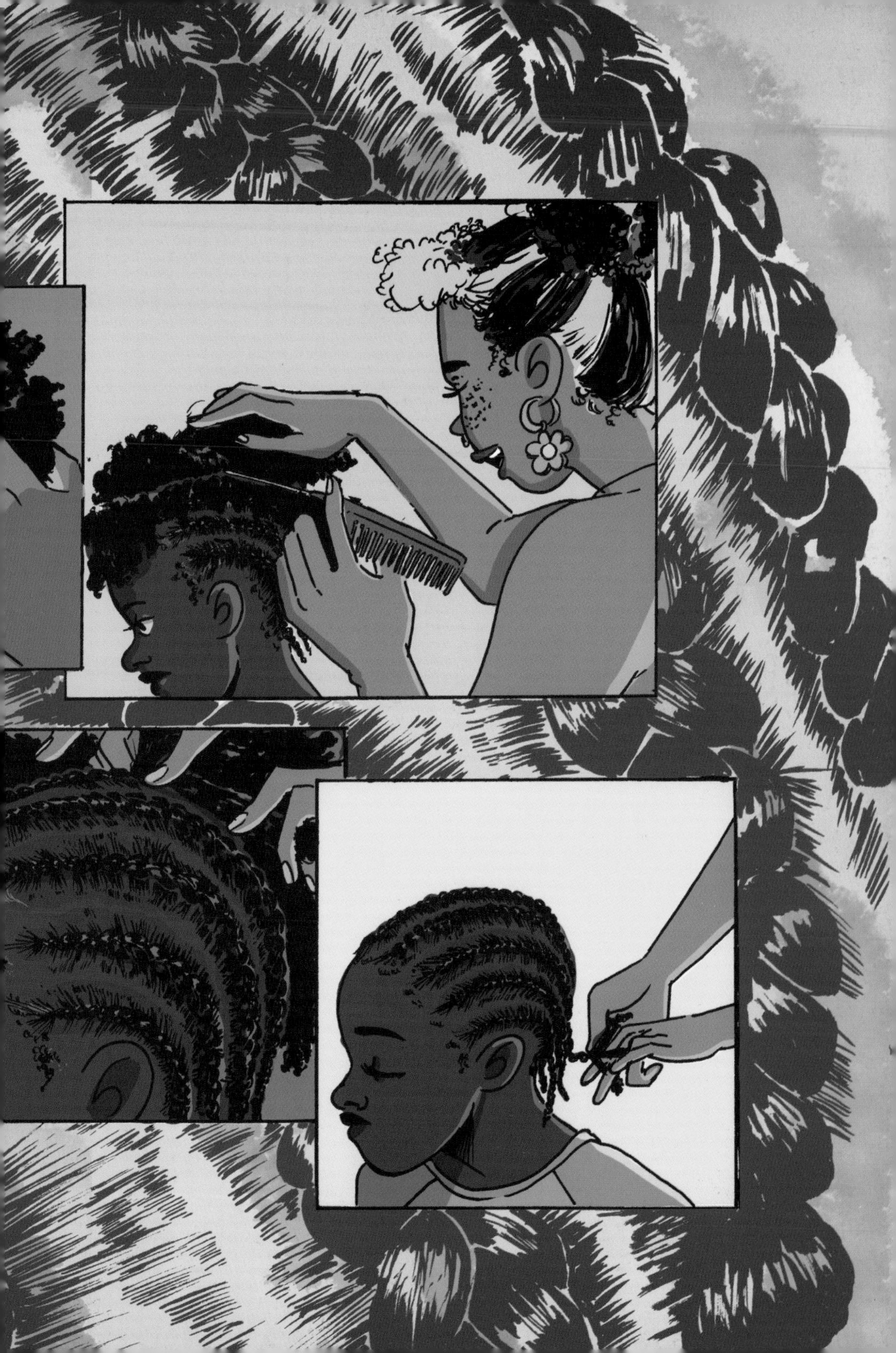

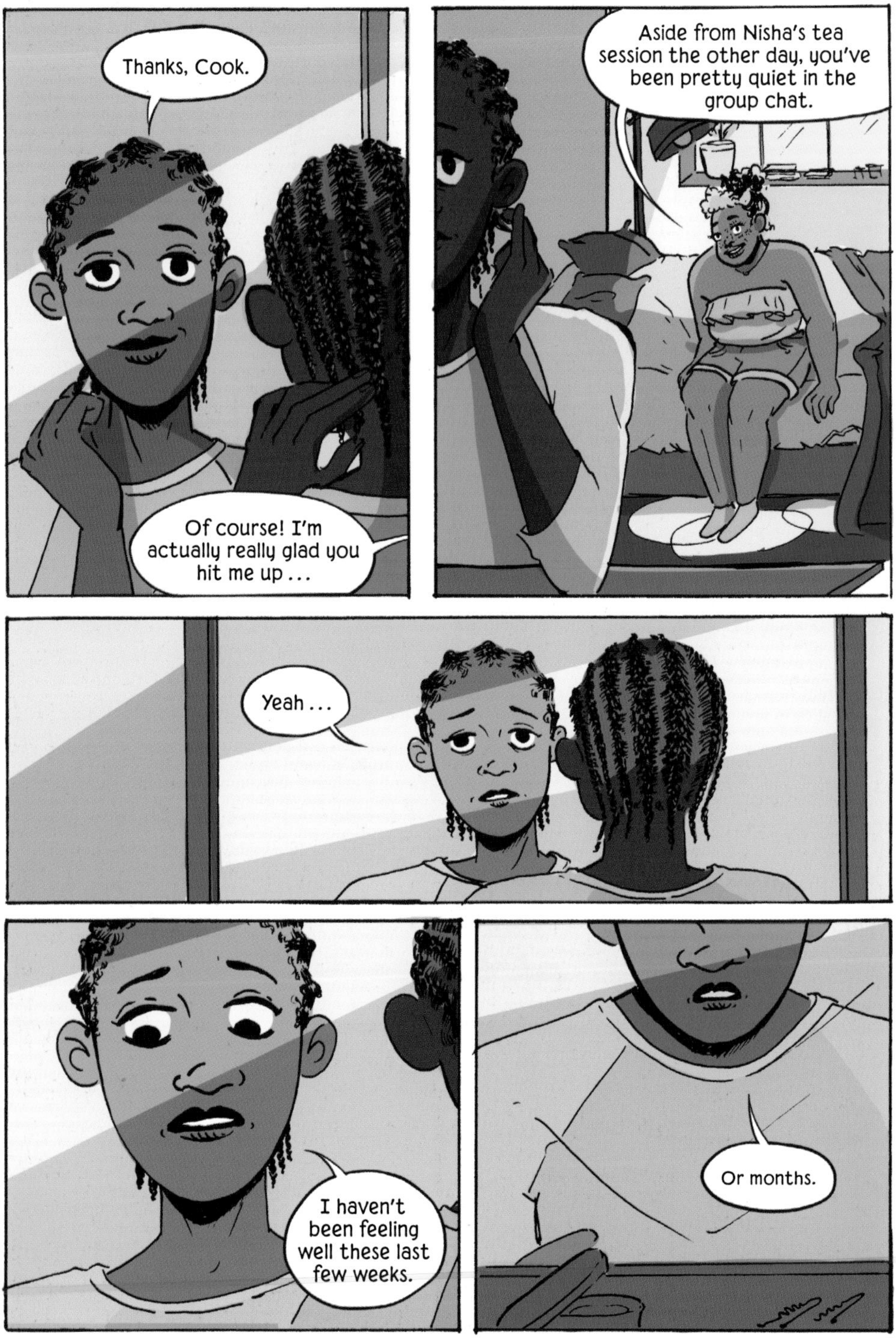
Thanks, Cook.
Of course! I'm actually really glad you hit me up . . .
Aside from Nisha's tea session the other day, you've been pretty quiet in the group chat.
Yeah . . .
I haven't been feeling well these last few weeks.
Or months.

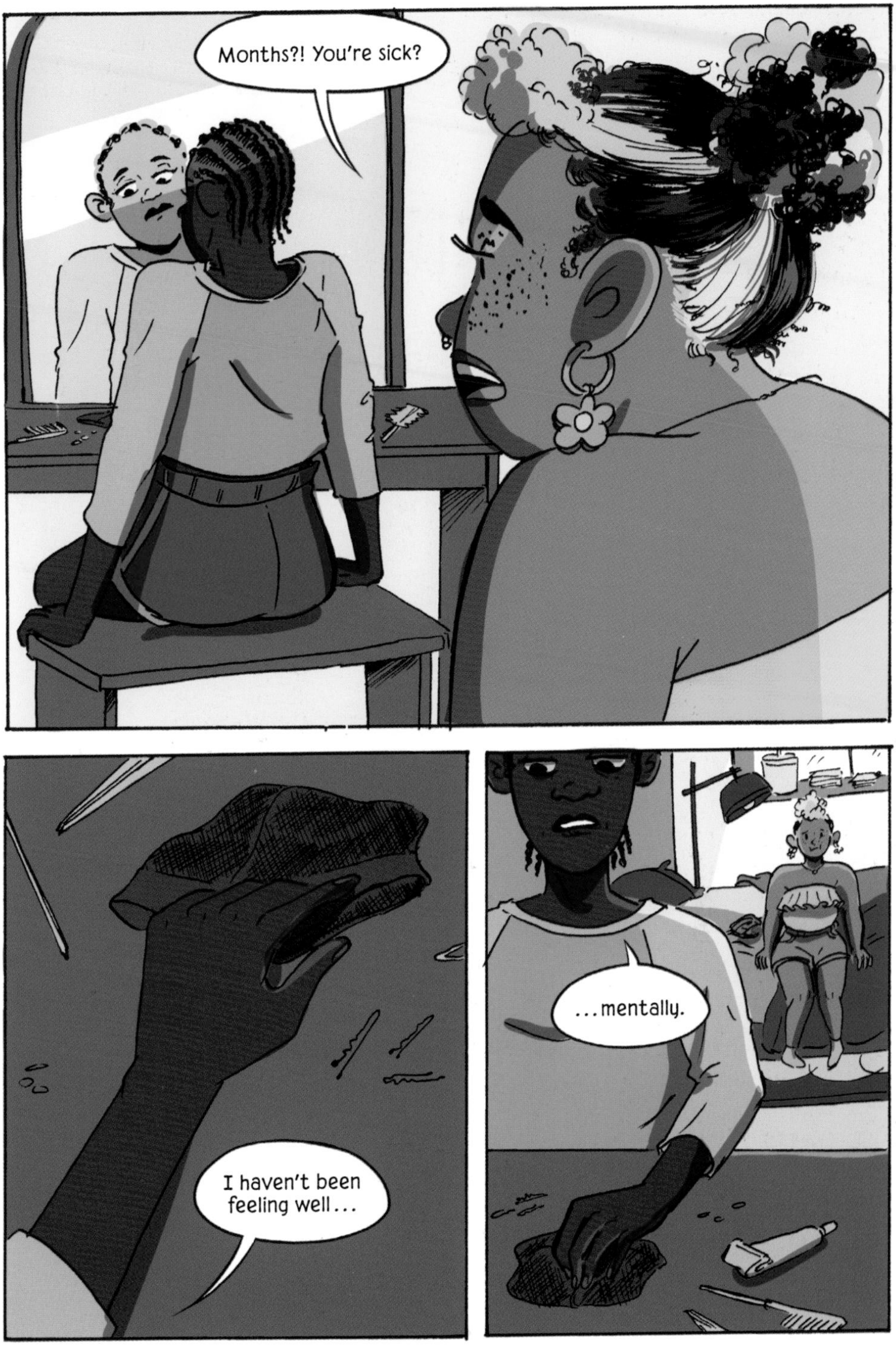
Months?! You're sick?
I haven't been feeling well...
...mentally.

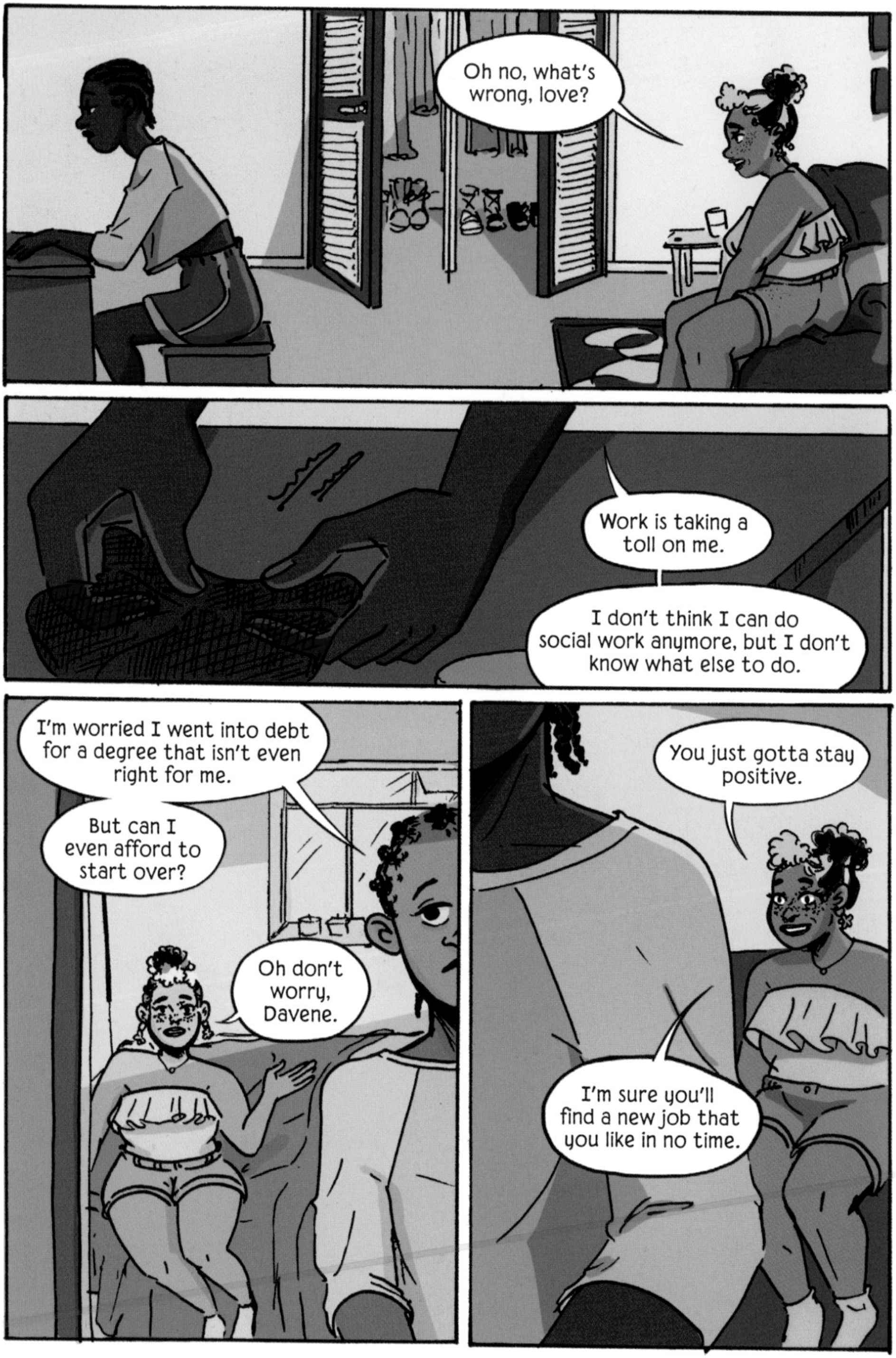
Oh no, what's wrong, love?
Work is taking a toll on me.
I don't think I can do social work anymore, but I don't know what else to do.
I'm worried I went into debt for a degree that isn't even right for me.
But can I even afford to start over?
Oh don't worry, Davene.
You just gotta stay positive.
I'm sure you'll find a new job that you like in no time.

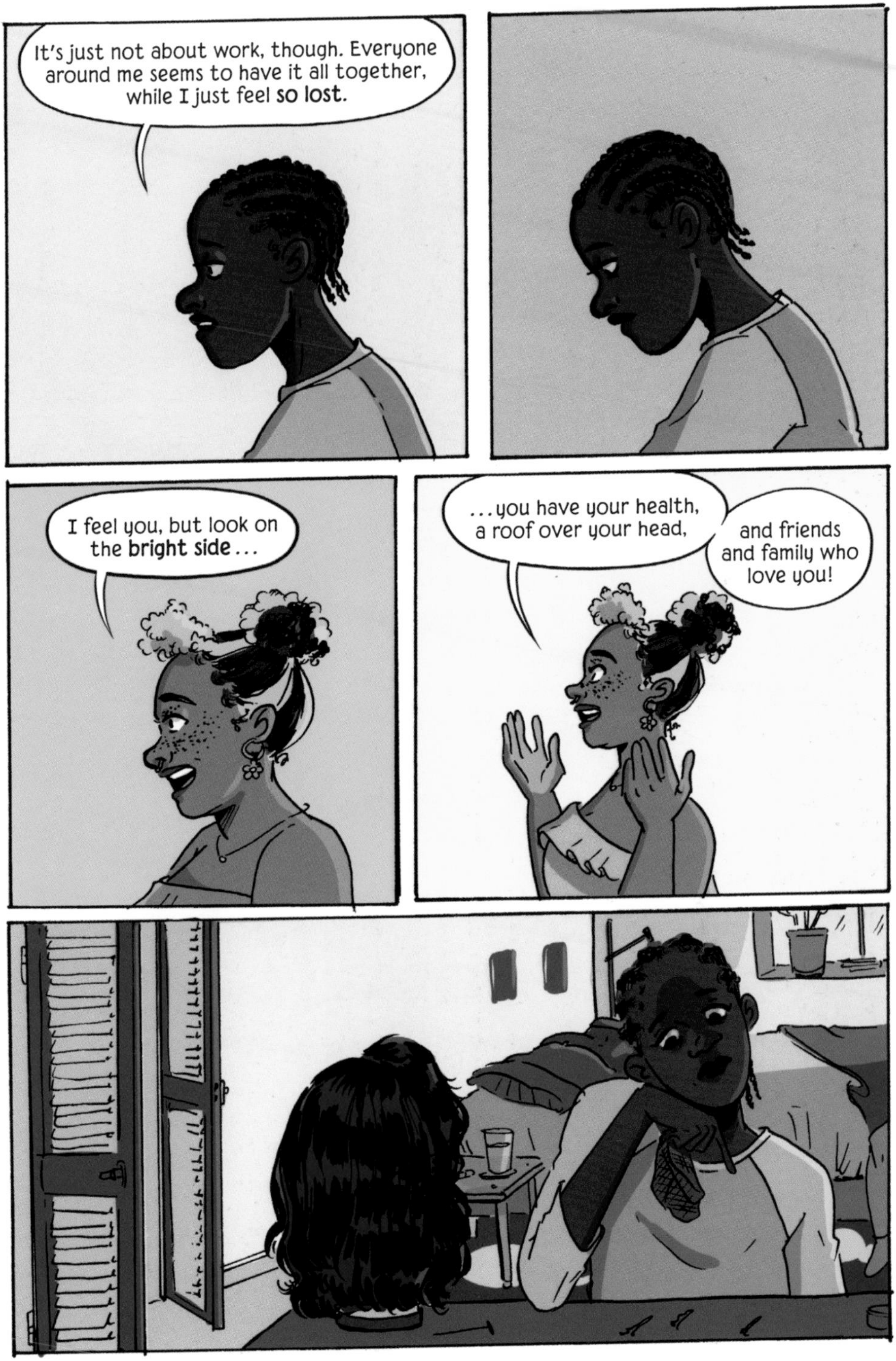

It's just not about work, though. Everyone around me seems to have it all together, while I just feel so lost.
I feel you, but look on the bright side . . .
. . . you have your health, a roof over your head,
and friends and family who love you!

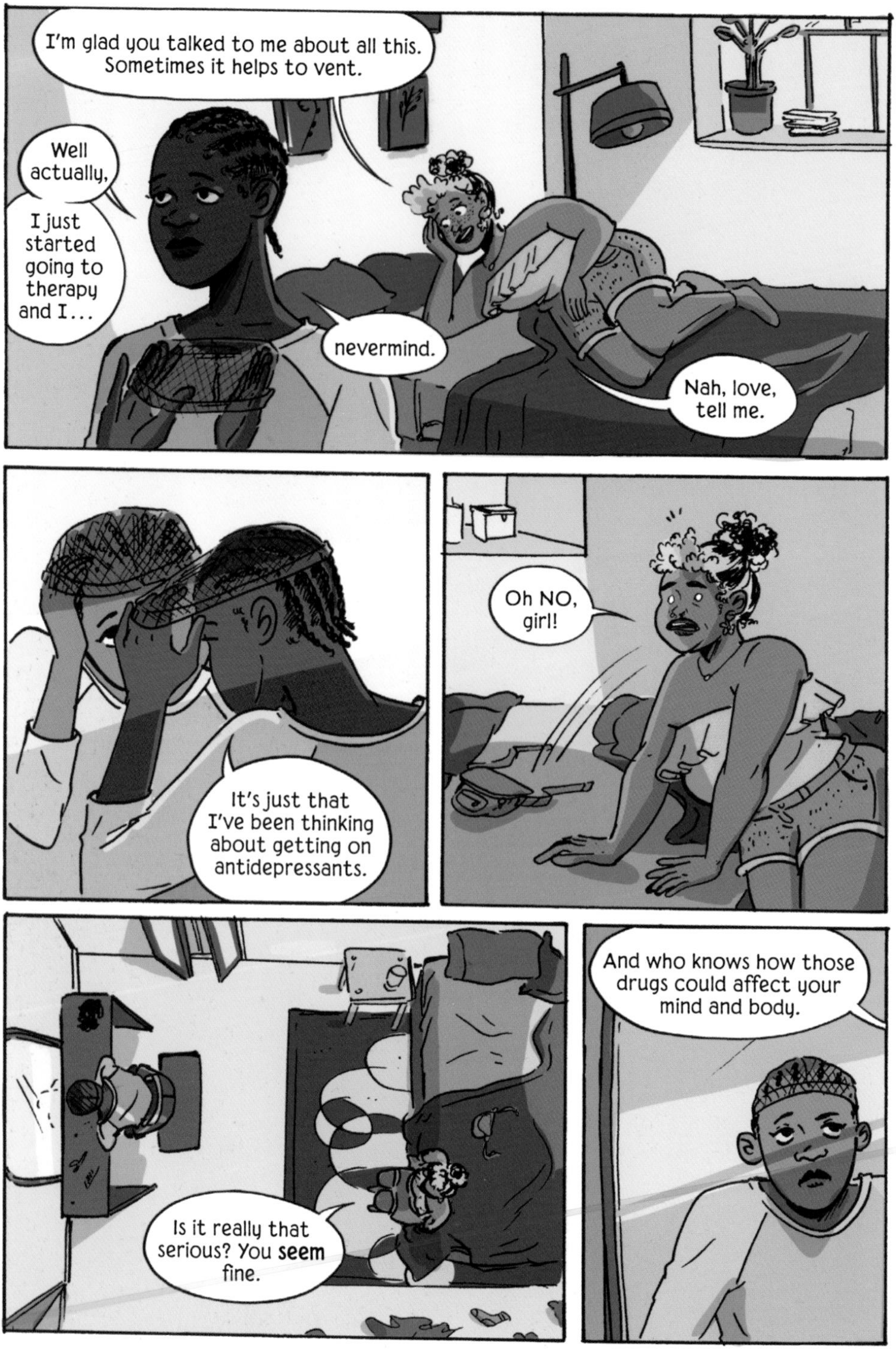
I'm glad you talked to me about all this. Sometimes it helps to vent.
Well actually,
I just started going to therapy and I...
nevermind.
Nah, love, tell me.
It's just that I've been thinking about getting on antidepressants.
Oh NO, girl!
Is it really that serious? You **seem** fine.
And who knows how those drugs could affect your mind and body.

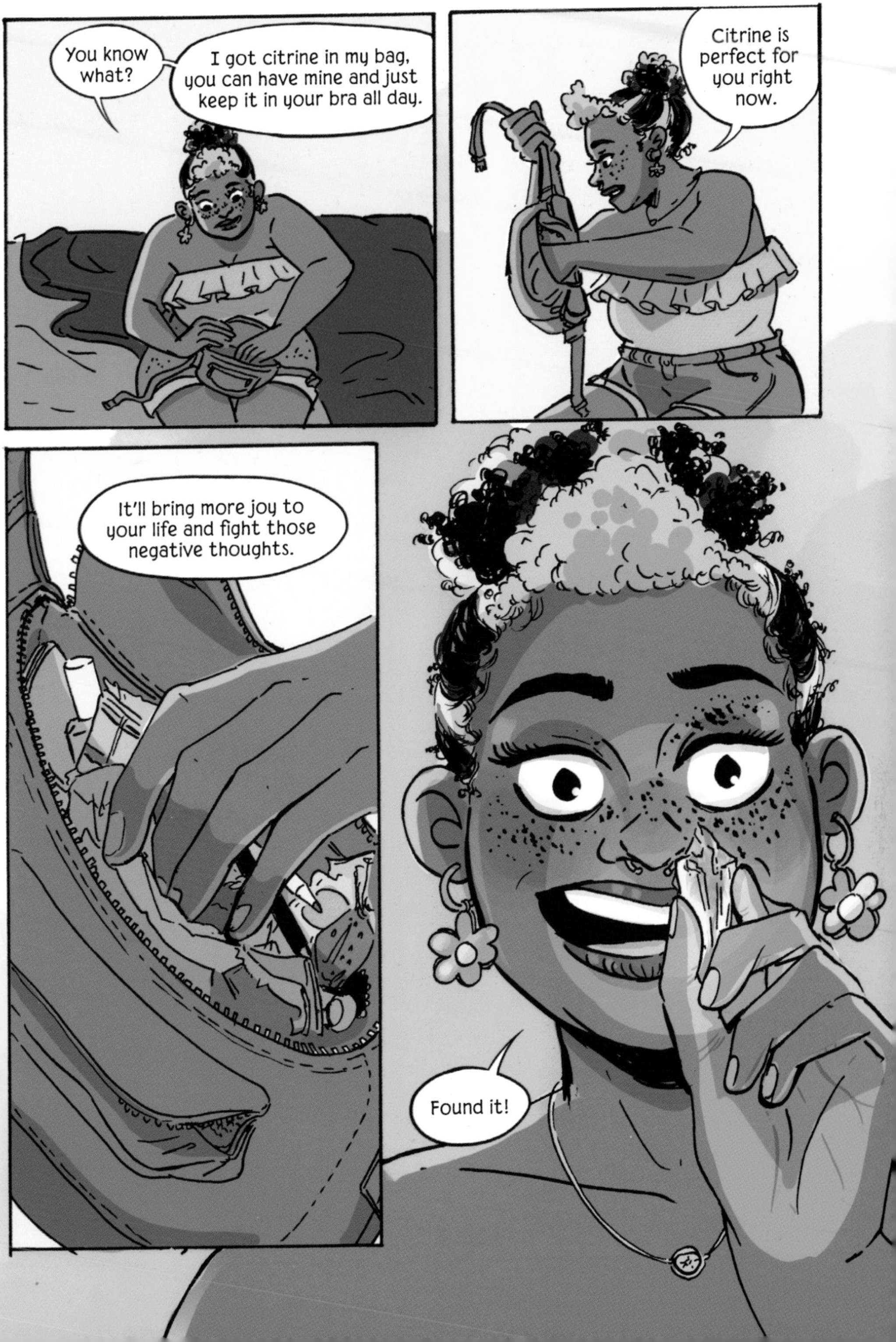

You know what?
I got citrine in my bag, you can have mine and just keep it in your bra all day.
Citrine is perfect for you right now.
It'll bring more joy to your life and fight those negative thoughts.
Found it!

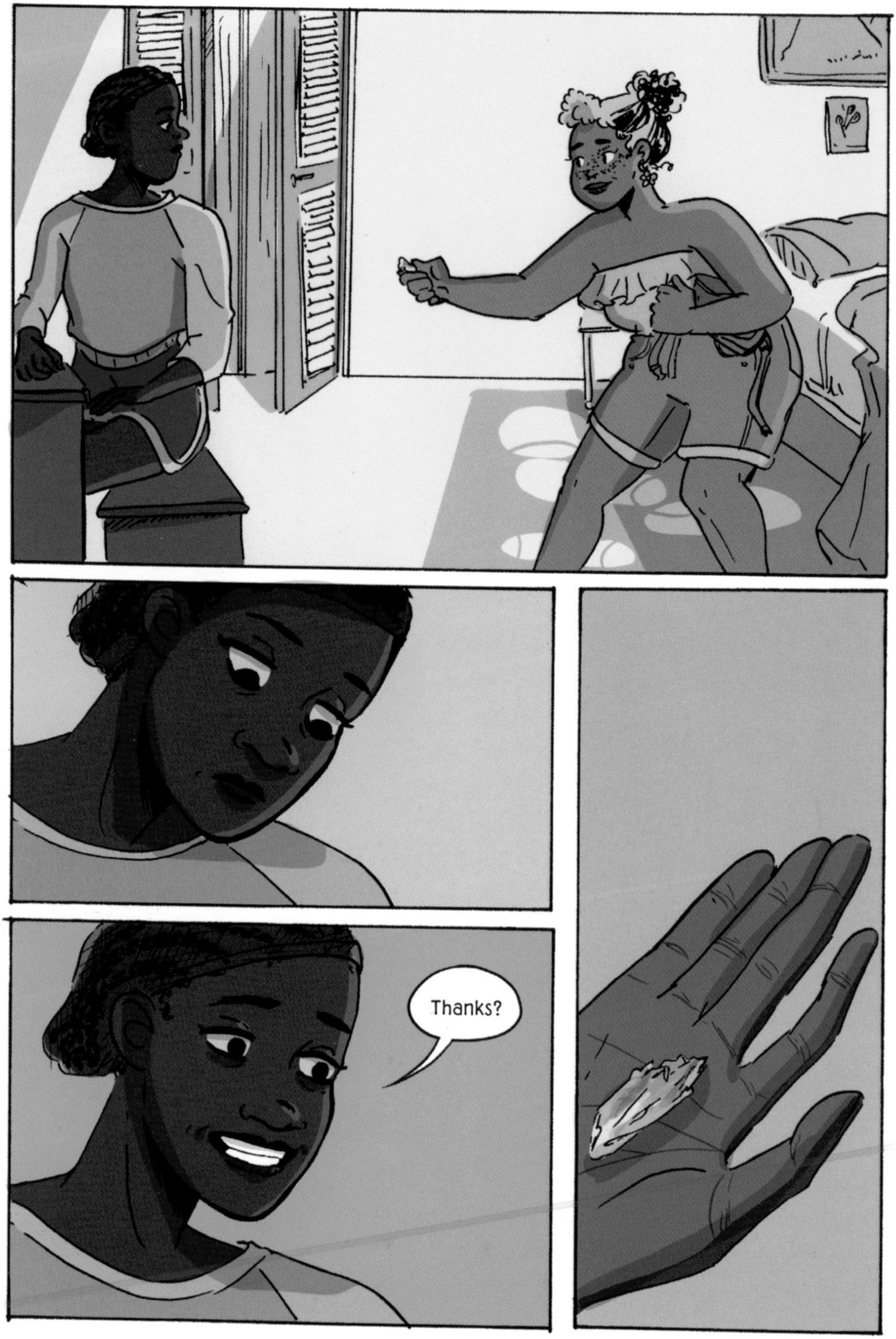
Thanks?

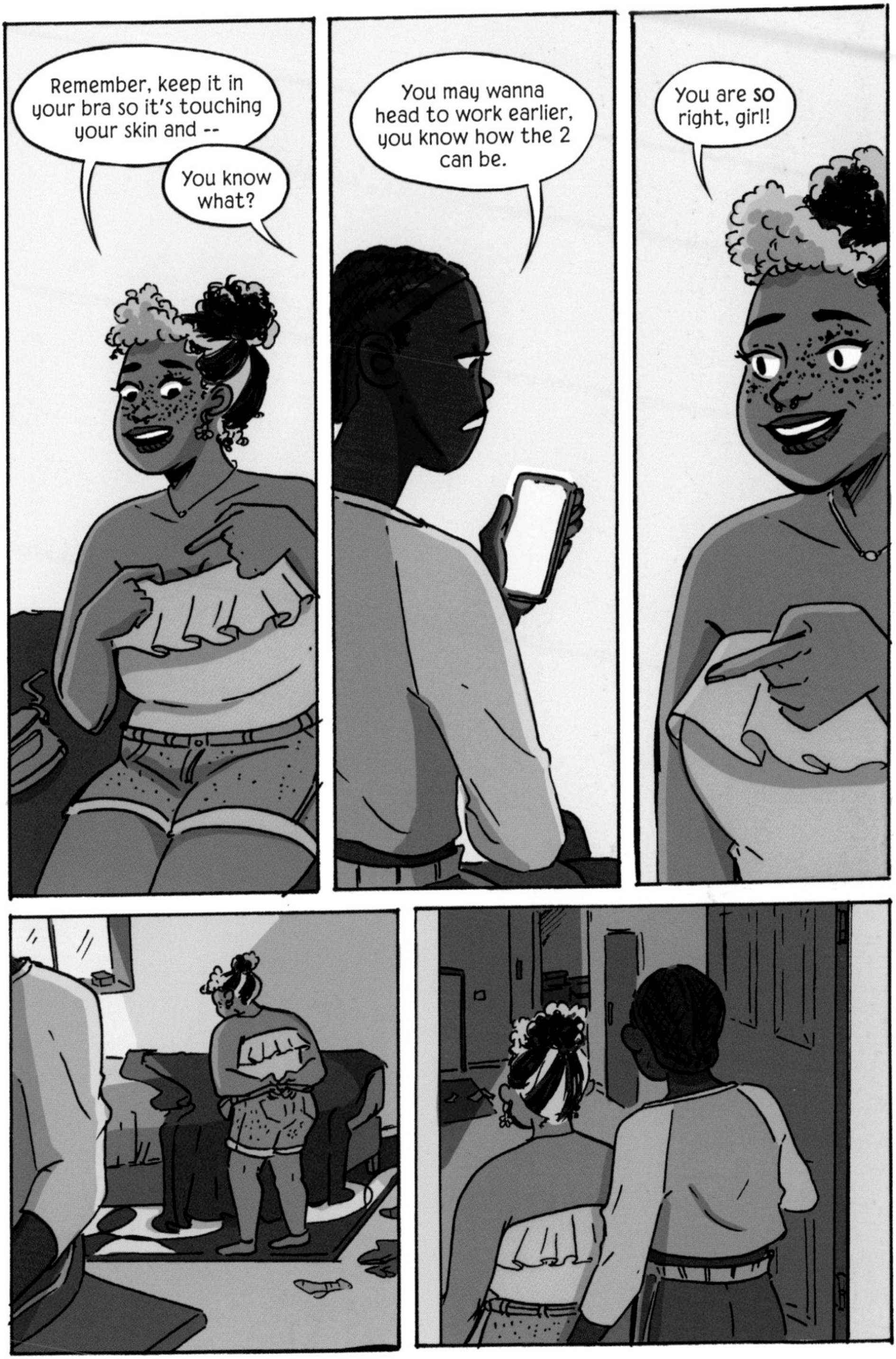
Remember, keep it in your bra so it's touching your skin and --
You know what?
You may wanna head to work earlier, you know how the 2 can be.
You are SO right, girl!

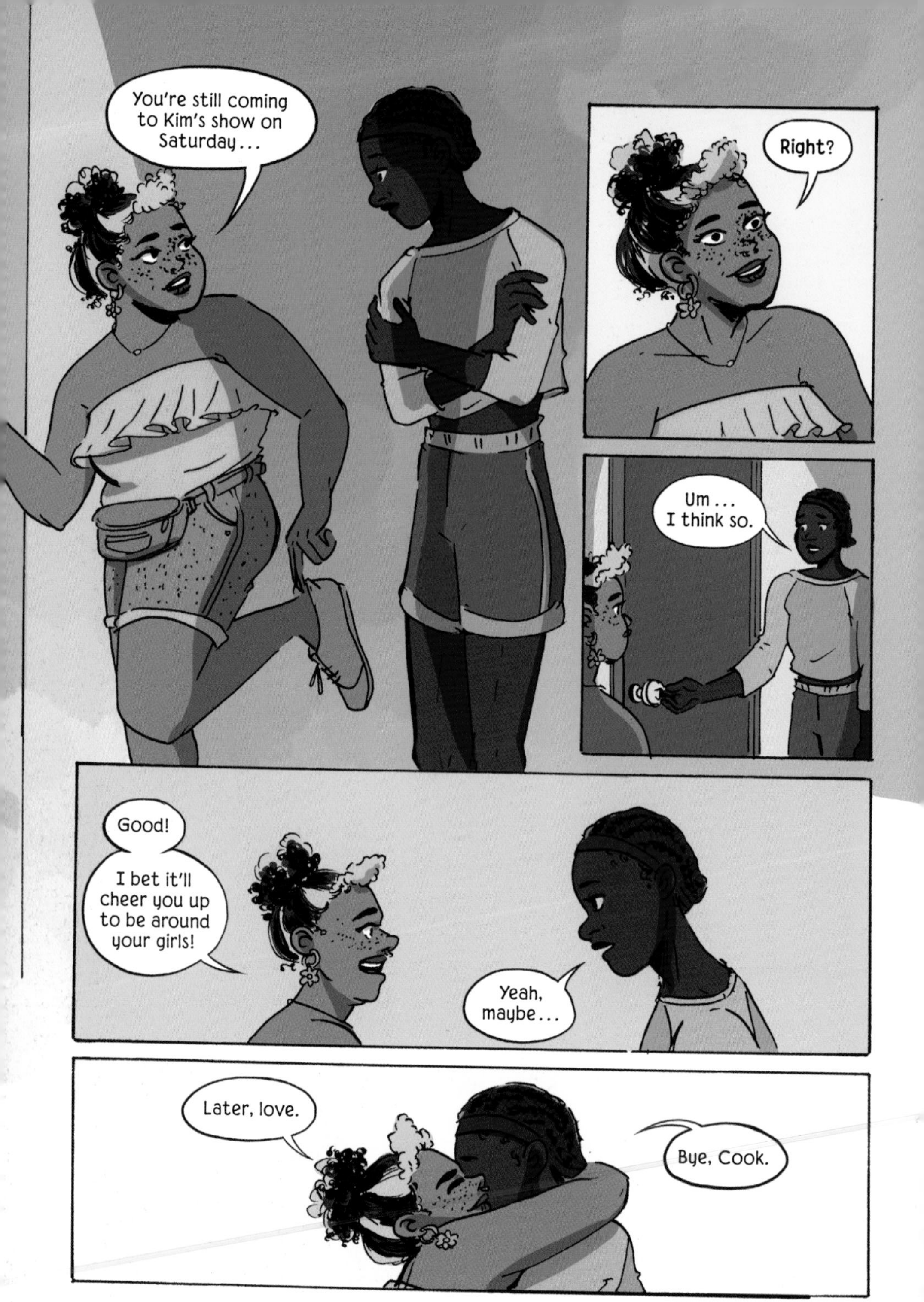
You're still coming to Kim's show on Saturday...
Right?
Um... I think so.
Good!
I bet it'll cheer you up to be around your girls!
Yeah, maybe...
Later, love.
Bye, Cook.

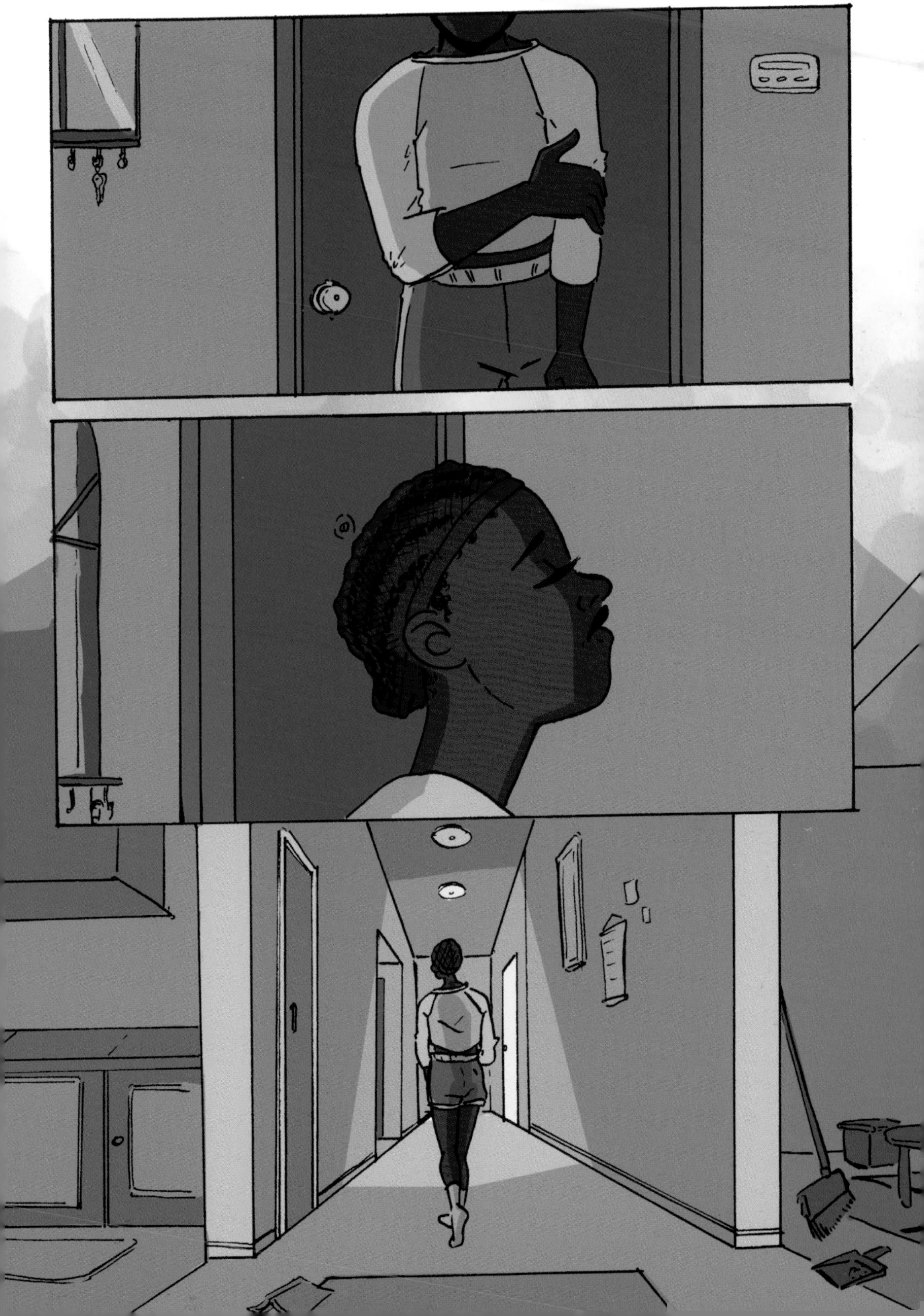

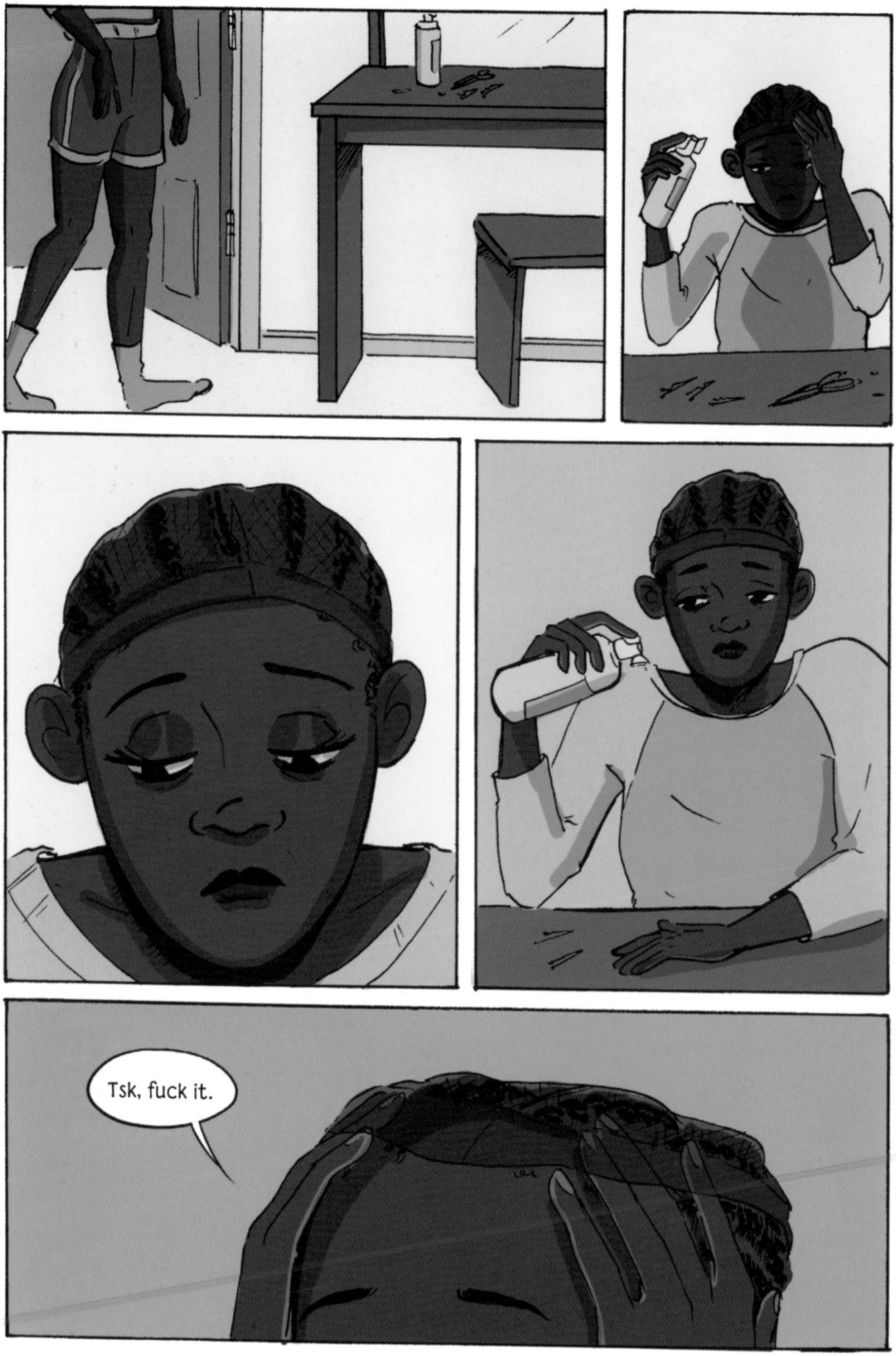
Tsk, fuck it.

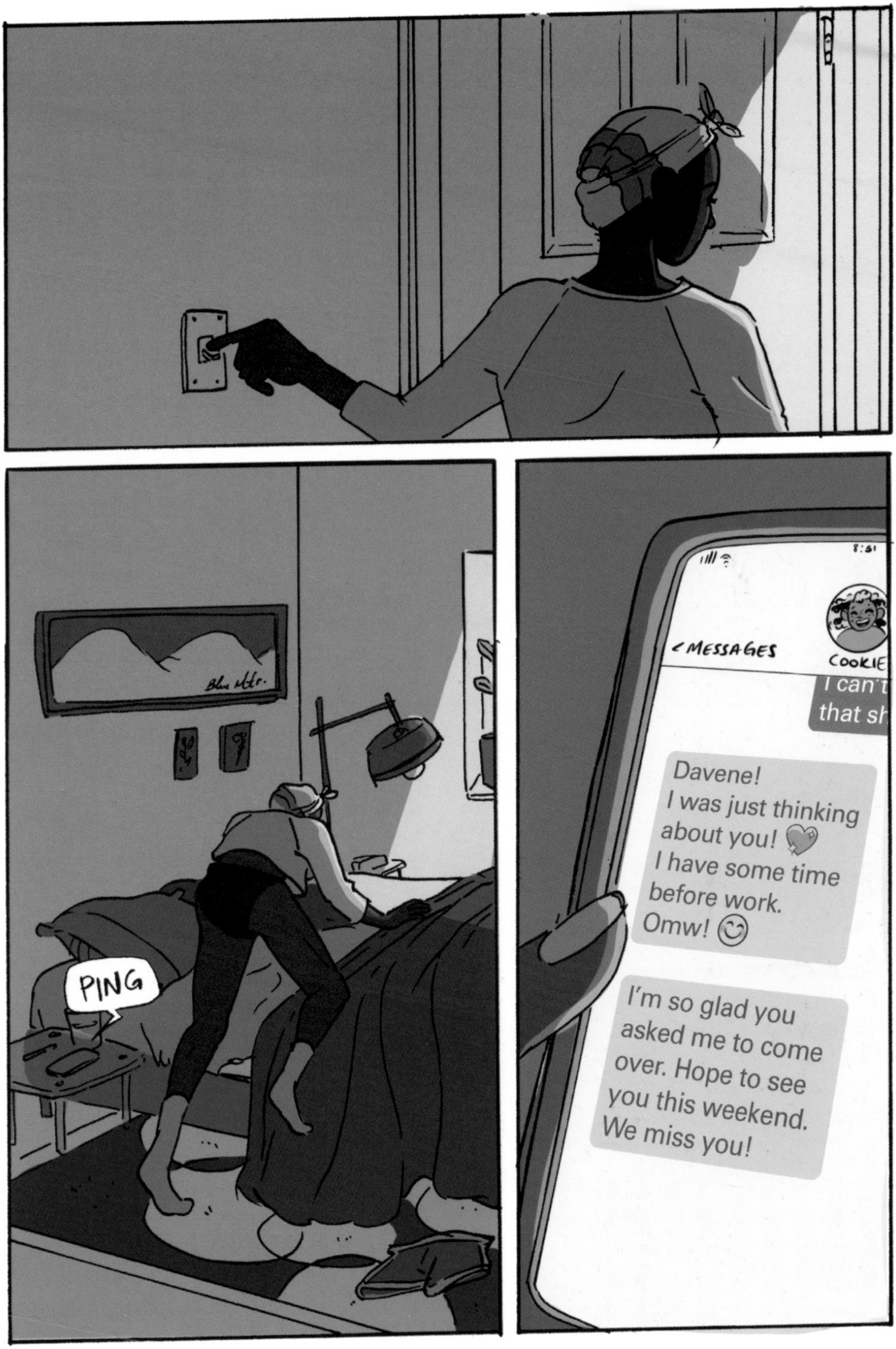
PING
<MESSAGES
COOKIE
Davene!
I was just thinking about you!
I have some time before work.
Omw!
I'm so glad you asked me to come over. Hope to see you this weekend. We miss you!

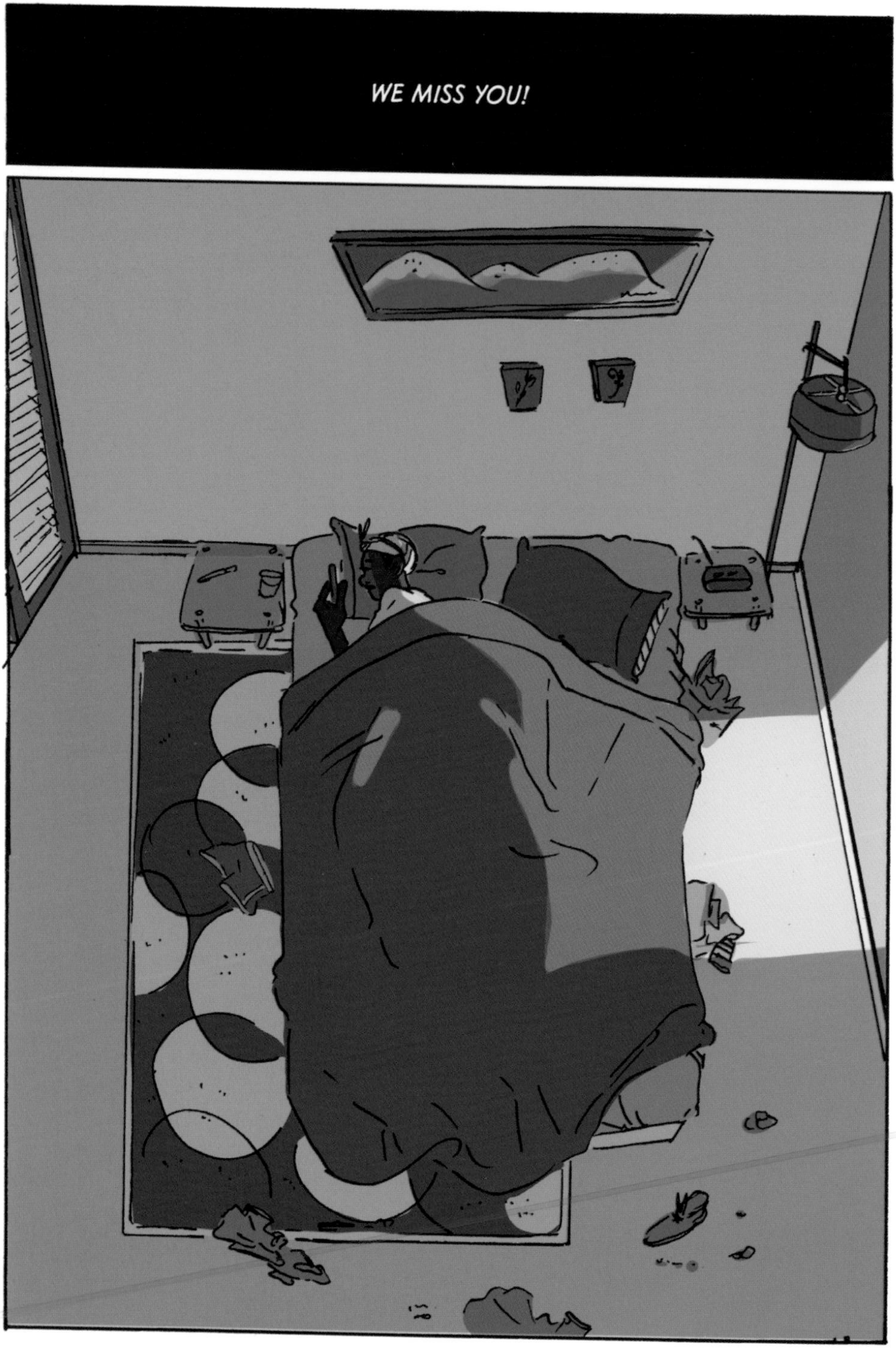
WE MISS YOU!

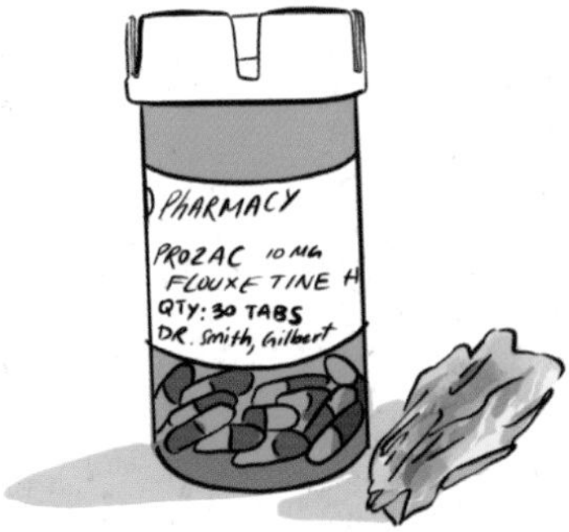
PHARMACY
PROZAC 10 MG
FLOUXETINE H
QTy: 30 TABS
DR. Smith, Gilbert

LA BENDICIÓN

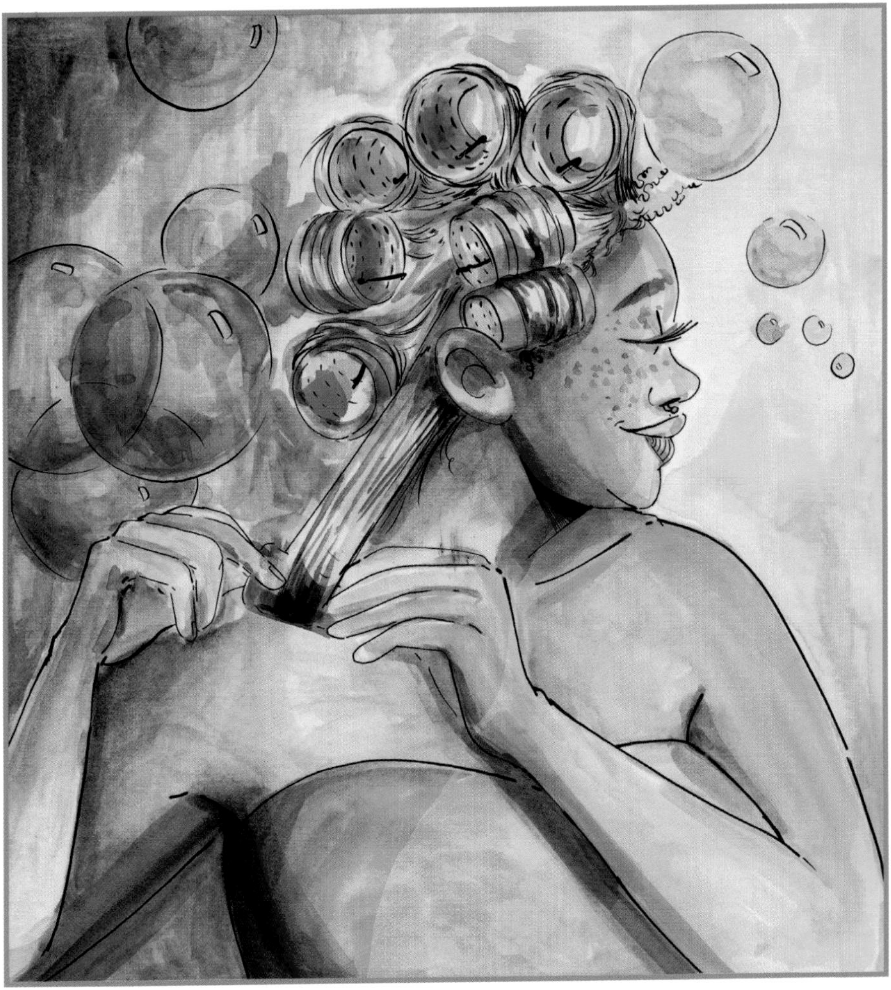

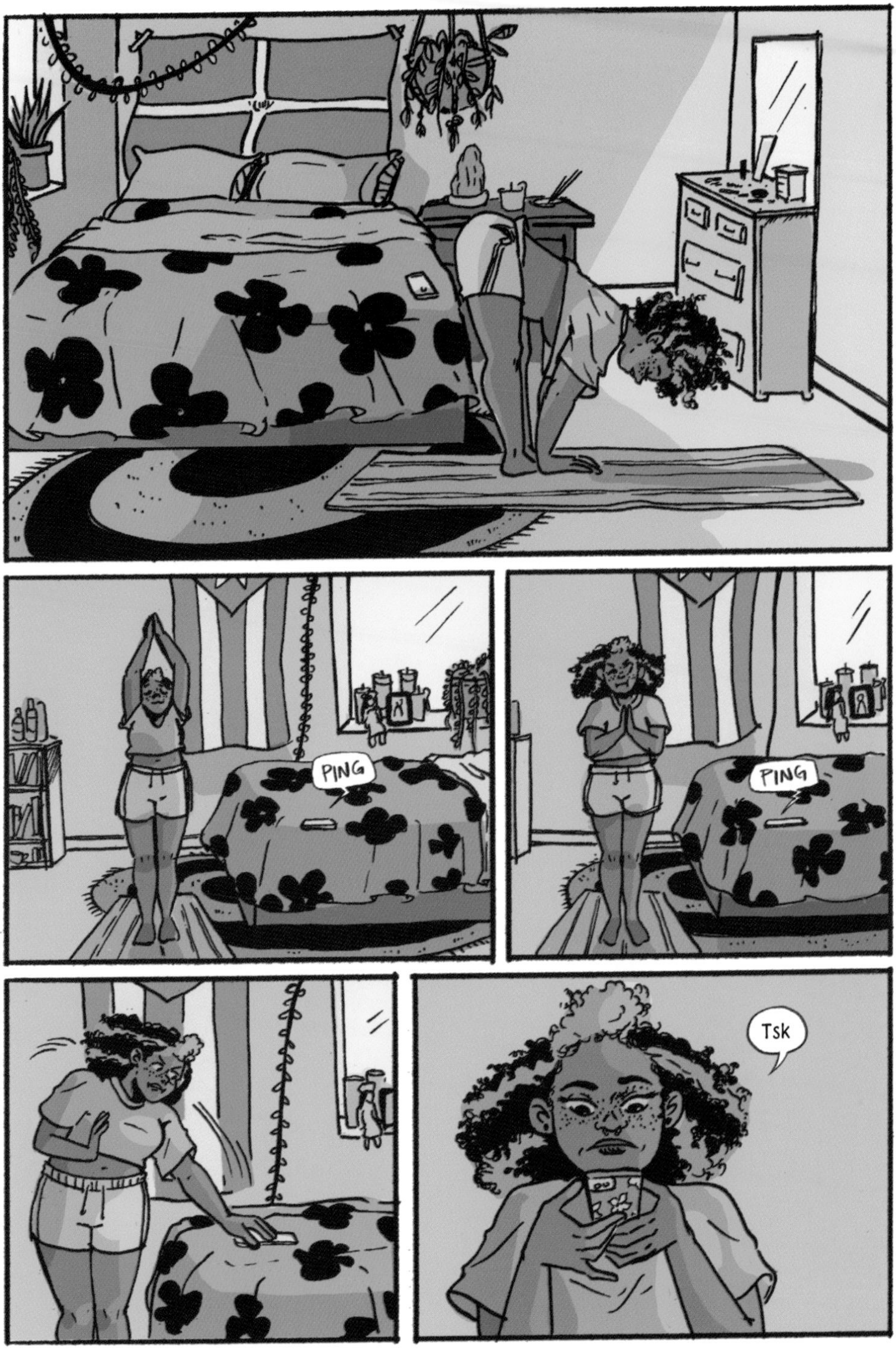
PING
PING
Tsk

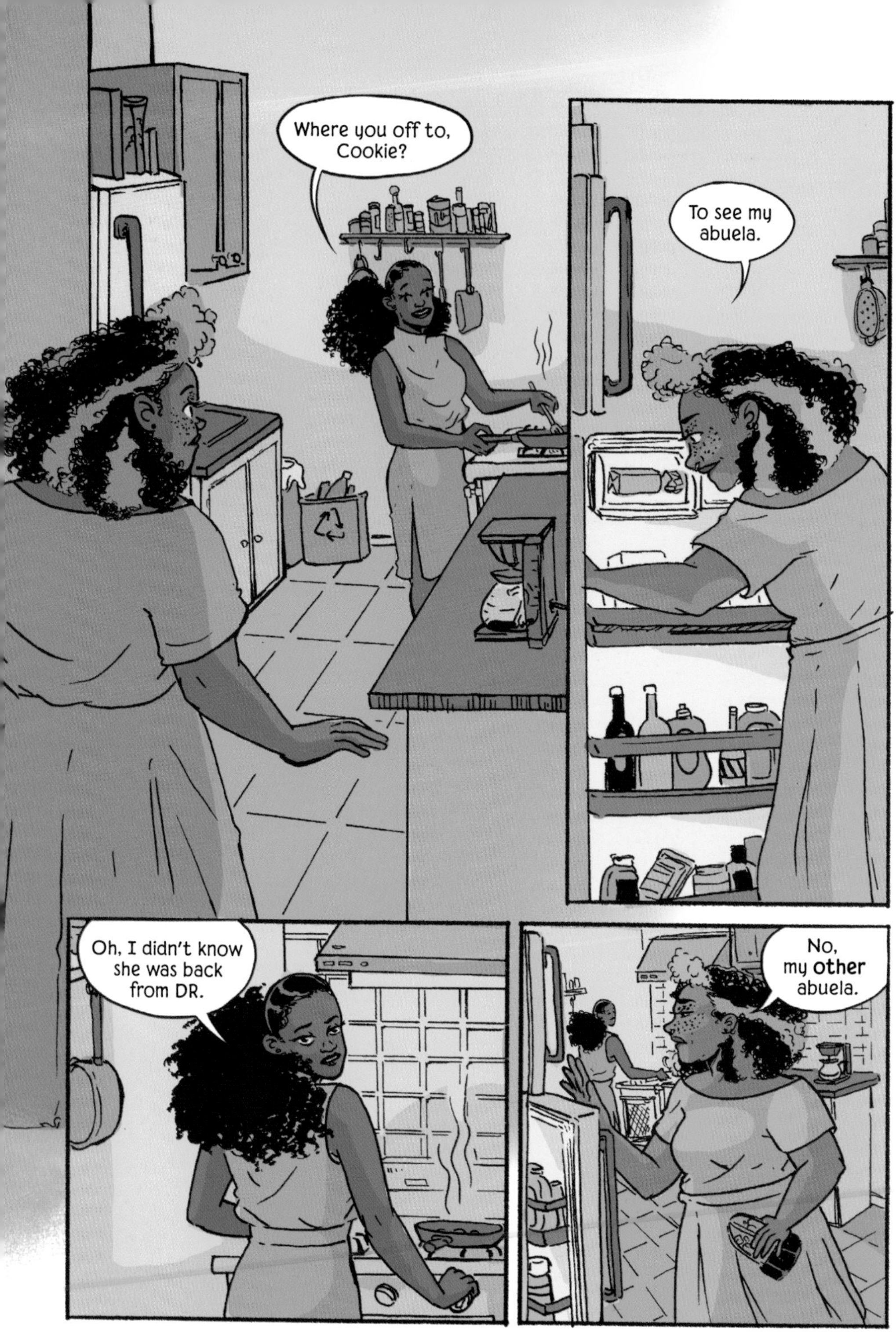
Where you off to, Cookie?
To see my abuela.
Oh, I didn't know she was back from DR.
No, my **other** abuela.

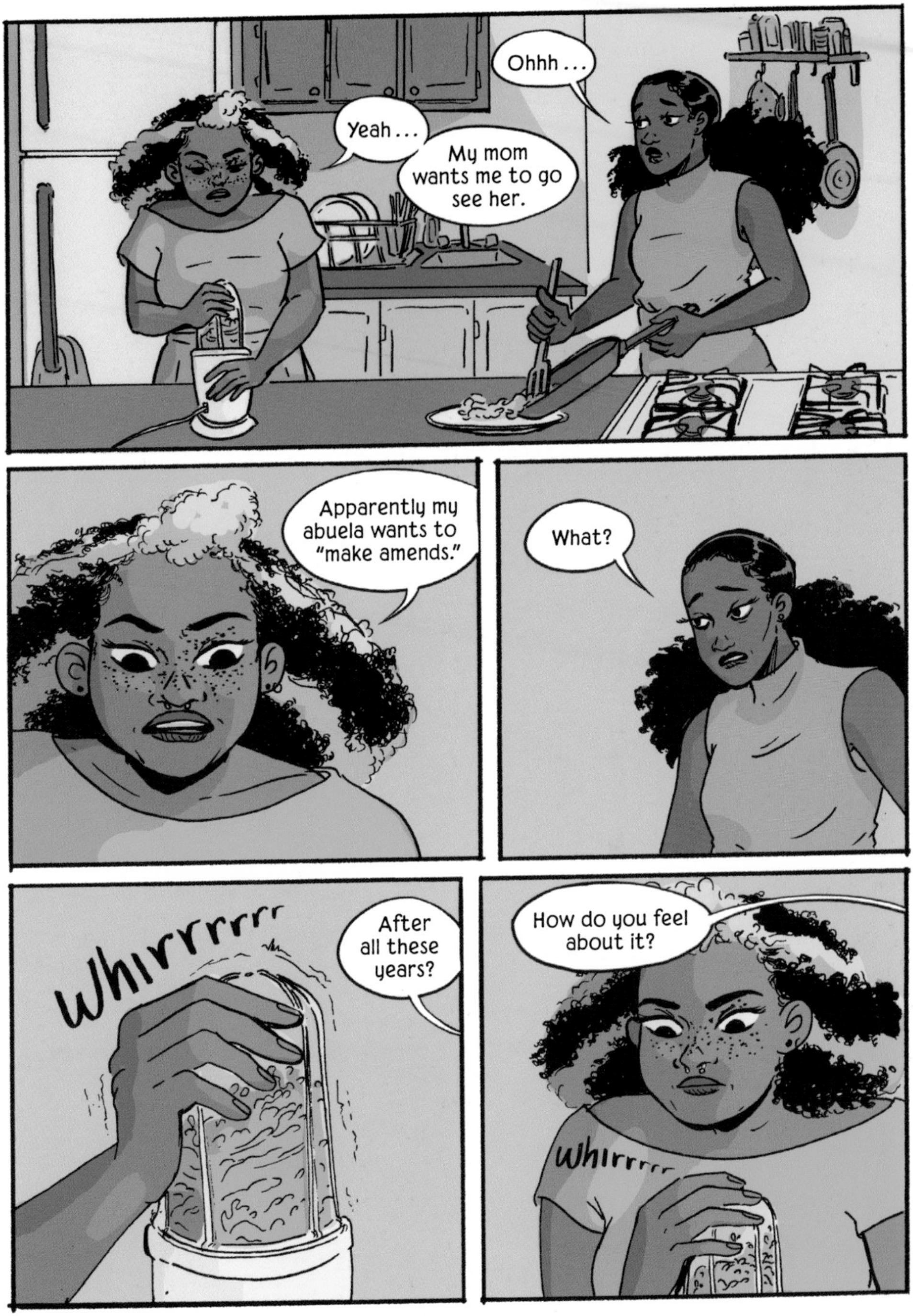
Ohhh . . .
Yeah . . .
My mom wants me to go see her.
Apparently my abuela wants to "make amends."
What?
Whirrrrrr
After all these years?
How do you feel about it?
Whirrrrr

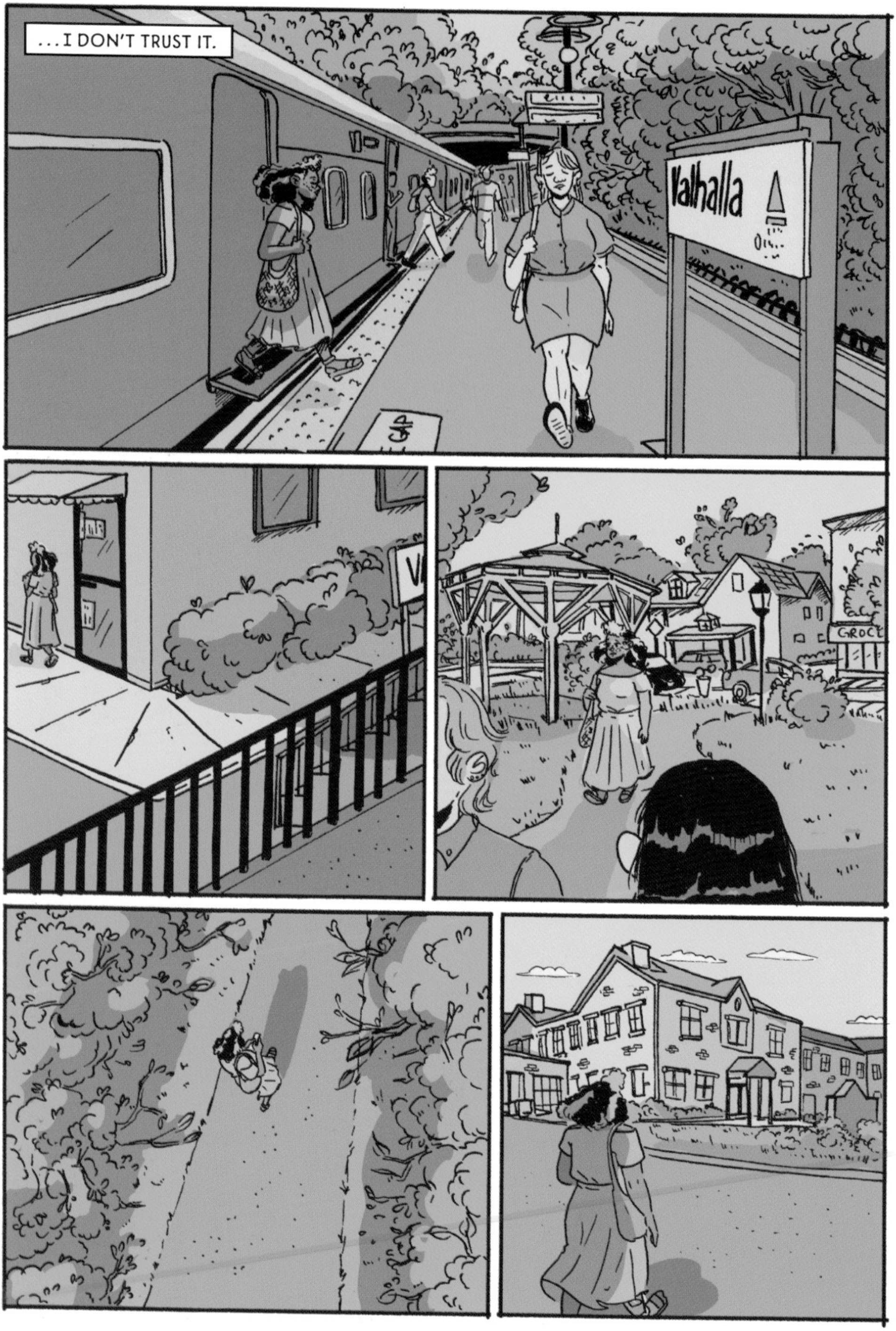
...I DON'T TRUST IT.
Valhalla
GROC

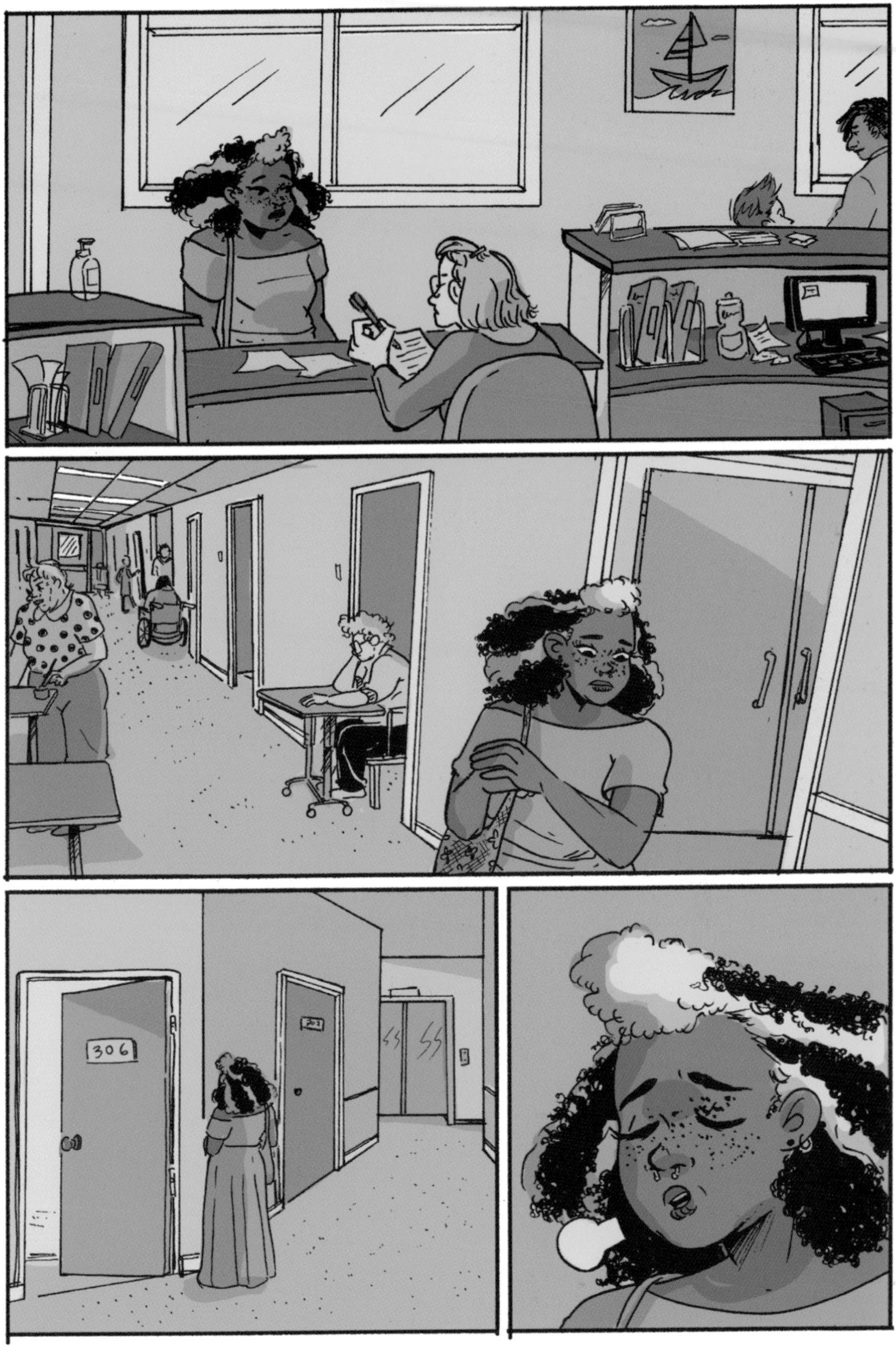
306

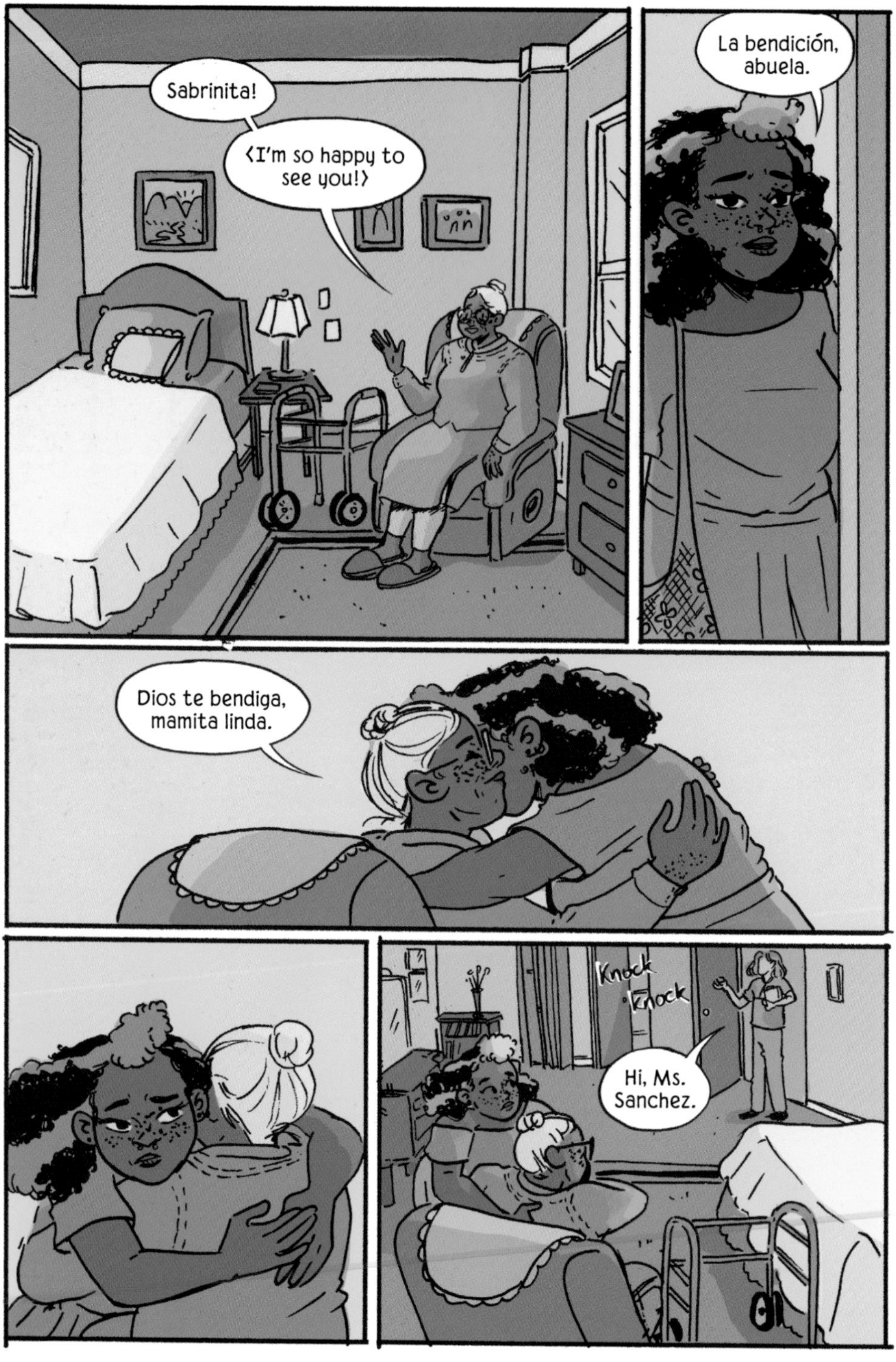
Sabrinita!
‹I'm so happy to see you!›
La bendición, abuela.
Dios te bendiga, mamita linda.
Knock knock
Hi, Ms. Sanchez.

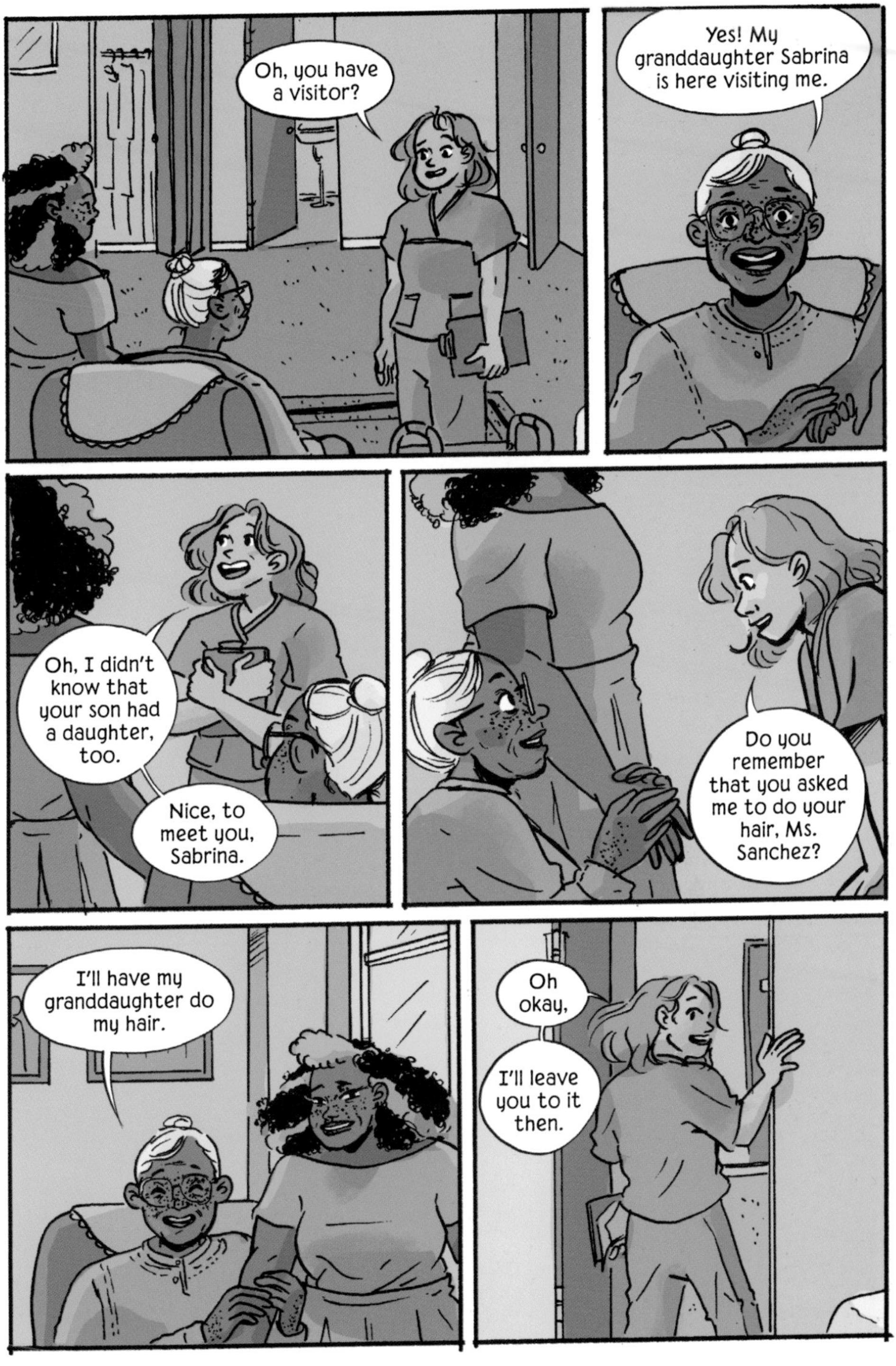
Oh, you have a visitor?
Yes! My granddaughter Sabrina is here visiting me.
Oh, I didn't know that your son had a daughter, too.
Nice, to meet you, Sabrina.
Do you remember that you asked me to do your hair, Ms. Sanchez?
I'll have my granddaughter do my hair.
Oh okay,
I'll leave you to it then.

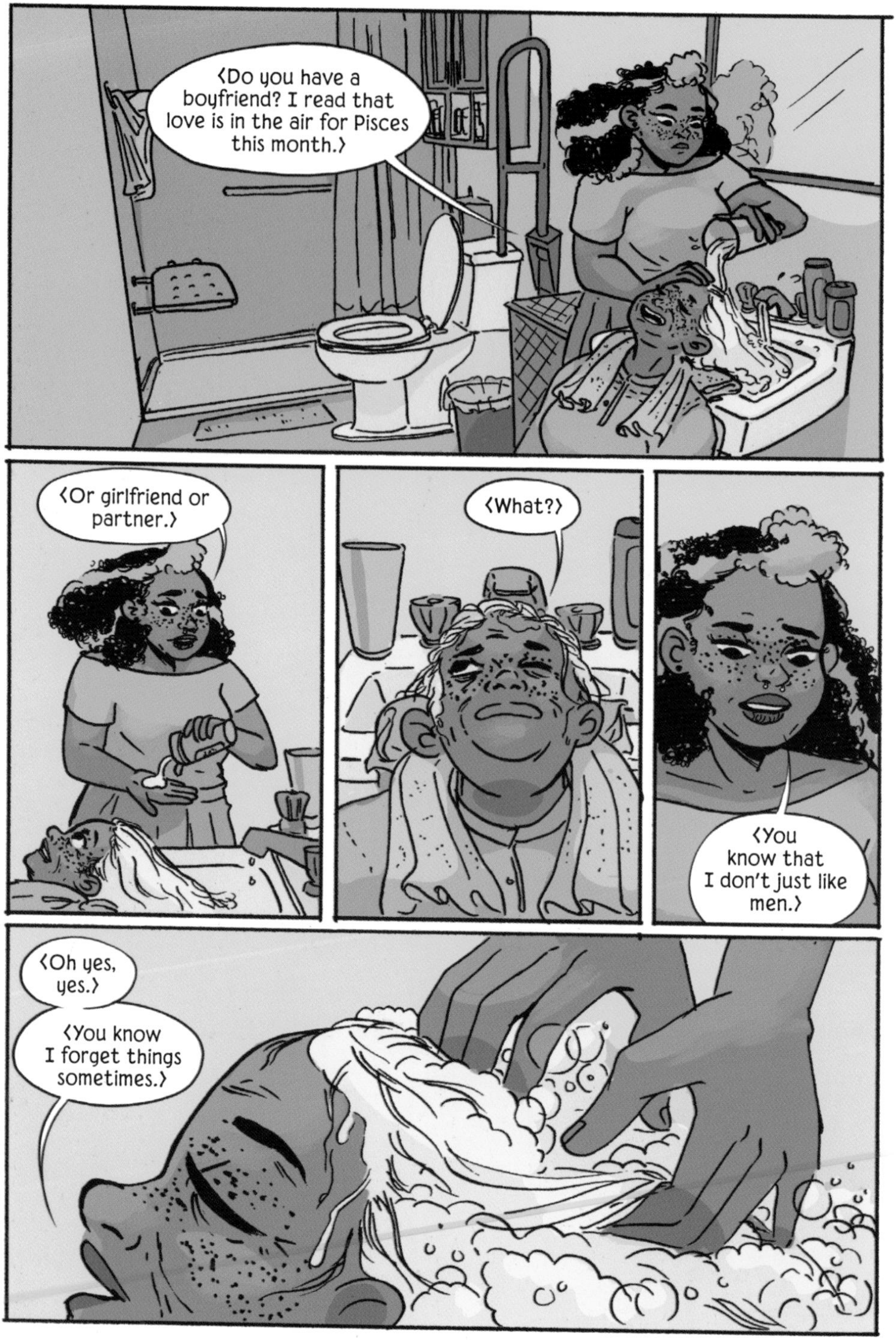

〈Do you have a boyfriend? I read that love is in the air for Pisces this month.〉
〈Or girlfriend or partner.〉
〈What?〉
〈You know that I don't just like men.〉
〈Oh yes, yes.〉
〈You know I forget things sometimes.〉

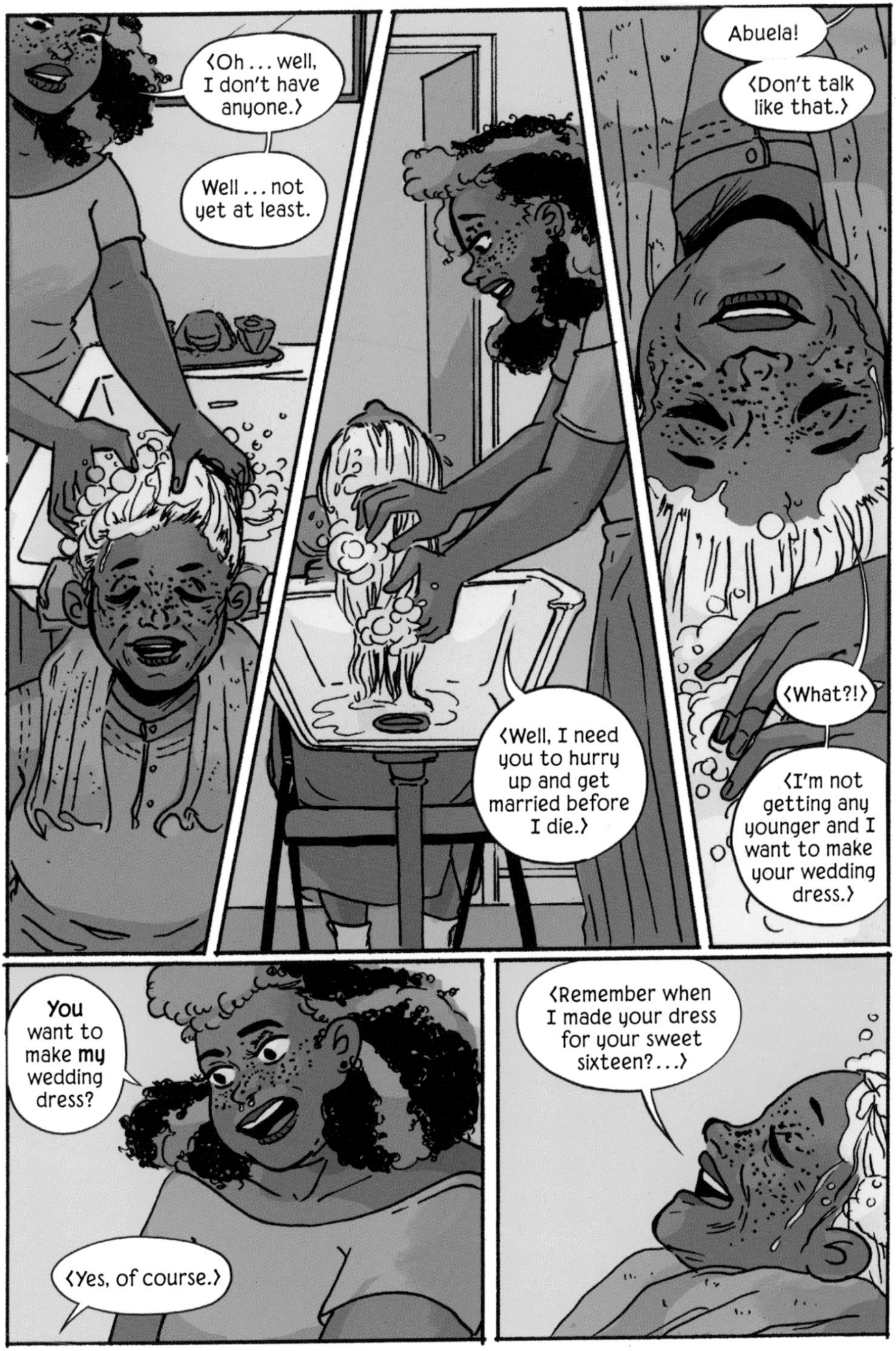

‹Oh . . . well, I don't have anyone.›
Well . . . not yet at least.
‹Well, I need you to hurry up and get married before I die.›
Abuela!
‹Don't talk like that.›
‹What?!›
‹I'm not getting any younger and I want to make your wedding dress.›
You want to make **my** wedding dress?
‹Yes, of course.›
‹Remember when I made your dress for your sweet sixteen? . . .›

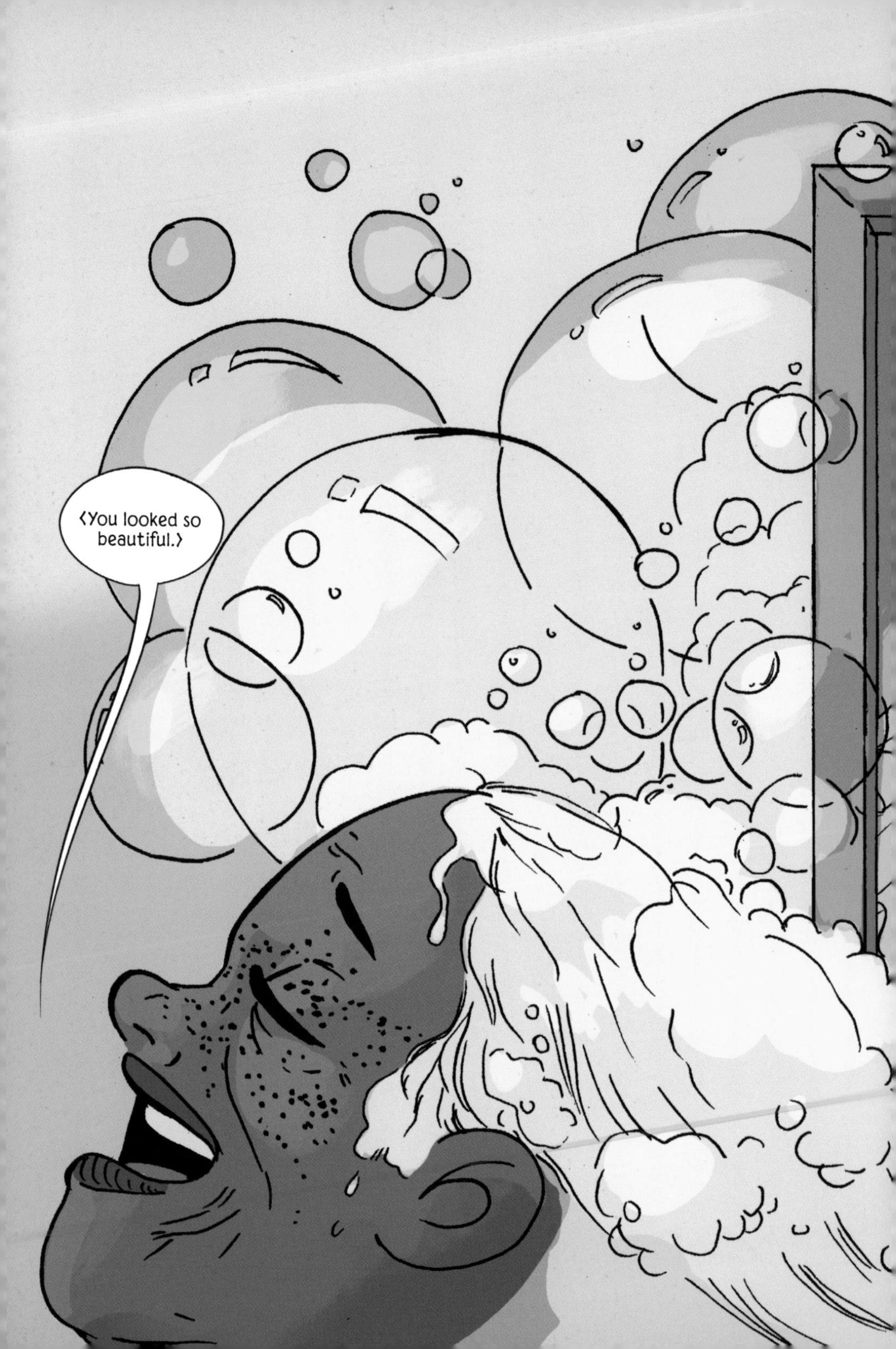
<You looked so beautiful.>

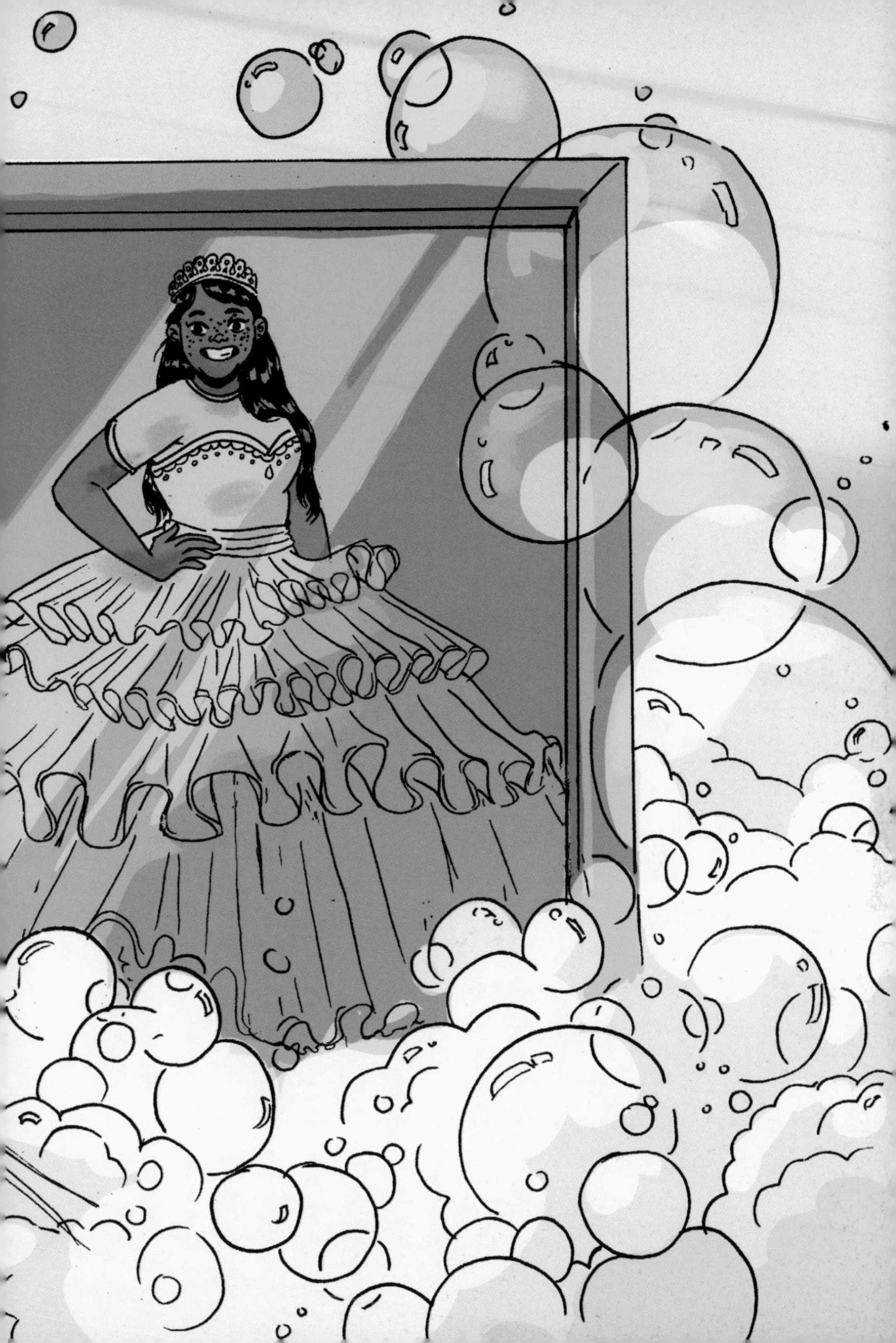

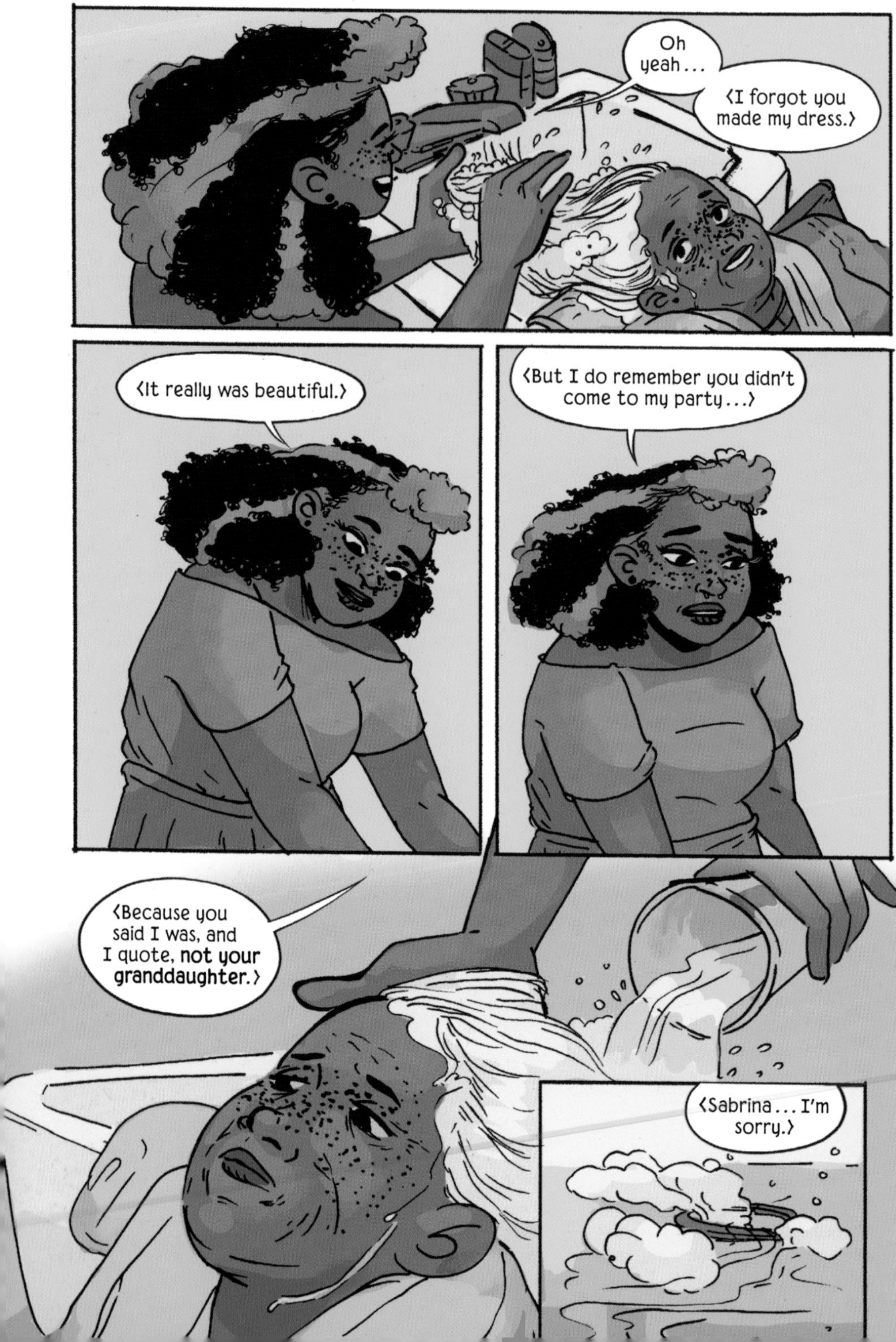
Oh yeah...
<I forgot you made my dress.>
<It really was beautiful.>
<But I do remember you didn't come to my party...>
<Because you said I was, and I quote, **not your granddaughter.**>
<Sabrina... I'm sorry.>

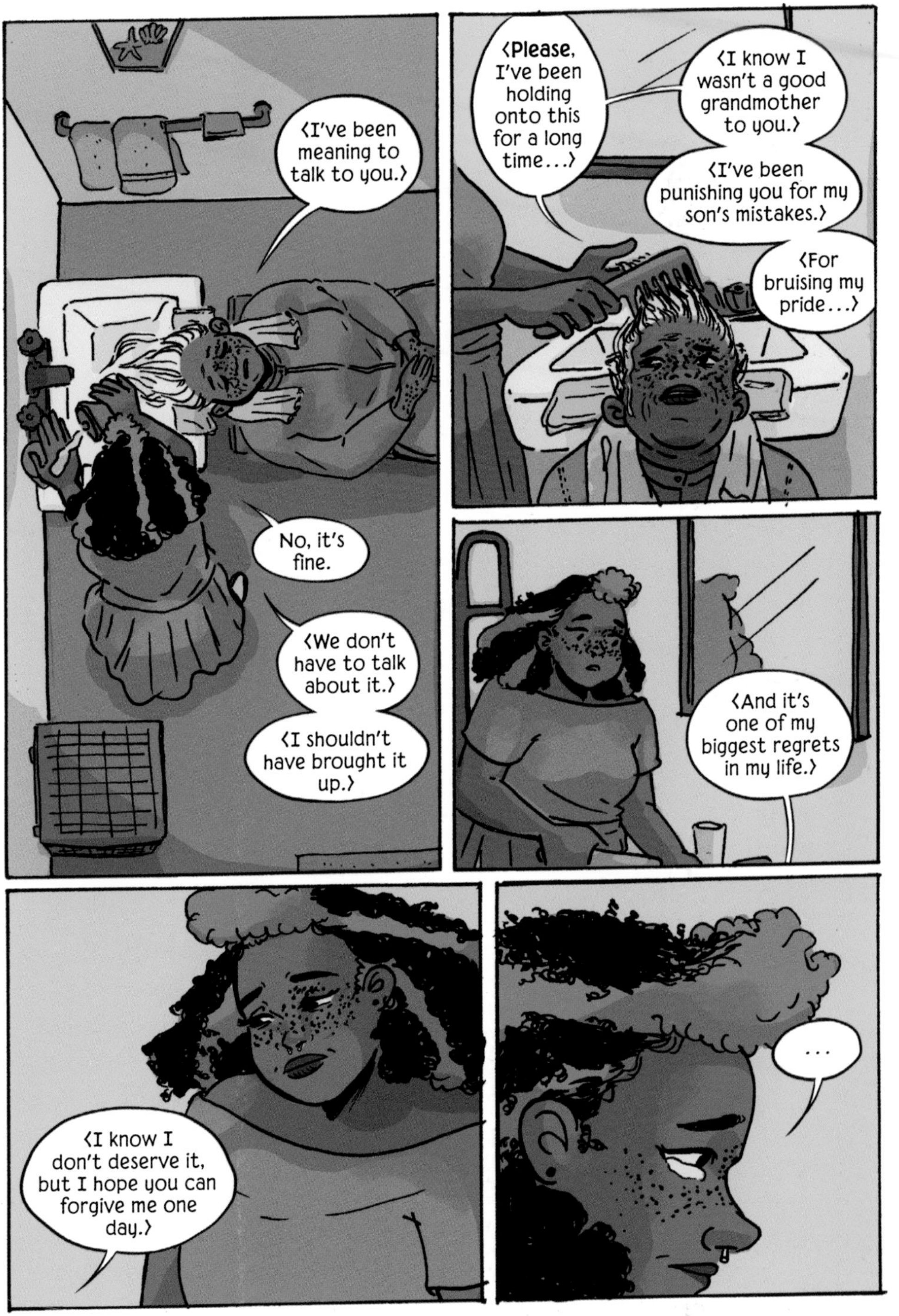

‹I've been meaning to talk to you.›
No, it's fine.
‹We don't have to talk about it.›
‹I shouldn't have brought it up.›
‹Please, I've been holding onto this for a long time...›
‹I know I wasn't a good grandmother to you.›
‹I've been punishing you for my son's mistakes.›
‹For bruising my pride...›
‹And it's one of my biggest regrets in my life.›
‹I know I don't deserve it, but I hope you can forgive me one day.›
...

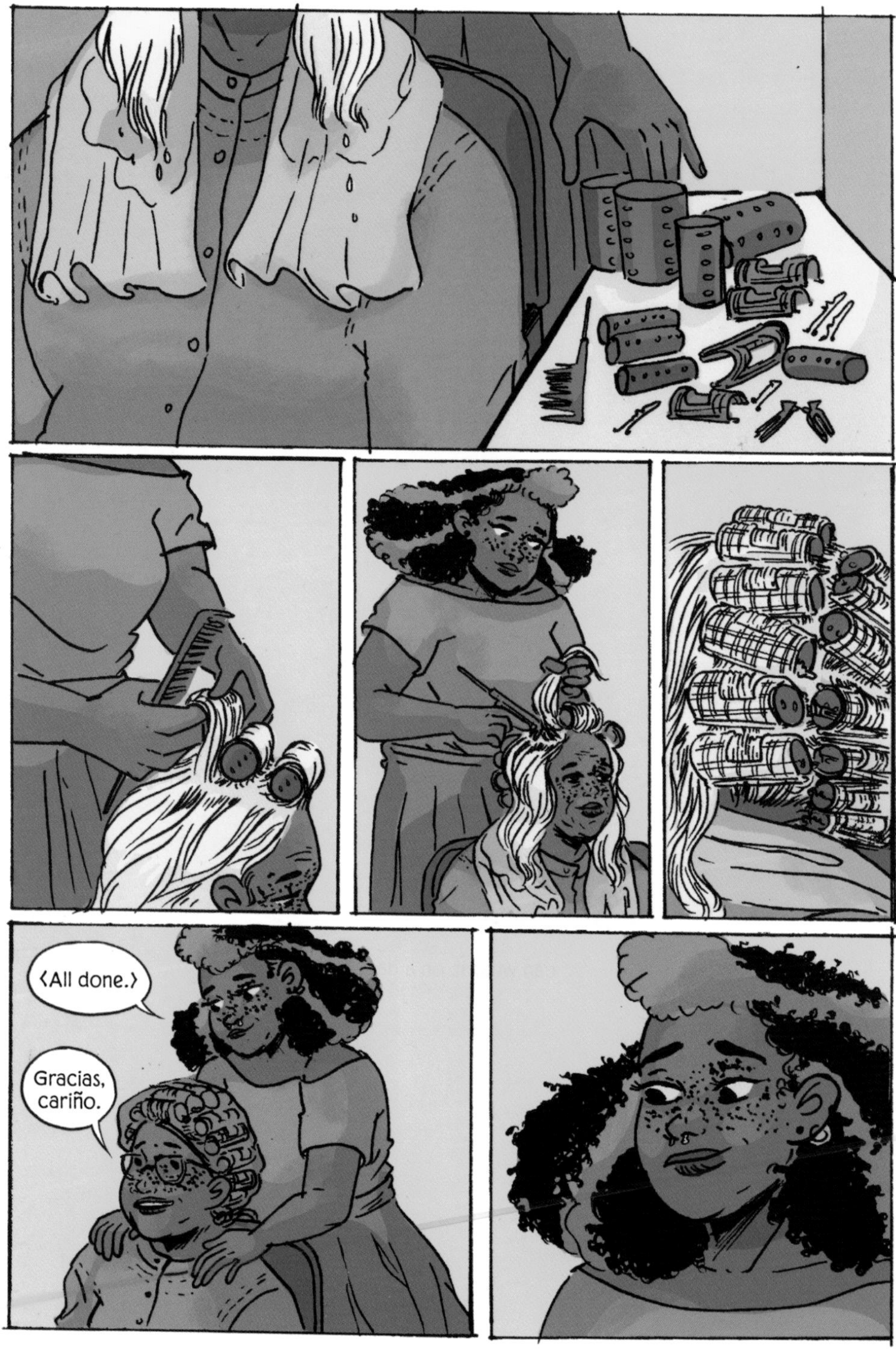

<All done.>
Gracias, cariño.

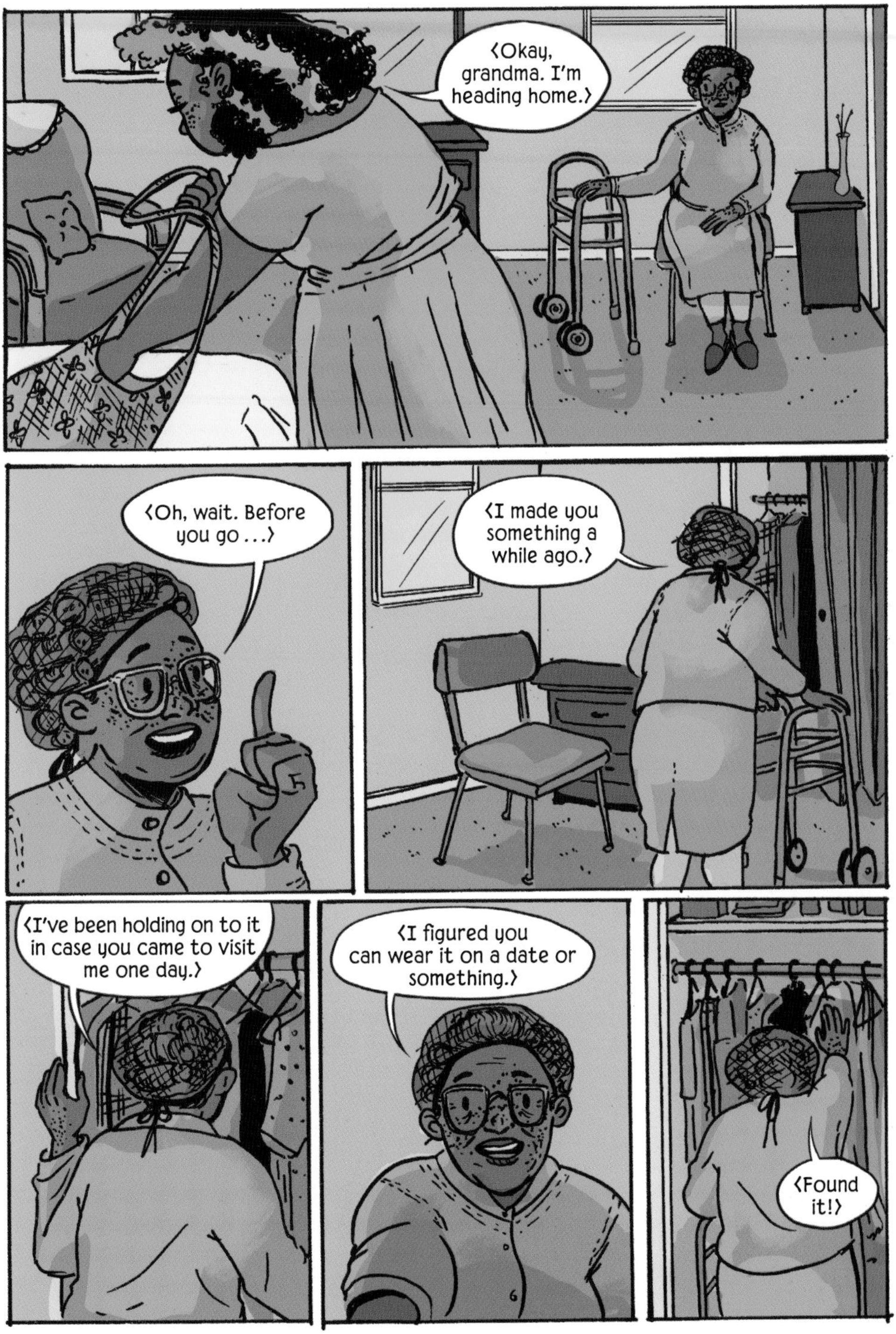
〈Okay, grandma. I'm heading home.〉
〈Oh, wait. Before you go . . .〉
〈I made you something a while ago.〉
〈I've been holding on to it in case you came to visit me one day.〉
〈I figured you can wear it on a date or something.〉
〈Found it!〉

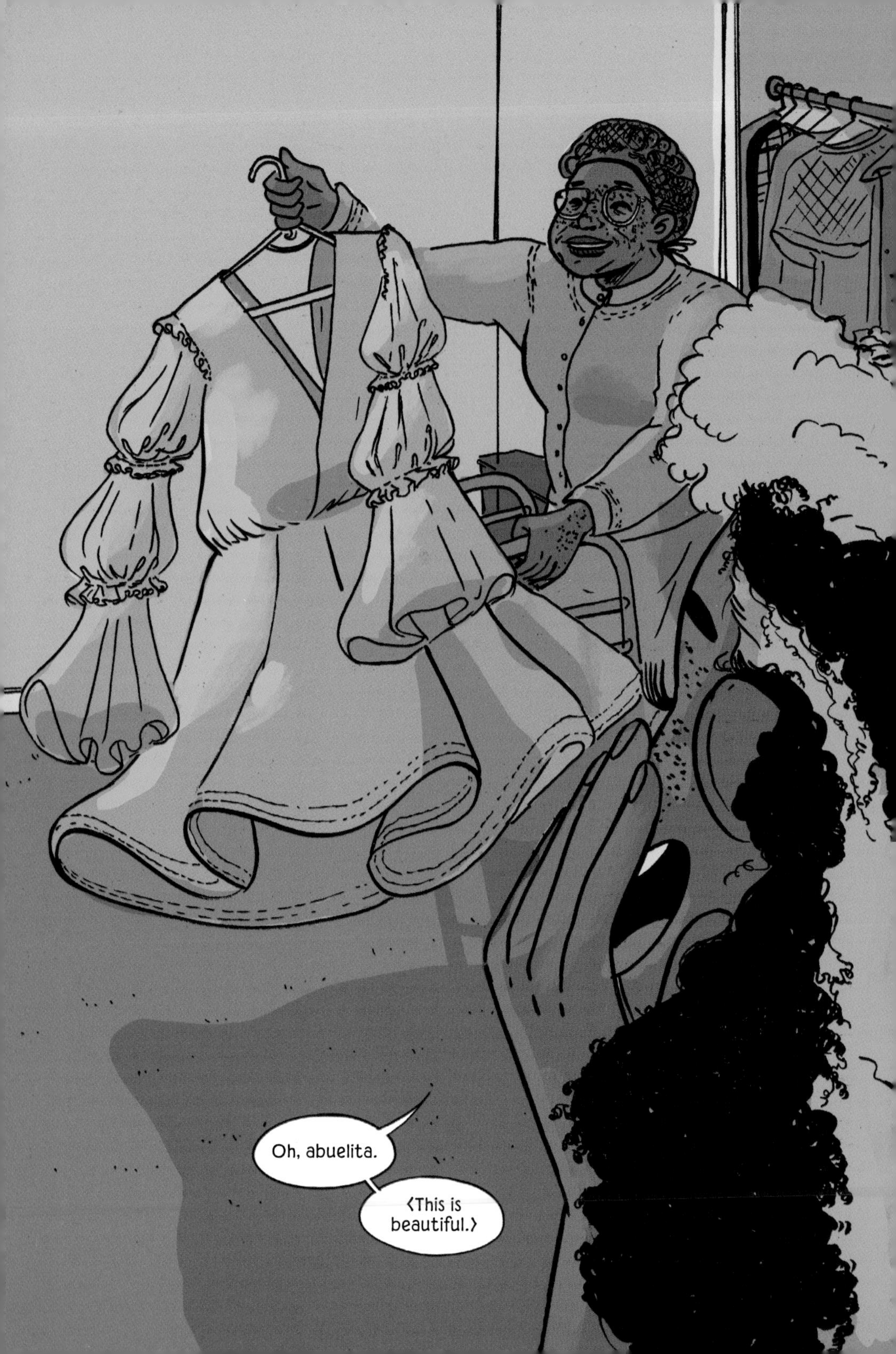
Oh, abuelita.
⟨This is beautiful.⟩

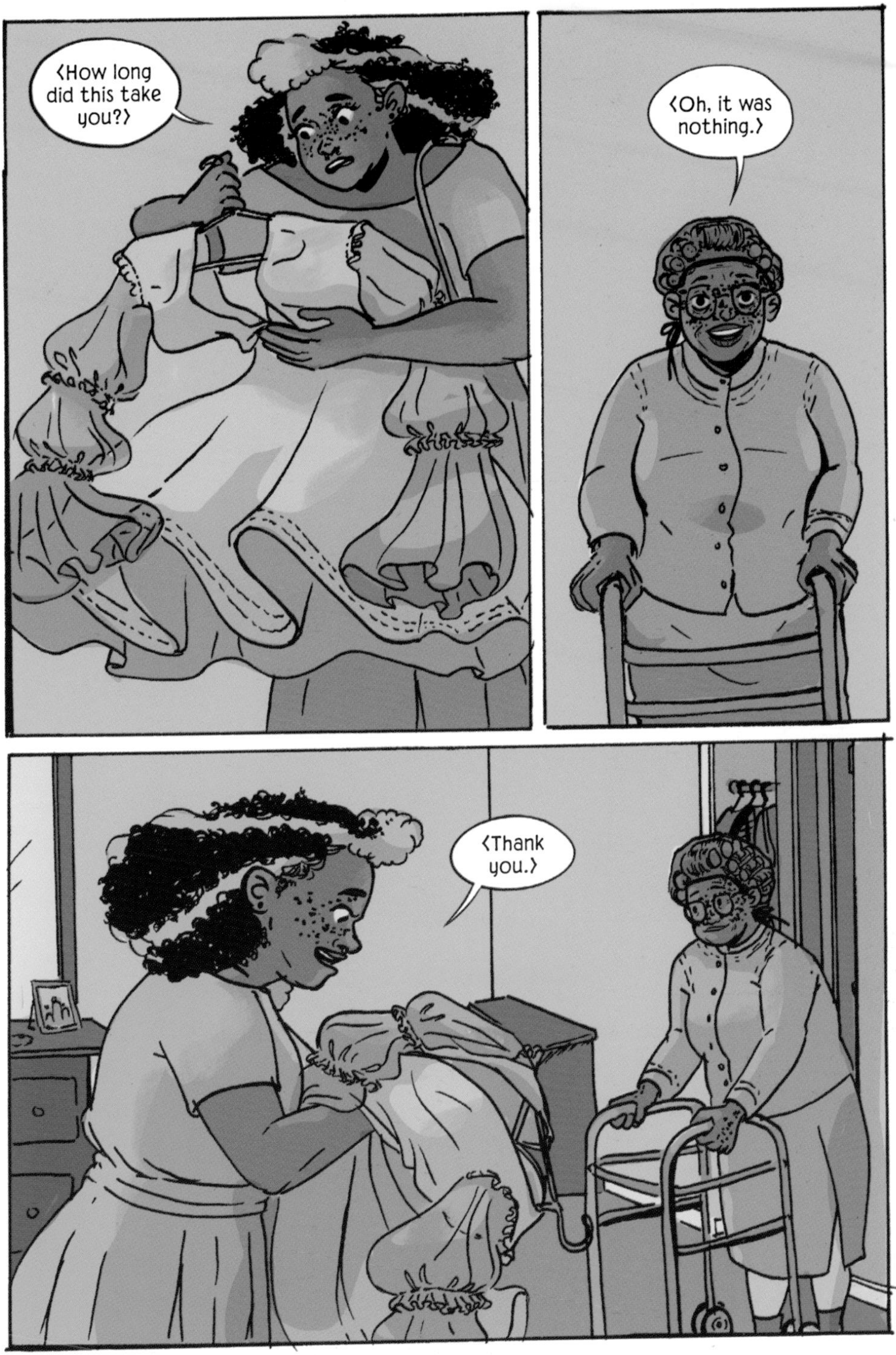
‹How long did this take you?›
‹Oh, it was nothing.›
‹Thank you.›

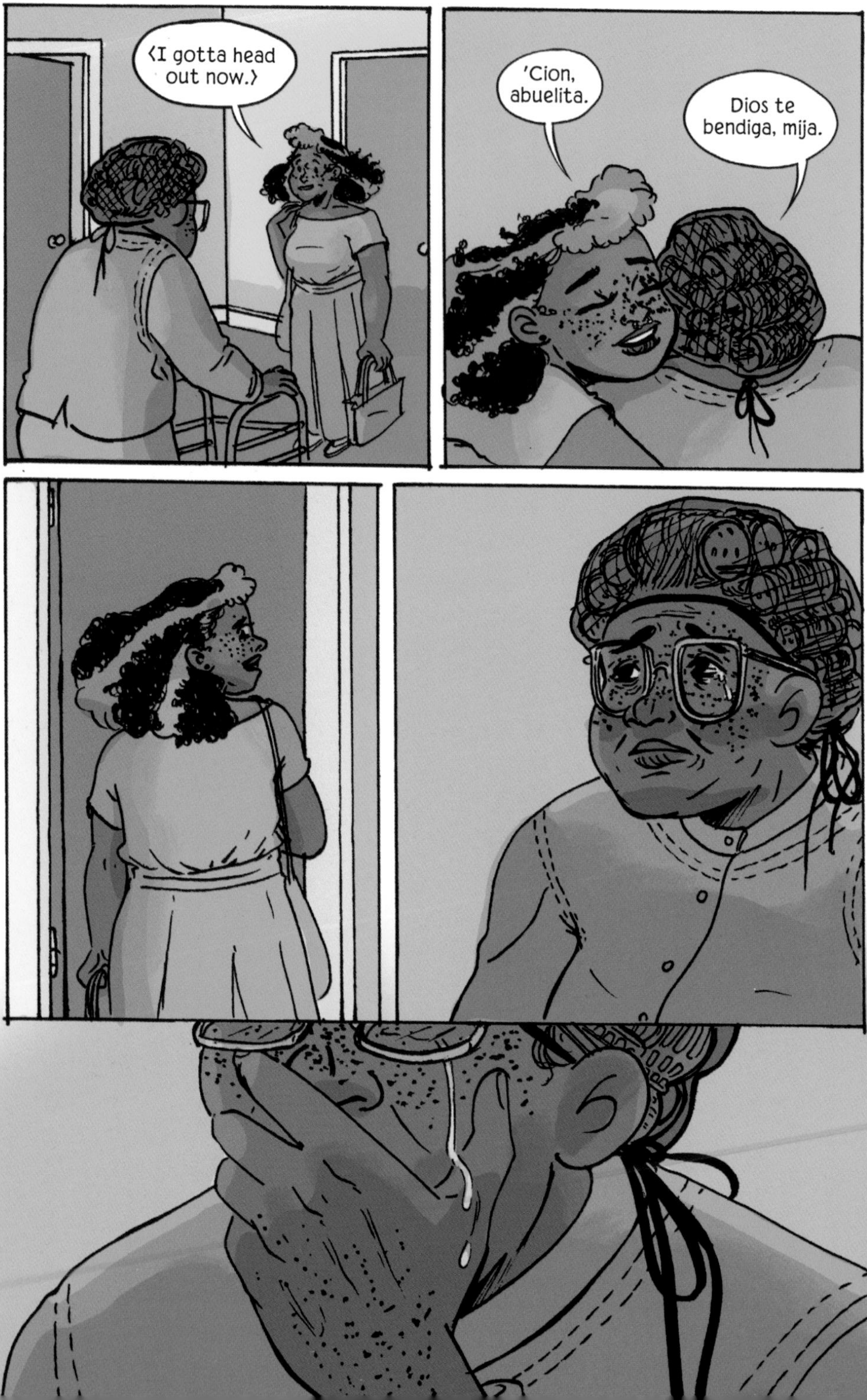

<I gotta head out now.>
'Cion, abuelita.
Dios te bendiga, mija.

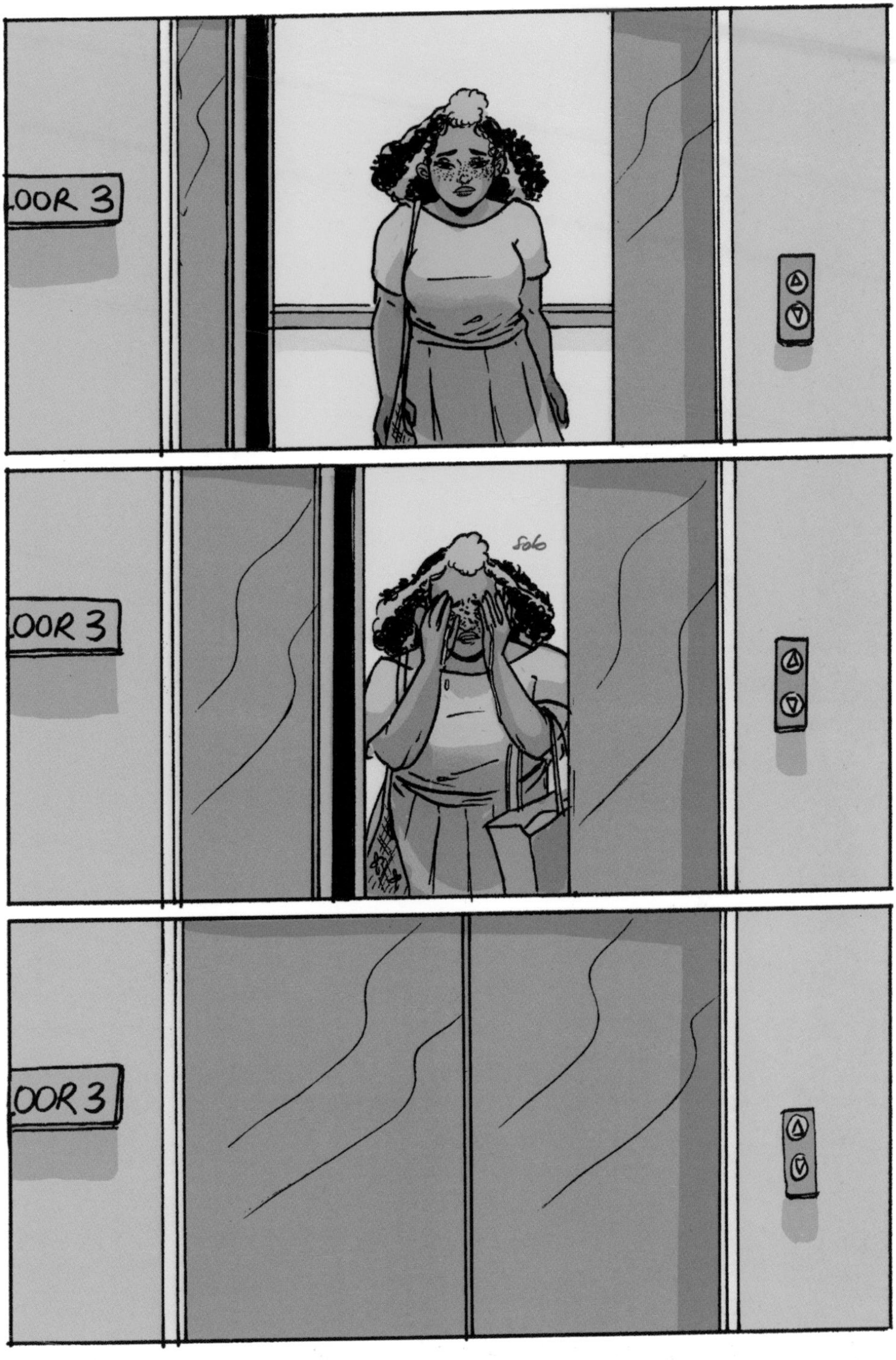

OOR 3
OOR 3
sob
OOR 3

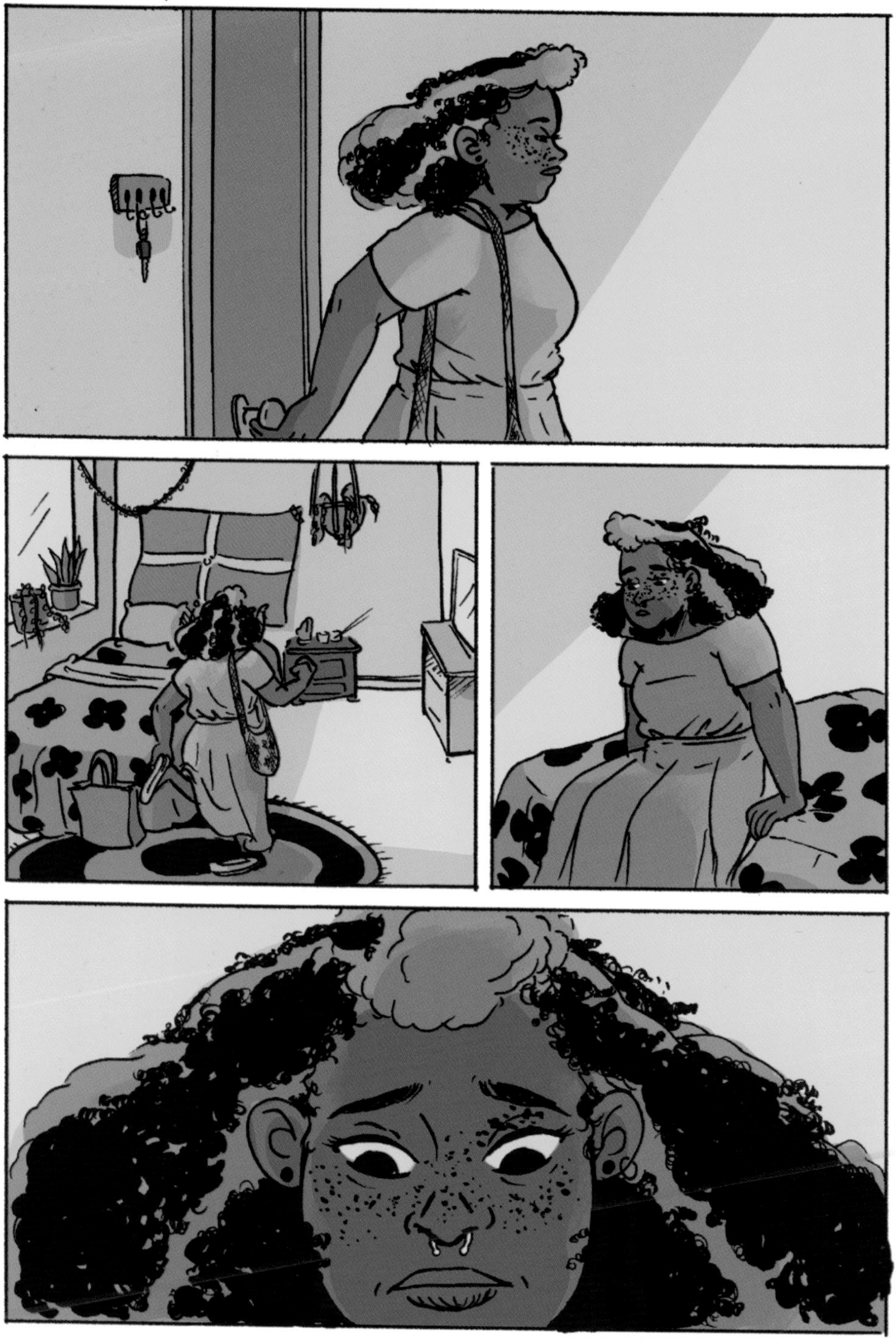

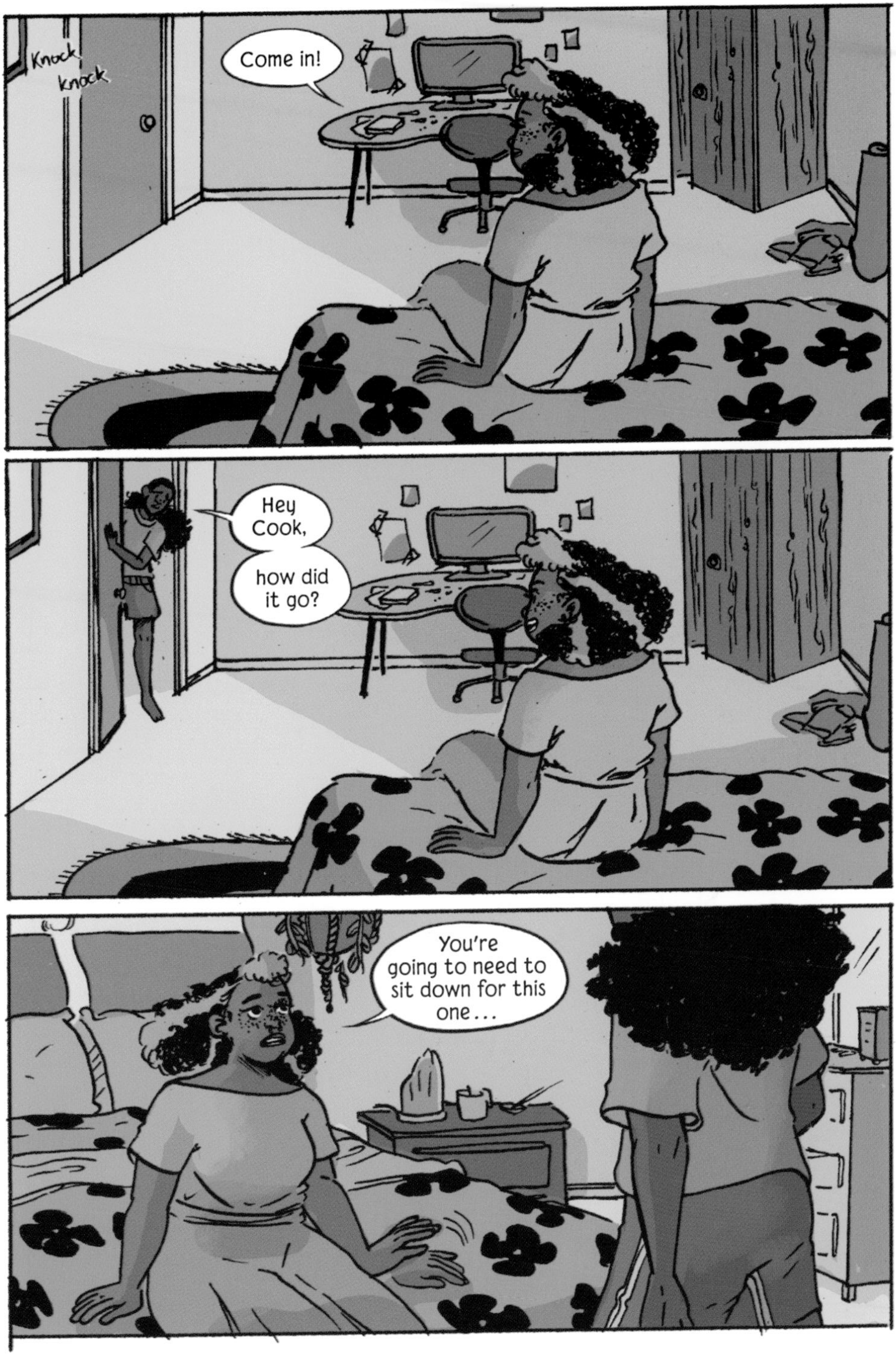
Knock knock
Come in!
Hey Cook,
how did it go?
You're going to need to sit down for this one...

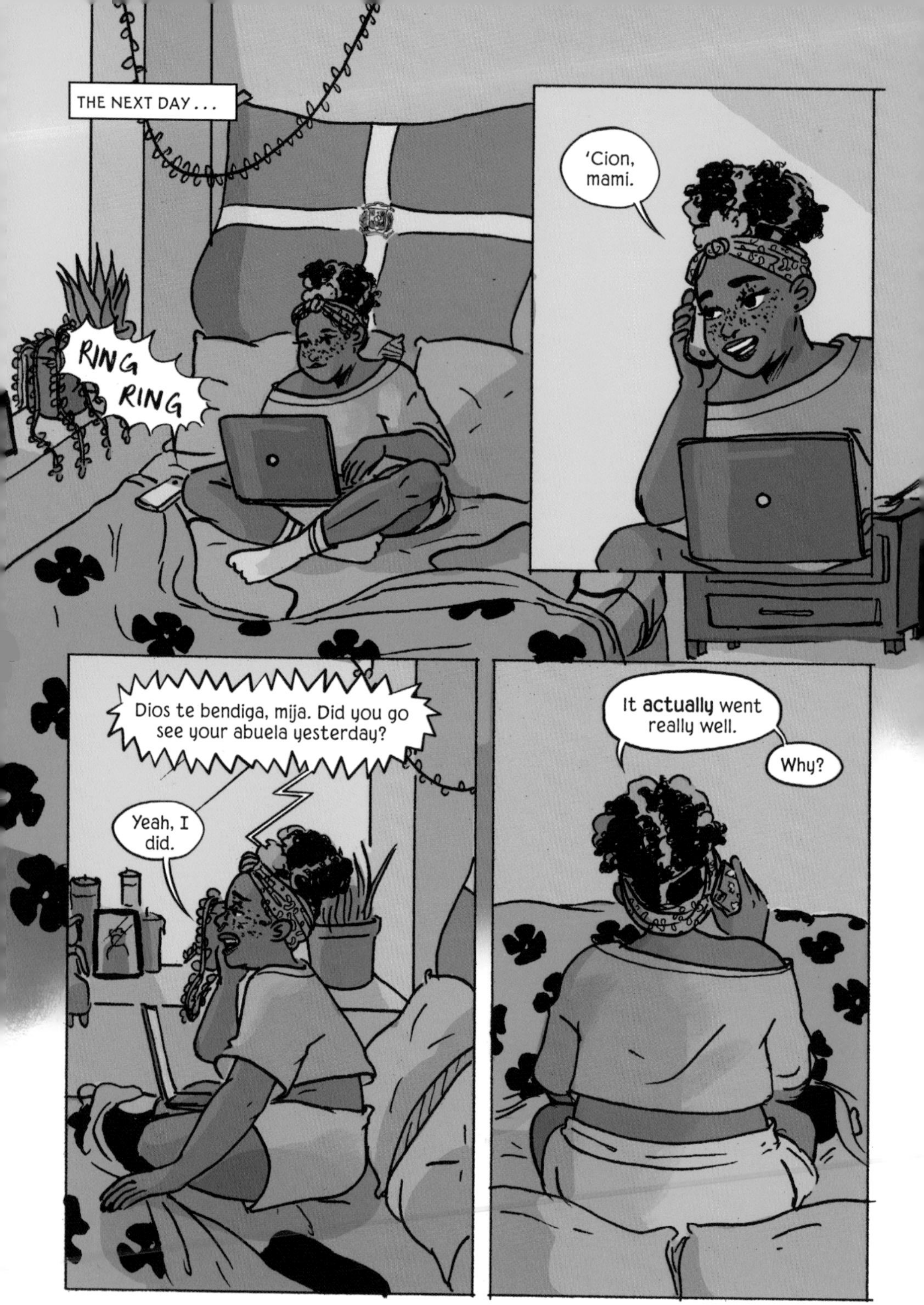
THE NEXT DAY . . .
RING RING
'Cion, mami.
Dios te bendiga, mija. Did you go see your abuela yesterday?
Yeah, I did.
It **actually** went really well.
Why?

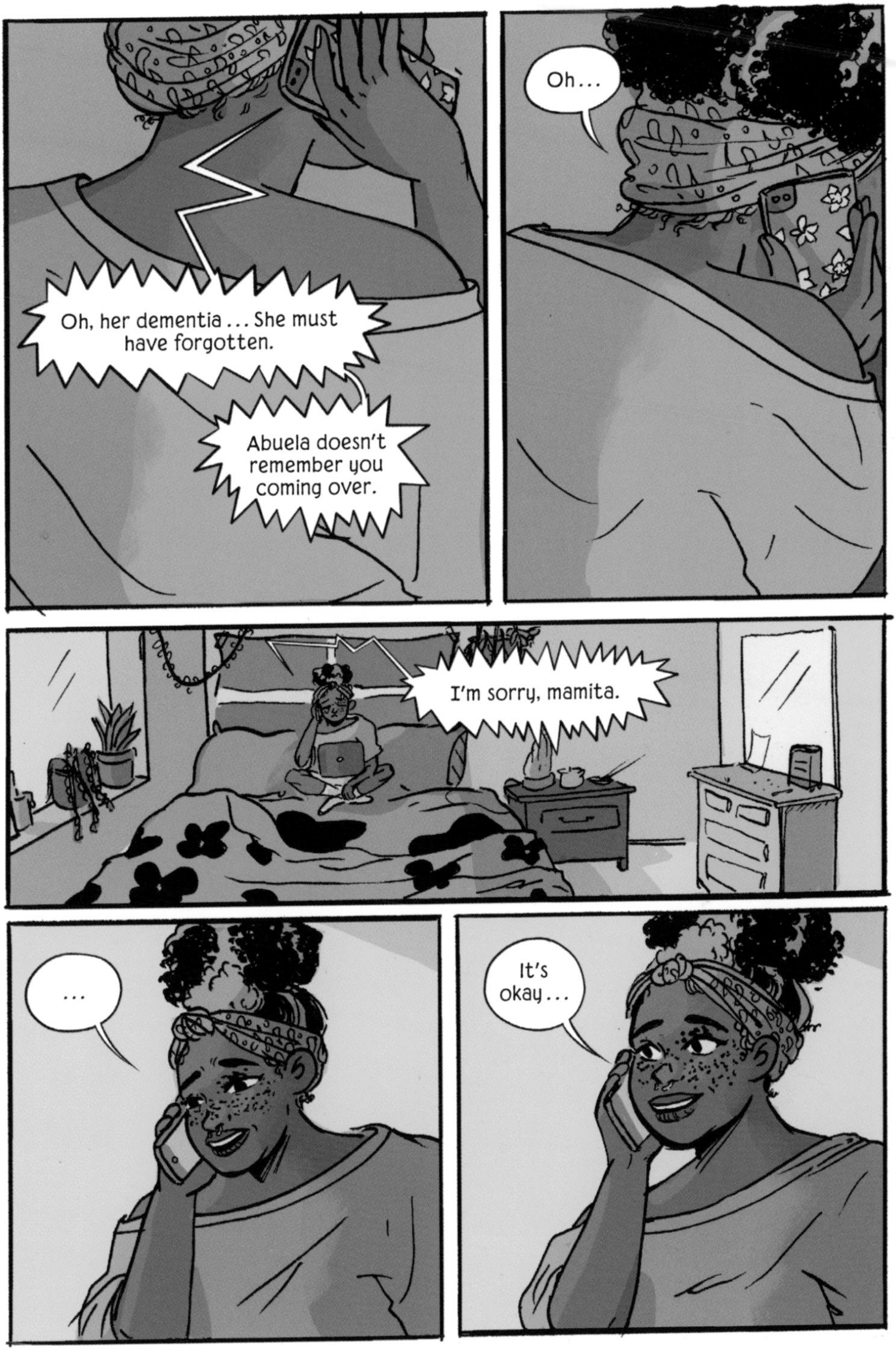
Oh, her dementia . . . She must have forgotten.
Abuela doesn't remember you coming over.
Oh . . .
I'm sorry, mamita.
. . .
It's okay . . .

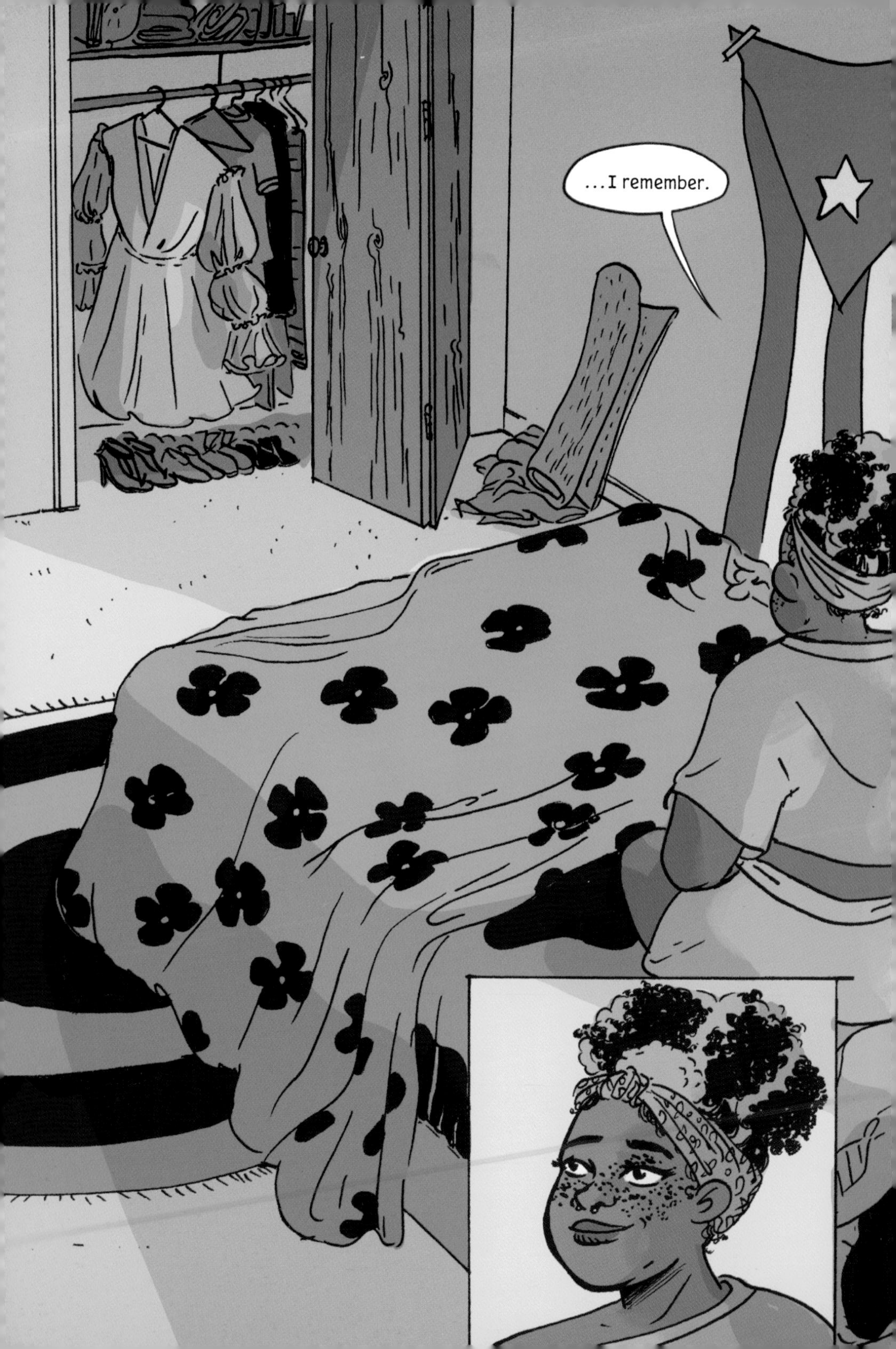
...I remember.

RIDE OR DIE

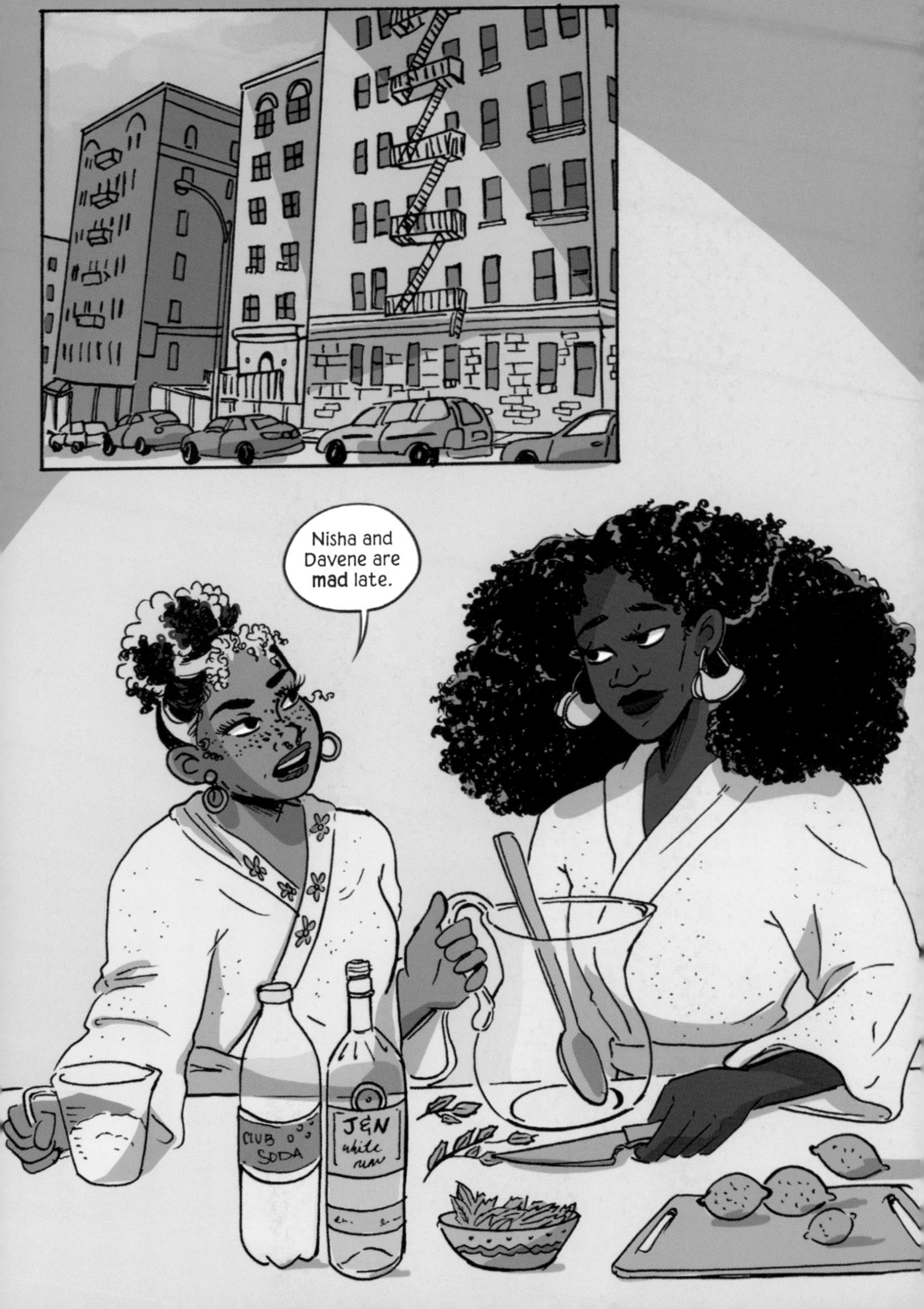
Nisha and Davene are mad late.
CLUB SODA
J&N white rum

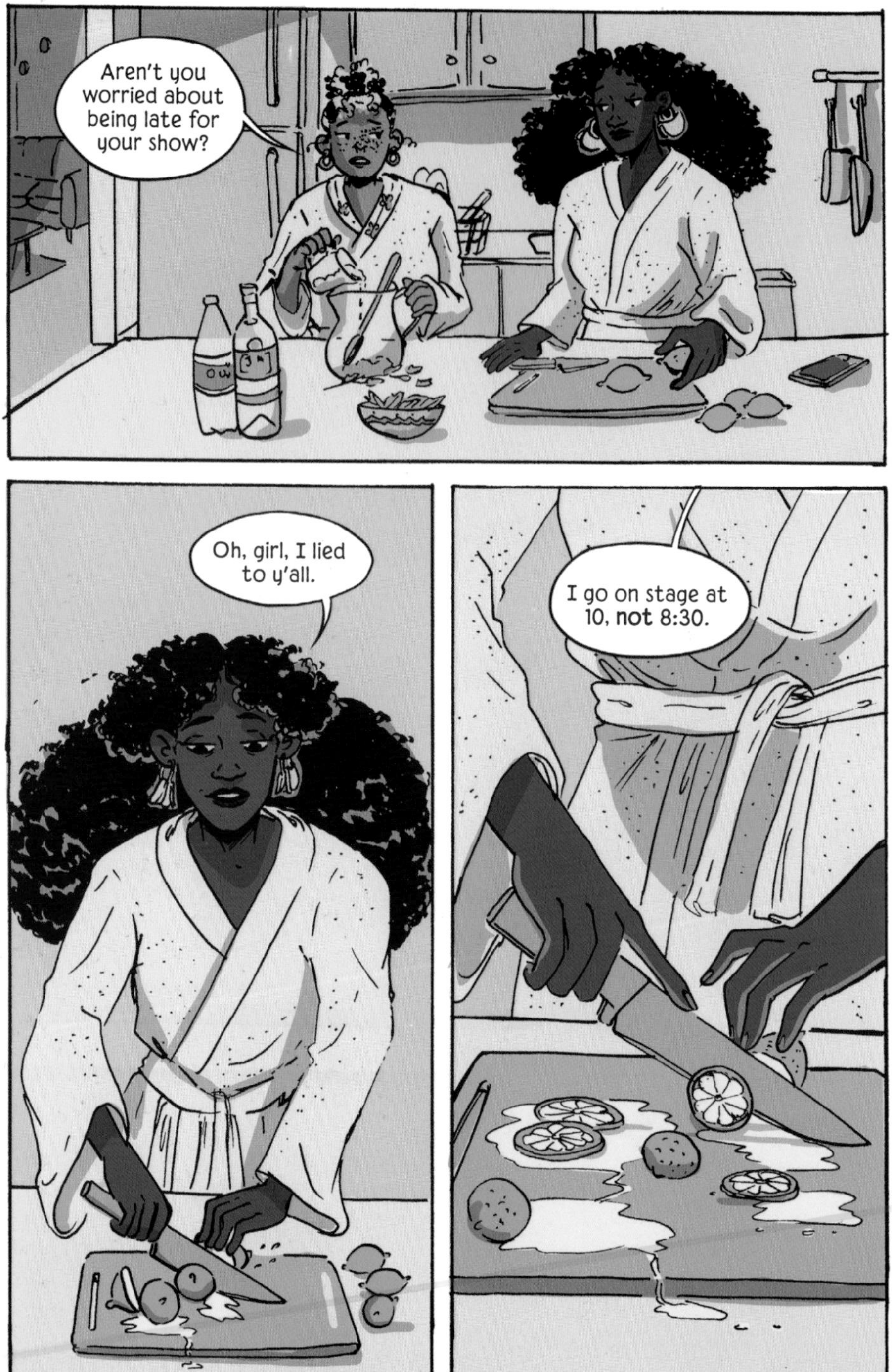
Aren't you worried about being late for your show?
Oh, girl, I lied to y'all.
I go on stage at 10, not 8:30.

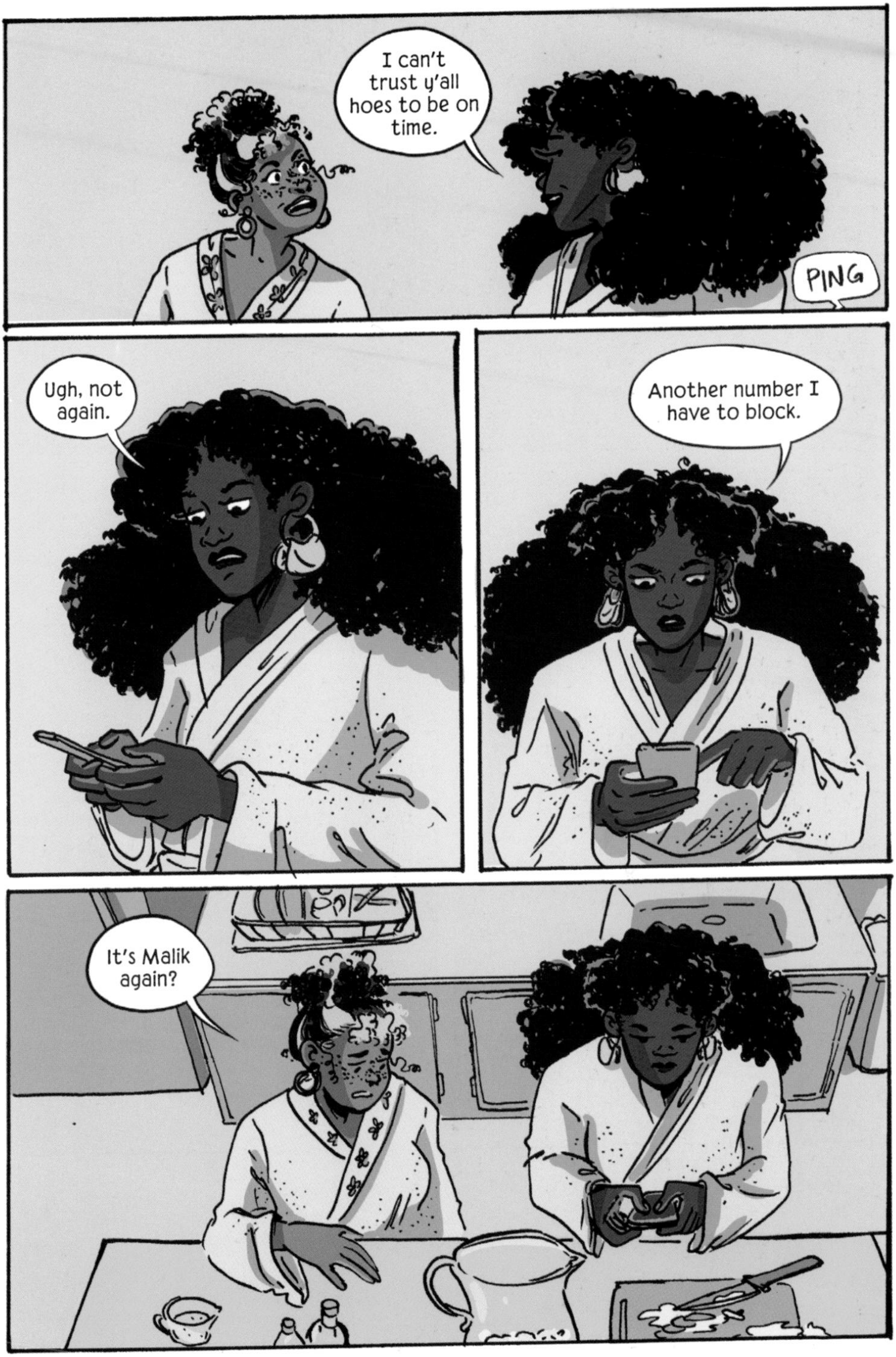
I can't trust y'all hoes to be on time.
PING
Ugh, not again.
Another number I have to block.
It's Malik again?

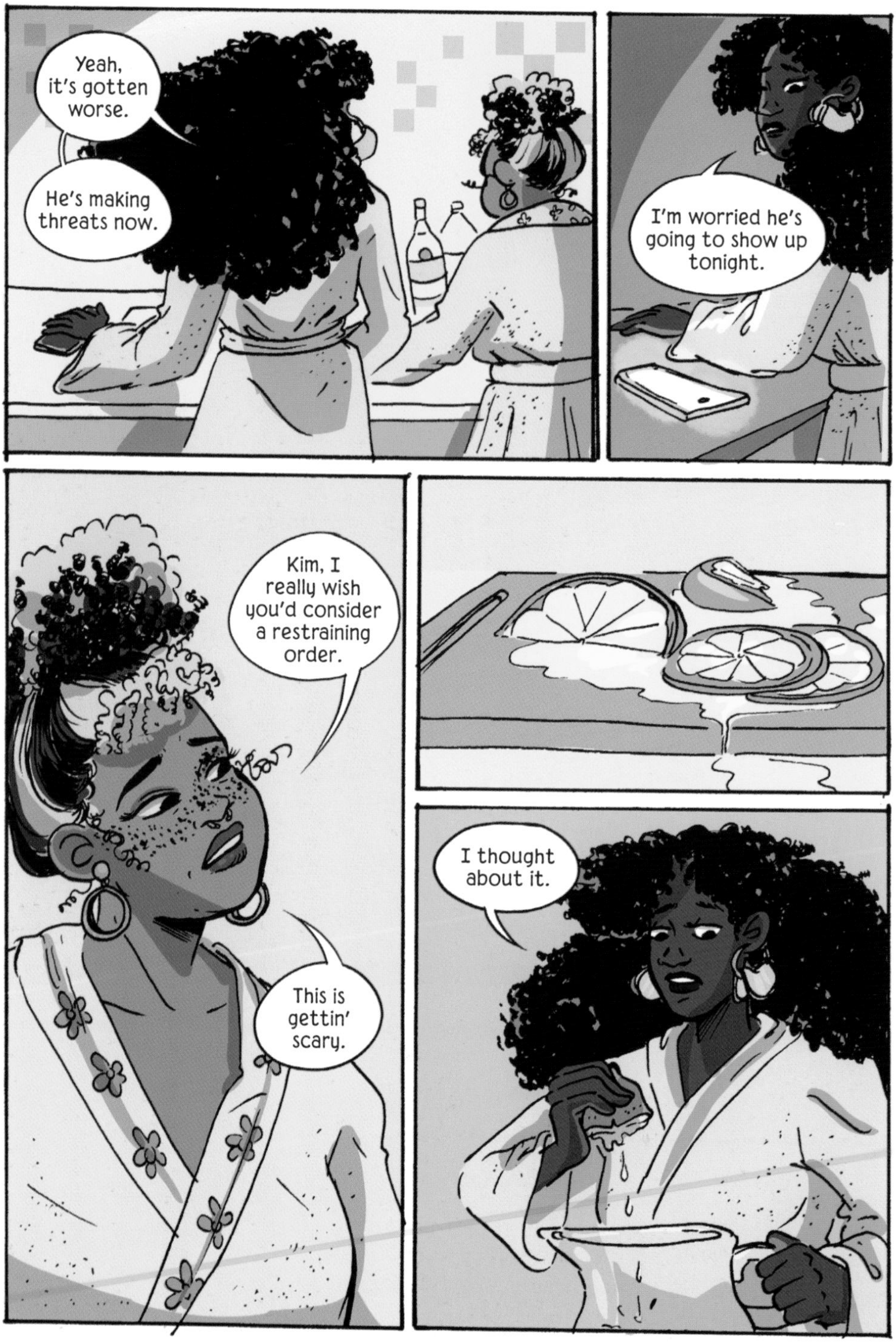
Yeah, it's gotten worse.
He's making threats now.
I'm worried he's going to show up tonight.
Kim, I really wish you'd consider a restraining order.
This is gettin' scary.
I thought about it.

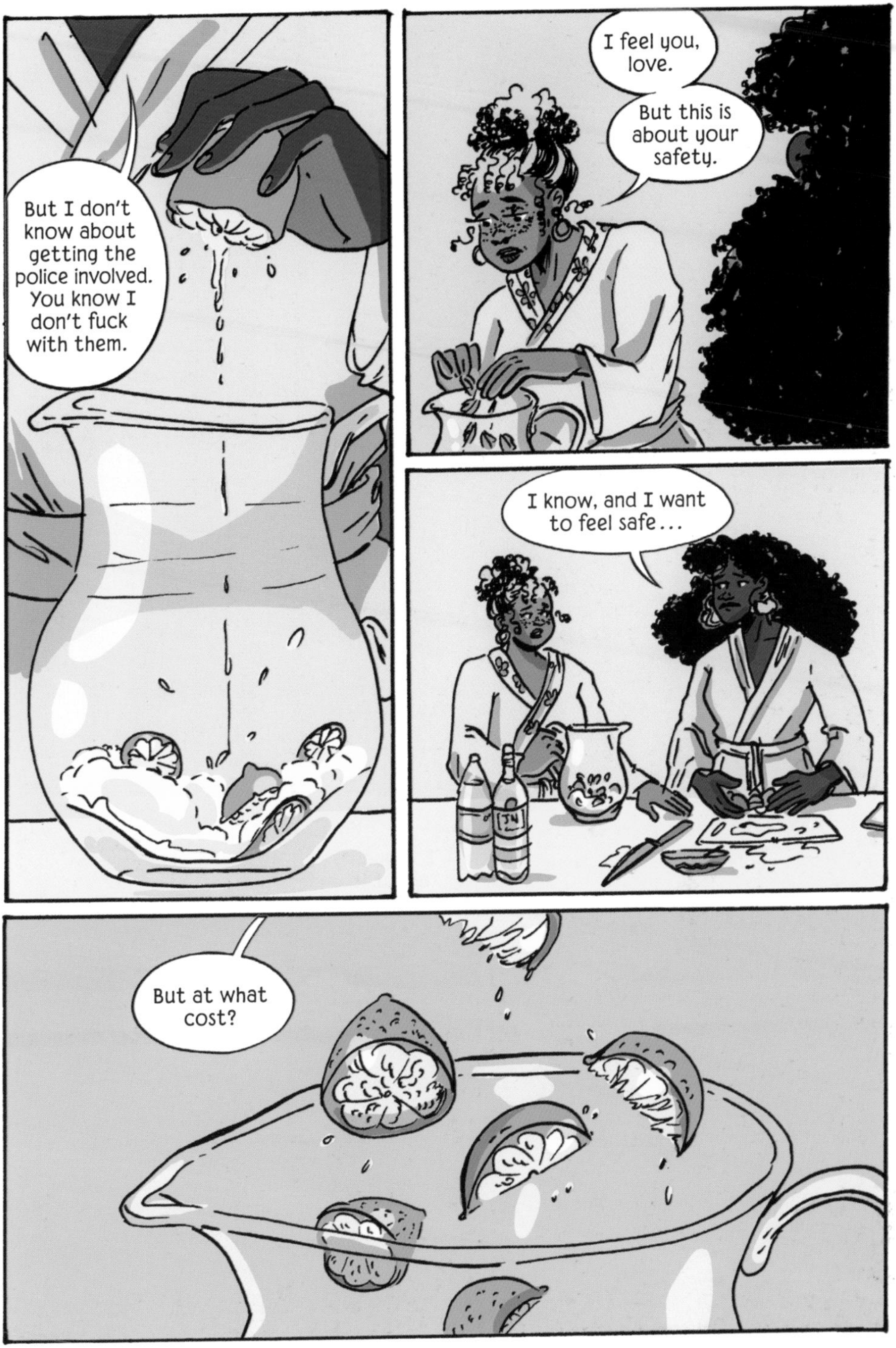
But I don't know about getting the police involved. You know I don't fuck with them.
I feel you, love.
But this is about your safety.
I know, and I want to feel safe...
But at what cost?

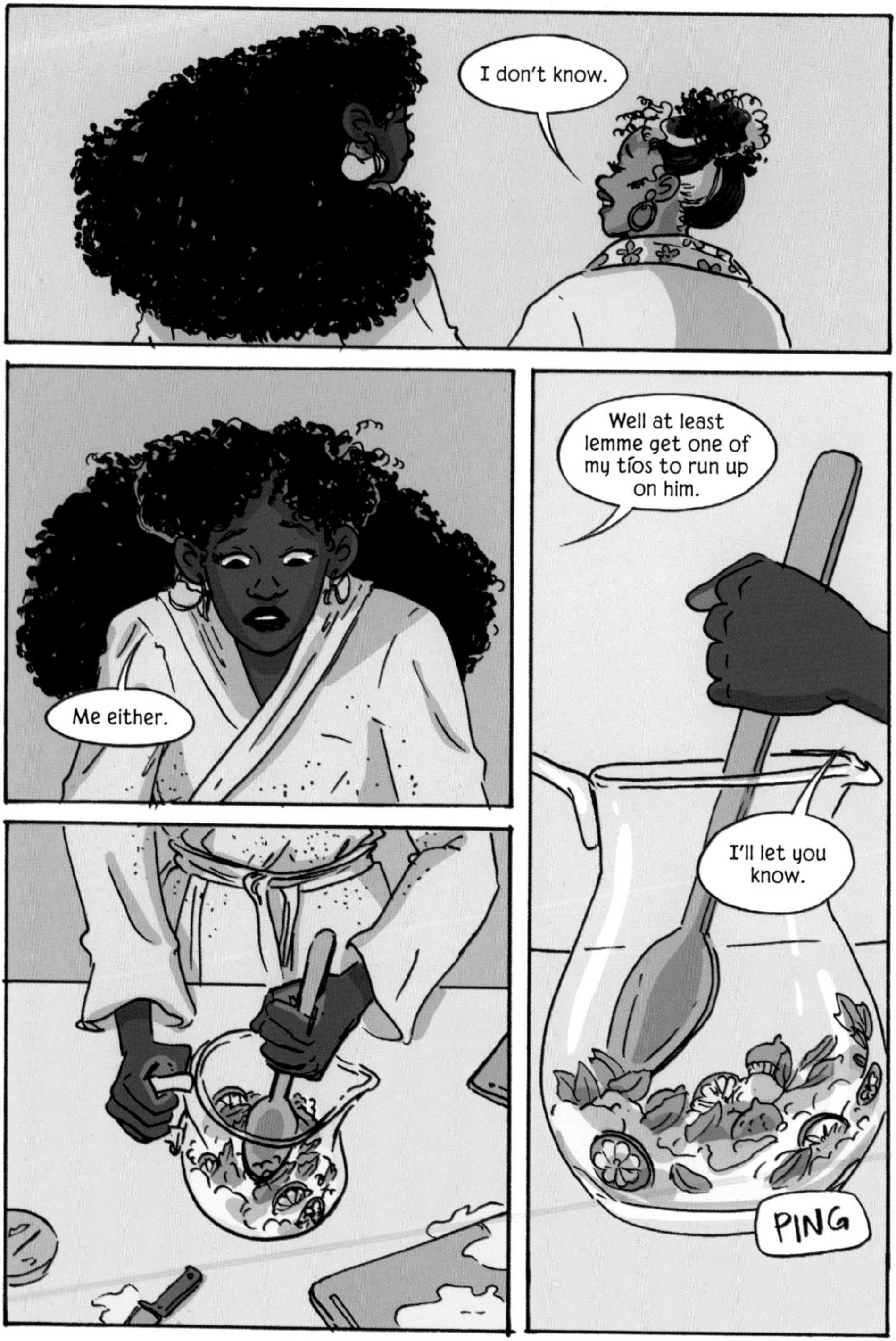
I don't know.
Me either.
Well at least lemme get one of my tíos to run up on him.
I'll let you know.
PING

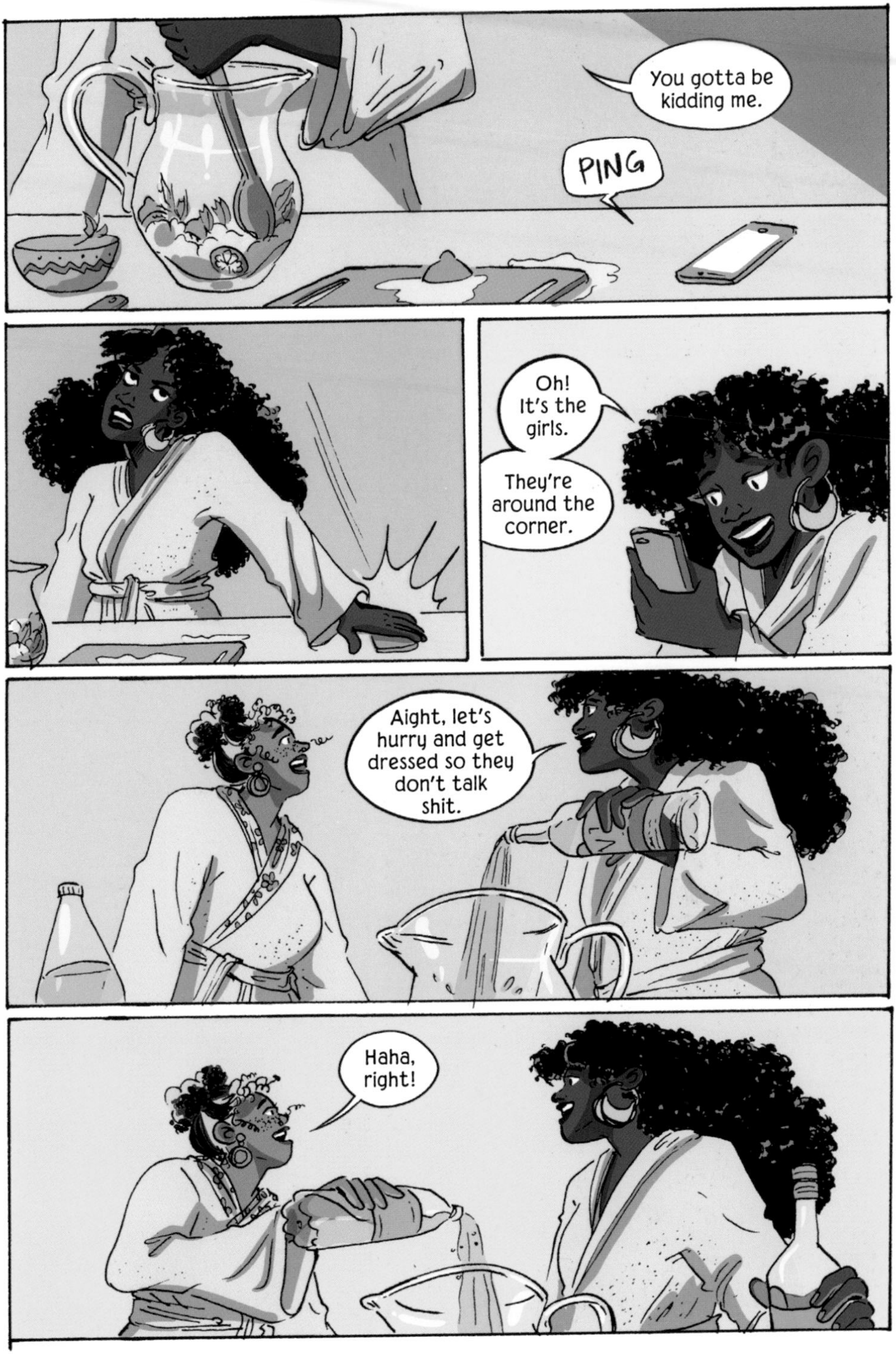
You gotta be kidding me.
PING
Oh! It's the girls.
They're around the corner.
Aight, let's hurry and get dressed so they don't talk shit.
Haha, right!

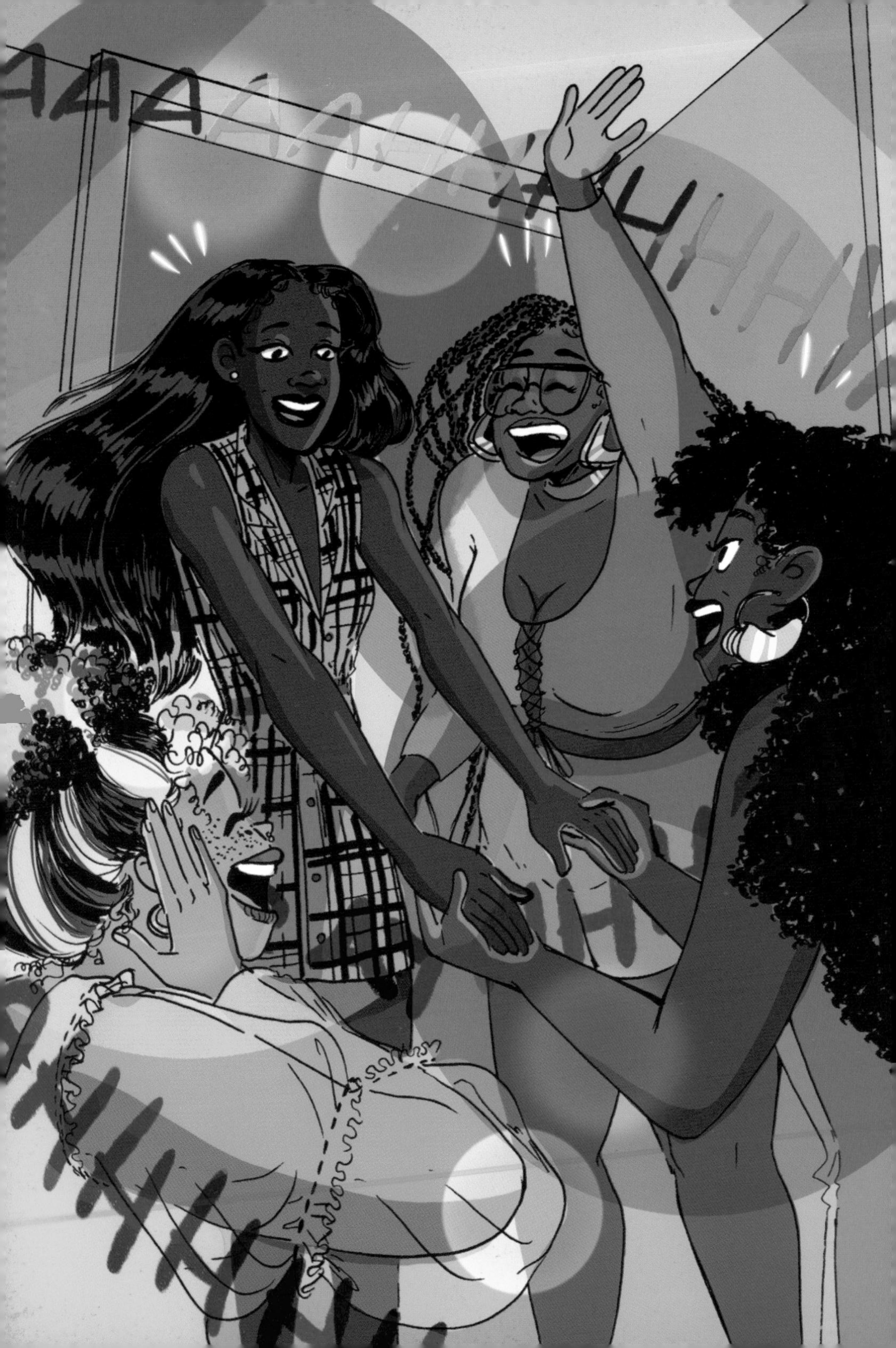

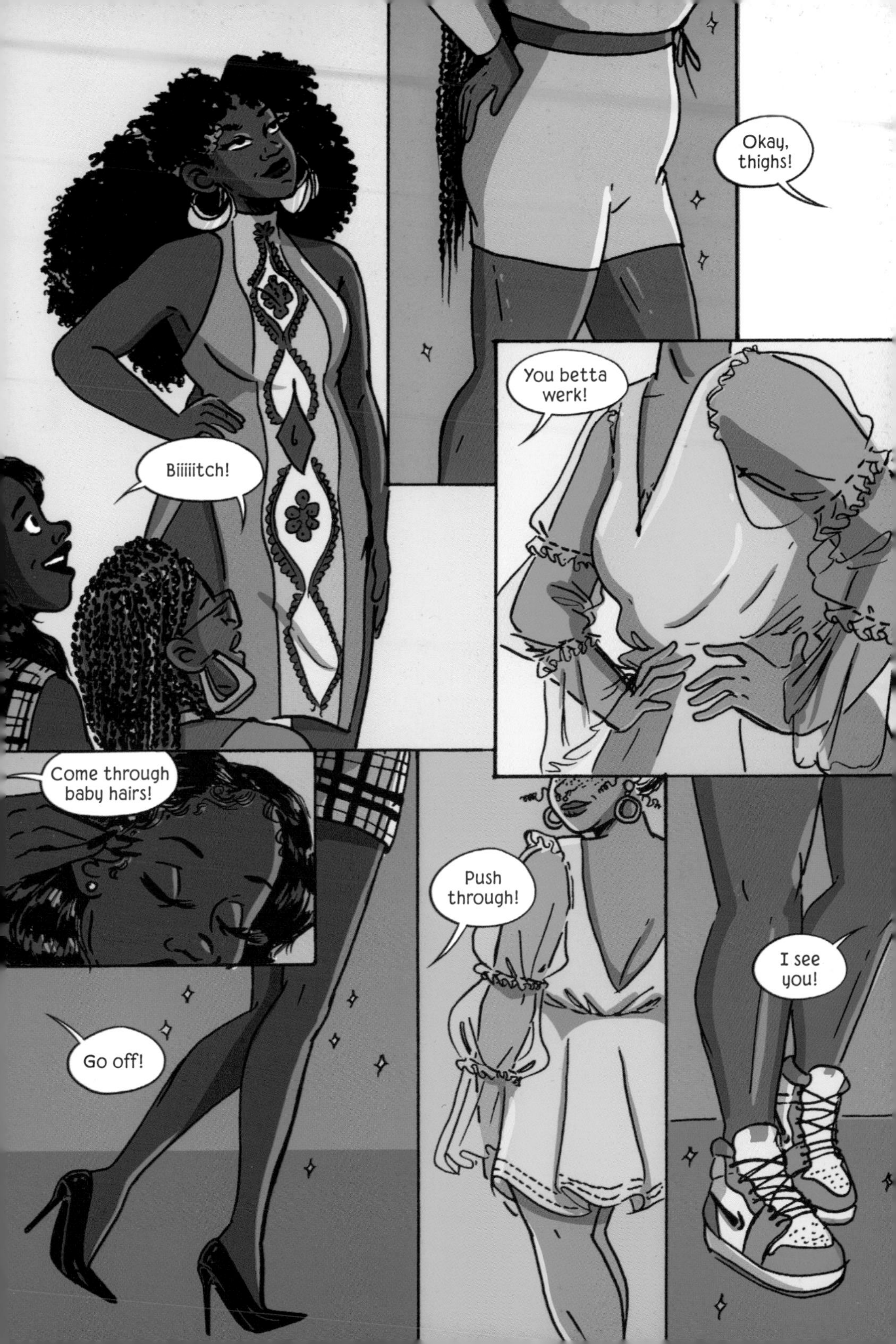
Okay, thighs!
You betta werk!
Biiiiitch!
Come through baby hairs!
Push through!
I see you!
Go off!

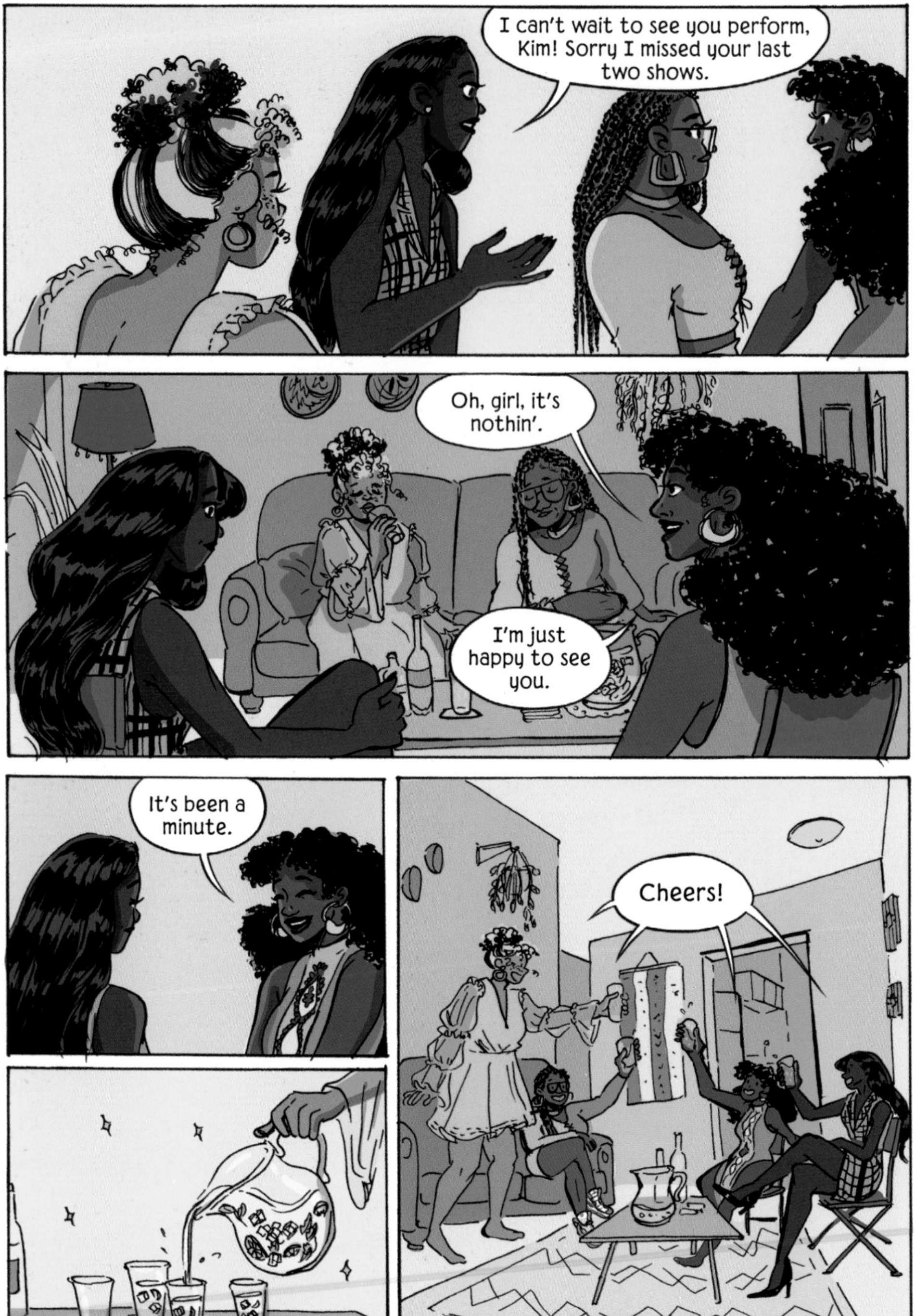
I can't wait to see you perform, Kim! Sorry I missed your last two shows.
Oh, girl, it's nothin'.
I'm just happy to see you.
It's been a minute.
Cheers!

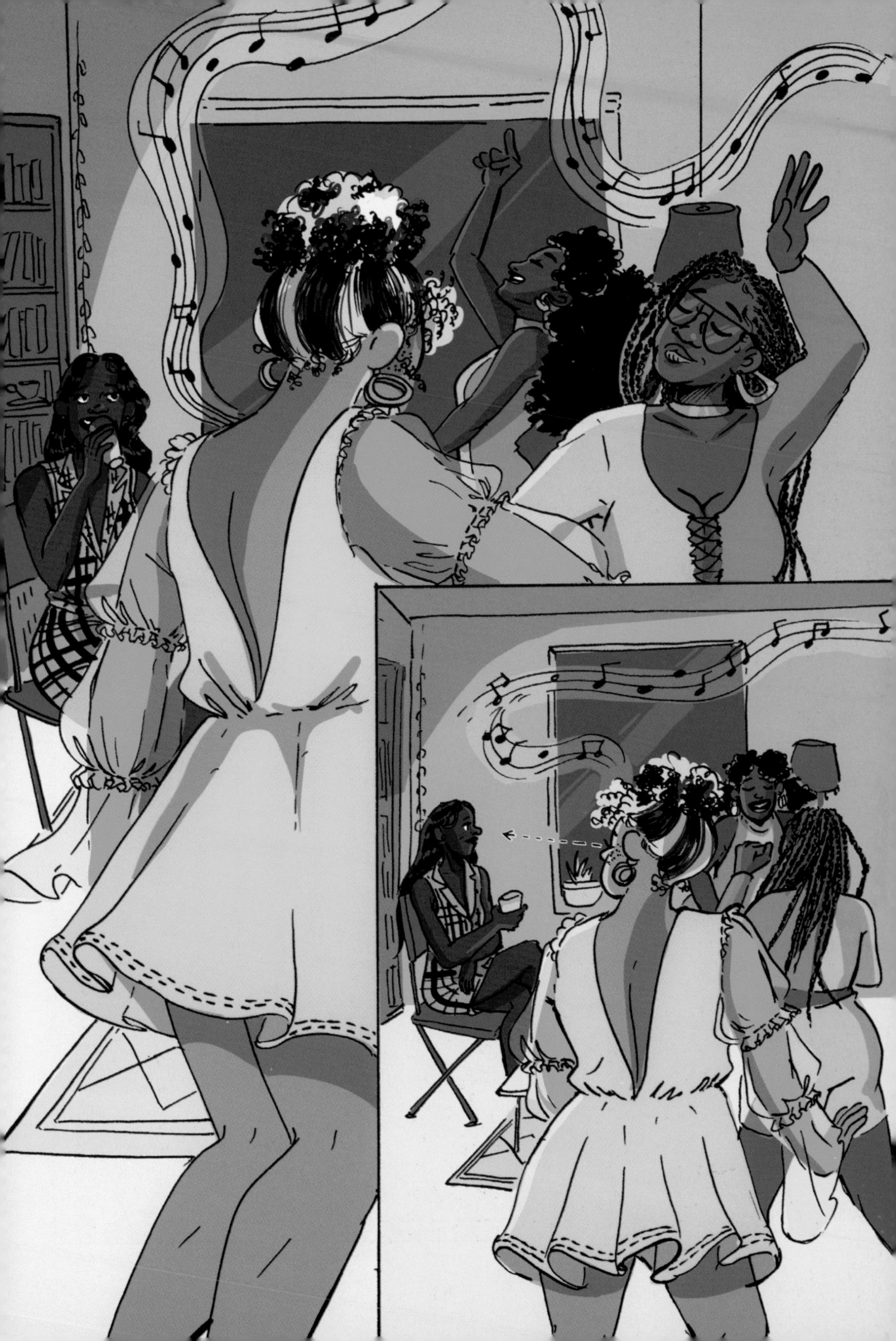

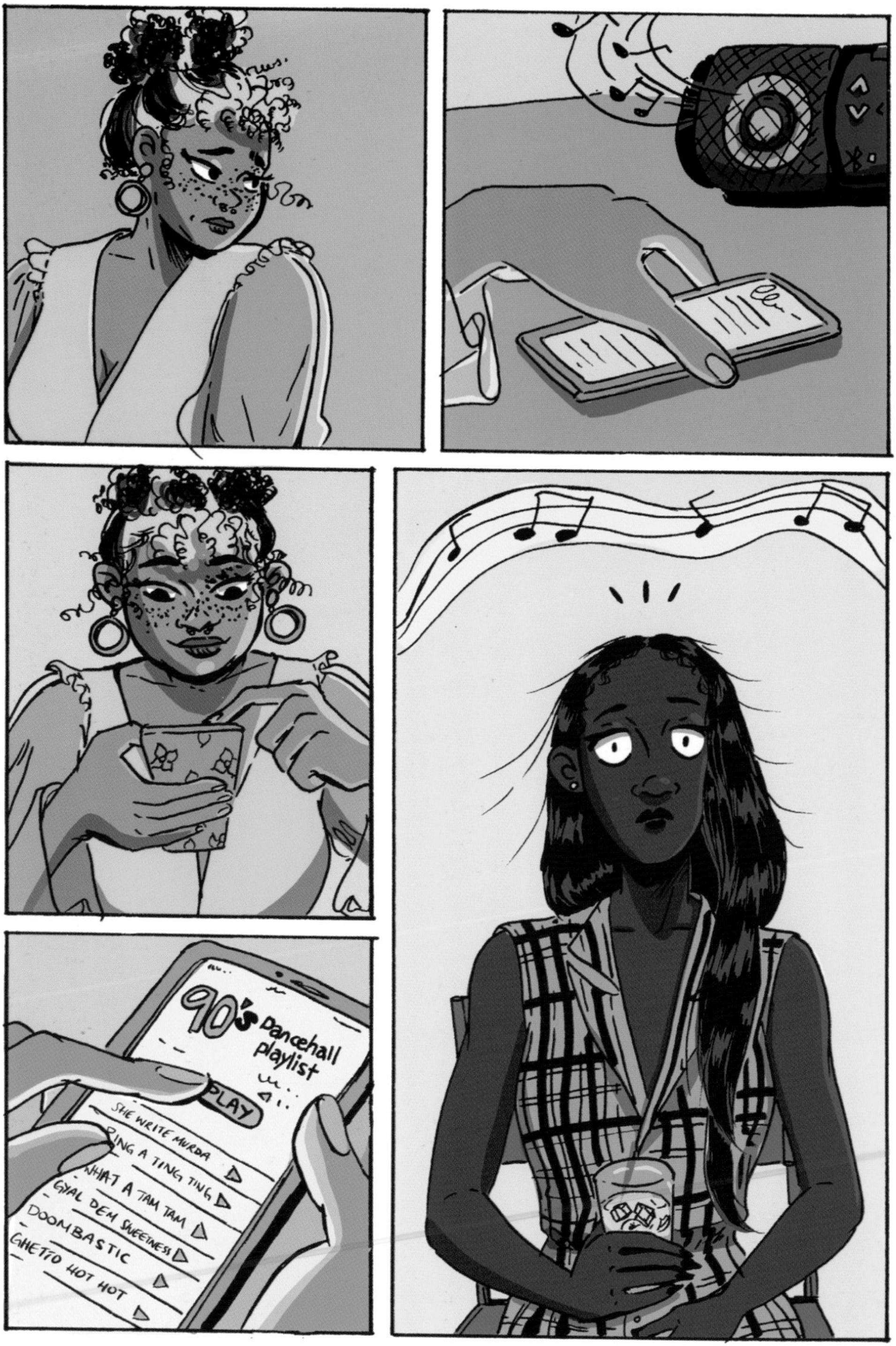

90's Dancehall playlist
PLAY
SHE WRITE MURDA
RING A TING TING
WHAT A TAM TAM
GYAL DEM SWEETNESS
DOOMBASTIC
GHETTO HOT HOT

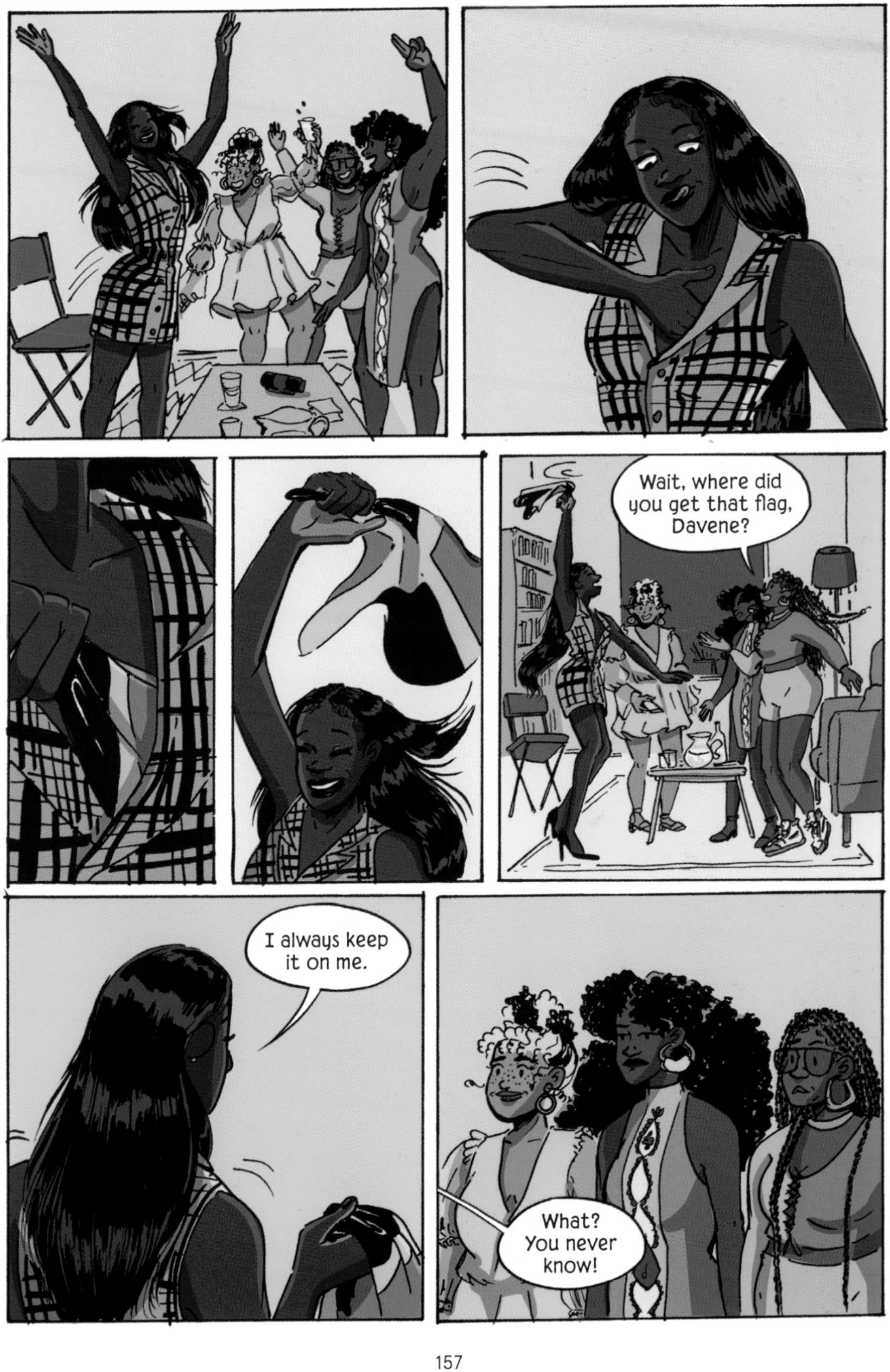
Wait, where did you get that flag, Davene?
I always keep it on me.
What? You never know!

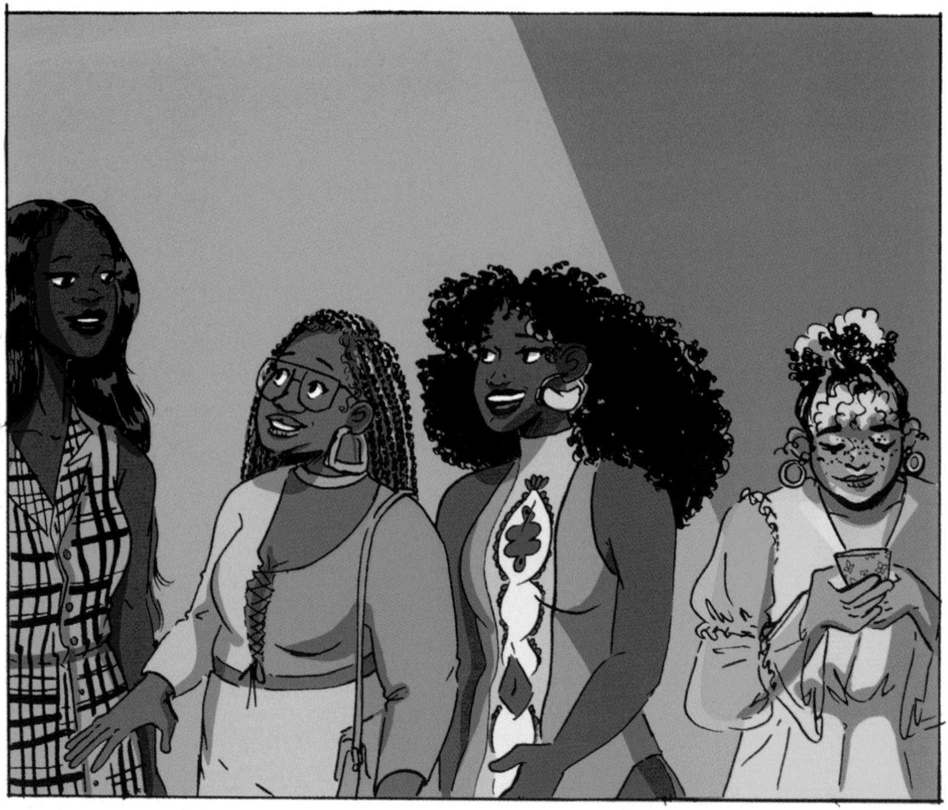

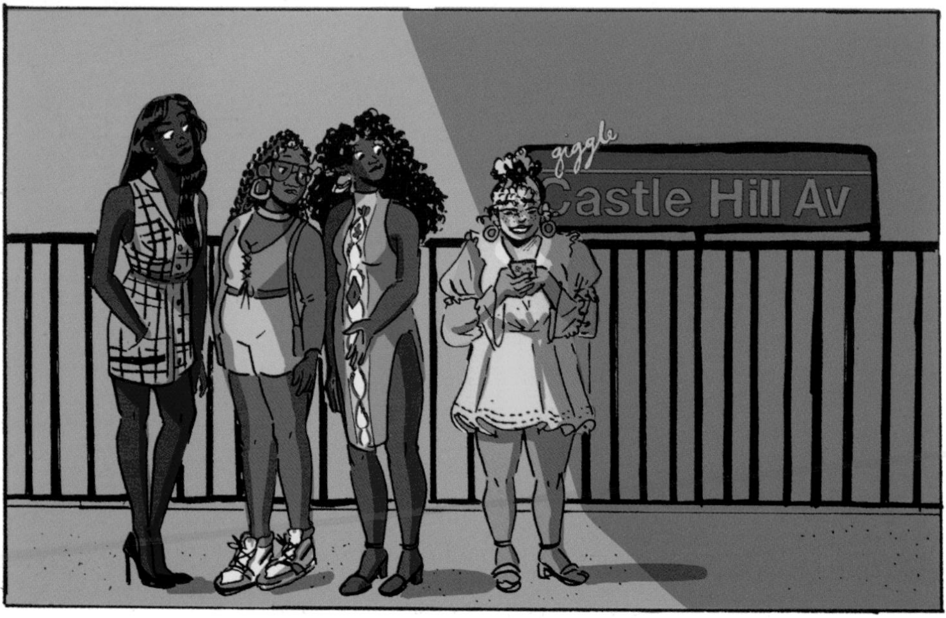
giggle
Castle Hill Av

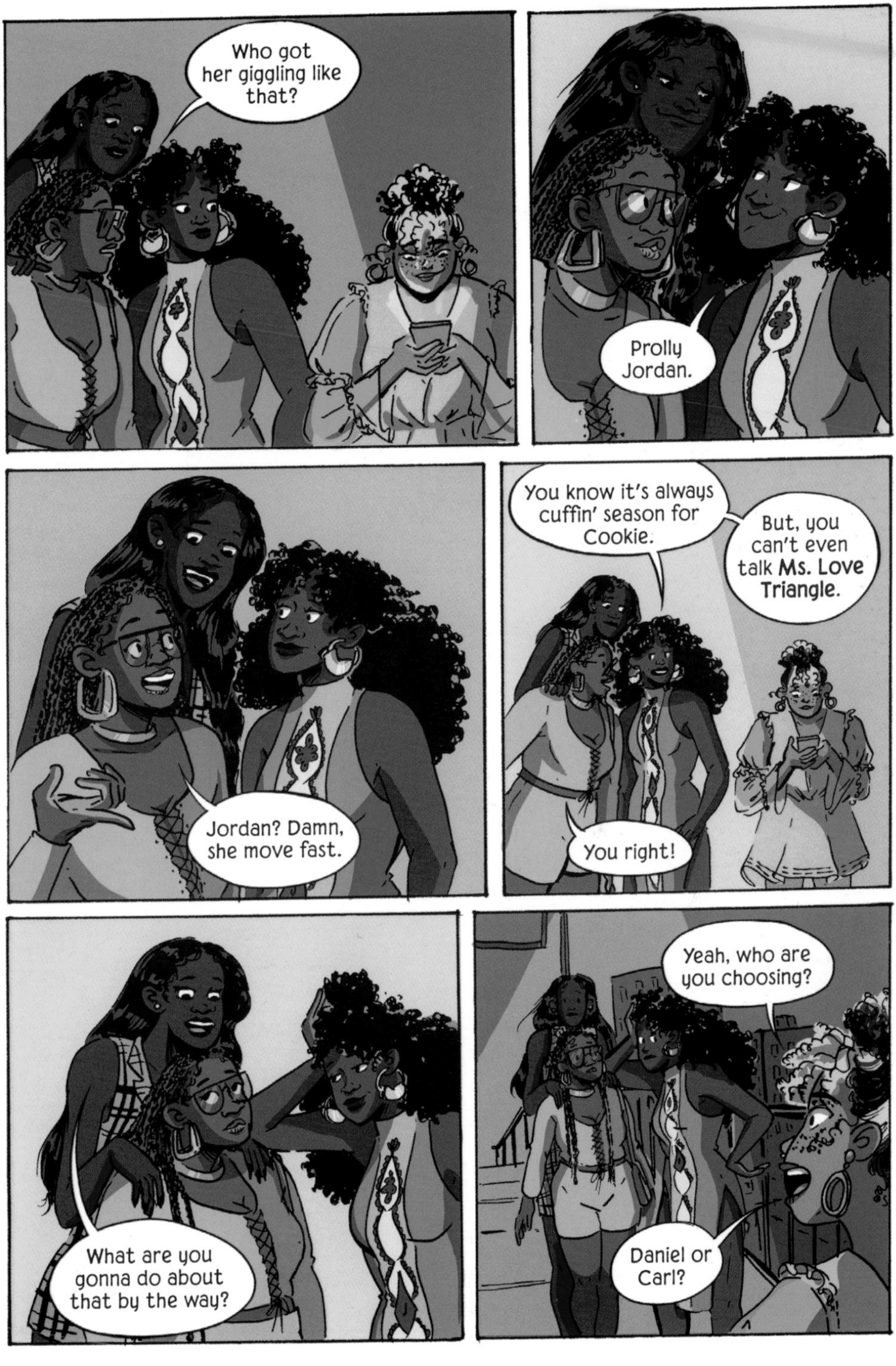
Who got her giggling like that?
Prolly Jordan.
Jordan? Damn, she move fast.
You know it's always cuffin' season for Cookie.
You right!
But, you can't even talk **Ms. Love Triangle**.
What are you gonna do about that by the way?
Yeah, who are you choosing?
Daniel or Carl?

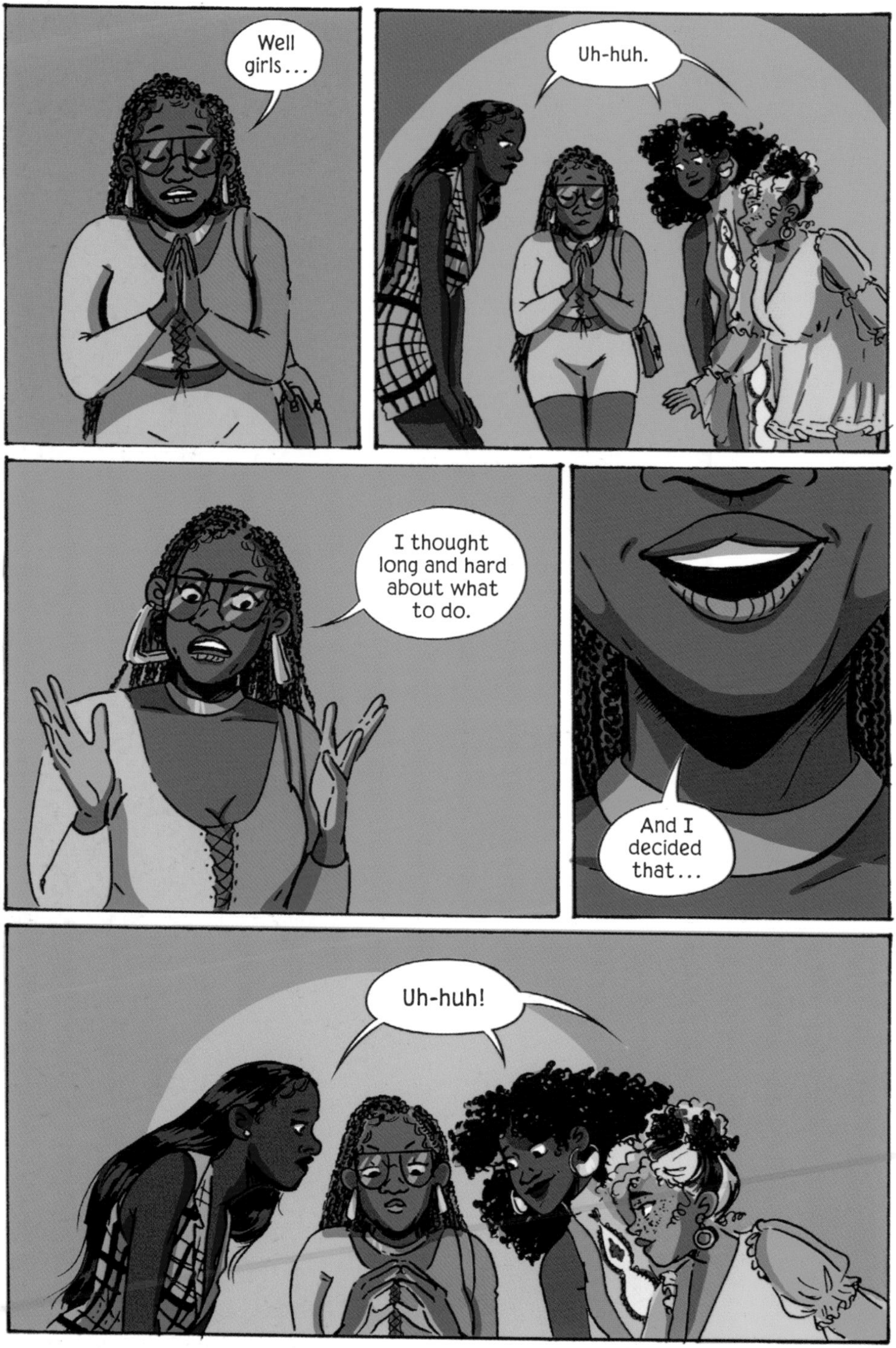

Well girls...
Uh-huh.
I thought long and hard about what to do.
And I decided that...
Uh-huh!

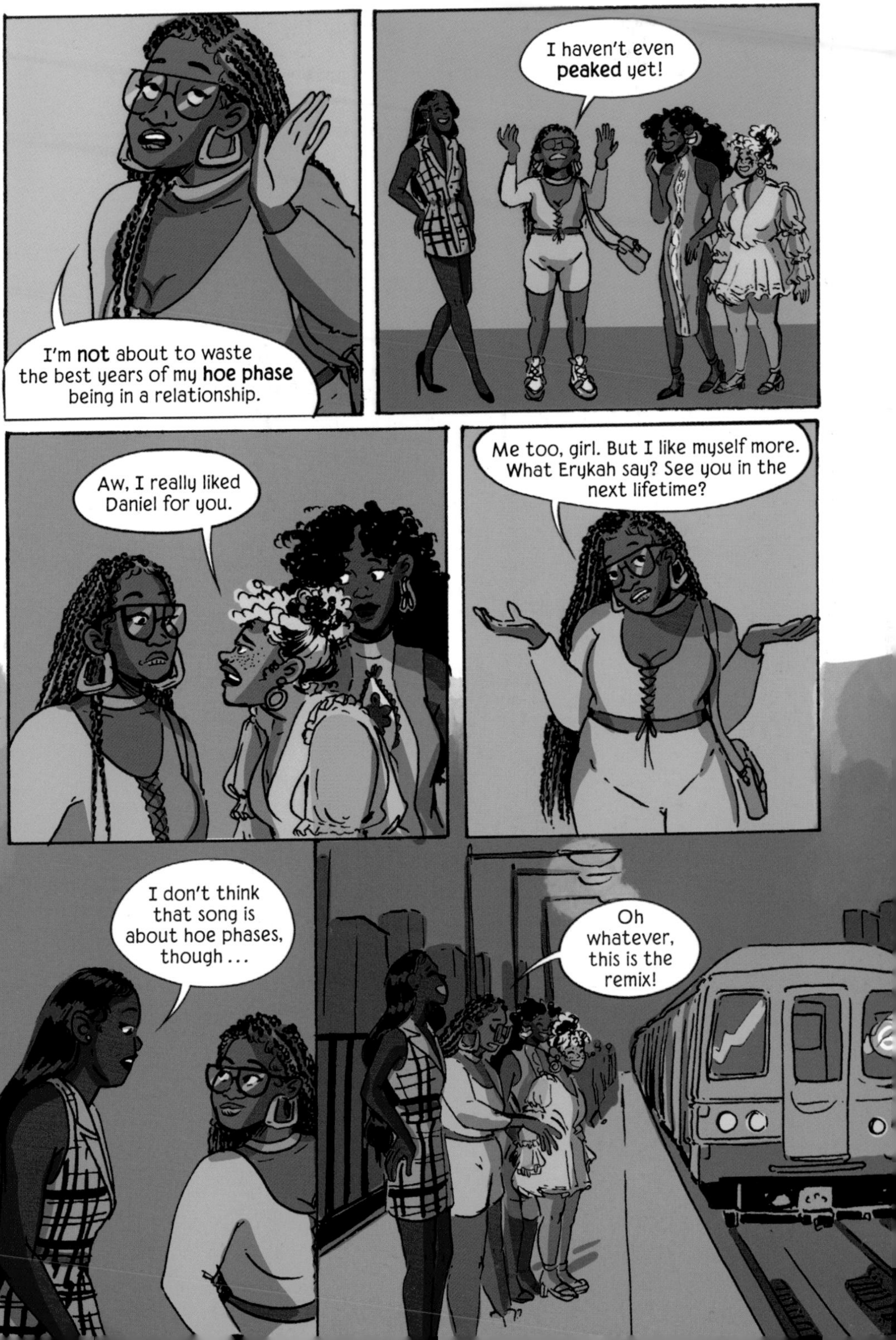
I'm **not** about to waste the best years of my **hoe phase** being in a relationship.
I haven't even **peaked** yet!
Aw, I really liked Daniel for you.
Me too, girl. But I like myself more. What Erykah say? See you in the next lifetime?
I don't think that song is about hoe phases, though . . .
Oh whatever, this is the remix!

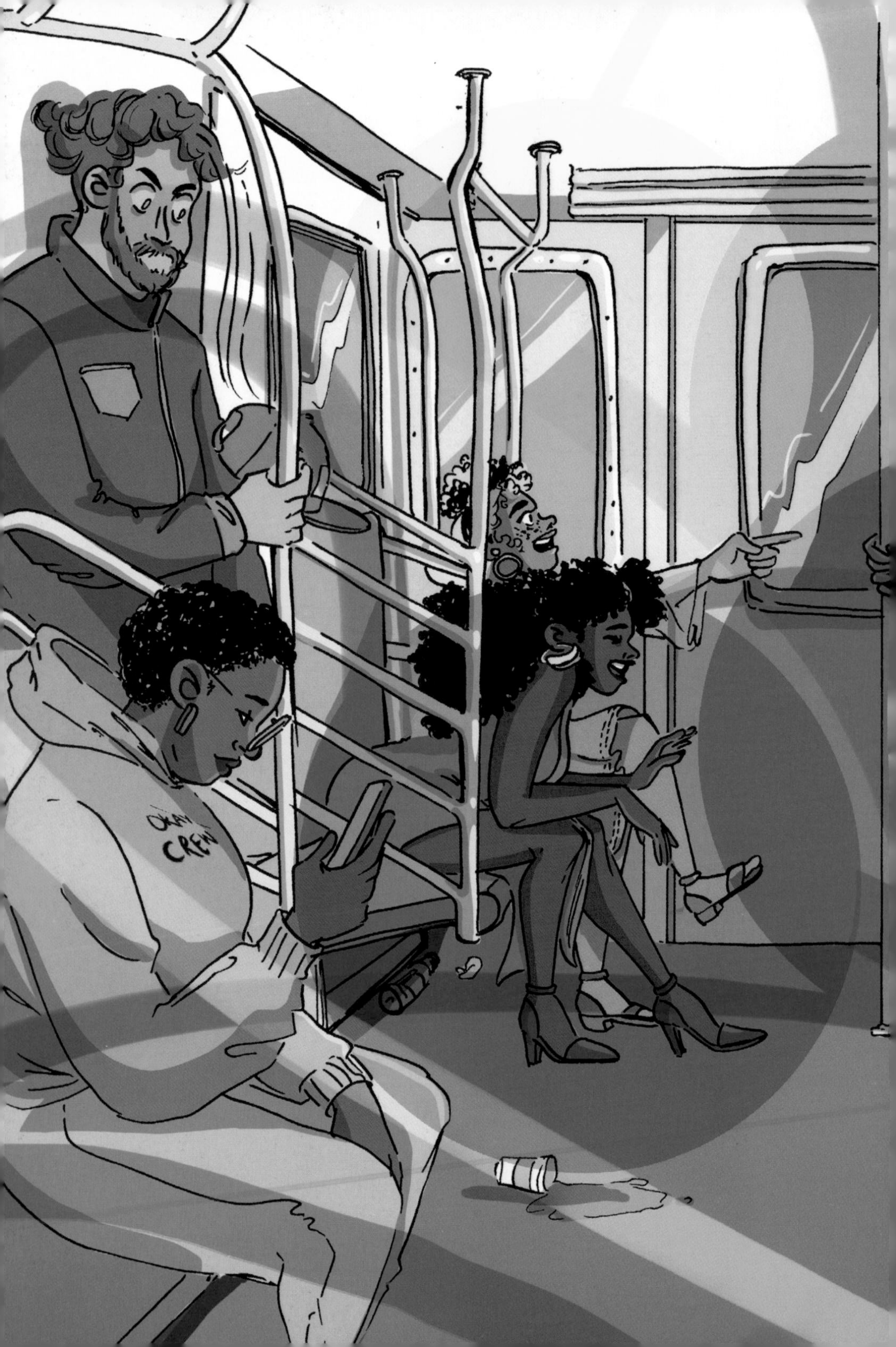

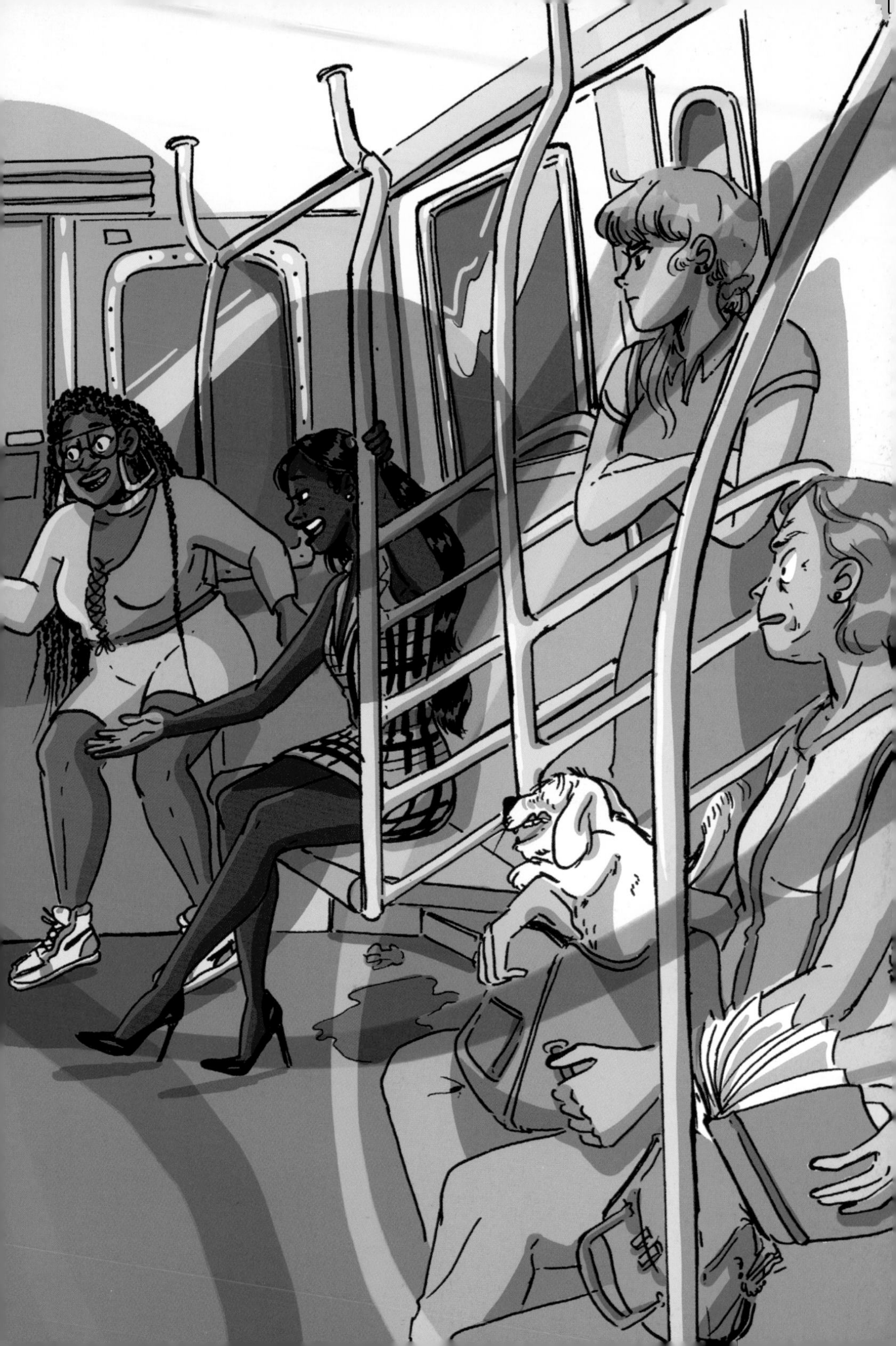

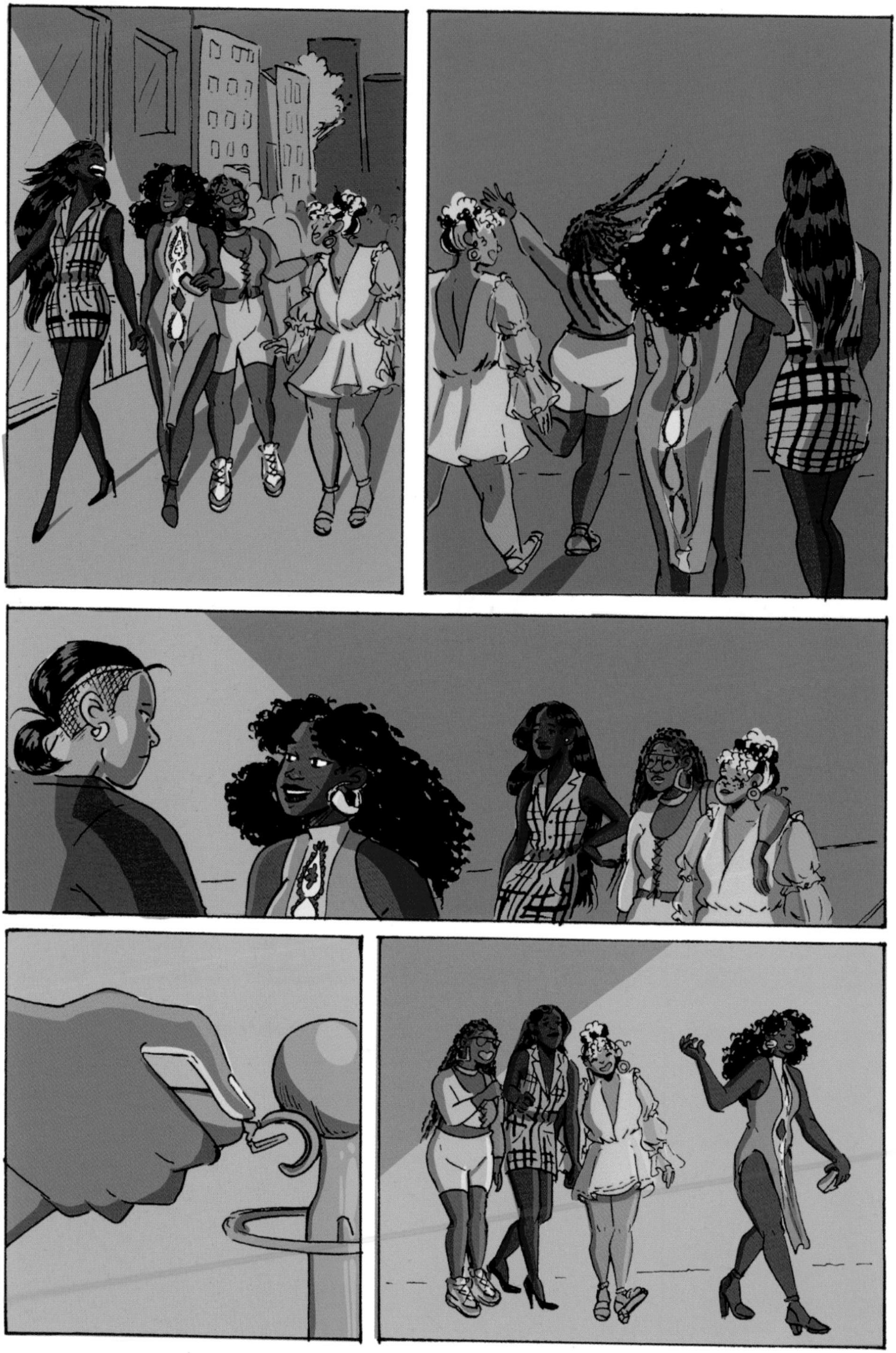

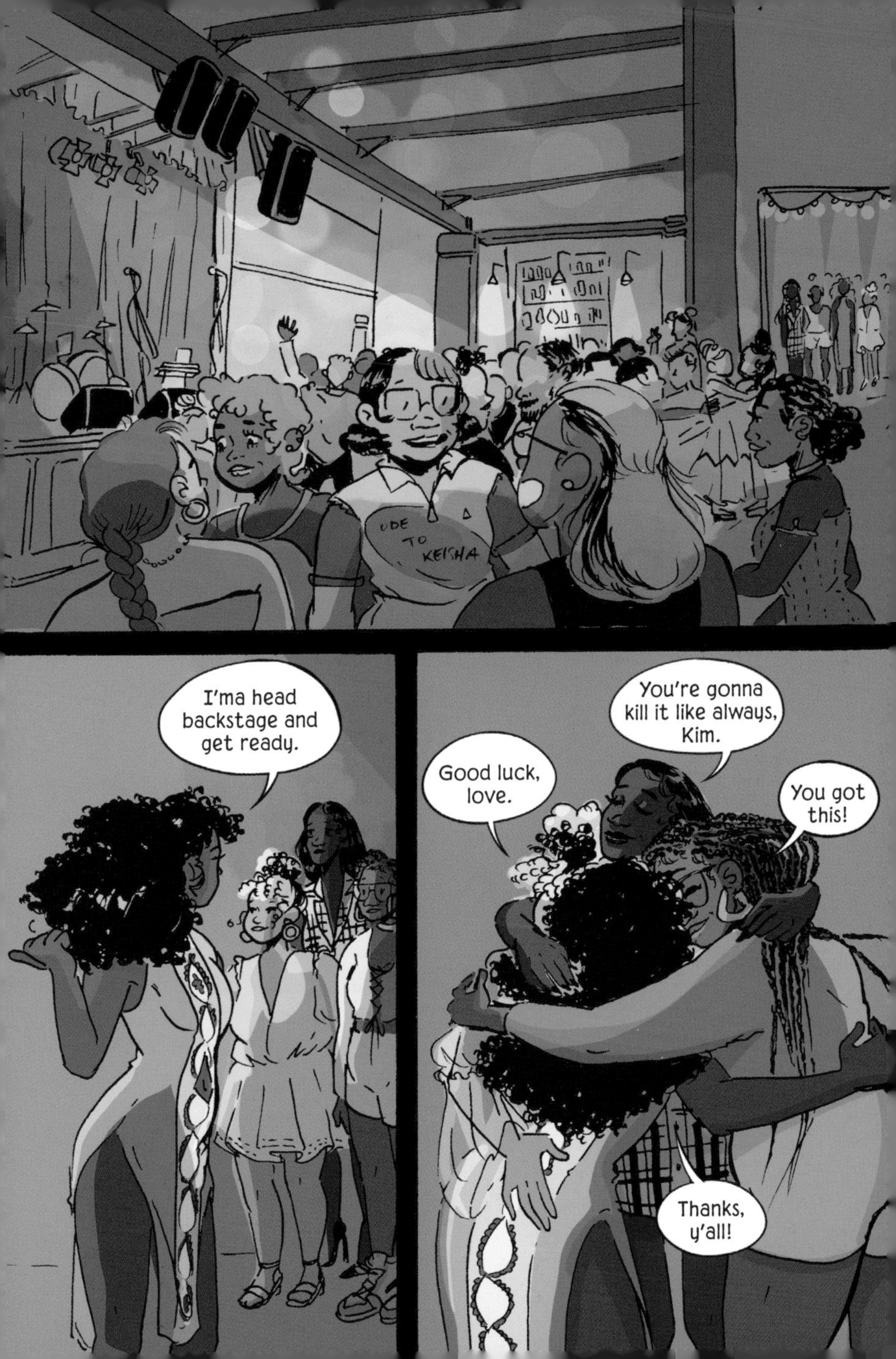
ODE TO KEISHA
I'ma head backstage and get ready.
Good luck, love.
You're gonna kill it like always, Kim.
You got this!
Thanks, y'all!

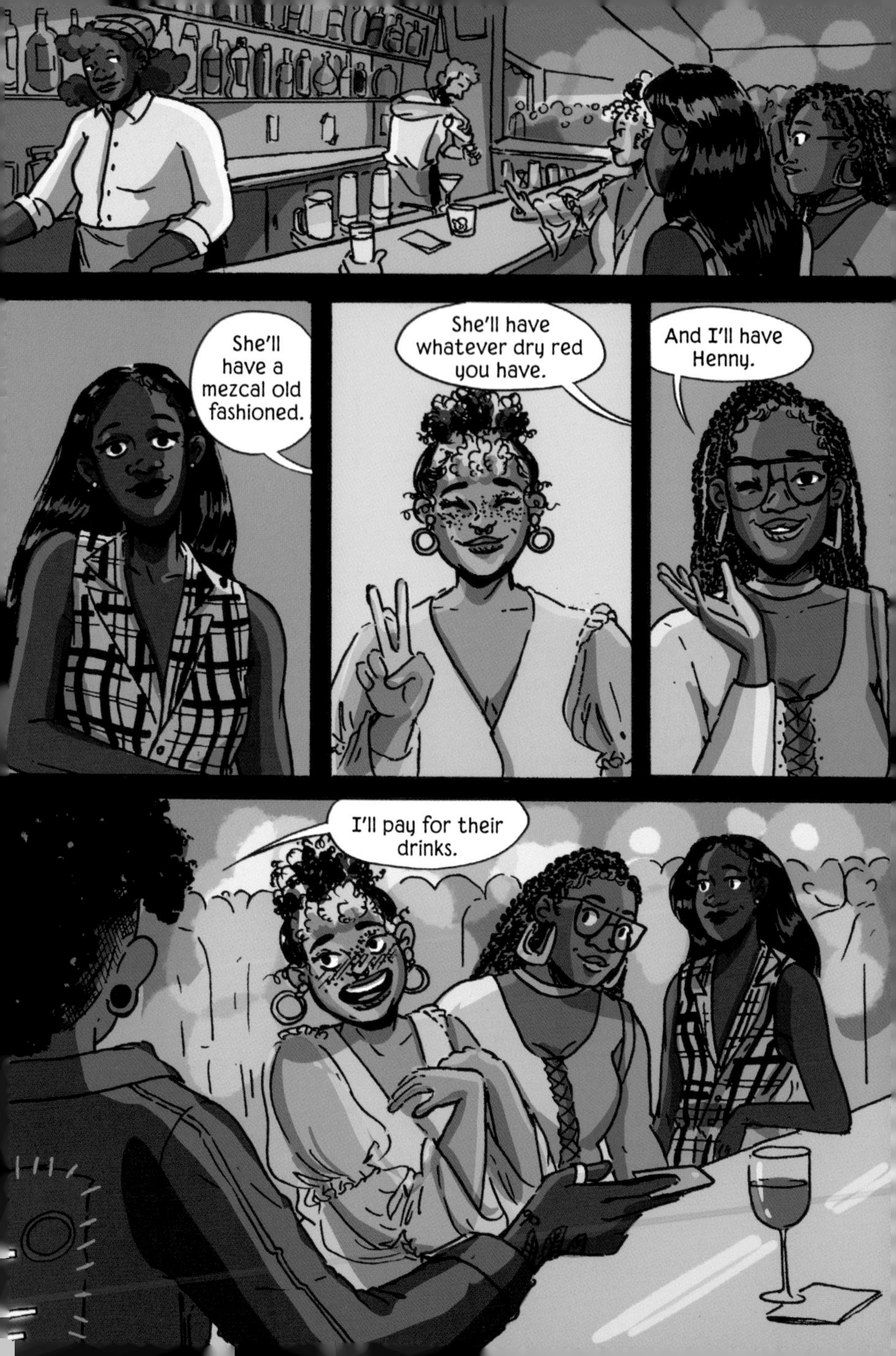

She'll have a mezcal old fashioned.
She'll have whatever dry red you have.
And I'll have Henny.
I'll pay for their drinks.

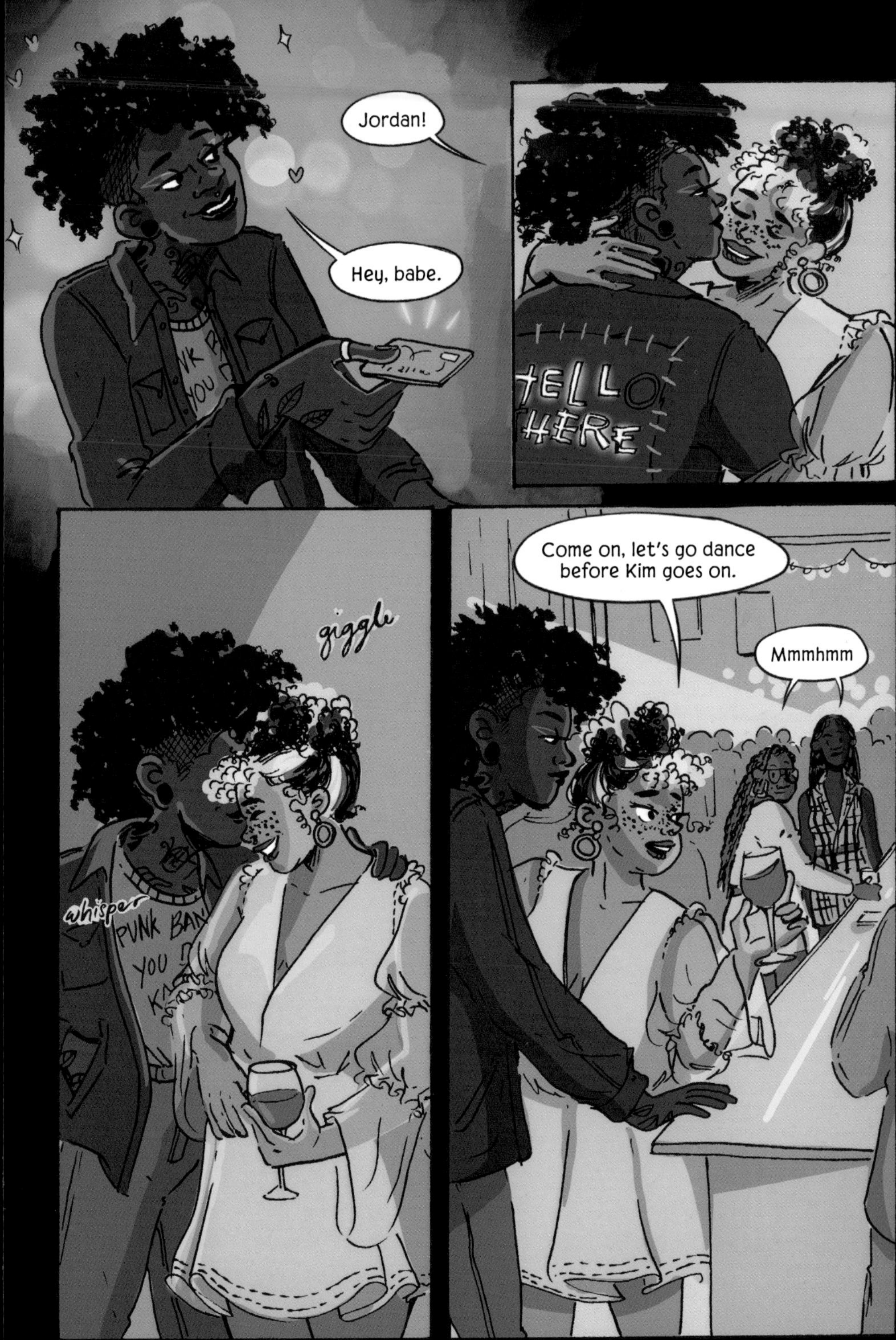
Jordan!
Hey, babe.
giggle
whisper
Come on, let's go dance before Kim goes on.
Mmmhmm

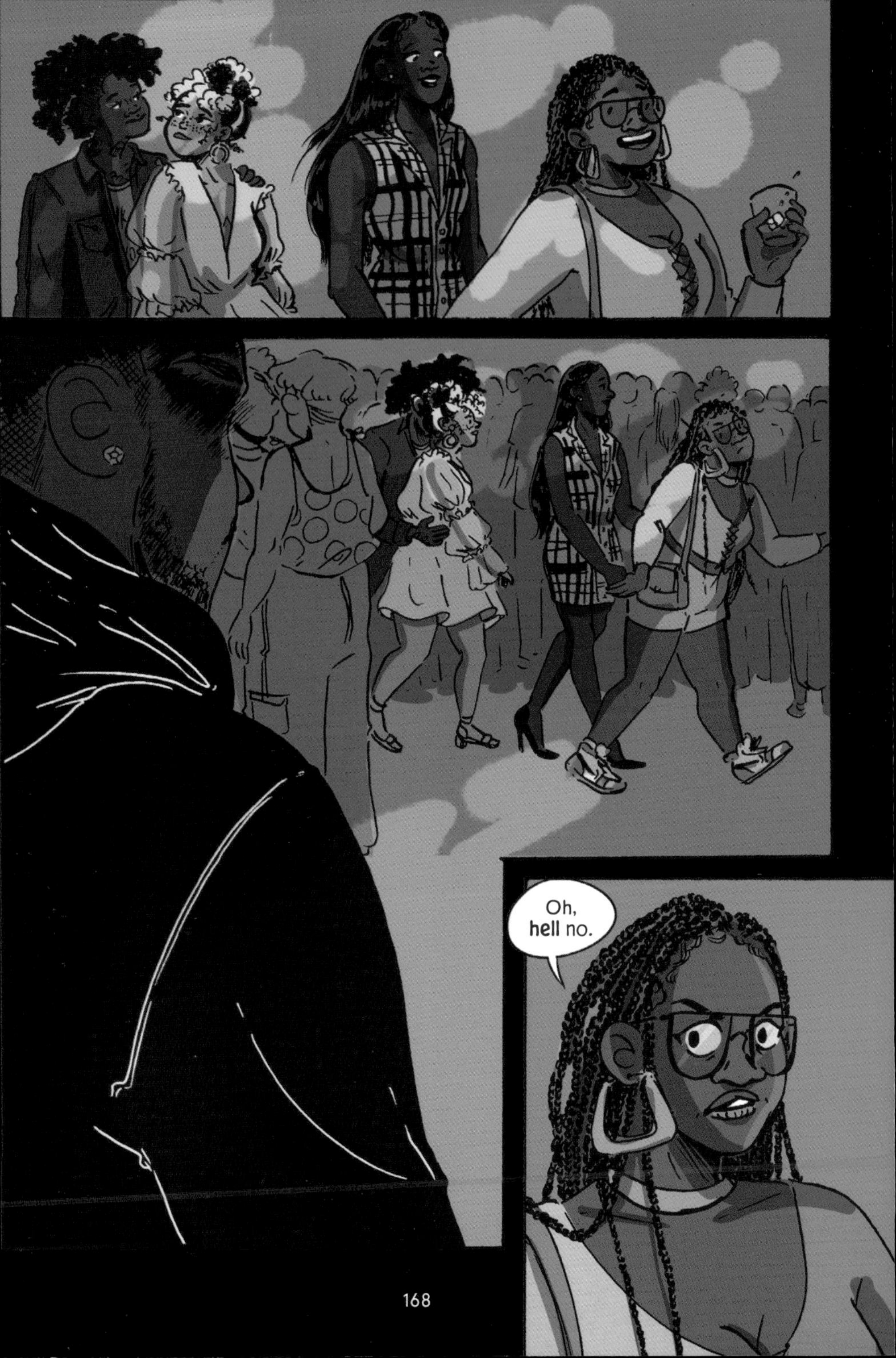
Oh, hell no.

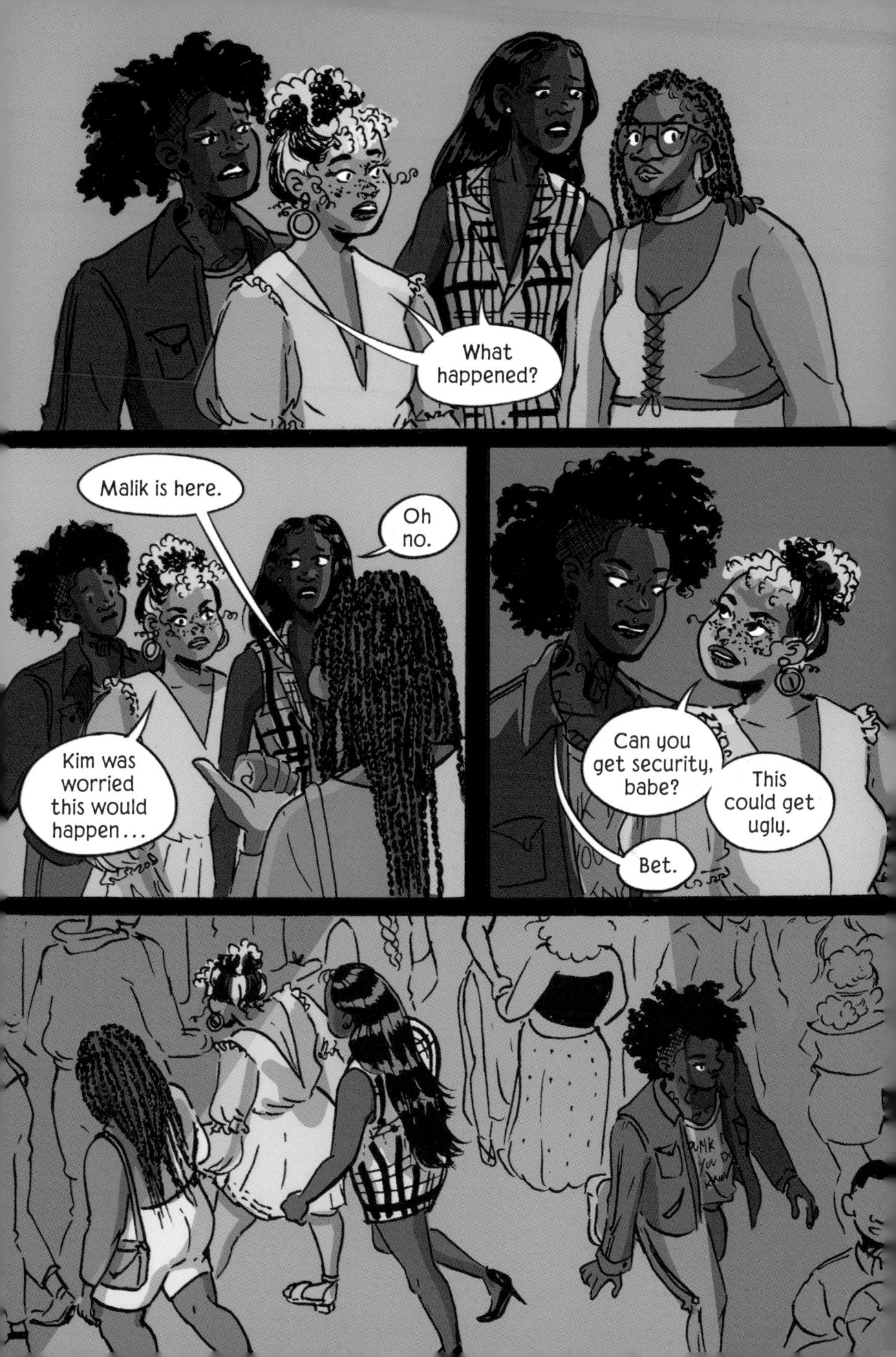
What happened?
Malik is here.
Oh no.
Kim was worried this would happen...
Can you get security, babe?
This could get ugly.
Bet.

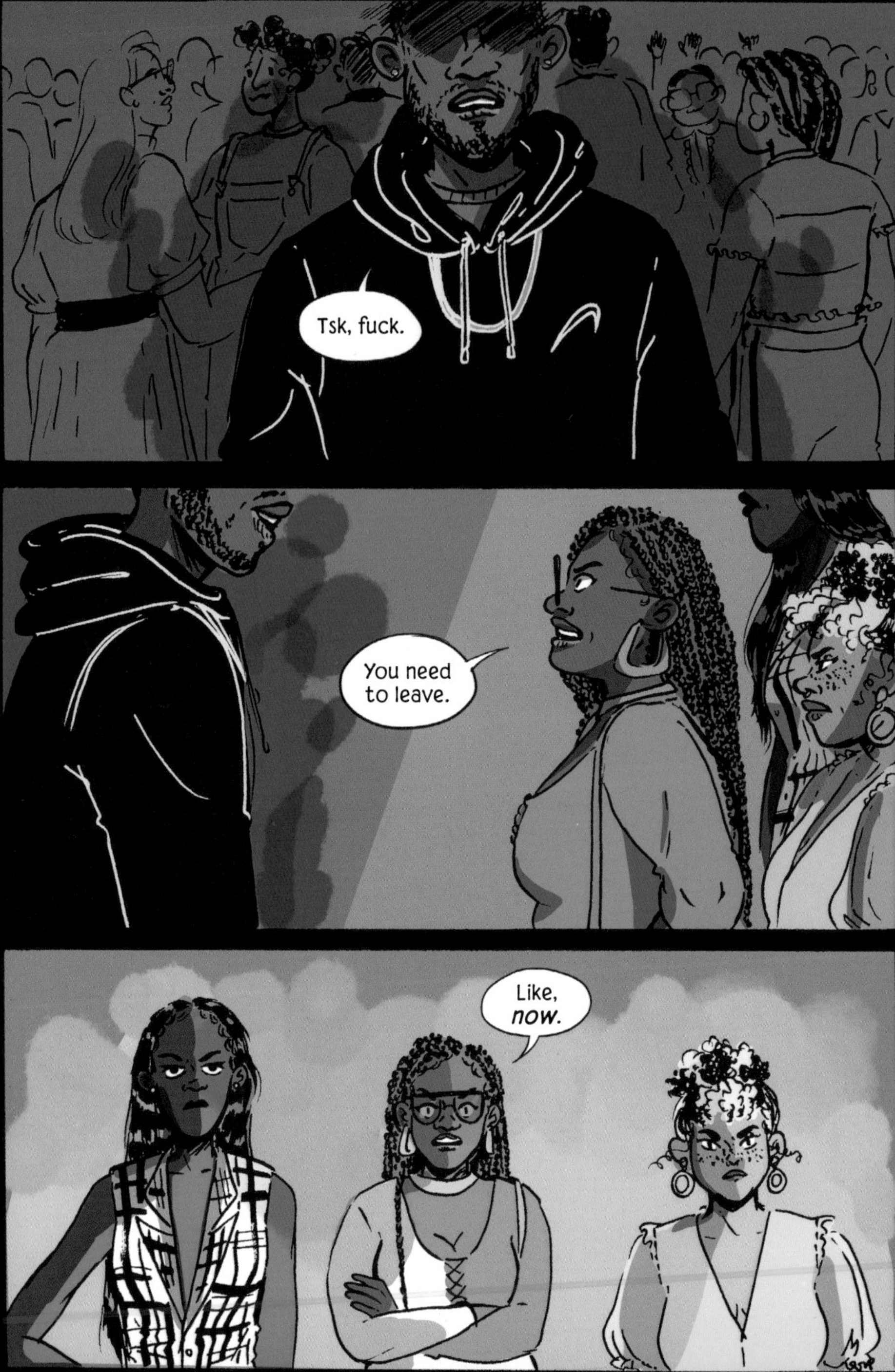
Tsk, fuck.
You need to leave.
Like, *now*.

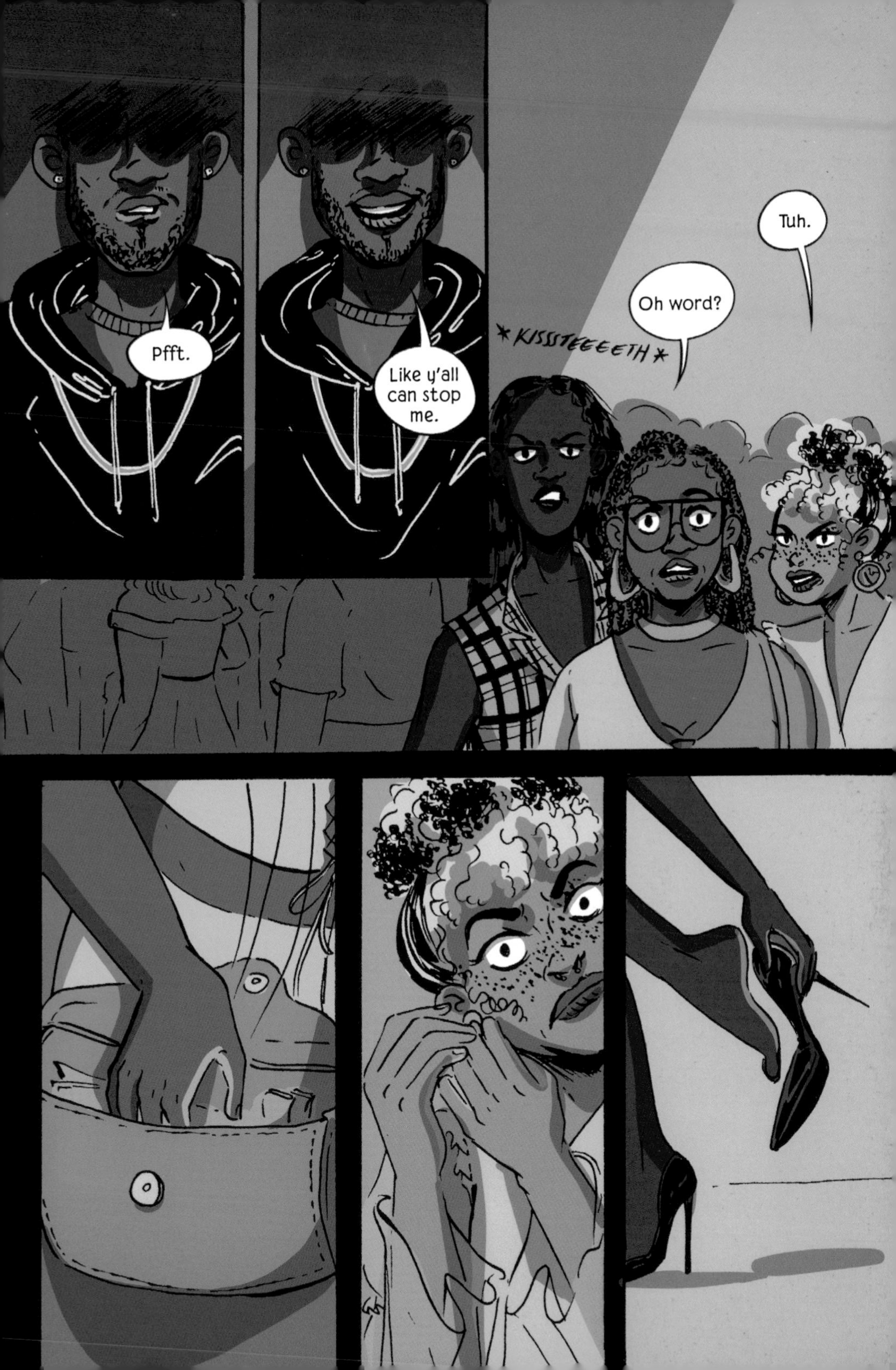
Pfft.
Like y'all can stop me.
KISSSTEEEEETH
Oh word?
Tuh.

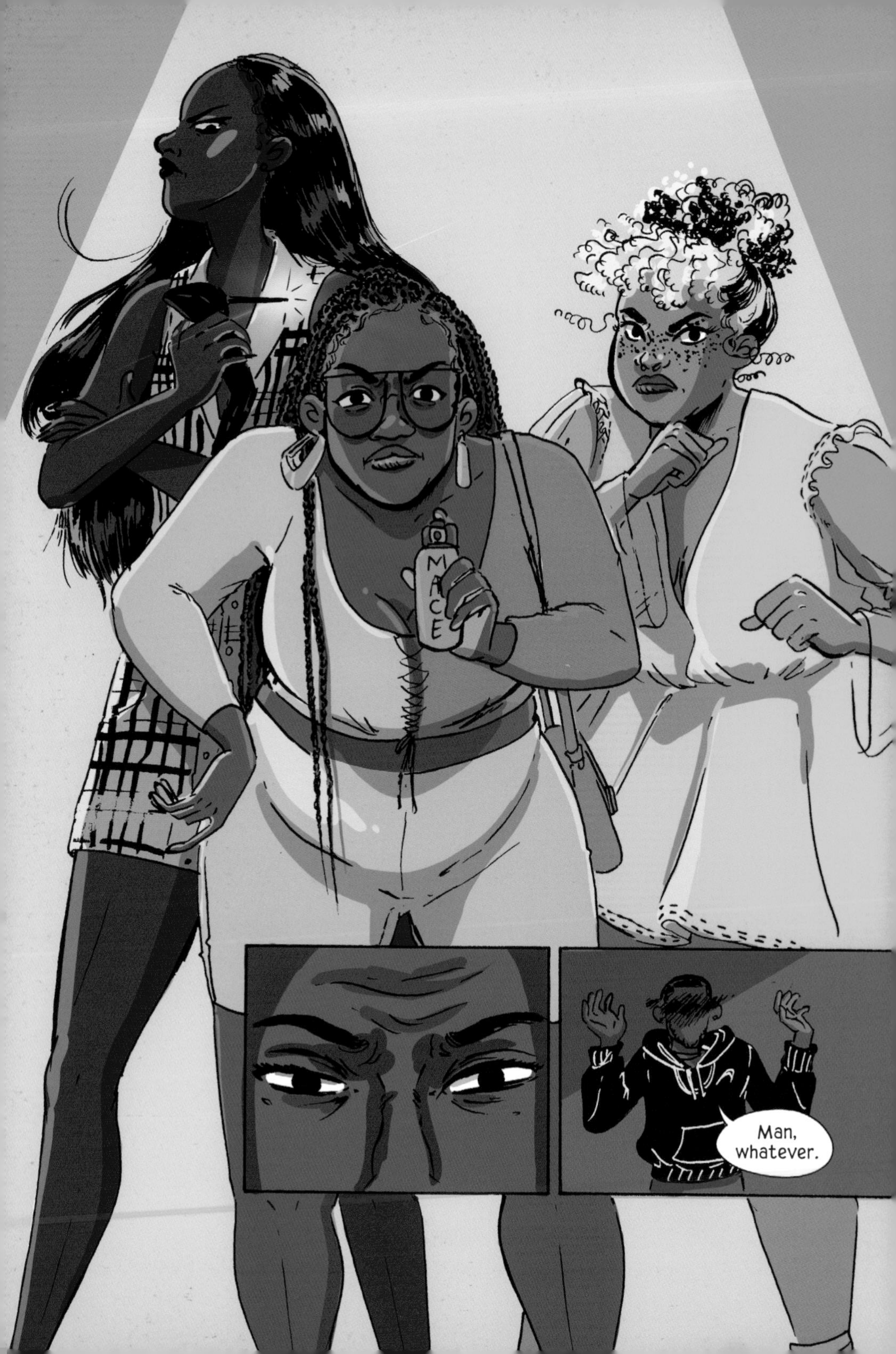
MACE
Man, whatever.

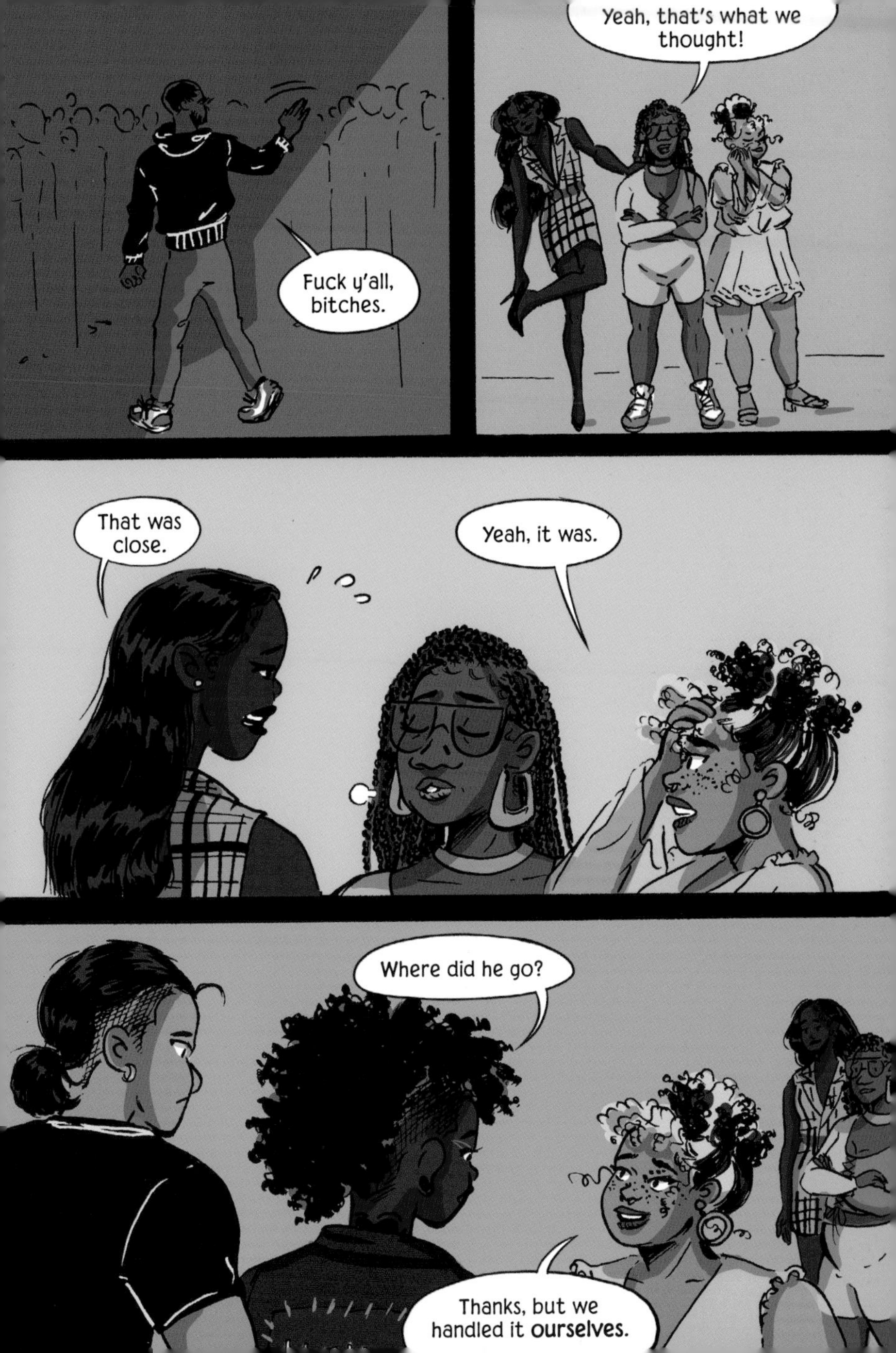
Fuck y'all, bitches.
Yeah, that's what we thought!
That was close.
Yeah, it was.
Where did he go?
Thanks, but we handled it **ourselves**.

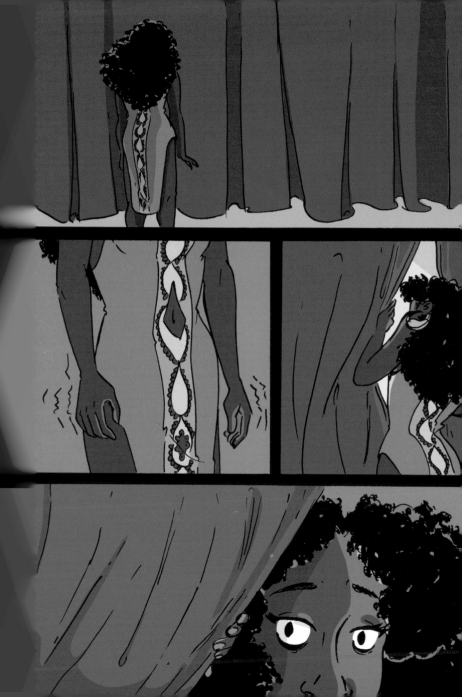

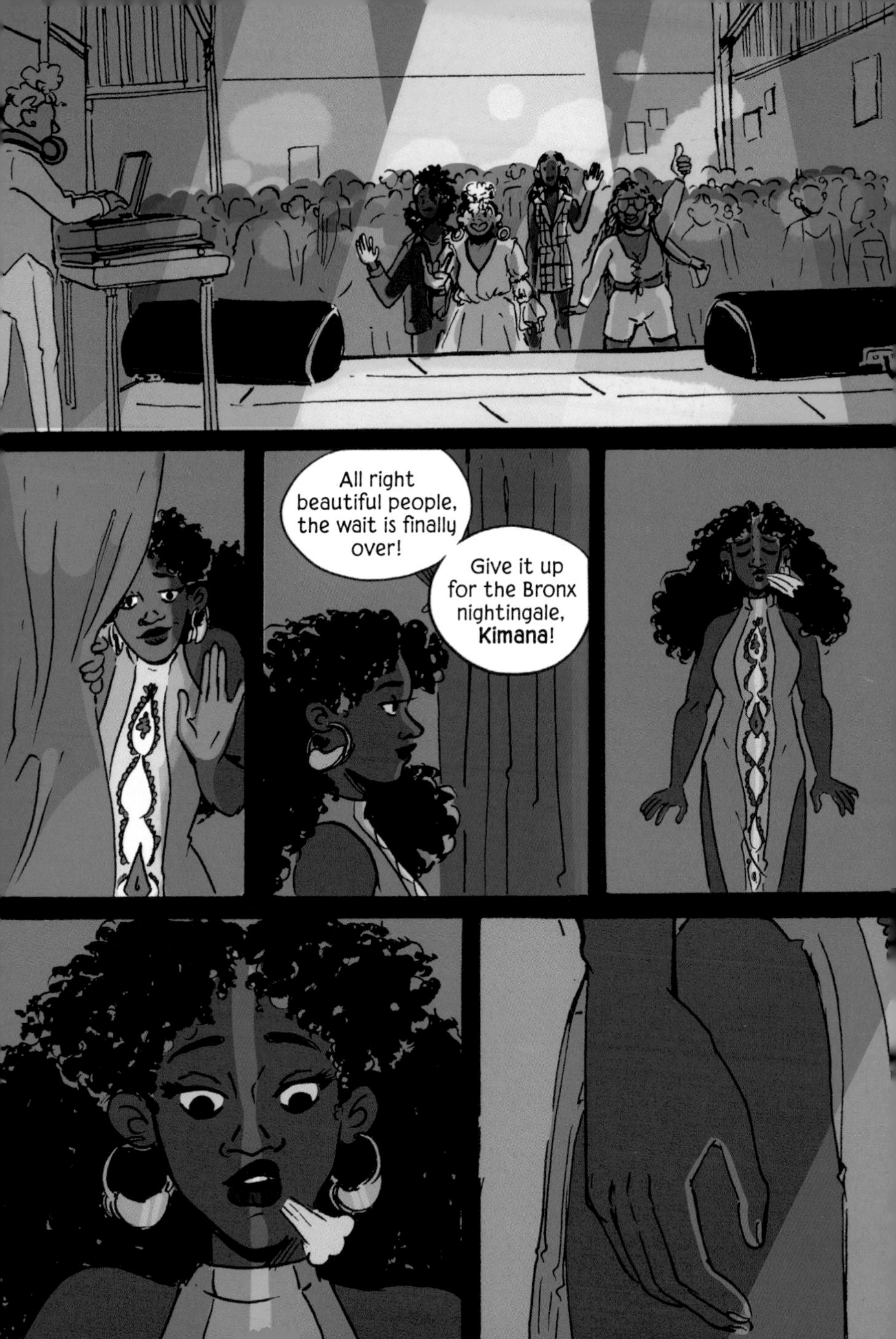
All right beautiful people, the wait is finally over!
Give it up for the Bronx nightingale, **Kimana**!

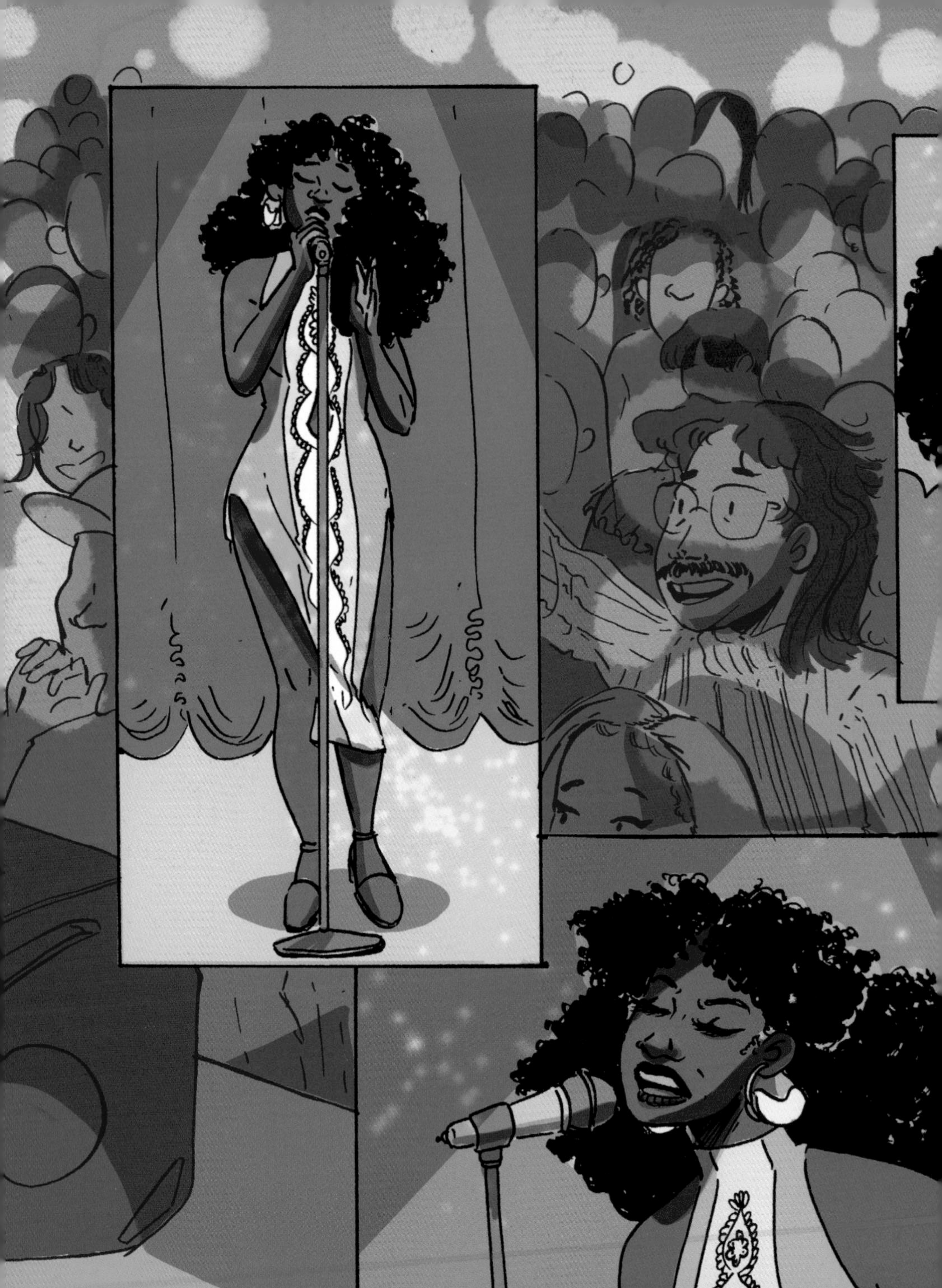

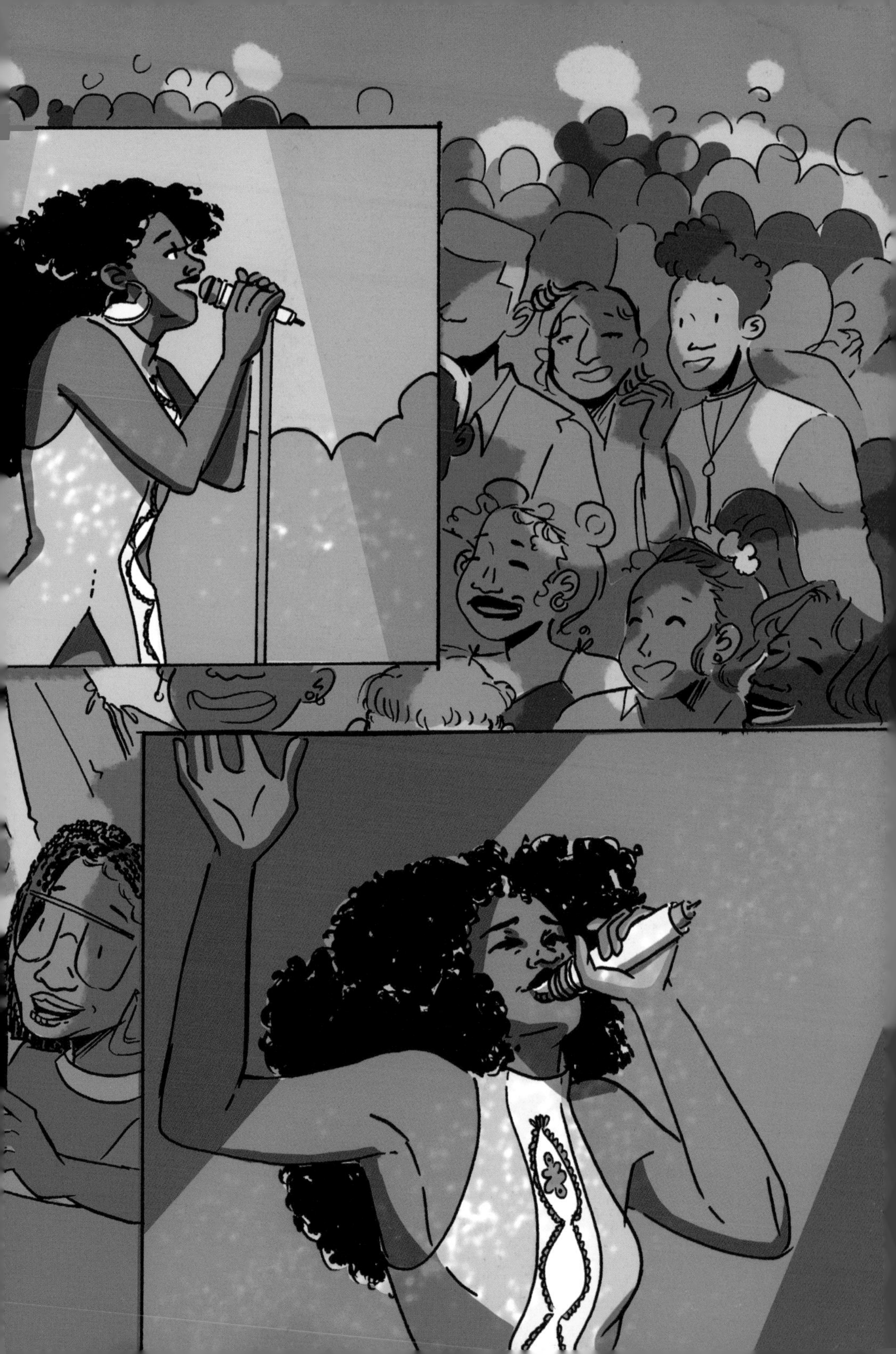

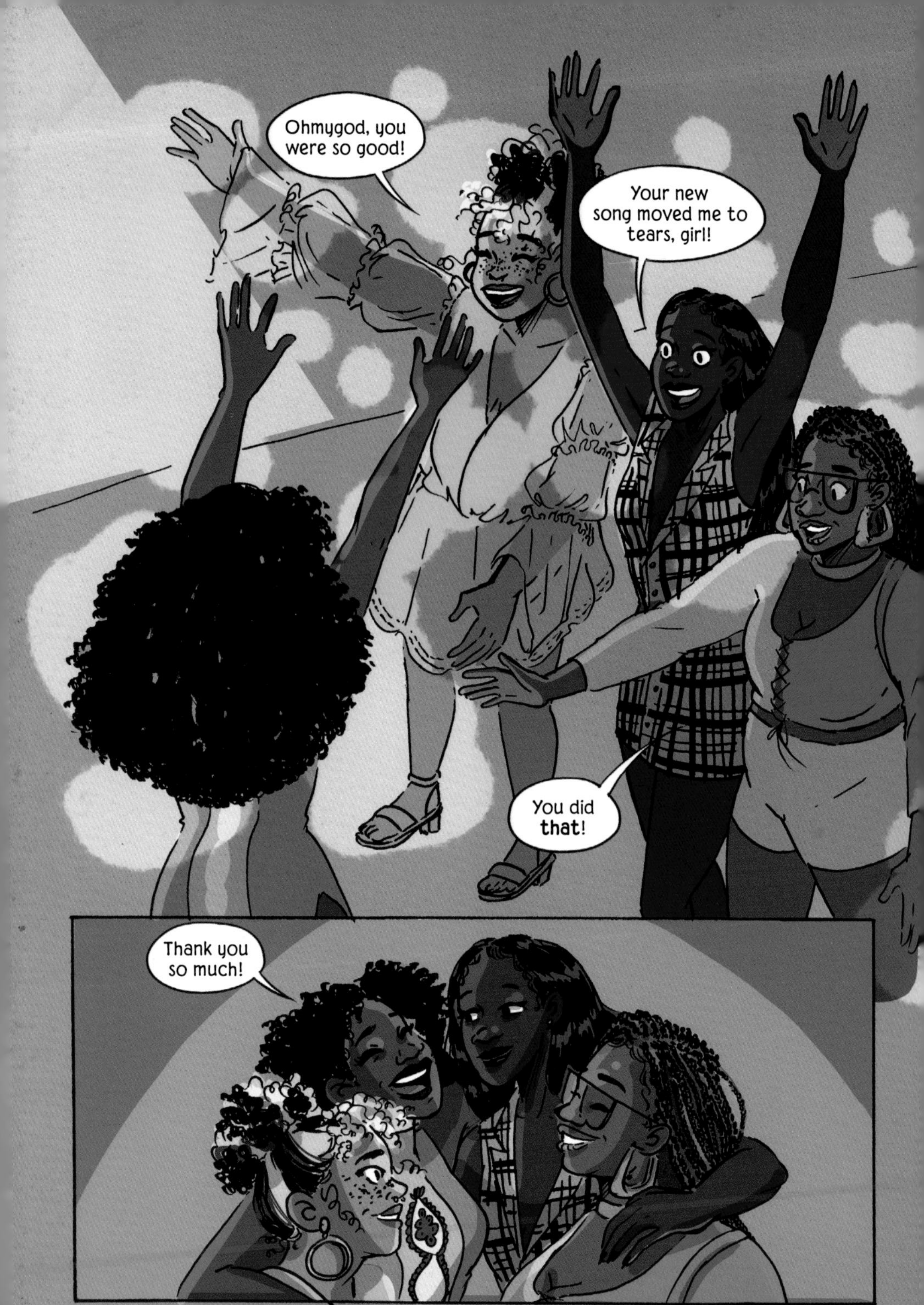
Ohmygod, you were so good!
Your new song moved me to tears, girl!
You did **that**!
Thank you so much!

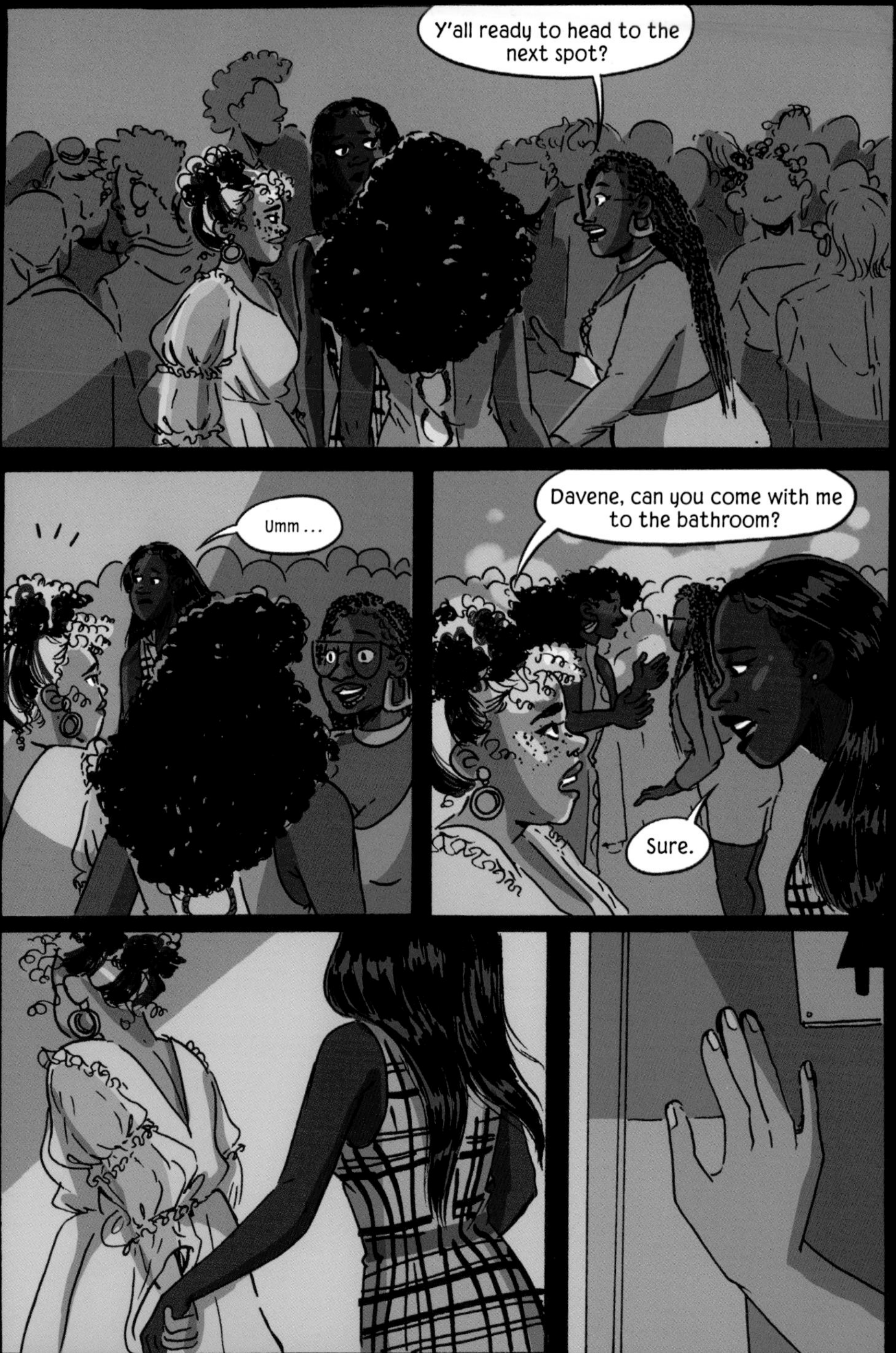
Y'all ready to head to the next spot?
Umm . . .
Davene, can you come with me to the bathroom?
Sure.

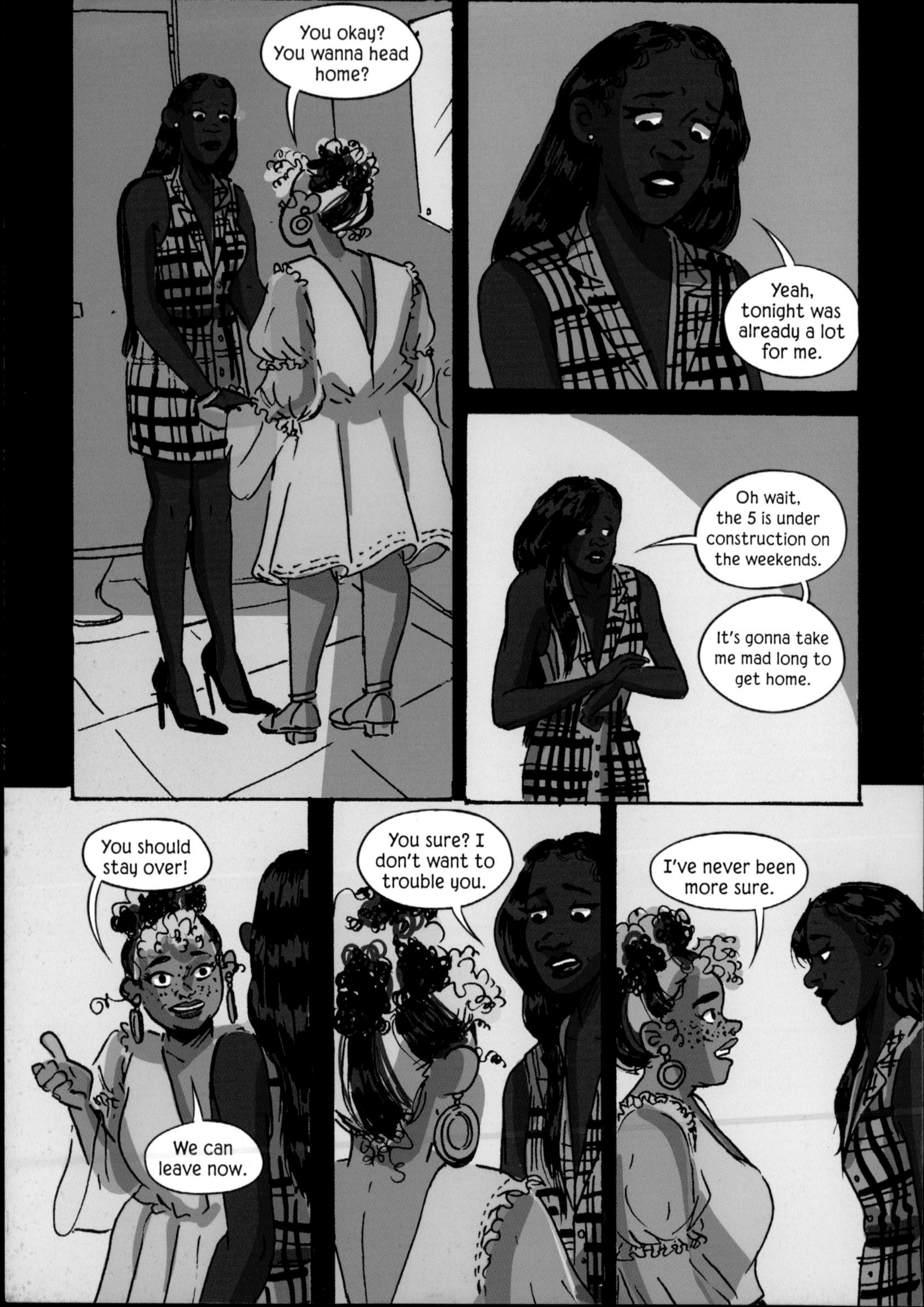
You okay? You wanna head home?
Yeah, tonight was already a lot for me.
Oh wait, the 5 is under construction on the weekends.
It's gonna take me mad long to get home.
You should stay over!
We can leave now.
You sure? I don't want to trouble you.
I've never been more sure.

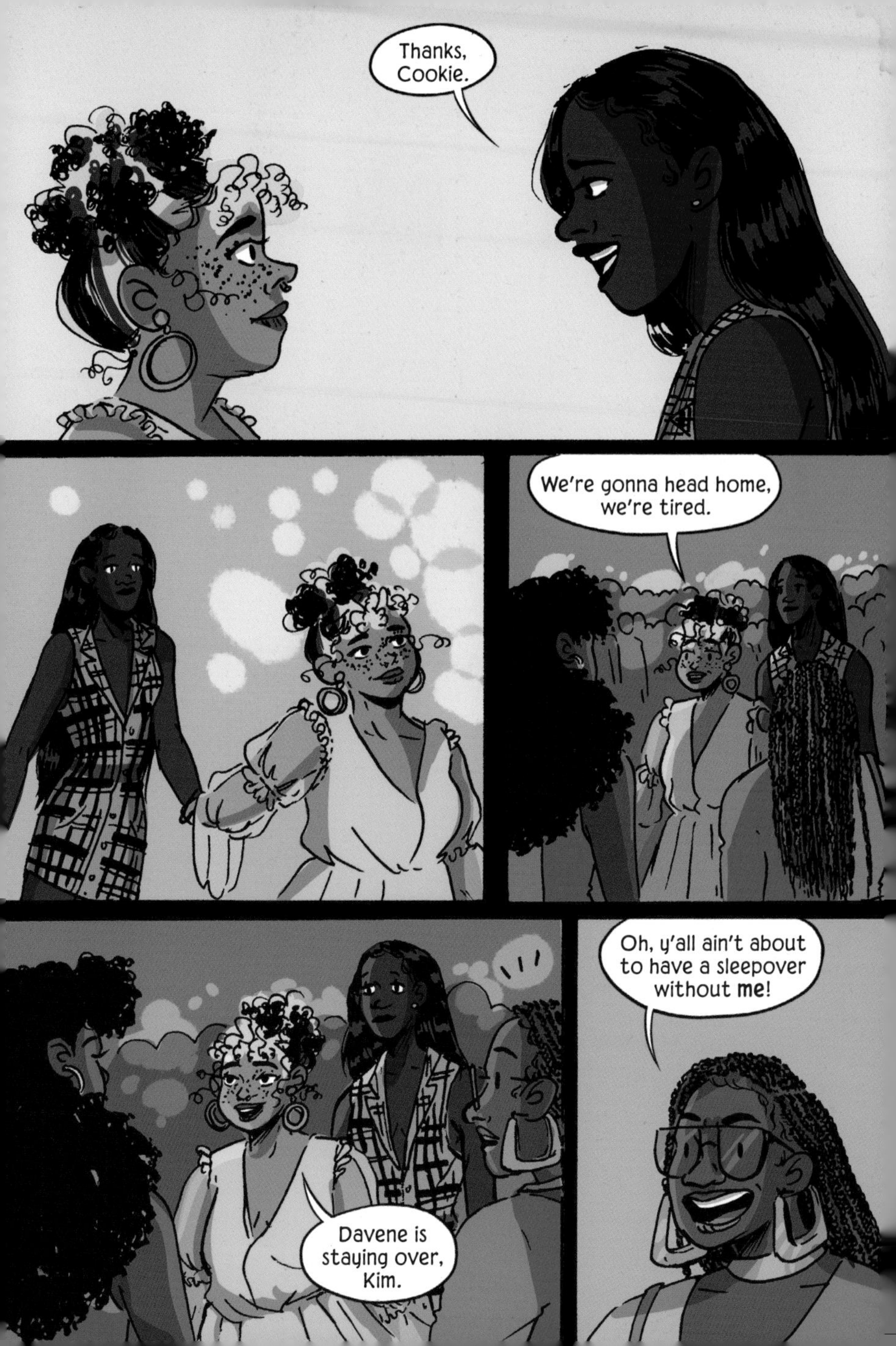

Thanks, Cookie.
We're gonna head home, we're tired.
Davene is staying over, Kim.
Oh, y'all ain't about to have a sleepover without **me**!

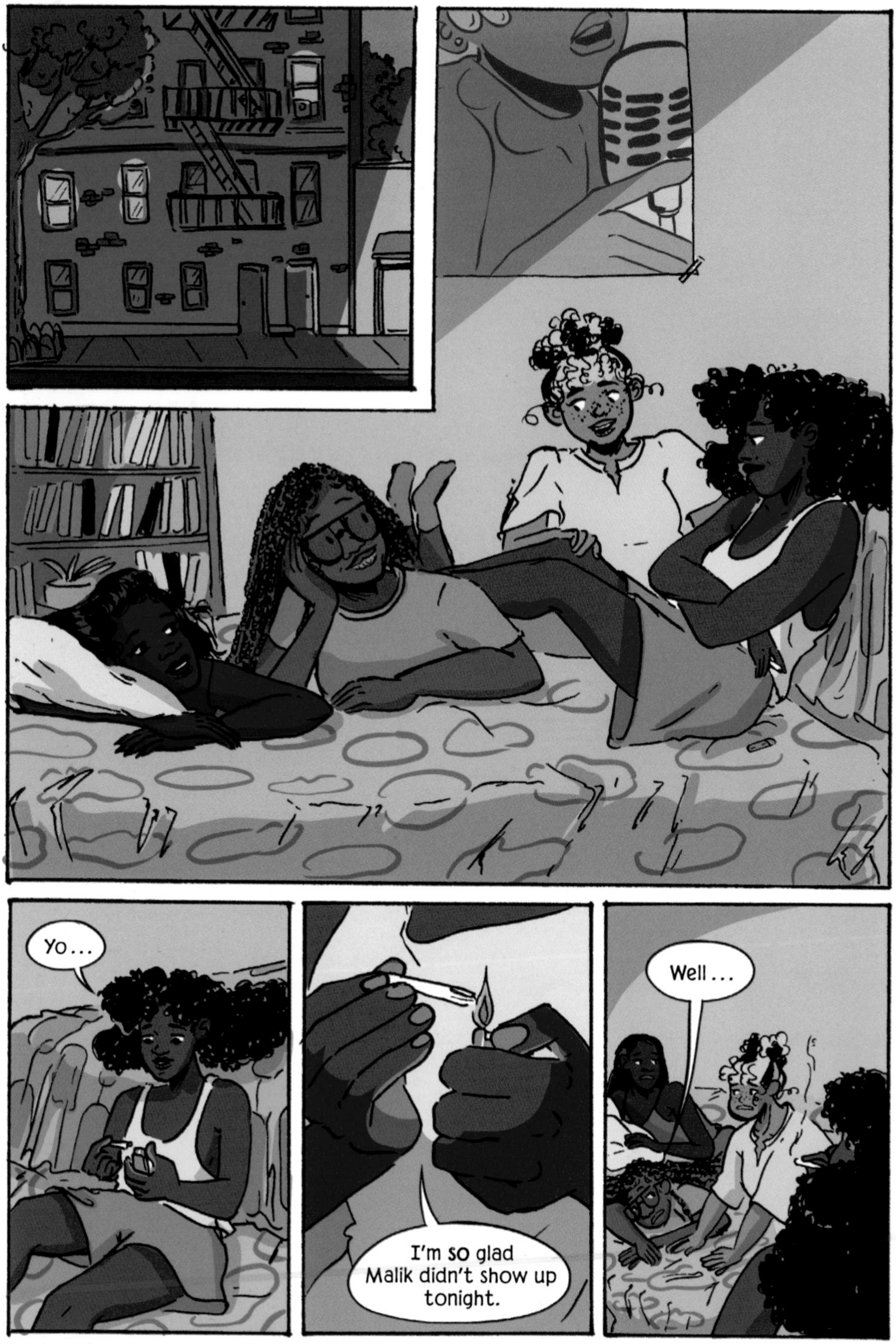
Yo . . .
I'm SO glad Malik didn't show up tonight.
Well . . .

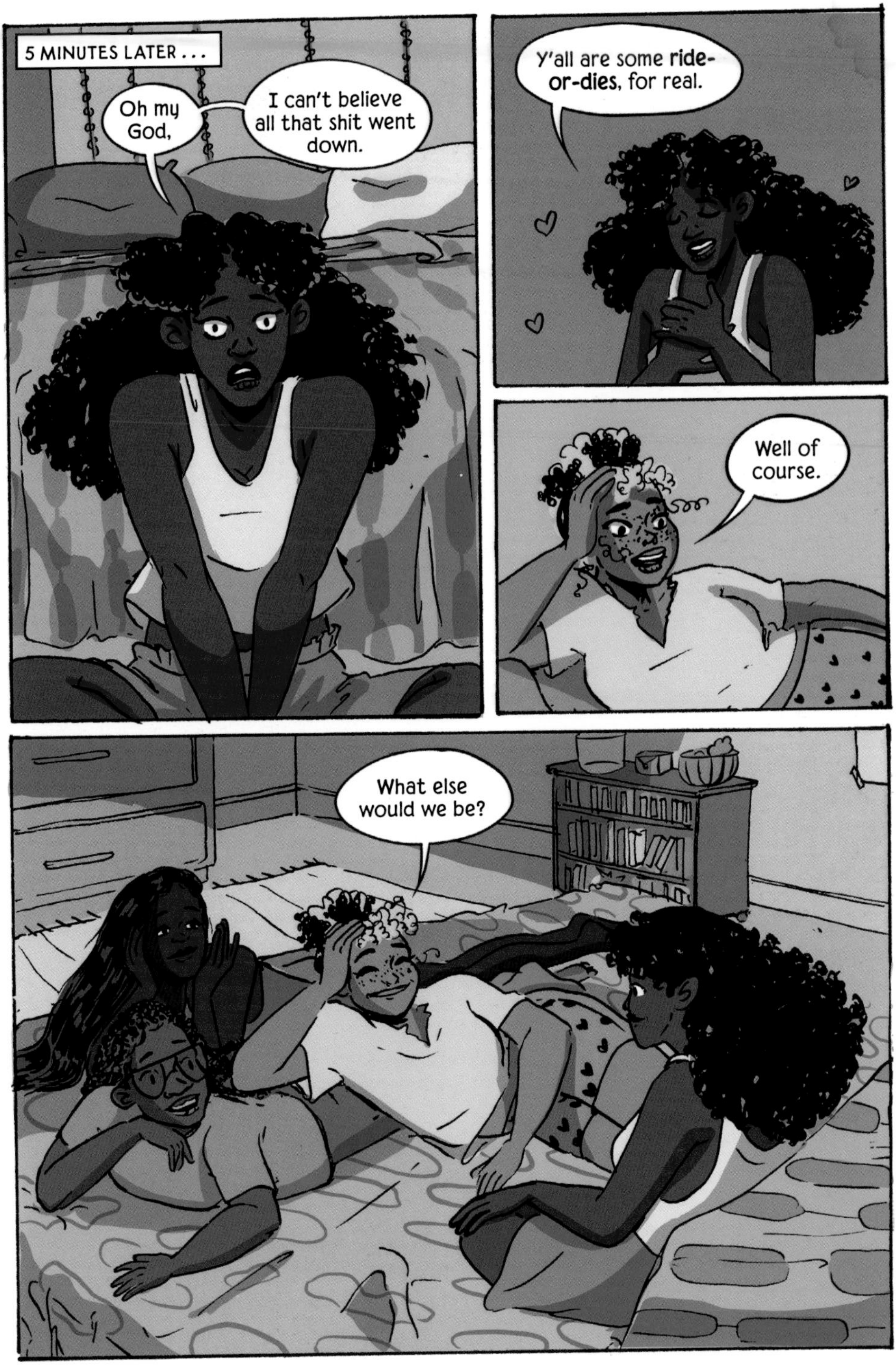
5 MINUTES LATER . . .
Oh my God,
I can't believe all that shit went down.
Y'all are some **ride-or-dies**, for real.
Well of course.
What else would we be?

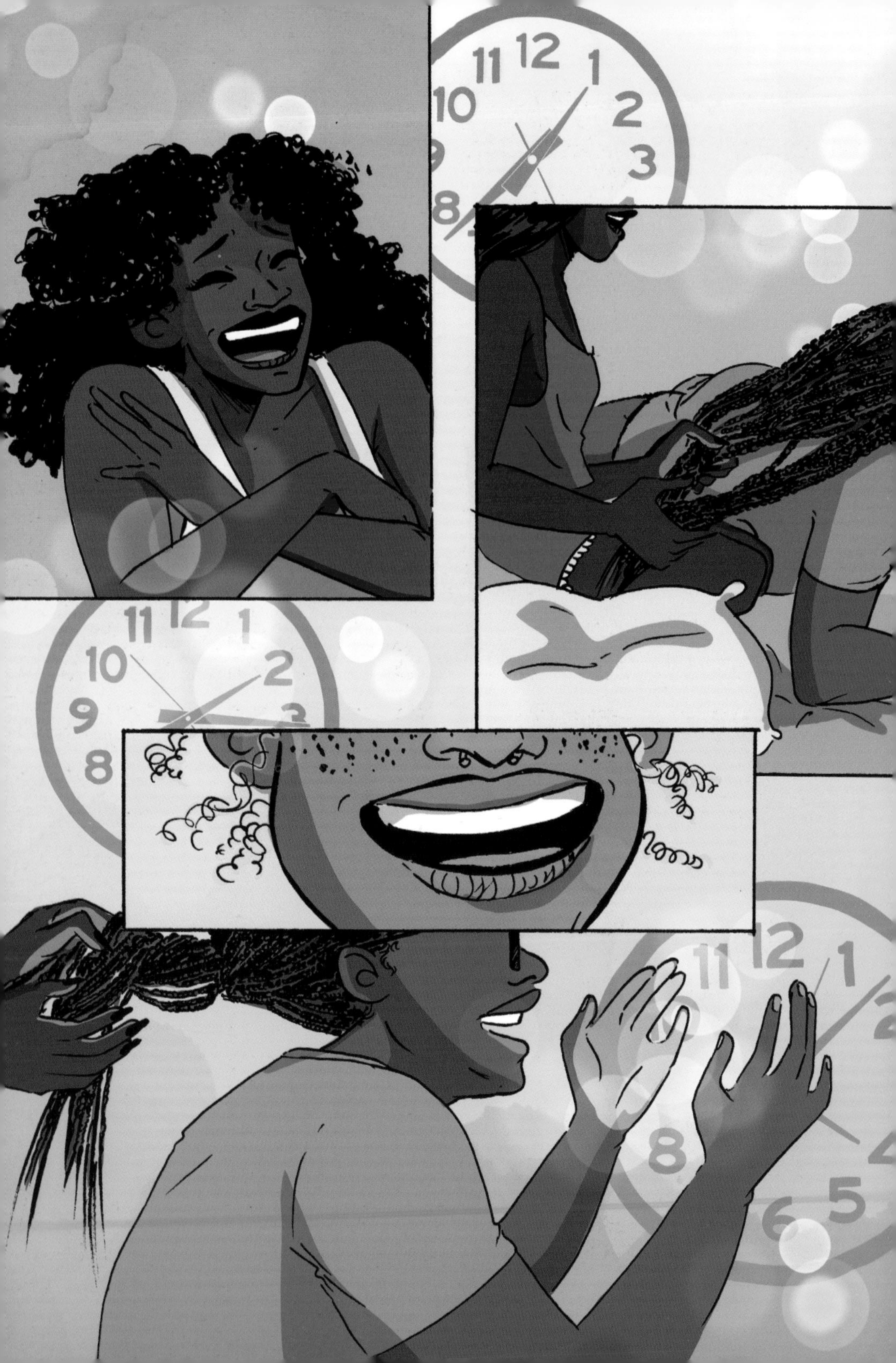

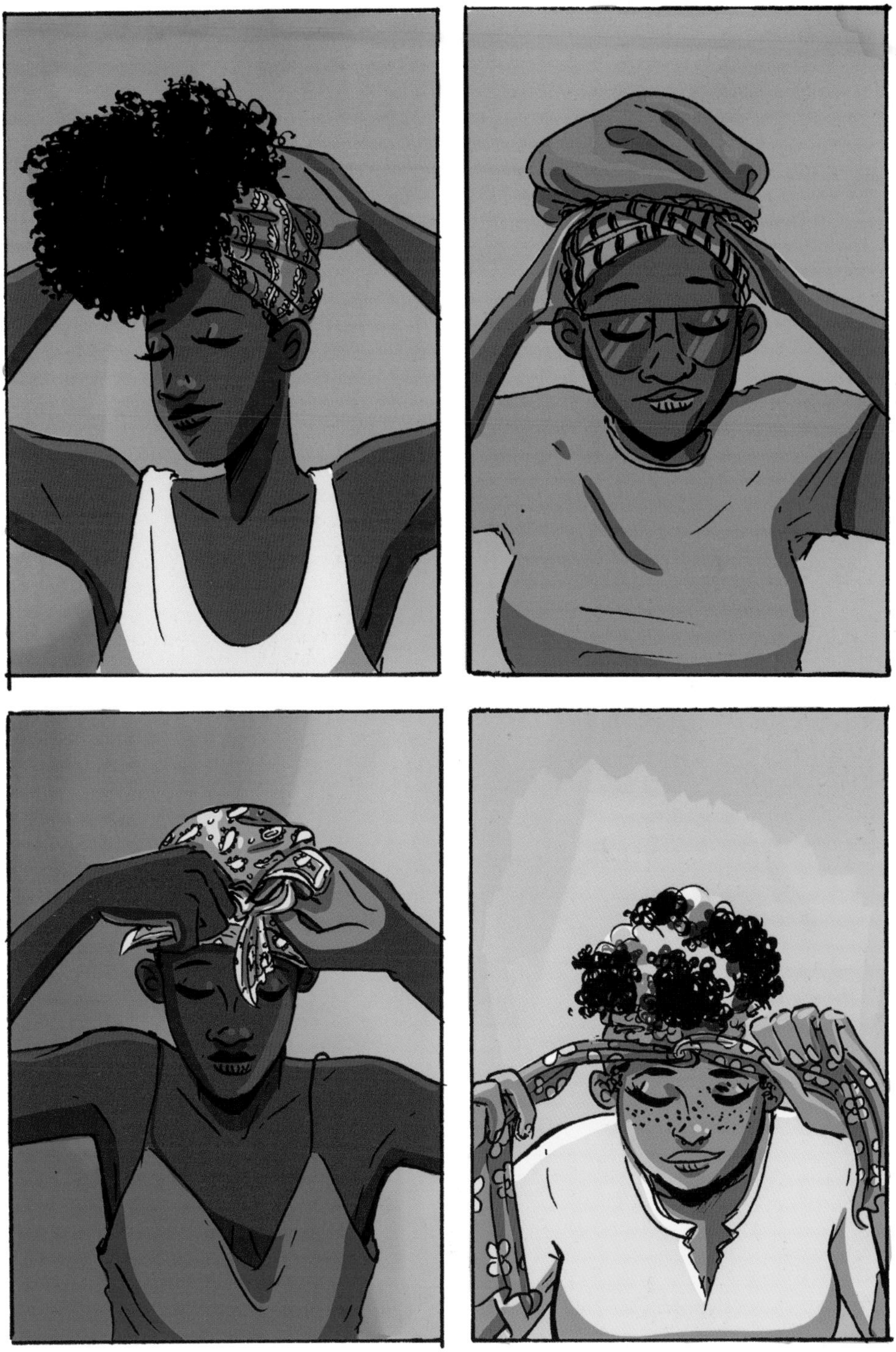

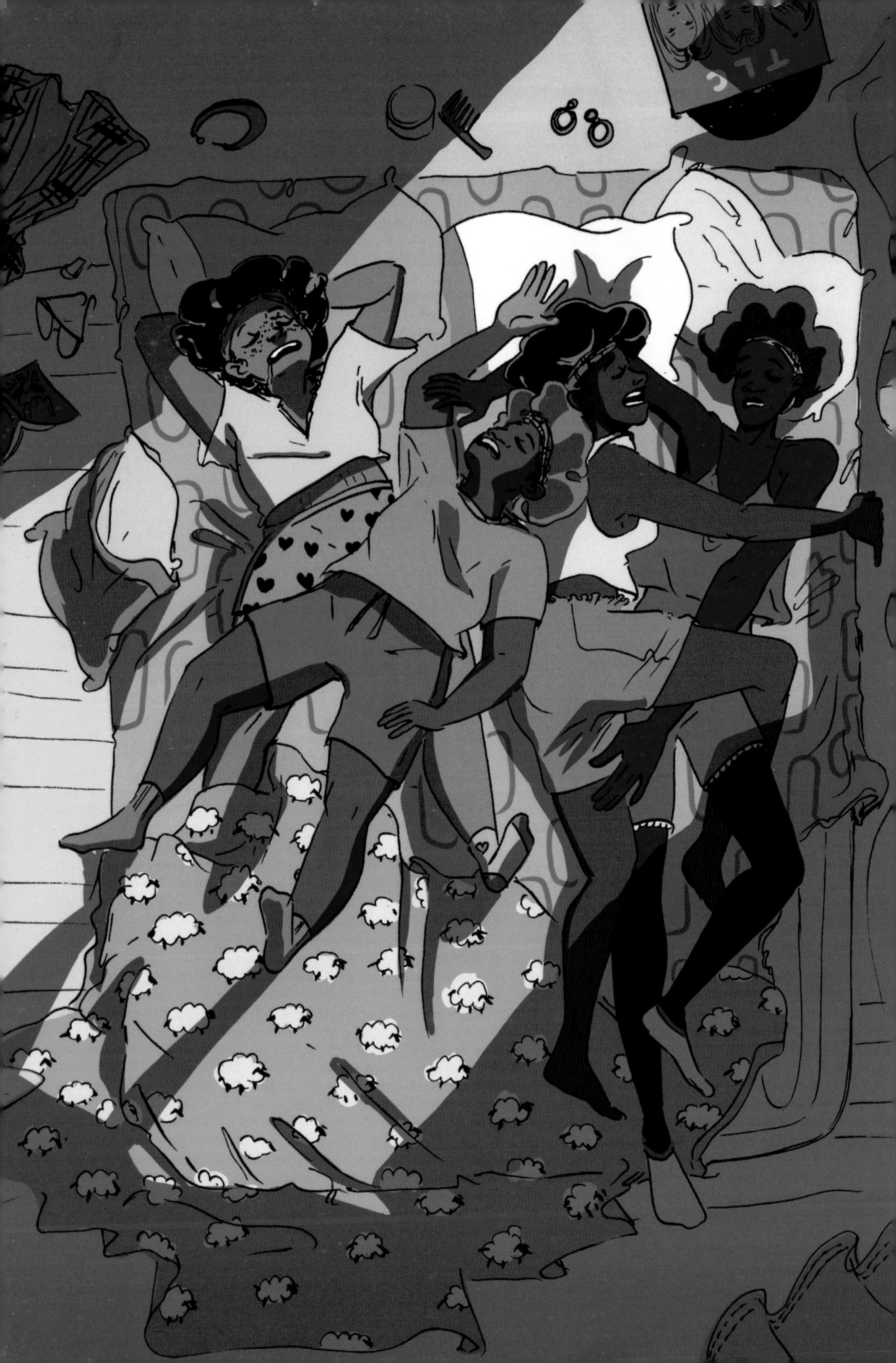
TLC

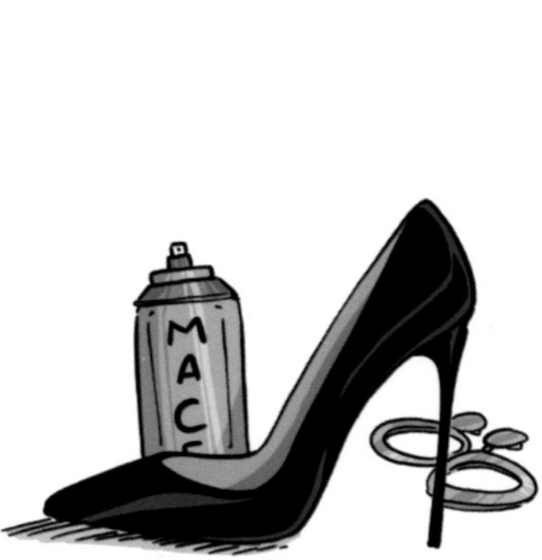
MAC

ACKNOWLEDGMENTS

Thank you to my parents for your constant love and support. To my brother, Myles, thank you for being the best brother and friend I could ask for. To my friends who fill my life with love, joy, and laughter. I don't know what I'd do without y'all. You inspire me so much.

Thank you to my partner, Jemar Souza, for always believing in me, especially when I didn't believe in myself. Thank you to Sahara Clement for believing *Wash Day* could and *should* be bigger. To my first editor, J.A. Micheline, and my agent, Jen Linnan. To the Chronicle team for giving Robyn and me the space to make *Wash Day Diaries* the way we wanted.

Robyn, thank you for everything you put into creating this beautiful comic with me. I've developed such a beautiful friendship with you because of our comic, and for that, I'm forever grateful. Thank you to everyone who backed the *Wash Day* Kickstarter and bought and shared the comic. We're here because of your support and we don't take that for granted.

Last but not least, I thank Black women and girls everywhere for being a constant source of inspiration and strength. I do what I do for us.

Jamila

To my parents, my brother and my grandmothers, my cousins, uncles and aunts, friends and Benson (my cat). The emotional support I needed to make it through this was flowing nonstop from you all and I am so grateful. I always feel loved and in turn was able to put that into this book.

Jamila I am so happy we have each other and I'm so happy that what started so long ago has made it this far. I look forward to what we do together next.

Robyn

CREDITS

Bex Glendining – Colorist
Bex Glendining (she/they) is a biracial queer, UK-based illustrator, comic artist, and colorist. When not working, they can usually be found building Gundams, playing video games with friends, or buying new plants.
lgions.com
Twitter/Instagram: @lgions

Kazimir Lee – Colorist
Kaz lives in Brooklyn with their family. Their work has appeared on The Nib, Oh Joy Sex Toy! and has garnered a Lambda Literary Award for Queer Erotica. They like country music, karaoke, and body horror. They are trying to do better.
Kazimirlee.com
Instagram: @kazzer.lee
Twitter: @iportmento

J.A. Micheline – *Wash Day* script editor
J. A. Micheline is a writer, editor, and critic based in New York City. As an editor, more than anything, she likes to consider the shapes of things.
Twitter: @elevenafter

Sahara Clement – Editor
Sahara Clement is an editor based in Philadelphia. Inspired by the power of books, she is passionate about finding creative ways to bring diverse and underrepresented stories to life. Like her kitten, Bean, she always tries to appreciate life's little joys.

Juliette Capra – Editor
Juliette Capra is a professional enthusiast and editor of comics, books, and more. She is delighted to find herself on the editorial side of her favorite medium with projects like *Wash Day Diaries*. She lives in the San Francisco Bay Area with her two cats, the fog, and a surprising amount of neighborhood wildlife.

Neil Egan – Designer and lettering layout
Neil is a graphic designer, art director, and life-long comics fan, who can't believe that his job is occasionally to collaborate with incredibly talented and wonderful comics creators to bring their vision to a final printed book. He lives in Oakland, California.

Angie Kang – Lettering assistance
Angie is a Chinese-American illustrator, designer, and writer based in San Francisco. She can be found on Instagram @anqiekanq, online at www.angiekang.net, or at the laundromat, separating quarters by where they were minted.

PROCESS PAGES

Script:

Here's a script excerpt from one of our favorite panels in *Group Chat*. This story was inspired by the dynamism and excitement that happens in storytelling amongst friends. Specifically, we wanted to highlight how lively storytelling is in group chats and represent that energy with visual elements as well as the dialogue.

Group Chat Page 10, Panel 2 Description

This is the panel where we'll start to play around visually with storytelling. KIM will interrupt NISHA'S story by physically pushing the flashback panel aside as if it's a curtain (described below). The flashback panel can be sort of bunched up to illustrate how the panel is like a curtain. KIM is technically outside of the panel so there won't be any border around her, it's like she's in the margins or behind the "flashback panel." We don't need to see KIM'S whole body; it could just be her head/upper body, whatever looks best. These images may help inspire this panel: [link].

Flashback panel: We're still outside of the gallery, but closer and from a different angle. We now see NISHA and DANIEL from a distance as they walk through the semi–crowded exhibit party. Since it's from a distance we don't need to clearly make out all of DANIEL's face and his features, we'll do that in the next panel. The focus is on NISHA AND DANIEL, so we may only make out some faces in the crowd clearly.

Kim:
Hold up, Daniel?!

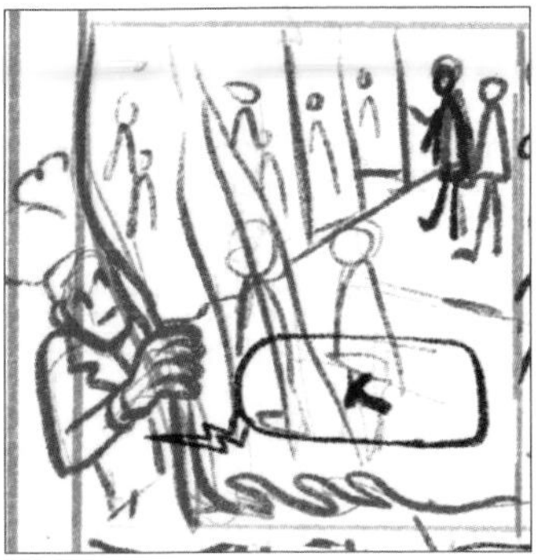

Thumbnail:

Thumbnails are the next process in making the comic. Here is where the first sketches of the layout are created.

```
Kim:
Hold up, Daniel?!
```

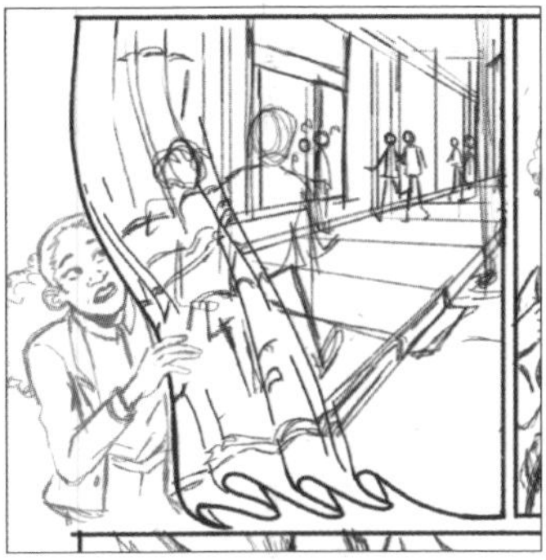

Pencils:

The penciling process refines the artwork and adds more details, and also serves as an underdrawing for inking.

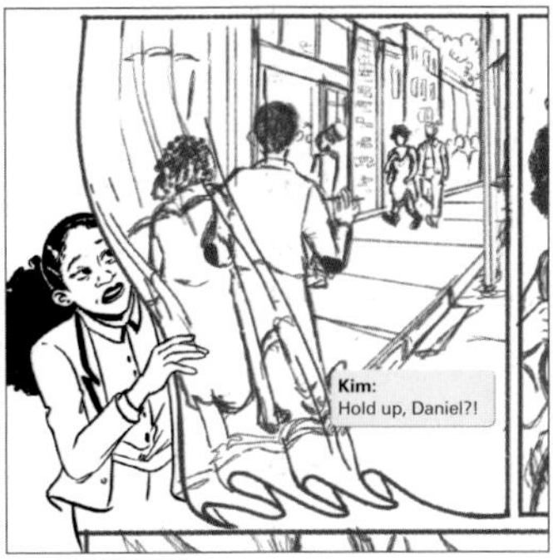
Kim:
Hold up, Daniel?!

Inks:

In this step of the process, you can see the difference in the inking styles of the "flashback scene" versus the "present scene."

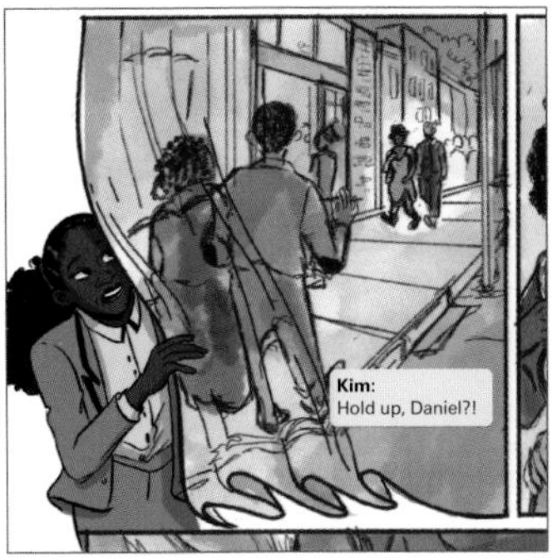
Kim:
Hold up, Daniel?!

Color:

Different coloring methods were also used to differentiate the past versus the present. For the flash-backs, a watercolor texture was used, and for the present scenes, we used flat digital colors.

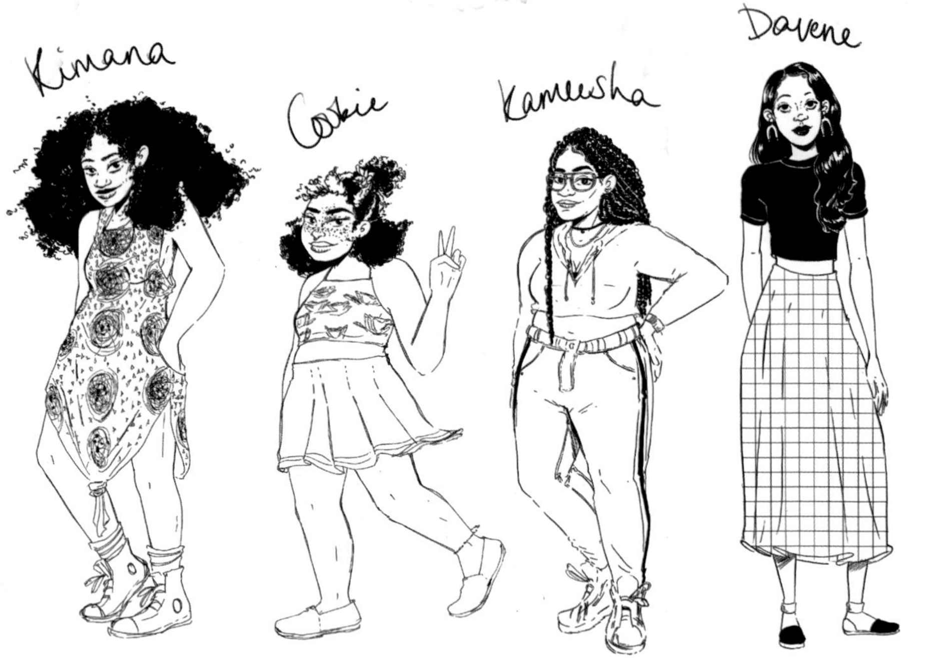
Kimana
Cookie
Kameesha
Davene

Our girls! <3 Tanisha's name changed as we developed the characters.

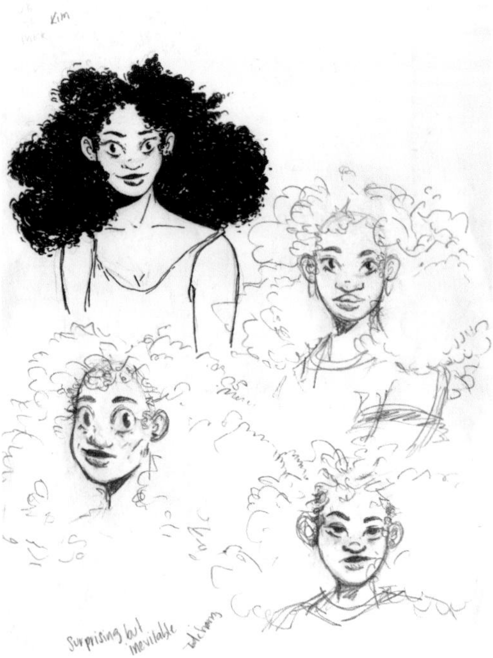

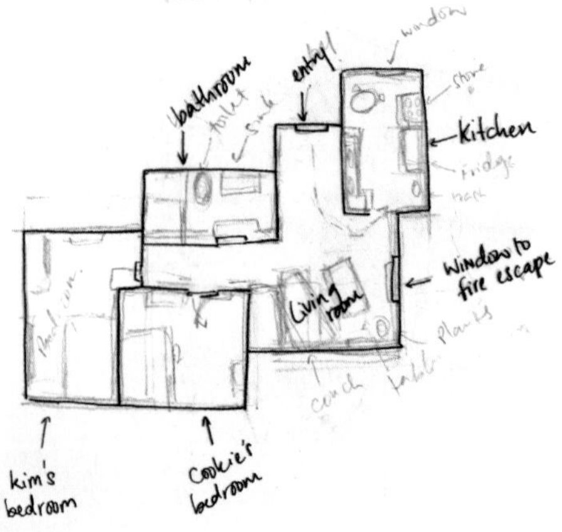
bathroom
entry!
window
Kitchen
Window to fire escape
Living room
kim's bedroom
Cookie's bedroom

The layout for Kim and Cookie's apartment.

This concept art shows t
acter design for the *Was*
other options we consid